Practical Programming in Tcl and Tk

Brent B. Welch

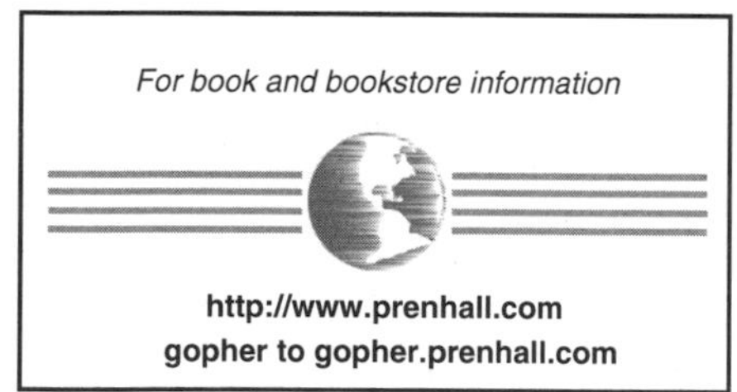

Prentice Hall PTR
Upper Saddle River, New Jersey 07458

Library of Congress Cataloging-in-Publication Data

Welch, Brent.
Practical programming in Tcl and Tk / Brent Welch.
p. cm.
Includes index.
ISBN 0-13-182007-9
1. Tcl (Computer program language) 2. Tk toolkit. I. Title
QA76.73.T44W45 1995
005.13'3—dc20 95-1159
CIP

Editorial/production supervision: *Kerry Reardon*
Cover design: *Design Source*
Manufacturing buyer: *Alexis R. Heydt*
Acquisitions editor: *Mark Taub*
Cover photo: *Alan Cober / The Stock Illustration Source, Inc*

Prentice-Hall, Inc.
A Simon & Schuster Company
Upper Saddle River, New Jersey 07458

The publisher offers discounts on this book when ordered in bulk quantities. For more information, contact:

Corporate Sales Department
Prentice Hall PTR
One Lake Street
Upper Saddle River, NJ 07458

Phone: 800-382-3419
Fax: 201-236-7141
E-mail: corpsales@prenhall.com

Printed in the United States of America

10 9 8 7 6 5 4 3 2

ISBN 0-13-182007-9

Prentice-Hall International (UK) Limited, *London*
Prentice-Hall of Australia Pty. Limited, *Sydney*
Prentice-Hall Canada Inc., *Toronto*
Prentice-Hall Hispanoamericana, S.A., *Mexico*
Prentice-Hall of India Private Limited, *New Delhi*
Prentice-Hall of Japan, Inc., *Tokyo*
Simon & Schuster Asia Pte. Ltd., *Singapore*
Editora Prentice-Hall do Brasil, Ltda., *Rio de Janeiro*

to

Jody
and
Christopher

Contents

List of Examples xix

List of Tables xxv

Preface xxix

1. Tcl Fundamentals 1

   Getting Started 1
   Tcl Commands 3
   Hello World 3
   Variables 4
   Command Substitution 4
   Math Expressions 5
   Backslash Substitution 6
   Grouping with Braces and Double Quotes 7
   Procedures 8
   A While Loop Example 9
   Grouping and Command Substitution 10
   More About Variable Substitution 11
   Comments 12
   Command Line Arguments 12
   Substitution and Grouping Summary 13
   Fine Points 14
   Reference 14
      Backslash Sequences 14
      Predefined Variables 15
      Arithmetic Operators 15
      Built-in Math Functions 16
      Core Tcl Commands 17

2. Strings and Pattern Matching 19

   The string Command 19
   Strings and Expresssions 20
   The append Command 21
   The format Command 21
   The scan Command 23
   String Matching 24
   Regular Expressions 25

The regexp Command 27
The regsub Command 28

3. Tcl Data Structures 29
More About Variables 29
The unset Command 30
Using info to Find Out About Variables 30
Tcl Lists 31
Constructing Lists: list, lappend, and concat 32
Getting List Elements: llength, lindex, and lrange 33
Modifying Lists: linsert and lreplace 34
Searching Lists: lsearch 34
Sorting Lists: lsort 35
The split and join Commands 35
Arrays 36
The array Command 37

4. Control Flow Commands 39
If Then Else 40
Switch 41
Comments in switch Commands 42
Foreach 43
While 44
For 44
Break and Continue 45
Catch 45
Error 46
Return 47

5. Procedures and Scope 49
The proc Command 49
Changing Command Names With rename 50
Scope 51
The global Command 52
Use Arrays for Global State 53
Call by Name Using upvar 53
Passing Arrays by Name 54

6. Eval 57
Construct Commands with list 57
Exploiting the concat Inside eval 59
Double-quotes and eval 60

The uplevel Command 60
Commands that Concatenate Their Arguments 61
The subst Command 62

7. Working with UNIX 63

Running UNIX Programs with exec 63
The auto_noexec Variable 65
Looking at the File System 65
Input/Output Command Summary 68
Opening Files for I/O 68
Opening a Process Pipeline 70
Reading and Writing 70
The puts and gets Commands 70
The read Command 71
Random Access I/O 72
Closing I/O streams 72
The Current Directory - cd and pwd 72
Matching File Names with glob 72
Expanding Tilde in File Names 73
The exit and pid Commands 73
Environment Variables 74

8. Reflection and Debugging 75

The info Command 75
Variables 76
Procedures 77
The Call Stack 77
Command Evaluation 78
Scripts and the Library 78
Version Numbers 78
Tracing Variable Values 79
Interactive Command History 80
History Syntax 81
A Comparison to /bin/csh History Syntax 82
Debugging 83
Don Libes' Debugger 84
Breakpoints by Pattern Matching 85
Deleting Break Points 86
Debugging Tk Scripts 86
The tkinspect Program 86
The tkerror Command 86
Performance Tuning 87

9. Script Libraries 89
The unknown Command 89
The tclIndex File 90
Using a Library: auto_path 91
Disabling the Library Facility: auto_noload 91
How Auto Loading Works 91
Dynamic Linking C Code 92
Interactive Conveniences 92
Auto Execute 92
History 93
Abbreviations 93
Tcl Shell Library Environment 93
Coding Style 94
A Module Prefix for Procedure Names 94
A Global Array for State Variables 94

10. Tk Fundamentals 95
Hello World In Tk 96
Naming Tk Widgets 98
Configuring Tk Widgets 98
Tk Widget Attributes and X Resources 99
The Tk Manual Pages 99
Summary Of The Tk Commands 100

11. Tk by Example 103
ExecLog 103
Window Title 105
A Frame for Buttons 105
Command Buttons 106
A Label and an Entry 106
Key Bindings and Focus 106
A Resizable Text and Scrollbar 107
The Run Procedure 107
The Log Procedure 108
The Stop Procedure 108
The Example Browser 109
More About Resizing Windows 110
Managing Global State 111
Searching Through Files 111
Cascaded Menus 112
A Read-Only Text Widget 112
A Tcl Shell 113

Naming Issues 114
Text Marks and Bindings 114

12. The Pack Geometry Manager 115

Packing Toward a Side 116
Shrinking Frames and Pack Propagate 116
Horizontal and Vertical Stacking 117
The Cavity Model 118
Packing Space and Display Space 119
The -fill Option 119
Internal Padding with -ipadx and -ipady 120
External Padding with -padx and -pady 122
Expand and Resizing 122
Anchoring 124
Packing Order 125
Pack Slaves and Pack Info 126
Pack the Scrollbar First 126
Choosing the Parent for Packing 127
Unpacking a Widget 127
Packer Summary 128
The pack Command 128
The Place Geometry Manager 129
The place Command 130
Window Stacking Order 131

13. Binding Commands to X Events 133

The bind Command 133
The bindtags Command 134
Using break and continue in Bindings 136
Defining New Binding Tags 136
Binding Precedence in Tk 3.6 136
Event Syntax 137
Keyboard Events 138
Detecting Modifiers in Tk 3.6 138
Mouse Events 139
Other Events 139
Modifiers 140
Modifiers in Tk 3.6 142
Event Sequences 142
Event Keywords 143

14. Buttons and Menus 145

Button Commands and Scope Issues 145
Buttons Associated with Tcl Variables 149
Button Attributes 151
Button Operations 153
Menus and Menubuttons 153
    Pop-up Menus 155
    Option Menus 155
Keyboard Traversal 155
Manipulating Menus and Menu Entries 156
Menu Attributes 157
A Menu by Name Package 158

15. Using X Resources 163

An Introduction to X Resources 163
    Warning: Order is Important! 165
Loading Option Database Files 165
Adding Individual Database Entries 166
Accessing the Database 166
User-Defined Buttons 167
User Defined Menus 168

16. Simple Tk Widgets 171

Frames and Toplevel Windows 171
    Attributes for Frames and Toplevels 172
The Label Widget 173
    Label Attributes 174
    Label Width and Wrap Length 174
The Message Widget 175
    Message Attributes 176
    Arranging Labels and Messages 177
The Scale Widget 177
    Scale Bindings 178
    Scale Attributes 178
    Programming Scales 179
The Scrollbar Widget 180
    Scrollbar Bindings 182
    Scrollbar Attributes 182
    Programming Scrollbars 183
    The Tk 3.6 protocol 184
The bell Command 184

17. Entry and Listbox Widgets 185
The Entry Widget 185
A Labeled Entry 185
Entry Attributes 188
Programming Entry Widgets 189
The Listbox Widget 191
Programming Listboxes 193
Listbox Bindings 197
Browse Select Mode 198
Single Select Mode 198
Extended Select Mode 199
Multiple Select Mode 200
Scroll Bindings 200
Listbox Attributes 201
Geometry Gridding 202

18. Focus, Grabs, and Dialogs 203
Input Focus 203
The focus Command 204
Focus Follows Mouse 204
Click to Type 205
Hybrid Models 205
Grabbing the Focus 205
Dialogs 206
The tkwait Command 206
Prompter Dialog 206
Keyboard Shortcuts and Focus 208
Destroying Widgets 208
Animation with the update Command 208
File Selection Dialog 209
Specifying Attributes with X Resources 212
Mouse and Key Bindings 212
Listing the Directory 214
Accepting a Name 215
Easy Stuff 217
File Name Completion 217

19. The Text Widget 219
Text Indices 219
Inserting and Deleting Text 220
Index Arithmatic 220
Text Marks 221

Text Tags 222
Tag Attributes 223
Mixing Attributes from Different Tags 224
Line Spacing and Justification 225
The Selection 227
Tag Bindings 227
Embedded Widgets 228
Text Bindings 230
Text Operations 232
Text Attributes 234

20. The Canvas Widget 235

Canvas Coordinates 235
Hello, World! 236
The Min Max Scale Example 238
Arc Items 241
Bitmap Items 242
Image Items 243
Line Items 244
Oval Items 246
Polygon Items 247
Rectangle Items 248
Text Items 249
Window Items 252
Canvas Operations 254
Generating Postscript 256
Canvas Attributes 258
Hints 259
Screen Coordinates vs. Canvas Coordinates 259
Large Coordinate Spaces 259
Scaling and Rotation 259
X Resources 260
Objects with Many Points 260
Selecting Canvas Items 260

21. Selections and the Clipboard 261

The selection Command 262
The clipboard Command 263
Interoperation with OpenLook 263
Selection Handlers 263
A Canvas Selection Handler 264

22. Callbacks and Handlers 267

The after Command 267
The fileevent Command 268
The send Command 269
  Send and X Authority 270
  The Sender Script 271
  Using Sender 272
  Communicating Processes 275

23. Tk Widget Attributes 277

Configuring Attributes 277
Size 278
Borders and Relief 280
The Focus Highlight 281
Padding and Anchors 281
Putting it all Together 282

24. Color, Images, and Cursors 285

Colors 286
Colormaps and Visuals 287
Bitmaps and Images 289
  The image Command 289
  Bitmap Images 290
  The bitmap Attribute 290
  Photo Images 291
The Mouse Cursor 294
The Text Insert Cursor 295

25. Fonts and Text Attributes 297

Fonts 297
Text Layout 300
Gridding, Resizing, and Geometry 301
Selection Attributes 301
A Font Selection Application 302
  Setup and Widget Layout 302
  Tracing Variables 304
  Listing Available Fonts 304
  Keeping Track of Fonts 305
  Creating the Menus 306
  The Font Sampler Display 306
  Selecting a Font 307

26. Window Managers and Window Information 309

The wm Command 309
  Size, Placement, and Decoration 310
  Icons 311
  Session State 312
  Miscellaneous 313
The winfo Command 314
  Sending Commands Between Applications 314
  Family Relationships 315
  Size 315
  Location 316
  Virtual Root Window 317
  Atoms and IDs 317
  Colormaps and Visuals 318
The tk Command 319

27. A User Interface to Bindings 321

A Pair of Listboxes Working Together 323
The Editing Interface 325
Saving and Loading Bindings 326

28. Managing User Preferences 329

App-Defaults Files 329
Defining Preferences 331
The Preferences User Interface 333
Managing the Preferences File 336
Tracing Changes to Preference Variables 337
Improving the Package 338

29. C Programming and Tcl 339

  Using the Tcl C Library 340
Application Structure 340
Tcl_Main and Tcl_AppInit 341
  The Standard Main in Tcl 7.3 342
A C Command Procedure 343
Managing the Result's Storage 344
Invoking Scripts From C 345
  Bypassing Tcl_Eval 345
Putting A Tcl Program Together 347
An Overview of the Tcl C library 347
  Application Initialization 348
  Creating and Deleting Interpreters 348

Creating and Deleting Commands 348
Managing the Result String 348
Lists and Command Parsing 348
Command Pipelines 349
Tracing the Actions of the Tcl Interpreter 349
Evaluating Tcl Commands 349
Manipulating Tcl Variables 349
Evaluating Expressions 350
Converting Numbers 350
Hash Tables 350
Dynamic Strings 352
Regular Expressions and String Matching 352
Tilde Substitution 352
Working with Signals 352

30. C Programming and Tk 353

Tk_Main and Tcl_AppInit 353
A Custom Main Program 355
A Custom Event Loop 358
An Overview of the Tk C library 359
Parsing Command Line Arguments 359
The Standard Application Setup 360
Creating Windows 360
Application Name for Send 360
Configuring Windows 360
Window Coordinates 360
Window Stacking Order 361
Window Information 361
Configuring Widget Attributes 361
Safe Handling of the Widget Data Structure 361
The Selection and Clipboard 361
Event Bindings 362
Event Loop Interface 362
Handling X Events 362
File Handlers 362
Timer Events 363
Idle Callbacks 363
Sleeping 363
Reporting Script Errors 363
Handling X Protocol Errors 363
Using the X Resource Database 363
Managing Bitmaps 364

Creating New Image Types 364
Using an Image in a Widget 364
Photo Image Types 364
Canvas Object Support 364
Geometry Management 365
String Identifiers (UIDS) 365
Colors and Colormaps 365
3D Borders 366
Mouse Cursors 366
Font Structures 366
Graphics Contexts 366
Allocate a Pixmap 366
Screen Measurements 366
Relief Style 367
Text Anchor Positions 367
Line Cap Styles 367
Line Join Styles 367
Text Justification Styles 367
Atoms 367
X Resource ID Management 367

31. Writing a Tk Widget in C 369

The Widget Data Structure 369
Specifying Widget Attributes 370
The Widget Class Command 373
The Widget Instance Command 374
Configuring and Reconfiguring Attributes 376
Displaying the Clock 378
The Window Event Procedure 381
Final Cleanup 382

32. Tcl Extension Packages 385

Extended Tcl 386
Adding TclX to Your Application 386
More UNIX System Calls 387
File Operations 387
New Loop Constructs 387
Command Line Additions 387
Debugging and Development Support 387
TCP/IP Access 388
File Scanning 388
Math Functions as Commands 388

List Operations 388
Keyed List Data Structure 389
String Utilities 389
XPG/3 Message Catalog 389
Memory Debugging 389
Expect: Controlling Interactive Programs 390
The Core Expect Commands 390
Pattern Matching 391
Important Variables 391
An Example expect Script 392
Debugging expect Scripts 393
Expect's Tcl Debugger 394
The Dbg C Interface 394
Handling SIGINT 395
BLT 396
Drag and Drop 397
Hypertext 397
Graphs 397
Table Geometry Manager 397
Bitmap Support 397
Background Exec 397
Busy Window 398
Tracing Tcl Commands 398
The Cutbuffer 398
Tcl-DP 398
Remote Procedure Call 399
Connection Setup 399
Sending Network Data 399
Using UDP 400
Event Processing 400
Replicated Objects 400
The [incr Tcl] Object System 401
Tcl_AppInit with Extensions 402
Other Extensions 405

33. Porting to Tk 4.0 407

wish 407
Obsolete Features 407
The cget Operation 408
Input Focus Highlight 408
Bindings 408
Scrollbar Interface 409

Pack info 409
Focus 409
Send 410
Internal Button Padding 410
Radio Button Value 410
Entry Widget 410
Menus 411
Listboxes 411
No geometry Attribute 411
Text Widget 412
Color Attributes 412
Canvas scrollincrement 412
The Selection 413
The bell Command 413

List of Examples

1.1 The "Hello, World!" example. 3
1.2 Tcl variables. 4
1.3 Command substitution. 4
1.4 Simple arithmetic. 5
1.5 Nested commands. 5
1.6 Built-in math functions. 6
1.7 Controlling precision with tcl_precision. 6
1.8 Quoting special characters with backslash. 6
1.9 Continuing long lines with backslashes 7
1.10 Grouping with double quotes vs. braces. 7
1.11 Defining a procedure. 8
1.12 A while loop. 9
1.13 Embedded command and variable substitution. 10
1.14 Embedded variable references. 11
1.15 Using /bin/sh to run a Tcl script. 12

2.1 Comparing strings. 21
2.2 Using regular expressions to parse a string. 27

3.1 Using set to return a variable value. 30
3.2 Using info to determine if a variable exists. 30
3.3 Constructing a list with the list command. 32
3.4 Using lappend to add elements to a list. 32
3.5 Using concat to splice together lists. 33
3.6 Double quotes compared to the list command. 33
3.7 Modifying lists with linsert and lreplace. 34
3.8 Deleting a list element by value. 34
3.9 Sorting a list using a comparison function. 35
3.10 Use split to turn input data into Tcl lists. 35
3.11 Using arrays. 36
3.12 Referencing an array indirectly. 37
3.13 Converting from an array to a list. 38

4.1 A conditional if-then-else command. 40
4.2 Chained conditional with elseif. 40
4.3 Using switch for an exact match. 41
4.4 Using switch with substitutions in the patterns. 42
4.5 Using switch with all pattern body pairs grouped with quotes... 42
4.6 Comments in switch commands. 42
4.7 Looping with foreach. 43
4.8 Parsing command line arguments. 43

4.9 Using `list` with `foreach`. 43
4.10 A `while` loop to read standard input. 44
4.11 A `for` loop. 44
4.12 A standard `catch` phrase. 45
4.13 A longer `catch` phrase. 46
4.14 Raising an error. 46
4.15 Preserving `errorInfo` when calling `error`. 47
4.16 Specifying `errorInfo` with `return`. 47

5.1 Default parameter values. 50
5.2 Variable number of arguments. 50
5.3 Variable scope and Tcl procedures. 51
5.4 A random number generator. 52
5.5 Using arrays for global state. 53
5.6 Print variable by name. 54
5.7 Improved `incr` procedure. 54
5.8 Using an array to implement a stack. 55

6.1 Using `list` to construct commands. 58
6.2 Using `eval` with `$args`. 59

7.1 Using `exec` on a process pipeline. 64
7.2 Comparing file modify times. 66
7.3 Creating a directory recursively. 67
7.4 Determining if pathnames reference the same file. 67
7.5 Opening a file for writing. 68
7.6 Opening a file using the POSIX access flags. 69
7.7 A more careful use of `open`. 70
7.8 Opening a process pipeline. 70
7.9 Prompting for input. 71
7.10 A read loop using `gets`. 71
7.11 A read loop using `read` and `split`. 71
7.12 Finding a file by name. 73
7.13 Printing environment variable values. 74

8.1 Printing a procedure definition. 77
8.2 Getting a trace of the Tcl call stack. 78
8.3 Tracing variables. 79
8.4 Creating array elements with array traces. 80
8.5 Interactive `history` usage. 81
8.6 Implementing special history syntax. 82
8.7 A Debug procedure. 83

9.1 Maintaining a `tclIndex` file. 90
9.2 Loading a `tclIndex` file. 92

10.1 "Hello, World!" Tk program. 97

11.1 Logging the output of a UNIX program. 104
11.2 A browser for the code examples in the book. 109
11.3 A Tcl shell in a text widget. 113

12.1 Two frames packed inside the main frame. 116
12.2 Turning off geometry propagation. 116
12.3 A horizontal stack inside a vertical stack. 117
12.4 Even more nesting of horizontal and vertical stacks. 117
12.5 Mixing `bottom` and `right` packing sides. 118
12.6 Filling the display into extra packing space. 119
12.7 Using horizontal fill in a menubar. 120
12.8 The effects of internal padding (`-ipady`). 121
12.9 Button padding vs. packer padding. 121
12.10 The look of a default button. 122
12.11 Resizing without the expand option. 123
12.12 Resizing with expand turned on. 123
12.13 More than one expanding widget. 124
12.14 Setup for anchor experiments. 124
12.15 The effects of non-center anchors. 125
12.16 Animating the packing anchors. 125
12.17 Controlling the packing order. 126
12.18 Packing into other relatives. 127

13.1 Bindings on different binding tags. 135
13.2 Output from the UNIX *xmodmap* program. 141
13.3 Emacs-like binding convention for Meta and Escape. 142

14.1 A troublesome button command. 146
14.2 Fixing the troublesome situation. 147
14.3 A button associated with a Tcl procedure. 148
14.4 Radiobuttons and checkbuttons. 150
14.5 A command on a radiobutton or checkbutton. 151
14.6 A menu sampler. 154
14.7 A simple menu-by-name package. 159
14.8 Adding menu entries. 159
14.9 A wrapper for cascade entries. 160
14.10 Using the menu-by-name package. 160
14.11 Keeping the accelerator display up-to-date. 161

15.1 Reading an option database file. 165
15.2 A file containing resource specifications. 166
15.3 Using resources to specify user-defined buttons. 167
15.4 `ButtonResources` defines buttons based on resources. 168
15.5 Using `ButtonResources`. 168
15.6 Specifying menu entries via resources. 169
15.7 Defining menus from resource specifications. 170

16.1 A label that displays different strings....173
16.2 The message widget formats long lines of text....175
16.3 Controlling the text layout in a message widget. 176
16.4 A scale widget. 177
16.5 A text widget and two scrollbars. 181

17.1 A command entry....186
17.2 A listbox with two scrollbars....191
17.3 A listbox with scrollbars and better alignment. 192
17.4 Choosing items from a listbox. 196

18.1 Setting focus-follows-mouse input focus model. 205
18.2 A simple dialog....207
18.3 A feedback procedure....209
18.4 A file selection dialog....210
18.5 Specifying attributes with X resources....212
18.6 Event bindings for the dialog....213
18.7 Listing a directory for `fileselect`. 214
18.8 Accepting a file name. 216
18.9 Simple support routines....217
18.10 File name completion. 217

19.1 Tag configurations for basic character styles. 224
19.2 Line spacing and justification in the text widget. 225
19.3 An active text button....228
19.4 Delayed creation of embedded widgets....229

20.1 A large scrollable canvas. 236
20.2 The canvas "Hello, World!" example. 236
20.3 A min max scale canvas example....238
20.4 Moving the markers for the min max scale. 240
20.5 Canvas `arc` items. 242
20.6 Canvas `bitmap` items. 243
20.7 Canvas `image` items....244
20.8 A canvas stroke drawing example....244
20.9 Canvas `oval` items....246
20.10 Canvas `polygon` items....247
20.11 Dragging out a box....248
20.12 Simple edit bindings for canvas `text` items. 250
20.13 Using a canvas to scroll a set of widgets. 252
20.14 Generating postscript from a canvas. 257

21.1 Paste the `PRIMARY` or `CLIPBOARD` selection. 261
21.2 A selection handler for canvas widgets. 264

22.1 A read event file handler....269

22.2 The sender application. 271
22.3 Using the sender application. 273
22.4 Hooking the browser to an `eval` server. 275
22.5 Making the shell into an `eval` server. 276

23.1 Equal-sized labels. 279
23.2 3D relief sampler. 280
23.3 Padding provided by labels and buttons. 282
23.4 Anchoring text in a label or button. 282
23.5 Borders and padding. 283

24.1 Resources for reverse video. 285
24.2 Computing a darker color. 287
24.3 Specifying an image for a widget. 289
24.4 Specifying a bitmap for a widget. 290
24.5 The built-in bitmaps. 291
24.6 The X cursor font. 294

25.1 `FindFont` matches an existing font. 299
25.2 Handling missing font errors. 299
25.3 `FontWidget` protects against font errors. 300
25.4 A gridded, resizable listbox. 301
25.5 A font selection application. 303
25.6 Using variable traces to fix things up. 304
25.7 Listing available fonts. 304
25.8 Determining possible font components. 305
25.9 Creating the radiobutton menu entries. 306
25.10 Setting up the label and message widgets. 306
25.11 The font selection procedures. 307

26.1 Gridded geometry for a canvas. 310
26.2 Telling other applications what your name is. 314

27.1 A user interface to widget bindings. 322
27.2 `Bind_Display` presents the bindings for a widget or class. 323
27.3 Related listboxes are configured to select items together. 324
27.4 Controlling a pair of listboxes with one scrollbar. 324
27.5 Drag-scrolling a pair of listboxes together. 325
27.6 An interface to define bindings. 325
27.7 Defining and saving bindings. 327

28.1 Preferences initialization. 330
28.2 Adding preference items. 331
28.3 Setting preference variables. 332
28.4 Using the preferences package. 332
28.5 A user interface to the preference items. 333
28.6 Interface objects for different preference types. 334

28.7 Displaying the help text for an item. 335
28.8 Saving preferences settings to a file. 336
28.9 Read settings from the preferences file. 337
28.10 Tracing a Tcl variable in a preference item. 338

29.1 A canonical Tcl `main` program and `Tcl_AppInit`. 341
29.2 The `RandomCmd` C command procedure. 343
29.3 Calling C command procedure directly. 345
29.4 A Makefile for a simple Tcl C program. 347
29.5 Using the `Hash` package. 351

30.1 A canonical Tk main program and `Tcl_AppInit`. 354
30.2 A custom Tk main program. 355
30.3 Using `Tk_DoOneEvent` with `TK_DONT_WAIT`. 359

31.1 The `Clock` widget data structure. 370
31.2 Configuration specs for the clock widget. 371
31.3 The `ClockCmd` command procedure. 373
31.4 The `ClockInstanceCmd` command procedure. 374
31.5 `ClockConfigure` allocates resources for the widget. 376
31.6 `ComputeGeometry` computes the widget's size. 378
31.7 The `ClockDisplay` procedure. 379
31.8 The `ClockEventProc` handles window events. 381
31.9 The `ClockDestroy` cleanup procedure. 382

32.1 A sample expect script. 392
32.2 A `SIGINT` handler. 395
32.3 Summary of [incr Tcl] commands. 401
32.4 `Tcl_AppInit` and extension packages. 403
32.5 Makefile for *supertcl*. 405

List of Tables

1-1 Backslash sequences. 14
1-2 Variables defined by *tclsh* and *wish*. 15
1-3 Arithmetic operators from highest to lowest precedence. 15
1-4 Built-in math functions. 16
1-5 Built-in Tcl Commands. 17

2-1 The `string` command. 20
2-2 Format conversions. 22
2-3 Format flags. 23
2-4 Regular expression syntax. 25

3-1 List-related commands. 31
3-2 The `array` command. 38

7-1 Summary of the `exec` syntax for I/O redirection. 64
7-2 The `file` command options. 65
7-3 Tcl commands used for file access. 68
7-4 Summary of the `open` access arguments. 69
7-5 Summary of `POSIX` flags for the access argument. 69

8-1 The `info` command. 76
8-2 The `history` command. 81
8-3 Special `history` syntax. 81
8-4 Debugger commands. 84

10-1 Tk widget-creation commands. 100
10-2 Tk widget-manipulation commands. 101

12-1 The `pack` command. 129
12-2 Packing options. 129
12-3 The `place` command. 130
12-4 Placement options. 131

13-1 Event types. 137
13-2 Event modifiers. 141
13-3 A summary of the event keywords. 143

14-1 Resource names of attributes for all button widgets. 151
14-2 Button operations. 153
14-3 Menu operations. 156
14-4 Menu entry index keywords 157
14-5 Menu attribute resource names. 157
14-6 Attributes for menu entries. 158

16-1 Frame and toplevel attribute resource names. 172
16-2 Label attribute resource names. 174
16-3 Message attribute resource names. 176
16-4 Scale bindings. 178
16-5 Scale attribute resource names. 178
16-6 Scale operations. 179
16-7 Scrollbar bindings. 182
16-8 Scrollbar attribute resource names. 182
16-9 Scrollbar operations. 183

17-1 Entry bindings. 187
17-2 Entry attribute resource names. 188
17-3 Entry indices. 189
17-4 Entry operations. 190
17-5 Listbox indices 194
17-6 Listbox operations. 194
17-7 The values for the `selectMode` of a listbox. 198
17-8 Bindings for `browse` selection mode. 198
17-9 Bindings for `single` selection mode. 198
17-10 Bindings for `extended` selection mode. 199
17-11 Bindings for `multiple` selection mode. 200
17-12 Listbox scroll bindings. 200
17-13 Listbox attribute resource names. 201

18-1 The `focus` command. 204
18-2 The `grab` command. 206
18-3 The `tkwait` command. 206

19-1 Text indices. 220
19-2 Index modifiers for text widgets. 221
19-3 Attributes for text tags. 223
19-4 Options to the `window create` operation. 229
19-5 Bindings for the text widget. 230
19-6 Operations for the text widget. 232
19-7 Text attribute resource names. 234

20-1 Arc attributes. 242
20-2 Bitmap attributes. 243
20-3 Image attributes. 244
20-4 Line attributes. 246
20-5 Oval attributes. 247
20-6 Polygon attributes. 248
20-7 Rectangle attributes. 249
20-8 Indices for canvas `text` items. 249
20-9 Canvas operations that apply to `text` items. 250
20-10 Text attributes 252
20-11 Operations on a `canvas` widget. 254

20-12 Canvas postscript options. 256
20-13 Canvas attribute resource names. 258

21-1 The selection command. 262
21-2 The clipboard command. 263

22-1 The after command. 268
22-2 The fileevent command. 269
22-3 Options to the send command. 269

23-1 Size attribute resource names. 278
23-2 Border and relief attribute resource names. 281
23-3 Highlight attribute resource names. 281
23-4 Layout attribute resource names. 282

24-1 Color attribute resource names. 286
24-2 Visual classes for X displays. 288
24-3 Summary of the image command. 289
24-4 Bitmap image options. 290
24-5 Photo image attributes. 291
24-6 Photo image operations. 292
24-7 Copy options for photo images. 293
24-8 Read options for photo images. 293
24-9 Write options for photo images. 293
24-10 Cursor attribute resource names. 295

25-1 X Font specification components. 298
25-2 Layout attribute resource names 301
25-3 Selection attribute resource names. 302

26-1 Size, placement and decoration window manager operations. . 311
26-2 Window manager commands for icons. 312
26-3 Session-related window manager operations. 313
26-4 Miscellaneous window manager operations. 313
26-5 send command information. 314
26-6 Window hierarchy information. 315
26-7 Window size information. 316
26-8 Window location information. 317
26-9 Virtual root window information. 317
26-10 Atom and window ID information. 318
26-11 Colormap and visual class information. 318

31-1 Configuration flags and corresponding C types. 372

33-1 Changes in color attribute names. 412

Preface

Tcl stands for *Tool Command Language*. Tcl is really two things: a scripting language, and an interpreter for that language that is designed to be easy to embed into your application. Tcl and its associated X windows toolkit, Tk, were designed and crafted by Professor John Ousterhout of the University of California, Berkeley. You can find these packages on the Internet, (as explained later), and use them freely in your application, even if it is commercial. The Tcl interpreter has been ported from UNIX to DOS, Windows, OS/2, NT, and Macintosh environments.

I first heard about Tcl in 1988 while I was Ousterhout's Ph.D. student at Berkeley. We were designing a network operating system, Sprite. While the students hacked on a new kernel, John wrote a new editor and terminal emulator. He used Tcl as the command language for both tools so users could define menus and otherwise customize those programs. This was in the days of X10, and he had plans for an X toolkit based on Tcl that would help programs cooperate with each other by communicating with Tcl commands. To me, this cooperation among tools was the essence of Tcl.

This early vision imagined that applications would be large bodies of compiled code and a small amount of Tcl used for configuration and high-level commands. John's editor, *mx*, and the terminal emulator, *tx*, followed this model. While this model remains valid, it has also turned out to be possible to write entire applications in Tcl. This is because of the Tcl/Tk shell, *wish*, that provides all the functionality of other shell languages, including running other programs, plus the ability to create a graphical user interface. For better or worse, it is now common to find applications that contain thousands of lines of Tcl script.

This book was written because, while I found it enjoyable and productive to use Tcl and Tk, there were times when I was frustrated. In addition, working at Xerox PARC, with many experts in languages and systems, I was compelled to understand both the strengths and weaknesses of Tcl and Tk. While many of my colleagues adopted Tcl and Tk for their projects, they were also just as quick to point out its flaws. In response, I have built up a set of programming techniques that exploit the power of Tcl and Tk while avoiding troublesome areas. Thus, this book is meant as a practical guide to help you get the most out of Tcl and Tk and avoid some of the frustrations I experienced.

Why Tcl?

As a scripting language, Tcl is similar to other UNIX shell languages such as the Bourne Shell (sh), the C Shell (csh), the Korn Shell (ksh), and Perl. Shell programs let you execute other programs. They provide enough programmability (variables, control flow, and procedures) to let you build complex scripts that assemble existing programs into a new tool tailored for your needs. Shells are wonderful for automating routine chores.

It is the ability to easily add a Tcl interpreter to your application that sets it apart from other shells. Tcl fills the role of an extension language that is used to configure and customize applications. There is no need to invent a command language for your new application, or struggle to provide some sort of user-programmability for your tool. Instead, by adding a Tcl interpreter, you structure your application as a set of primitive operations that can be composed by a script to best suit the needs of your users. It also allows other programs to have programmatic control over your application, leading to suites of applications that work well together.

There are other choices for extension languages that include Scheme, Elisp, and Python. Your choice between them is partly a matter of taste. Tcl has simple constructs and looks somewhat like C. It is easy to add new Tcl primitives by writing C procedures. In addition, the Tcl community has contributed many Tcl commands that you can access as-is. To me, the strength of the Tcl community is more important than the details of the language.

The Tcl C library has clean interfaces and is simple to use. The library implements the basic interpreter and a set of core scripting commands that implement variables, flow control, file I/O, and procedures (see page 17). In addition, your application can define new Tcl commands. These commands are associated with a C or C++ procedure that your application provides. The result is applications that are split into a set of primitives written in a compiled language, and exported as Tcl commands. A Tcl script is used to compose the primitives into the overall application. The script layer has access to shell-like capability to run other programs and access the file system, as well as call directly into the compiled part of the application through the application-specific Tcl commands you define. In addition, from the C programming level, you can call Tcl scripts, set and query Tcl variables, and even trace the execution of the Tcl interpreter.

There are many Tcl extensions freely available on the Internet. Most extensions include a C library that provides some new functionality, and a Tcl interface to the library. Examples include socket access for network programming, database access, telephone control, MIDI controller access, and *expect*, which adds Tcl commands to control interactive programs.

The most notable extension is Tk, a toolkit for X windows. Tk is currently being ported to Windows and Macintosh environments, too. Tk defines Tcl commands that let you create and manipulate user interface widgets. The script-based approach to user interface programming has three benefits:

- Development is fast because of the rapid turnaround; there is no waiting for long compilations.
- The Tcl commands provide a higher-level interface to X than most standard C library toolkits. Simple user interfaces require just a handful of commands to define them. At the same time, it is possible to refine the user interface in order to get every detail just so. The fast turnaround aids the refinement process.
- The user interface is clearly factored out from the rest of your application. The developer can concentrate on the implementation of the application core, and then fairly painlessly work up a user interface. The core set of Tk widgets is often sufficient for all your user interface needs. However, it is also possible to write custom Tk widgets in C, and again there are many contributed Tk widgets available on the network.

Tcl 7.4 and Tk 4.0

This book is up-to-date with Tcl version 7.4 and Tk version 4.0. There are occasional descriptions of Tk 3.6 features. The last chapter has some notes about porting scripts written in earlier versions of Tk.

Who Should Read This Book

This book is meant to be useful to the beginner in Tcl as well as the expert. For the beginner and expert alike I recommend careful study of Chapter One, *Tcl Fundamentals*. The programming model of Tcl is different from many programming languages. The model is based on string substitutions, and it is important that you understand it properly to avoid trouble in complex cases. The remainder of the book consists of examples that demonstrate how to use Tcl and Tk productively. For your reference, there are tables that summarize all the Tcl and Tk commands and widgets.

This book assumes that you have some UNIX and X background, although you should be able to get by even if you are a complete novice. Knowledge of UNIX shell programming will help, but it is not required. Where aspects of X are relevant, I provide some background information. Tcl has been widely ported, and the book will be helpful if you are using Tcl on a Macintosh, Windows machine, or some other environment.

How To Read This Book

This book is best used in a hands-on manner, at the computer, trying the examples. The book tries to fill the gap between the terse Tcl and Tk manual pages, which are complete but lack context and examples, and existing Tcl programs that may or may not be documented or well written.

I recommend the on-line manual pages for the Tcl and Tk commands. They provide a detailed reference guide to each command. This book summarizes much of the information from the manual pages, but it does not provide the complete details, which can vary from release to release.

I also recommend the book by John Ousterhout, *Tcl and the Tk Toolkit*, which provides a broad overview of all aspects of Tcl and Tk. There is some overlap with Ousterhout's book, although that book provides a more detailed treatment of C programming for Tcl, and this book provides more Tcl examples.

Ftp Archives

The primary site for the Tcl and Tk distributions is given below as a Universal Resource Location (URL). You can use FTP and login to the host (e.g., `ftp.cs.berkeley.edu`) under the `anonymous` user name. Give your email address as the password. The directory is in the URL after the host name (e.g., `ucb/tcl`).

```
ftp://ftp.cs.berkeley.edu/ucb/tcl
```

There are many sites that mirror this distribution. In addition, they provide an archive site for contributed Tcl commands, Tk widgets, and applications. There is also a set of Frequently Asked Questions files. As of this writing, these sites had Tcl sources:

```
ftp://ftp.aud.alcatel.com/tcl
ftp://syd.dit.csiro.au/pub/tk
ftp://ftp.ibp.fr/pub/tcl
ftp://src.doc.ic.ac.uk/packages/tcl/
ftp://ftp.luth.se/pub/unix/tcl/
ftp://ftp.switch.ch/mirror/tcl
ftp://ftp.sterling.com/programming/languages/tcl
ftp://ftp.sunet.se/pub/lang/tcl
mailto://ftpmail@ftp.sunet.se
ftp://ftp.cs.columbia.edu/archives/tcl
ftp://ftp.uni-paderborn.de/pub/unix/tcl
ftp://sunsite.unc.edu/pub/languages/tcl/
ftp://ftp.funet.fi/pub/languages/tcl/
```

You can also use a World Wide Web browser like *mosaic*, *netscape*, or *lynx* to access these sites. Enter the URL as specified above and you are presented with a directory listing of that location. From there you can change directories and fetch files.

If you do not have direct FTP access, you can use an email server for FTP. Send email to `ftpmail@decwrl.dec.com` with the message `Help` to get directions. If you are on BITNET, send email to `bitftp@pucc.princeton.edu`.

You can search for FTP sites that have Tcl by using the *archie* service that indexes the contents of anonymous FTP servers. Information about using *archie* can be obtained by sending mail to `archie@archie.sura.net` that contains the message `Help`.

World Wide Web

There are a number of pages on the World Wide Web about Tcl:

```
http://www.sco.com/IXI/of_interest/tcl/Tcl.html
http://web.cs.ualberta.ca/~wade/Auto/Tcl.html
```

Newsgroups

The `comp.lang.tcl` newsgroup is very active. It provides a forum for questions and answers about Tcl. Announcements about Tcl extensions and applications are posted frequently to this group.

Typographic Conventions

The more important examples are set apart with a title and horizontal rules, while others appear in-line. The examples use `courier` for Tcl and C code. When interesting results are returned by a Tcl command, those are presented below in *`oblique courier`*. The => is not part of the return value in the following example.

```
expr 5 + 8
=> 13
```

The `courier` font is also used when naming Tcl commands and C procedures within sentences.

The usage of a Tcl command is presented in the following example. The command name and constant keywords appear in `courier`. Variable values appear in *`courier oblique`*. Optional arguments are surrounded with question marks.

```
set varname ?value?
```

The name of a UNIX program is in italics:

xterm

Hot Tips

The icon in the margin marks a "hot tip" as judged by the reviewers of the book. The visual markers help you locate the more useful sections in the book. These are also listed in the index under Hot Tip.

On-line examples

The book comes with a floppy disk that has source for all of the examples. The floppy is in *tar* format, which you should be able to read on any UNIX system. On SunOS, use the following command to read the floppy:

```
% tar xvf /dev/rfd0c
```

The name of the floppy device may be different on your system.

You can also get the examples via FTP:

```
ftp://mercury.prenhall.com/pub/software/welch/tkbook.tar
```

Book Organization

The first chapter of this book describes the fundamental mechanisms that characterize the Tcl language. This is an important chapter that provides the basic grounding you will need to use Tcl effectively. Even if you have programmed in Tcl already, you should review this chapter.

Chapters 2-5 cover the basic Tcl commands in more detail, including string handling, regular expressions, data types, control flow, procedures and scoping issues. You can skip these chapters if you already know Tcl.

Chapter 6 discusses `eval` and more advanced Tcl coding techniques. If you are running into quoting problems, check out this chapter.

Chapter 7 describes the interface to the operating system for shell-like capabilities to run other programs and examine the file system. The I/O commands are described here.

Chapter 8 describes the facilities provided by the interpreter for introspection. You can find out about all the internal state of Tcl. The chapter describes development aids and debugging.

Chapter 9 describes the script library facility. If you do much Tcl programming, you should collect useful scripts into a library. This chapter also describes coding conventions to support larger scale programming efforts.

Chapter 10 is an introduction to Tk. It explains the relevant aspects of the X window system and the basic model provided by the Tk toolkit.

Chapter 11 illustrates Tk programming with a number of short examples. One of the examples is a browser for the code examples in this book.

Chapter 12 explains geometry management, which is responsible for arranging widgets on the screen. The chapter is primarily about the `pack` geometry manager. The simpler `place` geometry manager is described briefly.

Chapter 13 covers event binding. A binding registers a Tcl script that is executed in response to events from the X window system.

Chapter 14 describes the button and menu widgets. The chapter includes a simple menu package that hides some of details of setting up Tk menus.

Chapter 15 describes the X resource mechanism and how it relates to the Tk toolkit. The extended examples show how users can use resource specifications to define custom buttons and menus for an application.

Chapter 16 describes several simple Tk widgets: the frame, the toplevel, the label, the message, the scale, and the scrollbar. These widgets can be added to your interface with two or three commands. The `bell` command is also described here.

Chapter 17 describes the entry and listbox widgets. These are specialized text widgets that provide a single line of text input and a scrollable list of text items, respectively. You are likely to program specialized behavior for these widgets.

Chapter 18 covers the issues related to dialog boxes. This includes input focus and grabs for modal interactions. A file selection dialog box is presented as an example.

Chapter 19 describes the text widget, which is a general purpose text widget with advanced features for text formatting, editing, and embedded images.

Chapter 20 describes the canvas widget that provides a general drawing interface.

Chapter 21 explains how to use the selection mechanism for cut-and-paste. Tk supports different selections, including the `CLIPBOARD` selection used by OpenLook tools.

Chapter 22 describes the `after`, `fileevent`, and `send` commands. These commands let you create sophisticated application structures, including cooperating suites of applications.

Chapter 23 is the first of three chapters that review the attributes that are shared among the Tk widget set. This chapter describes sizing and borders.

Chapter 24 describes colors, images and cursors. It explains how to use the bitmap and color photo image types. The chapter includes a complete map of the X cursor font.

Chapter 25 describes fonts and other text-related attributes. The extended example is a font selection application.

Chapter 26 explains how to interact with the window manager using the `wm` command. The chapter describes all the information available through the `winfo` command.

Chapter 27 presents a user interface to the binding mechanism. You can browse and edit bindings for widgets and classes with the interface.

Chapter 28 builds upon Chapter 15 to create a user preferences package and an associated user interface. The preference package links a Tcl variable used in your application to an X resource specification.

Chapter 29 provides a short introduction to using Tcl at the C programming level. It gets you started with integrating Tcl into an existing application, and it provides a survey the facilities in the Tcl C library.

Chapter 30 introduces C programming with the Tk toolkit. It surveys the Tk C library.

Chapter 31 presents a sample digital clock Tk widget implementation in C.

Chapter 32 is a survey of several interesting Tcl extension packages. The packages extend Tcl to provide access to more UNIX functionality (TclX), control over interactive programs (Expect), network programming (Tcl-DP), more Tk widgets (BLT), and an object system ([incr Tcl]). The chapter concludes with a C program that integrates all of these extensions into one *supertcl* application.

Chapter 33 has notes about porting your scripts to Tk 4.0.

Thanks

I would like to thank my managers and colleagues at Xerox PARC for their patience with me as I worked on this book. The tips and tricks in this book came partly from my own work as I helped lab members use Tcl, and partly from them as they taught me. Dave Nichols' probing questions forced me to understand the basic mechanisms of the Tcl interpreter. Dan Swinehart and Lawrence Butcher kept me sharp with their own critiques. Ron Frederick and Berry Kerchival adopted Tk for their graphical interfaces and amazed me with their rapid results. Becky Burwell, Rich Gold, Carl Hauser, John Maxwell, Ken Pier, Marvin Theimer and Mohan Vishwanath made use of my early drafts, and their questions pointed out large holes in the text. Karin Petersen, Bill Schilit, and Terri Watson kept life interesting by using Tcl in very non-standard ways. I especially thank my managers, Mark Weiser and Doug Terry, for their understanding and support.

I thank John Ousterhout for Tcl and Tk, which are wonderful systems built with excellent craftsmanship. John was kind enough to provide me with an advance version of Tk 4.0 so I could learn about its new features well before its first beta release.

Thanks to the Tcl programmers out on the net, from which I learned many tricks. John LoVerso and Steven Uhler are the hottest Tcl programmers I know.

Many thanks to the patient reviewers of early drafts: Pierre David, Clif Flynt, Simon Kenyon, Eugene Lee, Don Libes, Lee Moore, Joe Moss, Hador Shemtov, Frank Stajano, Charles Thayer, and Jim Thornton.

Many folks contributed suggestions by email: Miguel Angel, Stephen Bensen, Jeff Blaine, Tom Charnock, Brian Cooper, Patrick D'Cruze, Benoit Desrosiers, Ted Dunning, Mark Eichin, Paul Friberg, Carl Gauthier, David Gerdes, Klaus Hackenberg, Torkle Hasle, Marti Hearst, Jean-Pierre Herbert, Jamie Honan, Norman Klein, Joe Konstan, Susan Larson, Håkan Liljegren, Lionel Mallet, Dejan Milojicic, Greg Minshall, Bernd Mohr, Will Morse, Heiko Nardmann, Gerd Neugebauer, TV Raman, Cary Renzema, Rob Riepel, Dan Schenk, Jean-Guy Schneider, Elizabeth Scholl, Karl Schwamb, Rony Shapiro, Peter Simanyi, Vince Skahan, Bill Stumbo, Glen Vanderburg, Larry Virden, Reed Wade, and Jim Wight. Unfortunately I could not respond to every suggestion, even some that were excellent. I am still open to comments about this edition. My email address is `welch@parc.xerox.com`.

Thanks to the editors and staff at Prentice Hall. Mark Taub has been very helpful as I progressed through my first book. Lynn Schneider and Kerry Reardon were excellent copy and production editors, respectively.

Finally, I thank my wonderful wife Jody for her love, kindness, patience, wit, and understanding as I worked long hours. Happily, many of those hours were spent working from home. My new son Christopher gets the credit for keeping me from degenerating into a complete nerd.

CHAPTER 1

Tcl Fundamentals

This chapter describes the basic syntax rules for the Tcl scripting language. It describes the basic mechanisms used by the Tcl interpreter: substitution and grouping. It touches lightly on the following Tcl commands: `source`, `puts`, `format`, `set`, `expr`, `string`, `while`, `incr`, and `proc`.

Tcl is a string-based command language. The language has only a few fundamental constructs and relatively little syntax, which makes it easy to learn. The basic mechanisms are all related to strings and string substitutions, so it is fairly easy to visualize what is going on in the interpreter. The model is a little different than some other languages you may already be familiar with, so it is worth making sure you understand the basic concepts.

Getting Started

With any Tcl installation there are typically two Tcl shell programs that you can use: *tclsh* and *wish*.[*] They are simple programs that are not much more than a read-eval-print loop. The first is a basic Tcl shell that can be used as a shell much like the C-shell or Bourne shell. *wish* is a Tcl interpreter that has been extended with the Tk commands used to create and manipulate X widgets. You can use *wish* to write applications that have a nice user interface. If you cannot find the basic Tcl shell, just run *wish* and ignore for the moment the empty window it pops up. Both shells print a % prompt and will execute Tcl commands interactively, printing the result of each top level command.

[*] You may have variations on these programs that reflect different extensions added to the shells. *tcl* and *wishx* are the shells that have Extended Tcl added, for example.

You may also find it easier to enter the longer examples into a file using your favorite editor. This lets you quickly try out variations and correct mistakes. Taking this approach you have three options. The first way is to use two windows, one running the Tcl interpreter and the other running your editor. Save your examples to a file and then execute them with the Tcl `source` command:

```
source filename
```

The second way is to create a stand-alone script much like an `sh` or `csh` script. The trick is in the first line of the file, which names the interpreter for the rest of the file. Support for this is built into the `exec` system call in UNIX. Begin the file with either of the following lines:

```
#!/usr/local/bin/tcl
```

or

```
#!/usr/local/bin/wish
```

Of course, the actual pathname for these programs may be different on your system. On most UNIX systems this pathname is limited to 32 characters, including the `#!`. The 32-character limit is a limitation of the UNIX `exec` system call. If you get the pathname wrong, you get a confusing "command not found" error, and if the pathname is too long you may end up with `/bin/sh` trying to interpret your script, giving you syntax errors. For a trick that works around the pathname length limitation, see page 12. If you have Tk version 3.6 or earlier, its version of *wish* requires a `-f` argument to make it read the contents of a file. The `-f` switch is ignored in Tk 4.0.

```
#!/usr/local/bin/wish -f
```

Your third option is to use the Tcl script library facility. Put all your Tcl files into one directory, (e.g., `~/tcl/book`). If you have the floppy disk that comes with the book, unpack the files there. On SunOS you can use these UNIX commands to read the floppy (the device may be different on other versions of UNIX):

```
% cd ~/tcl/book
% tar xvf /dev/rfd0c
```

The following Tcl command creates an index of the Tcl procedures in the directory. The floppy already has a `tclIndex` file, but if you add procedures you need to update the index with this command:

```
auto_mkindex ~/tcl/book *.tcl
```

The following command makes the Tcl procedures in the library available to your script. Put this command at the beginning of your script, before you use a procedure from one of the examples.

```
lappend auto_path ~/tcl/book
```

Chapter 9 explains the Tcl library facility in more detail.

Tcl Commands

The basic syntax for a Tcl command is:

```
command arg1 arg2 arg3 ...
```

The `command` is either the name of a built-in command or a Tcl procedure. White space (i.e., space or tab) is used to separate the command name and its arguments, and a newline or semicolon is used to terminate a command.

This basic model is extended with just a few pieces of syntax for *grouping*, which allows multiple words in one argument, and *substitution*, which is used with programming variables and nested command calls. The grouping and substitutions are the only mechanisms employed by the Tcl interpreter before it runs a command.

The arguments to a command are strings. Except for the substitutions described later in this chapter, the Tcl interpreter does not interpret the arguments to a command. In contrast, in other programming languages when you use an identifier you automatically gets its value, and you must use quotes to get a literal string. In Tcl, everything is a string, and you must explicitly ask for evaluation of variables and nested commands.

Hello World

Example 1–1 The "Hello, World!" example.

```
puts stdout {Hello, World!}
=> Hello, World!
```

In this example, the command is `puts`, which takes two arguments: an I/O stream identifier and a string. `puts` writes the string to the I/O stream along with a trailing newline character. There are two points to emphasize:

- Arguments are interpreted by the command. In the example, `stdout` is used to identify the standard output stream. The use of `stdout` as a name is a convention employed by `puts` and the other I/O commands. Also, `stderr` is used to identify the standard error output, and `stdin` is used to identify the standard input.
- Curly braces are used to group words together into a single argument. The `puts` command receives `Hello, World!` as its second argument. Note that the braces are not part of the value, which can be confusing. The braces are syntax for the interpreter, and they get stripped off before the value is passed to the command. Braces group all characters, including newlines and nested braces, until a matching brace is found. This property will be illustrated later.

Variables

The `set` command is used to assign a value to a variable. It takes two arguments: the first is the name of the variable and the second is the value. Variable names can be any length, and case *is* significant. You can use any character in a variable name. It is not necessary to declare Tcl variables before you use them. The interpreter will create the variable when it is first assigned a value. The value of a variable is obtained later with the dollar-sign syntax illustrated in the example:

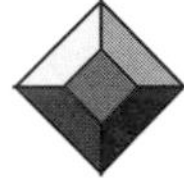

Example 1–2 Tcl variables.

```
set var 5
=> 5
set b $var
=> 5
```

The second `set` command assigns to variable `b` the value of variable `var`. The use of the dollar sign is our first example of substitution. You can imagine that the second `set` command gets rewritten by substituting the value of `var` for `$var` to obtain a new command.

```
set b 5
```

The actual implementation is a little different, but not much.

Command Substitution

The second form of substitution is *command substitution*. A nested command is delimited by square brackets, `[ ]`. The Tcl interpreter takes everything between the brackets and evaluates it as a command. It rewrites the outer command by replacing the square brackets and everything between them with the result of the nested command. This is similar to the use of backquotes in other shells, except that it has the additional advantage of supporting arbitrary nesting of other commands.

Example 1–3 Command substitution.

```
set len [string length foobar]
=> 6
```

In the example, the nested command is:

```
string length foobar
```

The `string` command performs various operations on strings. Here we are asking for the length of the string `foobar`.

Command substitution causes the outer command to be rewritten as if it were:

```
set len 6
```

If there are several cases of command substitution within a single command, the interpreter processes them from left to right. As each right bracket is encountered the command it delimits is evaluated.

Note that the spaces in the nested command are ignored for the purposes of grouping the arguments to `set`. In addition, if the result of the nested command contains any spaces or other special characters, they are not interpreted. These issues will be illustrated in more detail later in this chapter. The basic rule of thumb is that the interpreter treats everything from the left bracket to the matching right bracket as one lump of characters, and it replaces that lump with the result of the nested command.

Math Expressions

The Tcl interpreter itself does not evaluate math expressions. Instead, the `expr` command is used to evaluate math expressions. The interpreter treats `expr` just like any other command, and it leaves the expression parsing up to the `expr` implementation. The math syntax supported by `expr` is much like the C expression syntax, and a more complete summary of the expression syntax is given in the reference section at the end of this chapter.

The implementation of `expr` takes all its arguments, concatenates them into a single string, and then parses the string as a math expression. After `expr` computes the answer, the answer is formatted into a string and returned:

Example 1–4 Simple arithmetic.

```
expr 7.2 / 3
=> 2.4
```

The `expr` command primarily deals with integer, floating point, and boolean values. Logical operations return either 0 (false) or 1 (true). Integer values are promoted to floating point values as needed. Octal values are indicated by a leading zero. Hexadecimal values are indicated by a leading `0x`. Scientific notation for floating point numbers is supported. There is some support for string comparisons by `expr`, but the `string compare` command described in Chapter 2 is more reliable because `expr` may do conversions on strings that look like numbers.

You can include variable references and nested commands in math expressions. The following example uses `expr` to add `7` to the length of the string `foobar`. As a result of the inner-most command substitution, the `expr` command sees `6 + 7`, and `len` gets the value `13`:

Example 1–5 Nested commands.

```
set len [expr [string length foobar] + 7]
=> 13
```

The expression evaluator supports a number of built-in math functions. For a complete listing, see page 16. The following example computes the value of *pi*:

Example 1–6 Built-in math functions.

```
set pi [expr 2*asin(1.0)]
=> 3.14159
```

By default, six significant digits are used when returning a floating point value. This can be changed by setting the `tcl_precision` variable to the number of significant digits desired. Seventeen digits of precision is enough to ensure that no information is lost when converting back and forth between a string and an IEEE double precision number:

Example 1–7 Controlling precision with `tcl_precision`.

```
expr 1 / 3
=> 0
expr 1 / 3.0
=> 0.333333
set tcl_precision 17
=> 17
expr 1 / 3.0
=> 0.33333333333333331
```

Backslash Substitution

The final type of substitution done by the Tcl interpreter is *backslash substitution*. This is used to quote characters that have special meaning to the interpreter. For example, you can specify a literal dollar sign, brace, or bracket by quoting it with a backslash. You can also specify characters that are hard to type directly by giving their octal or hexadecimal value.

As a rule, however, if you find yourself using lots of backslashes, there is probably a simpler way to achieve the effect you are striving for. For example, you can group things with curly braces to turn off all interpretation of special characters. However, there are cases where backslashes are required.

Example 1–8 Quoting special characters with backslash.

```
set dollar \$
=> $
set x $dollar
=> $
```

In the example, the value of `dollar` does not affect the substitution done in the assignment to `x`. After the example, the value of `x` and `dollar` is the single character, `$`. This is a crucial property of the Tcl interpreter: *only a single round*

of interpretation is done. You do not have to worry about the value of variables.

You can also specify characters with their hexadecimal or octal value:

```
set escape \0x1b
set escape \033
```

The value of variable `escape` is the ASCII ESC character, which has character code `27`. The table on page 14 summarizes backslash substitutions.

Another common use of backslashes is to continue long commands on multiple lines. This is necessary because a newline terminates a command unless an argument is being grouped as described in the next section. A backslash as the last character in a line is converted into a space. In addition, all the white space at the beginning of the next line is replaced by this substitution. The backslash in the next example is required, otherwise the `expr` command gets terminated too soon.

Example 1–9 Continuing long lines with backslashes.

```
set totalLength [expr [string length $one] + \
      [string length $two]]
```

Grouping with Braces and Double Quotes

Double quotes and curly braces are used to group words together. The difference between double quotes and curly braces is that quotes allow substitutions to occur in the group, while curly braces prevent substitutions. This rule applies to command, variable, and backslash substitutions. In contrast, square brackets do not provide grouping, which is why the backslash is necessary in the previous example.

Example 1–10 Grouping with double quotes vs. braces.

```
set s Hello
=> Hello
puts stdout "The length of $s is [string length $s]."
=> The length of Hello is 5.
puts stdout {The length of $s is [string length $s].}
=> The length of $s is [string length $s].
```

In the second command of the example, the Tcl interpreter does variable and command substitution on the second argument to `puts`. In the third command, substitutions are prevented so the string is printed as-is.

In practice, grouping with curly braces is used when substitutions on the argument must be delayed until a later time (or never done at all). Examples include control flow statements and procedure declarations. Double quotes are useful in simple cases like the `puts` command previously shown.

Another common use of quotes is with the `format` command. This is similar to the C `printf` function. The first argument to `format` is a format specifier that often includes special characters like newlines, tabs, and spaces. The only way to effectively group these into a single argument to `format` is with quotes. The quotes allow the Tcl interpreter to do the backslash substitutions of `\n` and `\t` while ignoring spaces.

```
puts [format "Item: %s\t%5.3f" $name $value]
```

Here `format` is used to align a name and a value with a tab. The `%s` and `%5.3f` indicate how the remaining arguments to `format` are to be formatted. Note that the trailing `\n` usually found in a C `printf` call is not needed because `puts` provides one for us. For information about the `format` command, see Chapter 2.

Procedures

Tcl uses the `proc` command to define procedures. The basic syntax to define a procedure is:

```
proc name arglist body
```

The first argument is the name of the procedure being defined. The name is case sensitive, and in fact it can contain any characters. Procedure names and variable names do not conflict with each other. The second argument is a list of parameters to the procedure. The third argument is a command, or more typically a group of commands that form the procedure body. Once defined, a Tcl procedure is used just like any of the built-in commands.

Example 1–11 Defining a procedure.

```
proc diag {a b} {
    set c [expr sqrt($a * $a + $b * $b)]
    return $c
}
```

The `diag` procedure defined in the example computes the length of the diagonal side of a right triangle given the lengths of the other two sides. The `sqrt` function is one of many math functions supported by the `expr` command. The variable `c` is local to the procedure; it is only defined during execution of `diag`. Variable scope is discussed further in Chapter 5. It is not really necessary to use the variable `c` in this example. The procedure body could also be written as:

```
return [expr sqrt($a * $a + $b * $b)]
```

The `return` command is optional in this example because the Tcl interpreter returns the value of the last command in the body as the value of the procedure. So, the procedure body could be reduced to:

```
expr sqrt($a * $a + $b * $b)
```

Note the stylized use of curly braces in the example. Braces group the arguments `a` and `b` into a single argument list to form the second argument to the `proc` command. The curly brace at the end of the first line starts the third argument. In this case, the Tcl interpreter sees the opening left brace, causing it to ignore newline characters and gobble up text until a matching right brace is found. (Double quotes have the same property. They group characters, including newlines, until another double quote is found.) The result of the grouping is that the third argument to `proc` is a sequence of commands. When they are evaluated later, the embedded newlines will terminate each command. The other crucial effect of the curly braces around the procedure body is to delay any substitutions in the body until the time the procedure is called. For example, the variables `a`, `b`, and `c` are not defined until the procedure is called, so we do not want to do variable substitution at the time `diag` is defined.

The `proc` command supports additional features such as having variable numbers of arguments and default values for arguments. These are described in detail in Chapter 5.

A While Loop Example

To reinforce what we have learned so far, here is a longer example:

Example 1–12 A `while` loop.

```
set i 1 ; set product 1
while {$i <= 10} {
    set product [expr $product * $i]
    incr i
}
set product
=> 3628800
```

The semi-colon is used on the first line to remind you that it is a command terminator just like the newline character.

The example uses the `while` command to compute the product of a series of numbers. The first argument to `while` is a boolean expression, and its second argument is a sequence of commands, or *command body*, to execute. The `while` command evaluates the boolean expression, and then executes the body if the expression is true (non-zero). The `while` command continues to test the expression and then evaluates the command body until the expression is false (zero).

The same math expression evaluator used by the `expr` command is used by `while` to evaluate the boolean expression. There is no need to explicitly use the `expr` command in the first argument, even if you have a much more complex expression.

The `incr` command is used to increment the value of the loop variable `i`. The `incr` command can take an additional argument, a positive or negative integer by which to change the value of the variable. This is a handy command that saves us from the longer command:

```
set i [expr $i + 1]
```

Curly braces are used to group the two arguments to `while`. The loop body is grouped just like Example 1–11 grouped the procedure body. Curly braces around the boolean expression are crucial because they delay variable substitution until the `while` command implementation tests the expression. The following example is an infinite loop:

```
set i 1 ; while $i<=10 {incr i}
```

The loop will run indefinitely. The reason is that the Tcl interpreter will substitute for `$i` *before* `while` is called, so `while` gets a constant expression `1<=10` that will always be true. You can avoid these kinds of errors by adopting a consistent coding style that always groups expressions and command bodies with curly braces.

Expressions can include variable and command substitutions and still be grouped with curly braces because the expression parser does its own round of substitutions.* This is needed in the example so it can obtain the current value of `$i` in the boolean expression.

The last command in the example uses `set` with a single argument. When used in this way, the `set` command returns the current value of the named variable.

Grouping and Command Substitution

The following example demonstrates how command substitution affects grouping. A nested command is treated as one lump of characters, regardless of its internal structure. It is included with the surrounding group of characters when collecting arguments for the main command.

Example 1–13 Embedded command and variable substitution.

```
set x 7 ; set y 9
puts stdout $x+$y=[expr $x + $y]
=> 7+9=16
```

In the example the second argument to `puts` is:

```
$x+$y=[expr $x + $y]
```

The white space inside the nested command is ignored for the purposes of grouping the argument. The Tcl interpreter makes a single pass through the argument doing variable and command substitution. By the time it encounters the left bracket, it has already done some variable substitutions to obtain:

```
7+9=
```

At that point the interpreter calls itself recursively to evaluate the nested

* An argument to `expr` is subject to two rounds of substitution: one by the Tcl interpreter, and a second by `expr` itself. Ordinarily this is not a problem because math values do not contain the characters that are special to the Tcl interpreter. The fact that `expr` does substitutions on its arguments internally means that it is acceptable to group its arguments with curly braces.

command. Again, the $x and $y are substituted before calling expr. Finally, the result of expr is substituted for everything from the left bracket to the right bracket. The puts command gets the following as its second argument:

```
7+9=16
```

The point of this example is that the grouping decision about puts's second argument is made before the command substitution is done. The rule of thumb is: *grouping before substitution*. Even if the result of the nested command contained spaces or other special characters, they would be ignored for the purposes of grouping the arguments to the outer command. If you wanted the output to look nicer, with spaces around the + and =, then you would use double quotes to explicitly group the argument to puts:

```
puts stdout "$x + $y = [expr $x + $y]"
```

In contrast, it is never necessary to explicitly group a nested command with double quotes if it makes up the whole argument. The following is a redundant use of double quotes:

```
puts stdout "[expr $x + $y]"
```

In general, you can place a bracketed command anywhere. The following computes a command name:

```
[findCommand $x] arg arg
```

The following concatenates the results of two commands because there is no white space between the] and [.

```
set x [cmd1 arg][cmd2 arg]
```

More About Variable Substitution

Grouping and variable substitution interact the same as grouping and command substitution. Spaces or special characters in variable values do not affect grouping decisions because these decisions are made before the variable values are substituted.

Example 1–14 Embedded variable references.

```
set foo filename
set object $foo.o
=> filename.o
set a AAA
set b abc${a}def
=> abcAAAdef
set .o yuk!
set x ${.o}y
=> yuk!y
```

The Tcl interpreter makes some assumptions about variable names that make it easy to embed their values into other strings. By default, it assumes that variable names only contain letters, digits, and the underscore. The construct $foo.o represents a concatenation of the value of foo and the literal ".o".

If the variable reference is not delimited by punctuation or whitespace, then you can use curly braces to explicitly delimit the variable name. You can also use this to reference variables with funny characters in their name (although you probably do not want variables named like that).

Comments

Tcl uses the pound character, #, for comments. Unlike many languages, the # must occur at the beginning of a command. An easy trick to append a comment to the end of a command is to proceed the # with a semicolon to terminate the previous command:

```
# Here are some parameters
set rate 7.0     ;# The interest rate
set months 60    ;# The loan term
```

One subtle effect to watch out for is that a backslash effectively continues a comment line onto the next line of the script. In addition, a semi-colon inside a comment is not significant. Only a newline terminates comments:

```
# Here is the start of a Tcl comment \
and some more of it ; still in the comment
```

You can exploit this property to make a Tcl script work with the Bourne shell. The following trick comes from a posting to `comp.lang.tcl` by Kevin Kenny. A Bourne shell command that runs the Tcl interpreter is hidden in the comment as far as Tcl is concerned, but it is visible to `/bin/sh`. If you run into troubles with the 32 character limit on interpreter names, you can use this:

Example 1–15 Using `/bin/sh` to run a Tcl script.

```
#!/bin/sh
# The -f below is only necessary for wish built with Tk 3.6
# The backslash makes the next line a comment in Tcl \
exec /some/very/long/path/to/wish -f "$0" ${1+"$@"}
    ... Tcl script goes here ...
```

Command Line Arguments

The Tcl shells pass the command line arguments to the script as the value of the `argv` variable. The number of command line arguments is given by the `argc` variable. The name of the program, or script, is not part of `argv` nor is it counted by `argc`. Instead, it is put into the `argv0` variable. Table 1–2 lists all the predefined variables in the Tcl shells. `argv` is a list, so you use the `lindex` command described in Chapter 3 to extract items from the argument list:

```
set first [lindex $argv 0]
set second [lindex $argv 1]
```

Substitution and Grouping Summary

The following rules summarize the fundamental mechanisms of grouping and substitution that are performed by the Tcl interpreter before it invokes a command:

- A dollar sign, `$`, causes variable substitution. Variable names can be any length, and case is significant. If variable references are embedded into other strings, they can be distinguished with `${`*`varname`*`}` syntax.
- Square brackets, `[ ]`, cause command substitution. Everything between the brackets is treated as a command, and everything including the brackets is replaced with the result of the command. Nesting is allowed.
- The backslash character, `\`, is used to quote special characters. You can think of this as another form of substitution in which the backslash and the next character or group of characters are replaced with a new character.
- Substitutions can occur anywhere (unless prevented by curly brace grouping). A substitution can occur in the middle of a word. That is, part of the word can be a constant string, and other parts of it can be the result of substitutions. Even the command name can be affected by substitutions.
- Grouping with curly braces, `{ }`, prevents substitutions. Braces nest. The interpreter includes all characters between the matching left and right brace in the group, including newlines, semi-colons, and nested braces. The enclosing (i.e., outer-most) braces are not included in the group.
- Grouping with double-quotes, `" "`, allows substitutions. The interpreter groups everything until another double-quote is found, including newlines and semi-colons. The enclosing quotes are not included in the group of characters. A double-quote character can be included in the group by quoting it with a backslash, (e.g. `\"`).
- Grouping decisions are made before substitutions are performed. This means that the values of variables or command results do not affect grouping.
- A single round of substitutions is performed before command invocation. That is, the result of a substitution is not interpreted a second time. This rule is important if you have a variable value or a command result that contains special characters such as spaces, dollar-signs, square brackets or braces. Because only a single round of substitution is done, you do not have to worry about special characters in values causing extra substitutions.

Fine Points

- A common error is to forget a space between the right curly brace that ends one argument and the left curly brace that begins the next one. After a right curly brace there must be another right brace, a right square bracket, or whitespace. This is because white space is used as the separator, while the braces only provide grouping. This does not apply when braces are used to delimit a variable name.
- A double-quote is only significant when it comes after white space. That is, the interpreter only uses it for grouping in this case. As with braces, white space, a right bracket, or a right curly brace are the only characters allowed after the closing quote.
- Spaces are *not* required around the square brackets used for command substitution. For the purposes of grouping, the interpreter considers everything between the square brackets as part of the current group.
- When grouping with braces or double quotes, newlines and semi-colons are ignored for the purposes of command termination. They get included in the group of characters just like all the others.
- During command substitution, newlines and semi-colons *are* significant as command terminators. If you have a long command that is nested in square brackets, put a backslash before the newline if you want to continue the command on another line.

Reference

Backslash Sequences

Table 1–1 Backslash sequences.

\a	Bell. (0x7)
\b	Backspace. (0x8)
\f	Form feed. (0xc)
\n	Newline. (0xa)
\r	Carriage return. (0xd)
\t	Tab (0x9)
\v	Vertical tab. (0xb)
\<newline>	Replace the newline and whitespace on next line with a space.
\\	Backslash. ('\')
\ooo	Octal specification of character code. 1, 2, or 3 digits.
\xhh	Hexadecimal specification of character code. 1 or 2 digits.
\c	Replaced with literal *c* if *c* is not one of the cases listed above. In particular, \$, \", \{ and \[are used to obtain these characters.

Predefined Variables

Table 1–2 Variables defined by *tclsh* and *wish*.

`argc`	The number of command line arguments
`argv`	A list of the command line arguments
`argv0`	The name of the script being executed. If being used interactively, `argv0` is the name of the shell program.
`env`	An array of the environment variables. See page 74.
`tcl_interactive`	True (one) if the *tclsh* is prompting for commands.
`tcl_prompt1`	If defined, this is a command that outputs the prompt.
`tcl_prompt2`	If defined, this is a command that outputs the prompt if the current command is not yet complete.
`auto_path`	The search path for script library directories. See page 91.
`auto_index`	A map from command name to a Tcl command that defines it.
`auto_noload`	If set, the library facility is disabled.
`auto_noexec`	If set, the auto execute facility is disabled.
`geometry`	(*wish* only). The value of the `-geometry` argument.

Arithmetic Operators

Table 1–3 Arithmetic operators from highest to lowest precedence.

`- ~ !`	Unary minus, bitwise NOT, logical NOT.
`* / %`	Multiply, divide, remainder.
`+ -`	Add, subtract.
`<< >>`	Left shift, right shift.
`< > <= >=`	Comparison: less, greater, less or equal, greater or equal.
`== !=`	Equal, not equal.
`&`	Bitwise AND.
`^`	Bitwise XOR.
`|`	Bitwise OR.
`&&`	Logical AND.
`||`	Logical OR.
x`?`*y*`:`*z*	If *x* then *y* else *z*.

Built-in Math Functions

Table 1–4 Built-in math functions.

`acos(x)`	Arc-cosine of *x*.
`asin(x)`	Arc-sine of *x*.
`atan(x)`	Arc-tangent of *x*.
`atan2(y,x)`	Rectangular (*x*, *y*) to polar(*r*, *th*). atan2 gives *th*.
`ceil(x)`	Least integral value greater than or equal to *x*.
`cos(x)`	Cosine of *x*.
`cosh(x)`	Hyperbolic cosine of *x*.
`exp(x)`	Exponential, e^x.
`floor(x)`	Greatest integral value less than or equal to *x*.
`fmod(x,y)`	Floating point remainder of *x*/*y*.
`hypot(x,y)`	Returns `sqrt(x*x + y*y)`. *r* part of polar coordinates.
`log(x)`	Natural log of *x*.
`log10(x)`	Log base 10 of *x*.
`pow(x,y)`	*x* to the *y* power, x^y.
`sin(x)`	Sine of *x*.
`sinh(x)`	Hyperbolic sine of *x*.
`sqrt(x)`	Square root of *x*.
`tan(x)`	Tangent of *x*.
`tanh(x)`	Hyperbolic tangent of *x*.
`abs(x)`	Absolute value of *x*.
`double(x)`	Promote *x* to floating point.
`int(x)`	Truncate *x* to an integer.
`round(x)`	Round *x* to an integer.

Core Tcl Commands

The pages given in Table 1–5 are the primary reference for the command.

Table 1–5 Built-in Tcl Commands.

Command	Pg.	Description
`append`	21	Append arguments to a variable's value. No spaces added.
`array`	37	Query array state and search through elements.
`break`	45	Premature loop exit.
`catch`	45	Trap errors.
`cd`	72	Change working directory.
`close`	72	Close an open I/O stream.
`concat`	32	Concatenate arguments with spaces between. Splices lists.
`continue`	45	Continue with next loop iteration.
`error`	46	Raise an error.
`eof`	68	Check for end-of-file.
`eval`	57	Concatenate arguments and evaluate them as a command.
`exec`	63	Fork and execute a UNIX program.
`exit`	73	Terminate the process.
`expr`	5	Evaluate a math expression.
`file`	65	Query the file system.
`flush`	68	Flush output from an I/O stream's internal buffers.
`for`	44	Loop construct similar to C `for` statement.
`foreach`	43	Loop construct over a list of values.
`format`	21	Format a string similar to C `sprintf`.
`gets`	70	Read a line of input from an I/O stream.
`glob`	72	Expand a pattern to matching file names.
`global`	52	Declare global variables.
`history`	80	Command-line history control.
`if`	40	Conditional command. Allows `else` and `elseif` clauses.
`incr`	9	Increment a variable by an integer amount.
`info`	75	Query the state of the Tcl interpreter.
`join`	35	Concatenate list elements with a given separator string.
`lappend`	32	Add elements to the end of a list.
`lindex`	33	Fetch an element of a list.

Table 1–5 Built-in Tcl Commands. (Continued)

`linsert`	34	Insert elements into a list.
`list`	32	Create a list out of the arguments.
`llength`	33	Return the number of elements in a list.
`lrange`	33	Return a range of list elements.
`lreplace`	34	Replace elements of a list.
`lsearch`	34	Search for an element of a list that matches a pattern.
`lsort`	35	Sort a list.
`open`	68	Open a file or process pipeline for I/O.
`pid`	73	Return the process ID.
`proc`	49	Define a Tcl procedure.
`puts`	70	Output a string to an I/O stream.
`pwd`	72	Return the current working directory.
`read`	71	Read blocks of characters from an I/O stream.
`regexp`	27	Regular expression matching.
`regsub`	28	Substitutions based on regular expressions.
`rename`	50	Change the name of a Tcl command.
`return`	47	Return a value from a procedure.
`scan`	23	Similar to the C `sscanf` function.
`seek`	72	Set the seek offset of an I/O stream.
`set`	4	Assign a value to a variable.
`source`	1	Evaluate the Tcl commands in a file.
`split`	35	Chop a string up into list elements.
`string`	19	Operate on strings.
`subst`	62	Substitutions without command evaluation.
`switch`	41	Multi-way branch.
`tell`	72	Return the current seek offset of an I/O stream.
`time`	87	Measure the execution time of a command.
`trace`	79	Monitor variable assignments.
`unknown`	89	Unknown command handler.
`unset`	30	Undefine variables.
`uplevel`	60	Execute a command in a different scope.
`upvar`	53	Reference a variable in a different scope.
`while`	44	A loop construct.

CHAPTER 2

Strings and Pattern Matching

This chapter describes string manipulation and pattern matching. Tcl commands described: `string`, `append`, `format`, `scan`, `regexp`, `regsub`, and `glob`.

Strings are the basic data item in Tcl, so it should not be surprising that there are a large number of commands to manipulate strings. A closely related topic is pattern matching, in which string comparisons are made more powerful by matching a string against a pattern. Tcl supports two styles of pattern matching. Glob matching is a simple matching similar to that used in many shell languages. Regular expression matching is more complex and also more powerful.

The string Command

The general syntax of the Tcl `string` command is:

```
string operation stringvalue otherargs
```

The *operation* argument determines what `string` does, its second argument is a string value, and there may be additional arguments depending on the *operation*.

Some of the string operations involve character indices into the string. These count from zero. The `end` keyword refers to the last character in a string:

```
string range abcd 1 end
=> bcd
```

Table 2–1 summarizes the `string` command. Most of these commands are closely related to the string functions in the standard C library.

Table 2–1 The `string` command.

`string compare` *`str1 str2`*	Compare strings lexicographically. Returns 0 if equal, -1 if *`str1`* sorts before *`str2`*, else 1.
`string first` *`str1 str2`*	Return the index in *`str2`* of the first occurrence of *`str1`*, or -1 if *`str1`* is not found.
`string index` *`string index`*	Return the character at the specified *`index`*.
`string last` *`str1 str2`*	Return the index in *`str2`* of the last occurrence of *`str1`*, or -1 if *`str1`* is not found.
`string length` *`string`*	Return the number of characters in *`string`*.
`string match` *`pattern str`*	Return 1 if *`str`* matches the *`pattern`*, else 0. Glob-style matching is used. See page 24.
`string range` *`str i j`*	Return the range of characters in *`str`* from *`i`* to *`j`*.
`string tolower` *`string`*	Return *`string`* in lower case.
`string toupper` *`string`*	Return *`string`* in upper case.
`string trim` *`string`* `?`*`chars`*`?`	Trim the characters in *`chars`* from both ends of *`string`*. *`chars`* defaults to whitespace.
`string trimleft` *`string`* `?`*`chars`*`?`	Trim the characters in *`chars`* from the beginning of *`string`*. *`chars`* defaults to whitespace.
`string trimright` *`string`* `?`*`chars`*`?`	Trim the characters in *`chars`* from the end of *`string`*. *`chars`* defaults to whitespace.
`string wordend` *`str ix`*	Return the index in *`str`* of the character after the word containing the character at index *`ix`*.
`string wordstart` *`str ix`*	Return the index in *`str`* of the first character in the word containing the character at index *`ix`*.

Strings and Expresssions

Strings can be compared with `expr` using the comparison operators. However, there are a number of subtle issues that can cause problems. First, you must quote the string value so the expression parser can identify it as a string type. Then you must group the expression with curly braces to prevent the double quotes from being stripped off by the main interpreter:

```
if {$x == "foo"}
```

Ironically, despite the quotes, the expression evaluator first converts items to numbers if possible, and then converts them back if it detects a case of string comparison. This can lead to unexpected conversions between strings that look like hexadecimal or octal numbers:

```
if {"0xa" == "10"} { puts stdout ack! }
=> ack!
```

A safe way to compare strings is the `string compare` command. This command also operates faster because the unnecessary conversions are eliminated. Like the C library `strcmp` function, `string compare` returns 0 if the strings are equal, -1 if the first string is lexicographically less than the second, or 1 if the first string is greater than the second:

Example 2–1 Comparing strings.

```
if {[string compare $s1 $s2] == 0} {
    # strings are equal
}
```

The append Command

The `append` command takes a variable name as its first argument, and concatenates its remaining arguments onto the current value of the named variable. The variable is created if it did not already exist:

```
set foo z
append foo a b c
=> zabc
```

The command provides an efficient way to add items to the end of a string. It works by exploiting the memory allocation scheme used internally by Tcl, which allocates extra space for string growth.

The format Command

The `format` command is similar to the C `printf` function. It formats a string according to a format specification:

```
format spec value1 value2 ...
```

The `spec` argument includes literals and keywords. The literals are placed in the result as-is, while each keyword indicates how to format the corresponding argument. The keywords are introduced with a percent sign, `%`, followed by zero or more modifiers and terminates with a conversion specifier. Example keywords include `%f` for floating point, `%d` for integer and `%s` for string format. Use `%%` to obtain a single percent character. The most general keyword specification for each argument contains up to six parts:

- position specifier
- flags
- field width
- precision
- word length
- conversion character.

These components are explained by a series of examples. The examples use double quotes around the `format` specification. This is because often the format contains white space, so grouping is required, as well as backslash substitutions like `\t` or `\n`, and the quotes allow substitution of these special characters. Table 2–2 lists the conversion characters:

Table 2–2 Format conversions.

`d`	Signed integer.
`u`	Unsigned integer.
`i`	Signed integer. The argument may be in hex (0x) or octal (0) format.
`o`	Unsigned octal.
`x` or `X`	Unsigned hexadecimal. 'x' gives lower-case results.
`c`	Map from an integer to the ASCII character it represents.
`s`	A string.
`f`	Floating point number in the format `a.b`.
`e` or `E`	Floating point number in scientific notation, `a.bE+-c`.
`g` or `G`	Floating point number in either `%f` or `%e` format, whichever is shorter.

A position specifier is *i*`$`, which means take the value from argument *i* as opposed to the normally corresponding argument. The position counts from 1. If a position is specified for one format keyword, the position must be used for all of them. If you group the format specification with double-quotes, you need to quote the `$` with a backslash:

```
set lang 2
format "%${lang}\$s" one un uno
=> un
```

The position specifier is useful for picking a string from a set, such as this simple language-specific example. The position is also useful if the same value is repeated in the formatted string.

The flags in a format are used to specify padding and justification. In the following examples, the `#` causes a leading `0x` to be printed in the hexadecimal value. The zero in `08` causes the field to be padded with zeros. Table 2–3 summarizes the the format flag characters.

```
format "%#x" 20
=> 0x14
format "%#08x" 10
=> 0x0000000a
```

Table 2–3 Format flags.

-	Left justify the field.
+	Always include a sign, either + or -.
space	Precede a number with a space, unless the number has a leading sign. Useful for packing numbers close together.
0	Pad with zeros.
#	Leading 0 for octal. Leading 0x for hex. Always include a decimal point in floating point. Do not remove trailing zeros (%g).

After the flags you can specify a minimum field width value. The value is padded to this width with spaces, or with zeros if the 0 flag is used:

```
format "%-20s %3d" Label 2
=> Label                  2
```

You can compute a field width and pass it to `format` as one of the arguments by using `*` as the field width specifier. In this case the next argument is used as the field width instead of the value, and the argument after that is the value that gets formatted.

```
set maxl 8
format "%-*s = %s" $maxl Key Value
=> Key      Value
```

The precision comes next, and it is specified with a period and a number. For `%f` and `%e` it indicates how many digits come after the decimal point. For `%g` it indicates the total number of significant digits used. For `%d` and `%x` it indicates how many digits will be printed, padding with zeros if necessary.

```
format "%6.2f %6.2d" 1 1
=>   1.00     01
```

(The storage length part comes last, but it is rarely useful because Tcl maintains all floating point values in double-precision, and all integers as long words.)

If you want to preserve enough precision in a floating point number so that scanning in the number later will result in the same thing, use `%17g`. (This magic number applies to double-precision IEEE format.)

The scan Command

The `scan` command is like the C `sscanf` procedure. It parses a string according to a format specification and assigns values to variables. It returns the number of successful conversions it made. The general form of the command is:

```
scan string format var ?var? ?var? ...
```

The format for `scan` is nearly the same as in the `format` command. There is no `%u` scan format. The `%c` scan format converts one character to its binary value. Unlike the C `sscanf` `%c`, it does not allow a field width.

The scan format includes a set notation. Use square brackets to delimit a set of characters. The set matches one or more characters that are copied into the variable. A dash is used to specify a range. The following scans a field of all lowercase letters.

```
scan abcABC {%[a-z]} result
=> 1
set result
=> abc
```

If the first character in the set is a right square bracket, then it is considered part of the set. If the first character in the set is ^, then characters *not* in the set match. Again, put a right square bracket right after the ^ to include it in the set. Nothing special is required to include a left square bracket in the set. As in the previous example, you will want to protect the format with braces, or use backslashes, because square brackets are special to the Tcl parser.

String Matching

The string match command implements *glob*-style pattern matching that is modeled after the filename pattern matching done by various UNIX shells. There are just three constructs used in glob patterns: match any number of any characters (*), match any single character (?), or match one of a set of characters ([*abc*]).* Any other characters in a pattern are taken as literals that must match the input exactly. To match all strings that begin with a:

```
string match a* alpha
=> 1
```

To match all two-letter strings:

```
string match ?? XY
=> 1
```

To match all strings that begin with either a or b:

```
string match {[ab]*} cello
=> 0
```

Be careful! Square brackets are also special to the Tcl interpreter, so you will need to wrap the pattern up in curly braces to prevent it from being interpreted as a nested command. Another approach is to put the pattern into a variable:

```
set pat {[ab]*x}
string match $pat box
=> 1
```

* The string match function does not support alternation in a pattern, such as the {a,b,c} syntax of the C-shell. The glob command, however, does support this form.

The pattern specifies a range of characters with the syntax `[x-y]`. For example, `[a-z]` represents the set of all lower-case letters, and `[0-9]` represents all the digits. This range is applied to the character set collating sequence.

If you need to include a literal `*`, `?`, or bracket in your pattern, preface it with a backslash:

```
string match {*\?} what?
=> 1
```

In this case the pattern is quoted with curly braces because the Tcl interpreter is also doing backslash substitutions. Without the braces, you would have to use two backslashes. They are replaced with a single backslash by Tcl before `string match` is called.

```
string match *\\? what?
```

Regular Expressions

The most powerful way to express patterns is with regular expressions. There is a general pattern specification syntax, which includes the ability to extract substrings from the matching string. This proves quite useful in picking apart data.

A pattern is a sequence of the following items:

- A literal character.
- A matching character.
- A repetition clause.
- An alternation clause.
- A subpattern grouped with parentheses.

Table 2–4 summarizes the syntax of regular expressions:

Table 2–4 Regular expression syntax.

.	Matches any character.
*	Matches zero or more instances of the previous pattern item.
+	Matches one or more instances of the previous pattern item.
?	Matches zero or one instances of the previous pattern item.
( )	Groups a sub-pattern. The repetition and alternation operators apply to the whole proceeding sub-pattern.
|	Alternation.
[ ]	Delimit a set of characters. Ranges are specified as [x-y]. If the first character in the set is ^, then there is a match if the remaining characters in the set are *not* present.
^	Anchor the pattern to the beginning of the string. Only when first.
$	Anchor the pattern to the end of the string. Only when last.

A number of examples of regular expressions follow. Any pattern that contains brackets, dollar sign, or spaces must be handled specially when used in a Tcl command. Typically I use curly braces around patterns, although the following examples do not quote anything.

The general wild-card character is the period, ".". It matches any single character. The following pattern matches all two-character strings:

```
..
```

The matching character can be restricted to a set of characters with the `[xyz]` syntax. Any of the characters between the two brackets is allowed to match. For example, the following matches either `Hello` or `hello`:

```
[Hh]ello
```

The matching set can be specified as a range over the ASCII character set with the `[x-y]` syntax, which is the same as with the glob mechanism. However, there is also the ability to specify the complement of a set. That is, the matching character can be anything except what is in the set. This is achieved with the `[^xyz]` syntax. Ranges and complements can be combined. The following matches anything except the upper and lowercase letters:

```
[^a-zA-Z]
```

Repetition is specified with `*`, for zero-or-more, `+`, for one-or-more, and `?`, for zero-or-one. These operators apply to the previous item, which is either a matching character, which could involve the set syntax, or a subpattern grouped with parentheses. The following matches a string that contains `b` followed by zero or more `a`'s:

```
ba*
```

While the following matches a string that has one or more sequences of `ab`:

```
(ab)+
```

The pattern that matches anything is:

```
.*
```

Alternation is specified with `|`, a pipe symbol. Another way to match either `Hello` or `hello` is:

```
hello|Hello
```

In general, a pattern does not have to match the whole string. If you need more control than this, then you can anchor the pattern to the beginning of the string by starting the pattern with `^`, or to the end of the string by ending the pattern with `$`. You can force the pattern to match the whole string by using both. All strings that begin with spaces or tabs are matched with:

```
^( |\t)+
```

If a pattern can match several parts of a string, the matcher takes the match that occurs earliest in the input string. Then, if there is more than one match from that same point, the matcher takes the longest possible match. The rule of thumb is: *first, then longest*.

The regexp Command

The `regexp` command provides direct access to the regular expression matcher. Its syntax is:

```
regexp ?flags? pattern string ?match sub1 sub2...?
```

The return value is 1 if some part of the string matches the pattern, it is 0 otherwise.

The *pattern* argument is a regular expression as described in the previous section. If this contains `$` or `[`, you must be careful. The easiest thing to do is group your patterns with curly braces. However, if your pattern contains backslash sequences like `\n` or `\t` you should group with double quotes so the Tcl interpreter can do those substitutions. In that case, use `\[` and `\$` in your patterns.

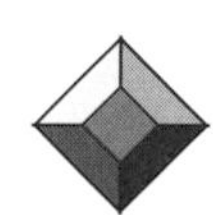

If *string* matches *pattern*, then the results of the match are stored in the variables named in the command. These match variable arguments are optional. If present, *match* is set to be the part of the string that matched the pattern. The remaining variables are set to be the substrings of *string* that matched the corresponding subpatterns in *pattern*. The correspondence is based on the order of left parentheses in the pattern to avoid ambiguities that can arise from nested subpatterns.

The *flags* are optional and constrain the match as follows:

- If `-nocase` is specified, then upper case characters in *string* are treated as lower case during the match.
- If `-indices` is specified, then the match variables each contain a pair of numbers that are the indices delimiting the match within *string*. Otherwise, the matching string itself is copied into the match variables.
- If your pattern begins with `-`, then you can use `--` to separate the flags from the pattern.

Example 2–2 Using regular expressions to parse a string.

```
set env(DISPLAY) corvina:0.1
regexp {([^:]*):} $env(DISPLAY) match host
=> 1
set match
=> corvina:
set host
=> corvina
```

The example uses `regexp` to pick the hostname out of the `DISPLAY` environment variable, which has the form:

```
hostname:display.screen
```

The pattern involves a complementary set, `[^:]`, to match anything except a colon. It uses repetition, `*`, to repeat that zero or more times. It groups that part into a subexpression with parentheses. The literal colon ensures that the `DISPLAY` value matches the format we expect. The part of the string that matches the complete pattern is stored into the `match` variable. The part that matches the subpattern is stored into `host`. The whole pattern has been grouped with braces to quote the square brackets. Without braces it would be:

```
regexp (\[^:]*): $env(DISPLAY) match host
```

This is quite a powerful statement, and it is efficient. If we only had the `string` command to work with, we would have needed to resort to the following, which takes roughly twice as long to interpret:

```
set i [string first : $env(DISPLAY)]
if {$i >= 0} {
    set host [string range $env(DISPLAY) 0 [expr $i-1]]
}
```

Multiple subpatterns are allowed. We can improve our pattern so it extracts the display and screen number of the `DISPLAY` as well as the host:

```
regexp {([^:]*):(.+)} $env(DISPLAY) match host display
```

The regsub Command

The `regsub` command does string substitution based on pattern matching. Its syntax is:

```
regsub ?switches? pattern string subspec varname
```

The `regsub` command returns the number of matches and replacements, or 0 if there was no match. `regsub` copies *string* to *varname*, replacing occurrences of *pattern* with the substitution specified by *subspec*.

The optional switches include `-all`, which means to replace all occurrences of the pattern. Otherwise only the first occurrence is replaced. The `-nocase` switch means that upper-case characters in the string are converted to lowercase before matching. The `--` switch separates the pattern from the switches, which is necessary if your pattern begins with a `-`.

The replacement pattern, *subspec*, can contain literal characters as well as the following special sequences:

- `&` is replaced with the string that matched the pattern.
- `\1` through `\9` are replaced with the strings that match the corresponding subpatterns in *pattern*. Nine subpatterns are supported. The correspondence is based on the order of left parentheses in the pattern specification.

The following replaces a user's home directory with a ~:

```
regsub ^$env(HOME)/ $pathname ~/ newpath
```

The following constructs a C compile command line given a filename:

```
regsub {([^\.]*)\.c} file.c {cc -c & -o \1.o} ccCmd
```

The `\.` is used to specify a match against period. The `&` is replaced with `file.c`, and `\1` is replaced with `file`, which matches the pattern between the parentheses. The value assigned to `ccCmd` is:

```
cc -c file.c -o file.o
```

CHAPTER 3

Tcl Data Structures

This chapter describes two data structures used in Tcl: lists and arrays.

The basic data structure in Tcl is a string. In addition, there are two higher-level data structures, lists and arrays. Lists are implemented as strings. Their structure is defined by the syntax of the string. The syntax rules are the same as for commands, and in fact commands are just a particular instance of lists. Arrays are variables that have an index. The index is a string value, so you can think of arrays as maps from one string (the index) to another string (the value of the array element).

As a rule, lists are acceptable when they are short, or when you are building up a command to be evaluated later. Arrays are more convenient and efficient for larger collections of data.

More About Variables

Before we explore lists and arrays, we should consider simple variables in more detail. Use the `set` command to define variables of any type. In addition, the `set` command will return the value of a variable if it is only passed a single argument. It treats that argument as a variable name and returns the current value of the variable. The dollar-sign syntax used to get the value of a variable is really just an easy way to use the `set` command.

Example 3–1 Using `set` to return a variable value.

```
set var {the value of var}
=> the value of var
set name var
=> var
set name
=> var
set $name
=> the value of var
```

This is a somewhat tricky example. In the last command, `$name` gets substituted with `var`. Then the `set` command returns the value of `var`, which is `the value of var`. Nested `set` commands provide another way to achieve a level of indirection. The last `set` command above can be written as follows

```
set [set name]
=> the value of var
```

The unset Command

You can delete a variable with the `unset` command:

```
unset varName varName2 ...
```

Any number of variable names can be passed to the `unset` command. However, `unset` will raise an error if a variable is not already defined.

You can delete an entire array, or just a single array element with `unset`. Using `unset` on an array is a convenient way to clear out a big data structure.

Using info to Find Out About Variables

The existence of a variable can be tested with the `info exists` command. For example, because `incr` requires that a variable exists, you might have to test for the existence of the variable first.

Example 3–2 Using `info` to determine if a variable exists.

```
if ![info exists foobar] {
    set foobar 0
} else {
    incr foobar
}
```

In Chapter 5, page 54, there is an example that implements a new version of `incr`, which handles this case.

Tcl Lists

Unlike list data structures in other languages, Tcl lists are just strings with a special interpretation. By definition, a Tcl list has the same structure as a Tcl command. That is, a list is simply a string with list elements separated by white space. Braces or quotes can be used to group words with whitespace into a single list element. Because of the relationship between lists and commands, the list-related commands are used often when constructing Tcl commands.

The string representation of lists in Tcl has performance implications. The string representation must be reparsed on each list access, so be careful when you use large lists. If you find yourself maintaining large lists that must be frequently accessed, consider changing your code to use arrays instead.

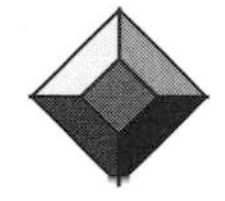

There are several Tcl commands related to lists, and these are described briefly in Table 3–1. Usage and examples for these commands are covered later in this chapter.

Table 3–1 List-related commands.

Command	Description
`list` *arg1 arg2* ...	Creates a list out of all its arguments.
`lindex` *list i*	Returns the *i*'th element from *list*.
`llength` *list*	Returns the number of elements in *list*.
`lrange` *list i j*	Returns the *i*'th through *j*'th elements from *list*.
`lappend` *listVar arg arg* ...	Append elements to the value of *listVar*.
`linsert` *list index arg arg* ...	Insert elements into *list* before the element at position *index*. Returns a new list.
`lreplace` *list i j arg arg* ...	Replace elements *i* through *j* of *list* with the *args*. Returns a new list.
`lsearch` *mode list value*	Return the index of the element in *list* that matches the *value* according to the mode, which is `-exact`, `-glob`, or `-regexp`. `-glob` is the default. Return -1 if not found.
`lsort` *switches list*	Sort elements of the list according to the switches: `-ascii, -integer, -real, -increasing, -decreasing, -command` *command*. Returns a new list.
`concat` *arg arg arg* ...	Join multiple lists together into one list.
`join` *list joinString*	Merge the elements of a list together by separating them with *joinString*.
`split` *string splitChars*	Split a string up into list elements, using (and discarding) the characters in *splitChars* as boundaries between list elements.

Constructing Lists: list, lappend, and concat

The `list` command constructs a list out of its arguments so that there is one list element for each argument. Although it might not seem like it at first glance, `list` is an important command because it ensures that the resulting list has the proper syntax. If any of the arguments contain special characters, the `list` command adds quoting to ensure they are parsed as a single element of the resulting list.

Example 3–3 Constructing a list with the `list` command.

```
set x {1 2}
=> 1 2
set x
=> 1 2
list $x \$ foo
=> {1 2} {$} foo
```

The braces used to group the list value into one argument to the `set` command are not part of the list value. At first this may be confusing. In the example, the interpreter strips off the outer braces that are used to group the second argument to `set`. However, the `list` command adds them back, which could lead you to believe that the braces are part of `x`'s value, but they are not.

The `lappend` command is used to append elements to the end of a list. It is efficient because it takes advantage of extra space allocated at the end of lists. Like `list`, `lappend` preserves the structure of its arguments. That is, it may add braces to group the values of its arguments so they retain their identity as list elements when they are appended onto the string representation of the list. The new elements added by `lappend` are peers of the existing list elements in the variable.

Example 3–4 Using `lappend` to add elements to a list.

```
lappend new 1 2
=> 1 2
lappend new 3 "4 5"
=> 1 2 3 {4 5}
set new
=> 1 2 3 {4 5}
```

The `lappend` command is unique among the list-related commands because its first argument is the name of a list-valued variable, while all the other commands take list values as arguments. You can call `lappend` with the name of an undefined variable and the variable will be created.

The `concat` command is useful for splicing together lists. It works by concatenating its arguments, separating them with spaces. This joins multiple lists into one where the top-level list elements in each input list are also top-level list elements (i.e., peers) in the resulting list:

Example 3–5 Using `concat` to splice together lists.

```
set x {4 5 6}
set y {2 3}
set z 1
concat $z $y $x
=> 1 2 3 4 5 6
```

Double quotes behave much like the `concat` command. The following example compares the use of `list`, `concat`, and double quotes:

Example 3–6 Double quotes compared to the `list` command

```
set x {1 2}
=> 1 2
set y "$x 3"
=> 1 2 3
set y [concat $x 3]
=> 1 2 3
set z [list $x 3]
=> {1 2} 3
```

The distinction between `list` and `concat` becomes important when Tcl commands are built dynamically. The basic rule is that `list` and `lappend` preserve list structure, while `concat` (or double quotes) eliminate one level of list structure. The distinction can be subtle because there are examples where `list` and `concat` return the same results. Unfortunately, this can lead to data-dependent bugs. Throughout the examples of this book you will see the `list` command used to safely construct lists. This issue is discussed more in Chapter 6.

Getting List Elements: llength, lindex, and lrange

The `llength` command returns the number of elements in a list.

```
llength {a b {c d} "e f g" h}
=> 5
```

The `lindex` command returns a particular element of a list. It takes an index; list indices count from zero. You can use the keyword `end` to specify the last element with `lindex`, `linsert`, `lrange`, and `lreplace`.

```
lindex {1 2 3} 0
=> 1
```

The `lrange` command returns a range of list elements. It takes a list and two indices as arguments.

```
lrange {1 2 3 {4 5}} 2 end
=> 3 {4 5}
```

Modifying Lists: linsert and lreplace

The `linsert` command inserts elements into a list value at a specified index. If the index is zero or less, then the elements are added to the front. If the index is equal to or greater than the length of the list, then the elements are appended to the end. Otherwise, the elements are inserted before the element that is current as position index.

`lreplace` replaces a range of list elements with new elements. If you don't specify any new elements, you effectively delete elements from a list.

Note: `linsert` and `lreplace` do not modify an existing list. Instead, they return a new list value. In the following example, the `lreplace` command does not change the value of `x`:

Example 3–7 Modifying lists with `linsert` and `lreplace`.

```
linsert {1 2} 0 new stuff
=> new stuff 1 2
set x [list a {b c} e d]
=> a {b c} e d
lreplace $x 1 2 B C
=> a B C d
lreplace $x 0 0
=> {b c} e d
```

Searching Lists: lsearch

`lsearch` returns the index of a value in the list, or -1 if it is not present. `lsearch` supports pattern matching in its search. Glob-style pattern matching is the default, and this can be disabled with the `-exact` flag. The semantics of the pattern matching done with the `-glob` and `-regexp` options is described in Chapter 2. In the following example, the glob pattern `l*` matches the value `list`.

```
lsearch {here is a list} l*
=> 3
```

The `lreplace` command is often used with `lsearch` to determine if the list already contains the elements. The example below uses `lreplace` to delete elements by not specifying any replacement list elements:

Example 3–8 Deleting a list element by value.

```
proc ldelete { list value } {
    set ix [lsearch -exact $list $value]
    if {$ix >= 0} {
        return [lreplace $list $ix $ix]
    } else {
        return $list
    }
}
```

Sorting Lists: lsort

You can sort a list in a variety of ways with `lsort`. The three basic types of sorts are specified with the `-ascii`, `-integer`, or `-real` options. The `-increasing` or `-decreasing` option indicate the sorting order. The default option set is `-ascii -increasing`. The list is not sorted in place. Instead, a new list value is returned.

You can provide your own sorting function for special-purpose sorting. For example, suppose you have a list of names, where each element is itself a list containing the person's first name, middle name (if any), and last name. The default sorts by everyone's first name. If you want to sort by their last name, you need to supply a sorting command.

Example 3–9 Sorting a list using a comparison function.

```
proc mycompare {a b} {
    set alast [lindex $a [expr [llength $a]-1]]
    set blast [lindex $b [expr [llength $b]-1]]
    set res [string compare $alast $blast]
    if {$res != 0} {
        return $res
    } else {
        return [string compare $a $b]
    }
}
set list {{Brent B. Welch} {John Ousterhout} {Miles Davis}}
=> {Brent B. Welch} {John Ousterhout} {Miles Davis}
lsort -command mycompare $list
=> {Miles Davis} {John Ousterhout} {Brent B. Welch}
```

The `mycompare` procedure extracts the last element from each of its arguments and compares those. If they are equal, then it just compares the whole of each argument.

The split and join Commands

The `split` command takes a string and turns it into a list by breaking it at specified characters. The `split` command provides a robust way to turn input lines into proper Tcl lists. Even if your data has space-separated words, you should be careful when using list operators on arbitrary input data. Otherwise, stray double quotes or curly braces in the input can result in invalid list structure and errors in your script.

Example 3–10 Use `split` to turn input data into Tcl lists.

```
set line {welch:*:3116:100:Brent Welch:/usr/welch:/bin/csh}
split $line :
=> welch * 3116 100 {Brent Welch} /usr/welch /bin/csh
set line {this is "not a tcl list}
```

```
lindex $line 1
=> is
lindex $line 2
=> unmatched open quote in list
lindex [split $line] 2
=> "not
```

The default separator character for `split` is white space. If there are multiple separator characters in a row, these result in empty list elements; the separators are not collapsed. The following command splits on commas, periods, spaces, and tabs. The backslash-space sequence is used to include a space in the set of characters. You could also group the argument to `split` with double quotes:

```
set line "\tHello, world."
split $line \ ,.\t
=> {} Hello {} world {}
```

The `join` command is the inverse of `split`. It takes a list value and reformats it with specified characters separating the list elements. In doing so, it removes any curly braces from the string representation of the list that are used to group the top-level elements. For example:

```
join {1 {2 3} {4 5 6}} :
=> 1:2 3:4 5 6
```

Arrays

Arrays are the other primary data structure in Tcl. An array is a variable with a string-valued index, so you can think of an array as a mapping from strings to strings. Internally an array is implemented with a hash table, so the cost of accessing each element is about the same. (It is slightly affected by the length of the index.)

The index of an array is delimited by parentheses. The index can have any string value, and it can be the result of variable or command substitution. Array elements are defined with `set`:

```
set arr(index) value
```

The value of an array element is obtained with `$` substitution:

```
set foo $arr(index)
```

Example 3–11 Using arrays.

```
set arr(0) 1
for {set i 1} {$i <= 10} {incr i} {
   set arr($i) [expr $i * $arr([expr $i-1])]
}
```

This example sets `arr(x)` to the product of `1 * 2 * ... * x`. The initial assignment of `arr(0)` defines `arr` as an array variable. It is an error to use a variable as both an array and a normal variable. The following would be an error after the previous example:

```
set arr 3
=> can't set "arr": variable is array
```

You can use an array element as you would a simple variable. For example, you can test for its existence with `info exists`, increment its value with `incr`, and append elements to it with `lappend`:

```
if [info exists stats($event)] {incr stats($event)}
```

If you have complex indices, use a comma to separate different parts of the index. Avoid putting a space after the comma. It is legal, but a space in an index value causes problems because *parentheses are not used as a grouping mechanism*. The space in the index needs to be quoted with a backslash, or the whole variable reference needs to be grouped:

```
set {arr(I'm asking for trouble)} {I told you so.}
```

Of course, if the array index is stored in a variable, then there is no problem with spaces in the variable's value. The following works well:

```
set index {I'm asking for trouble}
set arr($index) {I told you so.}
```

The name of the array can be the result of a substitution. If the name of the array is stored in another variable, then you must use `set` to reference the array elements, as shown in the following example. If you need to pass an array by name to a procedure, see the example on page 55, which uses a different solution.

Example 3–12 Referencing an array indirectly.

```
set name TheArray
=> TheArray
set ${name}(xyz) {some value}
=> some value
set x $TheArray(xyz)
=> some value
set x ${name}(xyz)
=> TheArray(xyz)
set x [set ${name}(xyz)]
=> some value
```

The array Command

The `array` command returns information about array variables. You can use it to iterate through array elements. The `array names` command is perhaps the most useful because it allows easy iteration through an array with a `foreach` loop. (`foreach` is described in more detail on page 43.)

```
foreach index [array names arr] { command body }
```

The order of the names returned by `array names` is arbitrary. It is essentially determined by the hash table implementation of the array. You can limit what names are returned by specifying a pattern argument. The pattern is the kind supported by the `string match` command, which is described on page 24.

It is also possible to iterate through the elements of an array one at a time using the search-related commands. The ordering is also random, and in practice I find the `foreach` over the results of `array names` much more convenient. If your array has an extremely large number of elements, or if you need to manage an iteration over long period of time, then the array search operations might be more appropriate.

The `array get` and `array set` operations are used to convert between an array and a list. The list returned by `array get` has an even number of elements. The first element is an index, and the next is the corresponding array value. The list elements continue to alternate between index and value.The list argument to `array set` must have the same structure. The ordering of the indexes is arbitrary. These commands are most useful when dumping an array contents to a file for storage.

Example 3–13 Converting from an array to a list.

```
set fruit(best) kiwi
set fruit(worst) peach
set fruit(ok) banana
array get fruit
=> ok banana best kiwi worst peach
```

Table 3–2 summarizes the `array` command.

Table 3–2 The `array` command.

`array exists` *arr*	Returns 1 if *arr* is an array variable.
`array get` *arr*	Returns a list that alternates between an index and the corresponding array value.
`array names` *arr ?pattern?*	Return the list of all indices defined for *arr*, or those that match the string match *pattern*.
`array set` *arr list*	Initialize the array *arr* from *list*, which should have the same form as the list returned by `get`.
`array size` *arr*	Return the number of indices defined for *arr*.
`array startsearch` *arr*	Return a search token for a search through *arr*.
`array nextelement` *arr id*	Return the value of the next element in *array* in the search identified by the token *id*. Returns an empty string if no more elements remain in the search.
`array anymore` *arr id*	Returns 1 if more elements remain in the search.
`array donesearch` *arr id*	End the search identified by *id*.

CHAPTER 4

Control Flow Commands

This chapter describes the Tcl commands that implement control structures: `if`, `switch`, `foreach`, `while`, `for`, `break`, `continue`, `catch`, `error`, and `return`.

Control flow in Tcl is achieved with commands, just like everything else. There are looping commands: `while`, `foreach`, and `for`. There are conditional commands: `if` and `switch`. There is an error handling command: `catch`. Finally, there are some commands to fine-tune control flow: `break`, `continue`, `return`, and `error`.

A control flow command often has a command body that is executed later, either conditionally or in a loop. In this case, it is important to group the command body with curly braces to avoid substitutions at the time the control flow command is invoked. Group with braces, and let the control flow command trigger evaluation at the proper time. A control flow command returns the value of the last command it chose to execute.

Another pleasant property of curly braces is that they group things together while including newlines. The examples use braces in a way that is both readable and convenient for extending the control flow commands across multiple lines.

Commands like `if`, `for`, and `while` involve boolean expressions. They use the `expr` command internally, so there is no need for you to invoke `expr` explicitly to evaluate their boolean test expressions.

If Then Else

The `if` command is the basic conditional command. If an expression is true then execute one command body, otherwise execute another command body. The second command body (the `else` clause) is optional. The syntax of the command is:

```
if boolean then body1 else body2
```

The `then` and `else` keywords are optional. In practice, I omit `then`, but use `else` as illustrated in the next example. I always use braces around the command bodies, even in the simplest cases:

Example 4–1 A conditional `if-then-else` command.

```
if {$x == 0} {
   puts stderr "Divide by zero!"
} else {
   set slope [expr $y/$x]
}
```

The style of this example takes advantage of the way the Tcl interpreter parses commands. Recall that newlines are command terminators, except when the interpreter is in the middle of a group defined by braces (or double quotes). The stylized placement of the opening curly brace at the end of the first and third line exploits this property to extend the `if` command over multiple lines.

The first argument to `if` is a boolean expression. As a matter of style this expression is grouped with curly braces. The expression evaluator performs variable and command substitution on the expression. Using curly braces ensures that these substitutions are performed at the proper time. It is possible to be lax in this regard, with constructs such as:

```
if $x break continue
```

This is a sloppy, albeit legitimate `if` command that will either break out of a loop or continue with the next iteration depending on the value of variable `x`. Instead, always use braces around the command bodies to avoid trouble later when you modify the command. It also improves the readability of your code. The following is much better (use `then` if it suites your taste):

```
if {$x} { break } else { continue }
```

You can create chained conditionals by using the `elseif` keyword. Again, note the careful placement of curly braces that create a single `if` command:

Example 4–2 Chained conditional with `elseif`.

```
if {$key < 0} {
   incr range 1
} elseif {$key == 0} {
   return $range
} else {
   incr range -1
}
```

Any number of conditionals can be chained in this manner. However, the `switch` command provides a more powerful way to test multiple conditions.

Switch

The `switch` command is used to branch to one of many command bodies depending on the value of an expression. In addition, the choice can be made on the basis of pattern matching as well as simple comparisons. Pattern matching is discussed in more detail in Chapter 2. Any number of pattern-body pairs can be specified. If multiple patterns match, only the body of the first matching pattern is evaluated.

The general form of the command is:

```
switch flags value pat1 body1 pat2 body2 ...
```

You can also group all the pattern-body pairs into one argument:

```
switch flags value { pat1 body1 pat2 body2 ... }
```

There are four possible flags that determine how *value* is matched.

`-exact`	Match the *value* exactly to one of the patterns. (The default.)
`-glob`	Use glob-style pattern matching. See page 24.
`-regexp`	Use regular expression pattern matching. See page 25.
`--`	No flag (or end of flags). Useful when *value* can begin with `-`.

There are three approaches to grouping the pattern and body pairs. The differences among them have to do with the substitutions that are performed (or not) on the patterns. You should always group the command bodies with curly braces so that substitution occurs only on the body with the pattern that matches the value.

The first style groups all the patterns and bodies into one argument. This makes it easy to group the whole command without worrying about newlines, and it suppresses any substitutions on the patterns:

Example 4–3 Using `switch` for an exact match.

```
switch -exact -- $value {
    foo { doFoo; incr count(foo) }
    bar { doBar; return $count(foo)}
    default { incr count(other) }
}
```

If the pattern associated with the last body is `default`, then this command body is executed if no other patterns match. Note that the `default` keyword only works on the last pattern-body pair. If you use the `default` pattern on an earlier body, it will be treated as a pattern to match the literal string `default`.

The second style is useful if you have variable references or backslash sequences in the patterns that you need to have substituted. However, you must use backslashes to escape the newlines in the command:

Example 4–4 Using `switch` with substitutions in the patterns.

```
switch -regexp -- $value \
    ^$key { body1 }\
    \t### { body2 }\
    {[0-9]*} { body3 }
```

In this example the first and second patterns have substitutions performed to replace `$key` with its value and `\t` with a tab character. The third pattern is quoted with curly braces to prevent command substitution; square brackets are part of the regular expression syntax, too. (See page 25.)

A third style allows substitutions on the patterns without needing to quote newlines, but you must add a backslash before any double-quotes that appear in the patterns or bodies:

Example 4–5 Using `switch` with all pattern body pairs grouped with quotes.

```
switch -glob -- $value "
    ${key}* { puts stdout \"Key is $value\" }
    X* -
    Y* { takeXorYaction $value }
"
```

If the body associated with a pattern is just a dash, `-`, then the `switch` command "falls through" to the body associated with the next pattern. You can tie together any number of patterns in this manner.

Comments in switch Commands

A comment can only occur where the Tcl parser expects a command to begin. This restricts the location of comments in a `switch` command. You must put them inside the command body associated with a pattern. If you put a comment at the same level as the patterns, the `switch` command will try to interpret the comment as one or more pattern-body pairs. The following example is incorrect:

Example 4–6 Comments in `switch` commands.

```
switch -- $value {
    # this comment confuses switch
    pattern { # this comment is ok }
}
```

Foreach

The `foreach` command loops over a command body assigning a loop variable to each of the values in a list. The syntax is:

`foreach loopVar valueList commandBody`

The first argument is the name of a variable, and the command body is executed once for each element in the loop with the loop variable taking on successive values in the list. The list can be entered explicitly, as in the next example:

Example 4–7 Looping with `foreach`.

```
set i 1
foreach value {1 3 5 7 11 13 17 19 23} {
    set i [expr $i*$value]
}
set i
=> 111546435
```

In the next example, a list-valued variable is used:

Example 4–8 Parsing command line arguments.

```
# argv is set by the Tcl shells
foreach arg $argv {
    switch -regexp -- $arg {
        -foo       {set fooOption 1}
        -bar       {barRelatedCommand}
        -([0-9]+)  {scan -%d $arg intValue}
    }
}
```

The variable `argv` is set by the Tcl interpreter to be a list of the command line arguments given when the interpreter was started. The loop looks for various command line options. The -- flag is *required* in this example because the `switch` command complains about a bad flag if the pattern begins with a - character. The `scan` command, which is similar to the C library `scanf` function, is used to pick a number out of one argument.

If the list of values is to contain variable values or command results, then the `list` command should be used to form the list. Avoid double-quotes because if any values or command results contain spaces or braces, the list structure will be reparsed, which can lead to errors or unexpected results.

Example 4–9 Using `list` with `foreach`.

```
foreach x [list $a $b [foo]] {
    puts stdout "x = $x"
}
```

The loop variable `x` will take on the value of `a`, the value of `b`, and the result of the `foo` command, regardless of any special characters or whitespace in those values.

While

The `while` command takes two arguments, a test and a command body:

```
while booleanExpr body
```

The `while` command repeatedly tests the boolean expression and then executes the body if the expression is true (non-zero). Because the test expression is evaluated again before each iteration of the loop, it is crucial to protect the expression from any substitutions before the while command is invoked. The following is an infinite loop (See also Example 1-11 in Chapter 1):

```
set i 0 ; while $i<10 {incr i}
```

The following behaves as expected:

```
set i 0 ; while {$i<10} {incr i}
```

It is also possible to put nested commands in the boolean expression. The following example uses `gets` to read standard input. The `gets` command returns the number of characters read, returning -1 upon end-of-file. Each time through the loop the variable `line` contains the next line in the file:

Example 4–10 A `while` loop to read standard input.

```
set numLines 0 ; set numChars 0
while {[gets stdin line] >= 0} {
    incr numLines
    incr numChars [string length $line]
}
```

For

The `for` command is similar to the C `for` statement. It takes four arguments:

```
for initial test final body
```

The first argument is a command to initialize the loop. The second argument is a boolean expression that determines if the loop body will execute. The third argument is a command to execute after the loop body:

Example 4–11 A `for` loop.

```
for {set i 0} {$i < 10} {incr i 3} {
    lappend aList $i
}
set aList
=> 0 3 6 9
```

Break and Continue

You can control loop execution with the `break` and `continue` commands. The `break` command causes immediate exit from a loop, while the `continue` command causes the loop to continue with the next iteration. Note that there is no `goto` command in Tcl.

Catch

Until now we have ignored the possibility of errors. In practice, however, a command will raise an error if it is called with the wrong number of arguments, or if it detects some error condition particular to its implementation. An uncaught error aborts execution of a script.[*] The `catch` command is used to trap such errors. It takes two arguments:

```
catch command ?resultVar?
```

The first argument to `catch` is a command body. The second argument is the name of a variable that will contain the result of the command, or an error message if the command raises an error. `catch` returns zero if there was no error caught, or one if it did catch an error.

It is important to use curly braces to group the command (as opposed to double-quotes) because `catch` invokes the full Tcl interpreter on the command, so any needed substitutions occurs then. If double-quotes are used, an extra round of substitutions occur before `catch` is even called. The simplest use of `catch` looks like the following:

```
catch { command }
```

A more careful `catch` phrase saves the result and prints an error message:

Example 4–12 A standard `catch` phrase.

```
if [catch { command arg1 arg2 ... } result] {
    puts stderr $result
} else {
    # command was ok, result is its return value
}
```

The most general `catch` phrase is shown in the next example. Multiple commands are grouped into a command body. The `errorInfo` variable is set by the Tcl interpreter after an error to reflect the stack trace from the point of the error:

[*] More precisely, the Tcl script unwinds and the current `Tcl_Eval` procedure returns `TCL_ERROR`. In Tk, errors that arise during event handling trigger a call to `tkerror`, a Tcl procedure you can implement in your application.

Example 4–13 A longer `catch` phrase.

```
if [catch {
    command1
    command2
    command3
} result] {
    global errorInfo
    puts stderr $result
    puts stderr "*** Tcl TRACE ***"
    puts stderr $errorInfo
} else {
    # command body ok, result of last command is in result
}
```

These examples have not grouped the call to `catch` with curly braces. This is acceptable because `catch` always returns a 0 or a 1, so the `if` command will parse correctly. However, if we had used `while` instead of `if`, then curly braces would be necessary to ensure that the `catch` phrase was evaluated repeatedly.

Error

The `error` command raises an error condition that terminates a script unless it is trapped with the `catch` command. The command takes up to three arguments:

`error` *`message ?info? ?code?`*

The *`message`* becomes the error message stored in the result variable of the `catch` command.

If the *`info`* argument is provided, then the Tcl interpreter uses this to initialize the `errorInfo` global variable. That variable is used to collect a stack trace from the point of the error. If the *`info`* argument is not provided, then the `error` command itself is used to initialize the `errorInfo` trace.

Example 4–14 Raising an error.

```
proc foo {} {
    error bogus
}
foo
=> bogus
set errorInfo
=> bogus
    while executing
"error bogus"
    (procedure "foo" line 2)
    invoked from within
"foo"
```

In the previous example, the `error` command itself appears in the trace. One common use of the `info` argument is to preserve the `errorInfo` that is available after a `catch`. In the next example, the information from the original error is preserved:

Example 4–15 Preserving `errorInfo` when calling `error`.

```
if [catch {foo} result] {
    global errorInfo
    set savedInfo $errorInfo
    # Attempt to handle the error here, but cannot...
    error $result $savedInfo
}
```

The `code` argument specifies a concise, machine readable description of the error. It is stored into the global `errorCode` variable. It defaults to `NONE`. Many of the file system commands return an `errorCode` that has three elements: `POSIX`, the error name (e.g., `ENOENT`), and the associated error message:

```
POSIX ENOENT {No such file or directory}
```

In addition, your application can define error codes of its own. Catch phrases could examine the code in the global `errorCode` variable and decide how to respond to the error.

Return

The `return` command is used to return from a procedure. It is needed if return is to occur before the end of the procedure body, or if a constant value needs to be returned. As a matter of style, I also use return at the end of a procedure, even though a procedure returns the value of the last command executed in the body.

Exceptional return conditions can be specified with some optional arguments to `return`. The complete syntax is:

`return ?-code` *`c`*`? ?-errorinfo` *`i`*`? ?-errorcode` *`ec`*`?` *`string`*

The `-code` option value is one of `ok`, `error`, `return`, `break`, `continue`, or an integer. `ok` is the default if `-code` is not specified.

The `-code error` option makes `return` behave much like the `error` command. The `-errorcode` option sets the global `errorCode` variable, and the `-errorinfo` option initializes the `errorInfo` global variable. The difference is that there is no `error` command in the stack trace. Compare Example 4–14 with the next example:

Example 4–16 Specifying `errorInfo` with `return`.

```
proc bar {} {
    return -code error -errorinfo "I'm giving up" bogus
}
catch {bar} result
```

```
=> 1
set result
=> bogus
set errorInfo
=> I'm giving up
    invoked from within
"bar"
```

The `return`, `break`, and `continue` code options take effect in the caller of the procedure doing the exceptional return. If `-code return` is specified then the calling procedure returns. If `-code break` is specified, then the calling procedure breaks out of a loop, and if `-code continue` is specified then the calling procedure continues to the next iteration of the loop. These `-code` options to `return` enable the construction of new control structures entirely in Tcl. The following example implements the `break` command with a Tcl procedure:

```
proc break {} {
    return -code break
}
```

CHAPTER 5

Procedures and Scope

Commands covered: `proc`, `rename`, `global`, and `upvar`.

Procedures parameterize a commonly used sequence of commands. In addition, each procedure has a new local scope for variables. The scope of a variable is the range of commands over which it is defined. This chapter describes the Tcl `proc` command in more detail, and then goes on to consider issues of variable scope.

The proc Command

A Tcl procedure is defined with the `proc` command. It takes three arguments:

```
proc name params body
```

The first argument is the procedure name, which is added to the set of commands understood by the Tcl interpreter. The name is case sensitive, and can contain any characters. The second argument is a list of parameter names. The last argument is the body of the procedure.

Once defined, a Tcl procedure is used just like any other Tcl command. When it is called, each argument is assigned to the corresponding parameter and the body is evaluated. The result of the procedure is the result returned by the last command in the body. The `return` command can be used to return a specific value.

The parameter list for a procedure can include default values for parameters. This lets the caller leave out some of the command arguments.

Example 5–1 Default parameter values.

```
proc p2 {a {b 7} {c -2} } {
    expr $a / $b + $c
}
p2 6 3
=> 0
```

Here the procedure p2 can be called with one, two, or three arguments. If it is called with only one argument, then the parameters b and c take on the values specified in the proc command. If two arguments are provided, then only c gets the default value, and the arguments are assigned to a and b. At least one argument and no more than three arguments can be passed to p2.

A procedure can take a variable number of arguments by specifying the args keyword as the last parameter. When the procedure is called, the args parameter is a list that contains all the remaining values:

Example 5–2 Variable number of arguments.

```
proc argtest {a {b foo} args} {
    foreach param {a b args} {
        puts stdout "\t$param = [set $param]"
    }
}
argtest 1
=> a = 1
   b = foo
   args =
argtest 1 2
=> a = 1
   b = 2
   args =
argtest 1 2 3
=> a = 1
   b = 2
   args = 3
argtest 1 2 3 4
=> a = 1
   b = 2
   args = 3 4
```

Changing Command Names With rename

The rename command changes the name of a command.There are two main uses for rename. The first is to augment an existing procedure. Before you redefine it with proc, rename the existing command:

```
rename foo foo.orig
```

From within the new implementation of `foo` you can invoke the original command as `foo.orig`. Existing users of `foo` will transparently use the new version.

The other thing you can do with `rename` is completely hide a command by renaming it to the empty string. For example, you might not want users to execute UNIX programs, so you could disable `exec` with the following command:

```
rename exec {}
```

Scope

There is a single, global scope for procedure names.* You can define a procedure inside another procedure, but it is visible everywhere.There is a different name space for variables and procedures, so you could have a procedure and a variable with the same name without conflict. Chapter 9, on page 94, explains a naming convention to manage the names for procedures and global variables.

Each procedure has a local scope for variables. That is, variables introduced in the procedure only live for the duration of the procedure call. After the procedure returns, those variables are undefined. Variables defined outside the procedure are not visible to a procedure, unless the `upvar` or `global` scope commands are used. If the same variable name exists in an outer scope, it is unaffected by the use of that variable name inside a procedure.

Example 5–3 Variable scope and Tcl procedures.

```
set a 5
set b -8
proc p1 {a} {
    set b 42
    if {$a < 0} {
        return $b
    } else {
        return $a
    }
}
p1 $b
=> 42
p1 [expr $a*2]
=> 10
```

In the example, the variable `a` in the outer scope is different than the parameter `a` to `p1`. Similarly, the variable `b` in the outer scope is different than the variable `b` inside `p1`.

* This is in contrast to Pascal and other Algol-like languages that have nested procedures, and C that allows for file-private (static) procedures.

The global Command

Global scope is the top level scope. This scope is outside of any procedure. Variables defined at the global scope must be made accessible to the commands inside a procedure by using the `global` command. The syntax for `global` is:

```
global varName1 varName2 ...
```

The `global` command goes inside a procedure that needs to access the global variable. A common mistake is to have a single `global` command and expect that to apply to all procedures. However, a `global` command in the global scope has no effect. Instead, the `global` command makes a global variable visible in the current scope, so you must use it in all procedures that access the global variable.

The variable can be undefined at the time the `global` command is used. When the variable is defined, it becomes visible in the global scope. The following example uses an array to hold the state of a random number generator. The state has to persist between calls to `random`, so it is kept in a global array.

Example 5–4 A random number generator.*

```
proc randomInit { seed } {
   global rand
   set rand(ia) 9301;# Multiplier
   set rand(ic) 49297;# Constant
   set rand(im) 233280;# Divisor
   set rand(seed) $seed;# Last result
}
proc random {} {
   global rand
   set rand(seed) \
      [expr ($rand(seed)*$rand(ia) +
            $rand(ic)) % $rand(im)]
   return [expr $rand(seed)/double($rand(im))]
}
proc randomRange { range } {
   expr int([random]*$range)
}
randomInit [pid]
=> 5049
random
=> 0.517687
random
=> 0.217177
randomRange 100
=> 17
```

* Adapted from *Exploring Expect* by Libes, O'Reilly & Associates, Inc., 1995, and from *Numerical Recipes in C* by Press et. al., Cambridge University Press, 1988

Use Arrays for Global State

Tcl arrays are very flexible because there are no restrictions on the index value. A good use for arrays is to collect together a set of related variables, much as one would use a record in other languages. An advantage of using arrays in this fashion is that a `global` scope command applies to the whole array, which simplifies the management of global variables.

For example, in a larger Tk application, each module of the implementation may require a few global state variables. By collecting these together in an array that has the same name as the module, name conflicts between different modules are avoided. Also, in each of the module's procedures, a single `global` statement will suffice to make all the state variables visible. More advanced scope control mechanisms are introduced by various object systems for Tcl, such as [incr Tcl], which is described in Chapter 32.

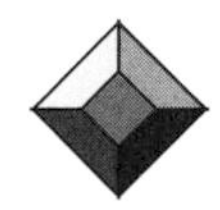

The following example uses an array to track the locations of some imaginary objects. (More interesting examples will be given in the context of some of the Tk widgets and applications.)

Example 5–5 Using arrays for global state.

```
proc ObjInit { o x y } {
    global obj
    set obj($o,x) $x
    set obj($o,y) $y
    set obj($o,dist) [expr sqrt($x * $x + $y * $y)]
}
proc ObjMove { o dx dy } {
    global obj
    if ![info exists obj($o,x)] {
        error "Object $o not initialized"
    }
    incr obj($o,x) $dx
    incr obj($o,y) $dy
    set obj($o,dist) [expr sqrt($obj($o,x) * $obj($o,x) + \
            $obj($o,y) * $obj($o,y))]
}
```

This example uses the global array `obj` to collect state variables, and it also parameterizes the index names with the name of an object. Remember to avoid spaces in the array indexes. The `incr` command and the `info exist` commands work equally well on array elements as on scalar variables.

Call by Name Using upvar

Use the `upvar` command when you need to pass the name of a variable into a procedure, as opposed to its value. Commonly this is used with array variables. The `upvar` command associates a local variable with a variable in a scope up the Tcl call stack. The syntax of the `upvar` command is:

```
upvar ?level? varName localvar
```

The *level* argument is optional, and it defaults to 1, which means one level up the Tcl call stack. You can specify some other number of frames to go up, or you can specify an absolute frame number with a `#number` syntax. Level `#0` is the global scope, so the `global foo` command is equivalent to:

```
upvar #0 foo foo
```

The variable in the uplevel stack frame can be either a scalar variable, an array element, or an array name. In the first two cases, the local variable is treated like a scalar variable. In the case of an array name, then the local variable is treated like an array. The following procedure uses `upvar` to print the value of a variable given its name.

Example 5–6 Print variable by name.

```
proc PrintByName { varName } {
   upvar $varName var
   puts stdout "$varName = $var"
}
```

You can use `upvar` to fix the `incr` command. One drawback of the built-in `incr` is that it raises an error if the variable does not exist. We can define a new version of `incr` that creates the variable as needed:

Example 5–7 Improved `incr` procedure.

```
proc incr { varName {amount 1}} {
   upvar $varName var
   if [info exists var] {
      set var [expr $var + $amount]
   } else {
      set var $amount
   }
   return $var
}
```

Passing Arrays by Name

The `upvar` command works on arrays. You can pass an array name to a procedure and use the `upvar` command to get an indirect reference to the array variable in the caller's scope. The array does not need to exist when the `upvar` command is called. In the following example, the `Push` and `Pop` procedures both guard against a non-existent array with the `info exists` command. When the first assignment to `S(top)` is done by `Push`, the array variable is created in the caller's scope. The example uses array indices in two ways. The `top` index records the depth of the stack. The other indices are numbers, so the construct `$S($S(top))` is used to reference the top of the stack.

Example 5–8 Using an array to implement a stack.

```
proc Push { stack value } {
	upvar $stack S
	if ![info exists S(top)] {
		set S(top) 0
	}
	set S($S(top)) $value
	incr S(top)
}
proc Pop { stack } {
	upvar $stack S
	if ![info exists S(top)] {
		return {}
	}
	if {$S(top) == 0} {
		return {}
	} else {
		incr S(top) -1
		set x $S($S(top))
		unset S($S(top))
		return $x
	}
}
```

CHAPTER 6

Eval

This chapter describes explicit calls to the interpreter with the `eval` command. An extra round of substitutions is performed that results in some useful effects. The chapter describes the potential problems with `eval` and the ways to avoid them. The `uplevel` command evaluates commands in a different scope. The `subst` command does substitutions but no command invocation.

Evaluation involves substitutions, and it is sometimes necessary to go through an extra round of substitutions. This is achieved with the `eval` and `subst` commands. The need for more substitutions can crop up in simple cases, such as dealing with the list-valued `args` parameter to a procedure. In addition, there are commands like `after`, `uplevel`, and the Tk `send` command that have similar properties to `eval`, except that the command evaluation occurs later or in a different context.

The `eval` command is used to re-interpret a string as a command. It is very useful in certain cases, but it can be tricky to assemble a command so it is evaluated properly by `eval`. The root of the quoting problems is the internal use of `concat` by `eval` and similar commands to put their arguments into one command string. The `concat` can lose some important list structure so that arguments are not passed through as you expect. One general strategy to avoid these problems is to use `list` and `lappend` to explicitly form the command. In other cases, the `concat` is useful in joining lists (e.g., `$args`) to make up a single command.

Construct Commands with list

The `eval` command results in another call to the Tcl interpreter. If you construct a command dynamically, you must use `eval` to interpret it. For example, suppose we want to construct the following command now, but execute it later:

```
puts stdout "Hello, World!"
```

In this case, it is sufficient to do the following:

```
set cmd {puts stdout "Hello, World!"}
=> puts stdout "Hello, World!"
# sometime later...
eval $cmd
=> Hello, World!
```

However, suppose that the string to be output is stored in a variable, but that variable will not be defined at the time `eval` is used. We can artificially create this situation like this:

```
set string "Hello, World!"
set cmd {puts stdout $string}
unset string
eval $cmd
=> can't read "string": no such variable
```

The solution to this problem is to construct the command using `list`, as shown in the folowing example:

Example 6–1 Using `list` to construct commands.

```
set string "Hello, World!"
set cmd [list puts stdout $string]
=> puts stdout {Hello, World!}
unset string
eval $cmd
=> Hello, World!
```

The trick is that `list` has formed a list containing three elements: `puts`, `stdout`, and the value of `string`. The substitution of `$string` occurs before `list` is called, and `list` takes care of grouping that value for us.

In contrast, compare this to the most widely used incorrect approach:

```
set cmd "puts stdout $string"
=> puts stdout Hello, World!
eval $cmd
=> bad argument "World!": should be "nonewline"
```

Using double quotes is equivalent to:

```
set cmd [concat puts stdout $string]
```

The problem here is that `concat` does not preserve list structure. The main lesson is that you should use `list` to construct commands if they contain variable values or command results that are substituted now, as opposed to later, when the command is evaluated.

Exploiting the concat Inside eval

This section illustrates cases where the `concat` doen by `eval` is useful in assembling a command by concatenating multiple lists into one list. A `concat` is done internally by `eval` if it gets more than one argument:

```
eval list1 list2 list3 ...
```

The effect of `concat` is to join all the lists into one list; a new level of list structure is *not* added. This is useful if the lists are fragments of a command. It is common to use this form of `eval` with the `args` construct in procedures. Use the `args` parameter to pass optional arguments through to another command. Invoke the other command with `eval` and the arguments in `$args` get concatenated onto the command properly. This technique is illustrated with a simple Tk example. At this point, all you need to know is that a command to create a button looks like this:

```
button .foo -text Foo -command foo
```

After a button is created, it is made visible by packing it into the display:

```
pack .foo -side left
```

The following does not work:

```
set args {-text Foo -command foo}
button .foo $args
=> unknown option "-text Foo -command foo"
```

The problem is that `$args` is a list value, and `button` gets the whole list as a single argument. Instead, `button` needs to get the elements of `$args` as individual arguments. In this case, you can use `eval` because it concatenates its arguments to form a single list before evaluation. The single list is, by definition, the same as a single Tcl command, so the `button` command parses correctly:

```
eval button .foo $args
=> .foo
```

Example 6–2 Using `eval` with `$args`.

```
# PackedButton creates and packs a button.
proc PackedButton {path txt cmd {pack {-side right}} args} {
   eval {button $path -text $txt -command $cmd} $args
   eval {pack $path} $pack
}
```

In `PackedButton`, both `pack` and `args` are list-valued parameters that are used as parts of a command. The internal `concat` done by `eval` is perfect for this situation. The simplest call to `PackedButton` is:

```
PackedButton .new "New" { New }
```

The quotes and curly braces are redundant in this case, but are retained to convey some type information. The `pack` argument takes on its default value, and the `args` variable is an empty list. The two commands executed by `PackedButton` are:

```
button .new -text New -command New
pack .new -side right
```

PackedButton creates a horizontal stack of buttons by default. The packing can be controlled with a packing specification:

```
PackedButton .save "Save" { Save $file } {-side left}
```

This changes the pack command to:

```
pack .new -side left
```

The remaining arguments, if any, are passed through to the button command. This lets the caller fine tune some of the button attributes:

```
PackedButton .quit Quit { Exit } {-side left -padx 5} \
    -background red
```

This changes the button command to:

```
button .new -text New -command New -background red
```

Double-quotes and eval

You may be tempted to use double-quotes instead of curly braces in your uses of eval. *Don't give in!* Using double quotes is, mostly likely, wrong. Suppose the first eval command is written like this:

```
eval "button $path -text $txt -command $cmd $args"
```

This happens to work with the following because txt and cmd are one-word arguments with no special characters in them:

```
PackedButton .quit Quit { Exit }
```

In the next call an error is raised:

```
PackedButton .save "Save" { Save $file }
=> can't read "file": no such variable
```

The danger is that the success of this approach depends on the value of the parameters. The value of txt and the value of cmd are subject to another round of substitutions and parsing. When those values contain spaces or special characters, the command gets parsed incorrectly.

To repeat, the safe construct is:

```
eval {button $path -text $txt -command $cmd} $args
```

As you may be able to tell, this was one of the more difficult lessons I learned, despite three uses of the word "concatenate" in the eval man page!

The uplevel Command

The uplevel command is similar to eval, except that it evaluates a command in a different scope than the current procedure. It is useful for defining new control structures entirely in Tcl. The syntax for uplevel is:

```
uplevel level command
```

As with upvar, the *level* parameter is optional and defaults to 1, which means to execute the command in the scope of the calling procedure. The other common use of level is #0, which means to evaluate the command in the global scope.

When you specify the *command* argument, you have to be aware of any substitutions that might be performed by the Tcl interpreter before uplevel is called. If you are entering the command directly, protect it with curly braces so that substitutions occur in the correct scope. The following affects the variable x in the caller's scope:

```
uplevel {set x [expr $x + 1]}
```

However, the following will use the value of x in the current scope to define the value of x in the calling scope, which is probably not what was intended:

```
uplevel "set x [expr $x + 1]"
```

It is common to have the command in a variable. This is the case when the command has been passed into your new control flow procedure as an argument. In this case you should evaluate the command one level up:

```
uplevel $cmd
```

Or, perhaps you have read the command from a user-interface widget. In this case, you should evaluate the command at the global scope:

```
uplevel #0 $cmd
```

Finally, if you are assembling a command from a few different lists, such as the args parameter, then you can use concat to form the command:

```
uplevel [concat $cmd $args]
```

The lists in $cmd and $args are concatenated into a single list, which is a valid Tcl command. Like eval, uplevel uses concat internally if it is given extra arguments, so you can leave out the explicit use of concat.

Commands that Concatenate Their Arguments

The uplevel command and two Tk commands, after and send, concatenate their arguments into a command and execute it later in a different context. Whenever I discover such a command I put it on my danger list and make sure I explicitly form a single command argument with list instead of letting the command concat items for me. Get in the habit now:

```
after 100 [list doCmd $param1 $param2]
send $interp [list doCmd $param1 $param2];# Safe!
```

The worst part of this is: concat and list can result in the same thing, so you can be led down the rosy garden path, only to get errors later when values change. The two previous examples always work. The next two work only if param1 and param2 have values that are single list elements:

```
after 100 doCmd $param1 $param2
send $interp doCmd $param1 $param2;# Unsafe!
```

If you use other Tcl extensions that provide eval-like functionality, carefully check their documentation to see if they contain commands that concat their arguments into a command. For example, Tcl-DP, which provides a network version of send, dp_send, also uses concat.

The subst Command

The subst command is used to do command and variable substitution, but without invoking any command. It is similar to eval in that it does a round of substitutions for you. However, it doesn't try to interpret the result as a command.

```
set a "foo bar"
subst {a=$a date=[exec date]}
=> a=foo bar date=Thu Dec 15 10:13:48 PST 1994
```

The subst command does not honor the quoting effect of curly braces:

```
subst {a=$a date={[exec date]}}
=> a=foo bar date={Thu Dec 15 10:15:31 PST 1994}
```

Instead, you must use backslashes to prevent variable and command substitution.

```
subst {a=\$a date=\[exec date]}
=> a=$a date=[exec date]
```

CHAPTER 7

Working with UNIX

This chapter describes how to use Tcl in a UNIX environment. Tcl commands:
exec, open, close, read, write, seek, tell, glob, pwd, and cd.

This chapter describes how to run programs and access the file system from Tcl. Although these commands were designed for UNIX, they are also implemented (perhaps with limitations) in the Tcl ports to other systems such as DOS and Macintosh. These capabilities enable your Tcl script to be a general purpose glue that assembles other programs into a tool that is customized for your needs.

Running UNIX Programs with exec

The exec command runs UNIX programs from your Tcl script.* For example:

```
set d [exec date]
```

The standard output of the program is returned as the value of the exec command. However, if the program writes to its standard error stream or exits with a non-zero status code, then exec raises an error.

The exec command supports a full set of *I/O redirection* and *pipeline* syntax. Each UNIX process normally has three I/O streams associated with it: standard input, standard output, and standard error. With I/O redirection you can divert these I/O streams to files or to I/O streams you have opened with the Tcl open command. A pipeline is a chain of UNIX processes that have the standard

* Unlike the C-shell exec command, the Tcl exec does not replace the current process with the new one. Instead, the Tcl library forks first and executes the program as a child process.

output of one command hooked up to the standard input of the next command in the pipeline. Any number of programs can be linked together into a pipeline.

Example 7–1 Using exec on a process pipeline.

```
set n [exec sort < /etc/passwd | uniq | wc -l 2> /dev/null]
```

The example uses exec to run three programs in a pipeline. The first program is sort, which takes its input from the file /etc/passwd. The output of sort is piped into uniq, which suppresses duplicate lines. The output of uniq is piped into wc, which counts the lines. The error output of the command is diverted to the null device to suppress any error messages.

Table 7–1 provides a summary of the syntax understood by the exec command. Note that a trailing & causes the program to run in the background. In this case the process identifier is returned by the exec command. Otherwise, the exec command blocks during execution of the program and the standard output of the program is the return value of exec. The trailing newline in the output is trimmed off, unless you specify -keepnewline as the first argument to exec.

Table 7–1 Summary of the exec syntax for I/O redirection.

-keepnewline	(First argument.) Do not discard trailing newline from the result.
|	Pipe standard output from one process into another.
|&	Pipe both standard output and standard error output.
< *fileName*	Take input from the named file.
<@ *fileId*	Take input from the I/O stream identified by *fileId*.
<< *value*	Take input from the given value.
> *fileName*	Overwrite *fileName* with standard output.
2> *fileName*	Overwrite *fileName* with standard error output.
>& *fileName*	Overwrite *fileName* with both standard error and standard out.
>> *fileName*	Append standard output to the named file.
2>> *fileName*	Append standard error to the named file.
>>& *fileName*	Append both standard error and standard output to the named file.
>@ *fileId*	Direct standard output to the I/O stream identified by *fileId*.
2>@ *fileId*	Direct standard error to the I/O stream identified by *fileId*.
>&@ *fileId*	Direct both standard error and standard output to the I/O stream.
&	As the last argument, indicates pipeline should run in background.

If you look closely at the I/O redirection syntax, you'll see that it is built up from a few basic building blocks. The basic idea is that | stands for pipeline, > for output, and < for input. The standard error is joined to the standard output by `&`. Standard error is diverted separately by using `2>`. You can use your own I/O streams by using `@`.

The auto_noexec Variable

The Tcl shell programs are set up by default to attempt to execute unknown Tcl commands as UNIX programs. For example, you can get a directory listing by typing:

```
ls
```

instead of:

```
exec ls
```

This is handy if you are using the Tcl interpreter as a general shell. It can also cause unexpected behavior when you are just playing around. To turn this off, define the `auto_noexec` variable:

```
set auto_noexec anything
```

Looking at the File System

The `file` command provides several ways to check the status of files in the UNIX file system. For example, you can find out if a file exists, and what type of file it is. In fact, essentially all the information the `stat` system call returns is available with the `file` command. Table 7–2 provides a summary of the various forms of the `file` command:

Table 7–2 The `file` command options.

`file atime` *name*	Return access time as a decimal string.
`file dirname` *name*	Return parent directory of file *name*.
`file executable` *name*	Return 1 if *name* has execute permission, else 0.
`file exists` *name*	Return 1 if *name* exists, else 0.
`file extension` *name*	Return the part of *name* from the last dot (i.e., .) to the end.
`file isdirectory` *name*	Return 1 if *name* is a directory, else 0.
`file isfile` *name*	Return 1 if *name* is not a directory, symbolic link, or device, else 0.
`file lstat` *name var*	Place stat results about the link *name* into *var*.
`file mtime` *name*	Return modify time of *name* as a decimal string.
`file owned` *name*	Return 1 if current user owns the file *name*, else 0.

Table 7–2 The `file` command options. (Continued)

`file readable` *name*	Return 1 if *name* has read permission, else 0.
`file readlink` *name*	Return the contents of the symbolic link *name*.
`file rootname` *name*	Return all but the extension of *name* (i.e., up to but not including the last `.` in *name*).
`file size` *name*	Return the number of bytes in *name*.
`file stat` *name var*	Place stat results about *name* into array *var*. The elements defined for *var* are: `atime`, `ctime`, `dev`, `gid`, `ino`, `mode`, `mtime`, `nlink`, `size`, `type`, and `uid`.
`file tail` *name*	Return all characters after last `/` in *name*.
`file type` *name*	Return type identifier, which is one of: `file`, `directory`, `characterSpecial`, `blockSpecial`, `fifo`, `link`, or `socket`.
`file writable` *name*	Return 1 if *name* has write permission, else 0.

The following command uses `file mtime` to compare the modify times of two files. If you have ever resorted to piping the results of *ls -l* into *awk* in order to derive this information in other shell scripts, you will appreciate this example:

Example 7–2 Comparing file modify times.

```
proc newer { file1 file2 } {
    if ![file exists $file2] {
        return 1
    } else {
        # Assume file1 exists
        expr [file mtime $file1] > [file mtime $file2]
    }
}
```

A few of the options operate on pathnames as opposed to returning information about the file itself. You can use these commands on any string; there is no requirement that the pathnames refer to an existing file. The `dirname` and `tail` options are complementary. The first returns the parent directory of a pathname, while `tail` returns the trailing component of the pathname:

```
file dirname /a/b/c
=> /a/b
file tail /a/b/c
=> c
```

For a pathname with a single component, the `dirname` option returns "`.`", which is the name of the current directory.

The `extension` and `root` options are also complementary. The `extension` option returns everything from the last period in the name to the end (i.e., the file suffix including the period.) The `root` option returns everything up to, but not including, the last period in the pathname:

```
file root /a/b.c
=> /a/b
file extension /a/b.c
=> .c
```

The following `makedir` example uses the `file` command to determine if it is necessary to create the intermediate directories in a pathname. It calls itself recursively, using `file dirname` in the recursive step to create the parent directory. To do the actual work, it executes the *mkdir* program. An error can be raised in two places, explicitly by the `Makedir` procedure if it finds a non-directory in the pathname, or by the *mkdir* program if, for example, the user does not have the permissions to create the directory.

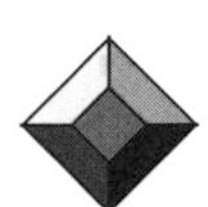

Example 7–3 Creating a directory recursively.

```
proc makedir { pathname } {
    if {[file isdirectory $pathname]} {
        return $pathname
    } elseif {[file exists $pathname]} {
        error "Non-directory $pathname already exists."
    } else {
        # Recurse to create intermediate directories
        makedir [file dirname $pathname]
        exec mkdir $pathname
        return $pathname
    }
}
```

The most general `file` command options are `stat` and `lstat`. They take a third argument that is the name of an array variable, and they initialize that array with elements and values corresponding to the results of the `stat` system call. The array elements defined are: `atime`, `ctime`, `dev`, `gid`, `ino`, `mode`, `mtime`, `nlink`, `size`, `type`, and `uid`. All the element values are decimal strings, except for `type`, which can have the values returned by the `type` option. See the UNIX manual page on the `stat` system call for a description of these attributes.

Example 7–4 Determining if pathnames reference the same file.

```
proc fileeq { path1 path2 } {
    file stat $path1 stat1
    file stat $path2 stat2
    expr [$stat1(ino) == $stat2(ino) && \
          $stat1(dev) == $stat2(dev)]
}
```

The example uses the device (`dev`) and inode (`ino`) attributes of a file to determine if two pathnames reference the same file.

Input/Output Command Summary

Table 7–3 lists the commands associated with file input/output:

Table 7–3 Tcl commands used for file access.

`open` *what ?access? ?permissions?*	Return stream ID for a file or pipeline.
`puts ?-nonewline?` *?stream? string*	Write a string.
`gets` *stream ?varname?*	Read a line.
`read` *stream ?numBytes?*	Read *numBytes* bytes, or all data.
`read -nonewline` *stream*	Read all bytes and discard the last `\n`.
`tell` *stream*	Return the seek offset.
`seek` *stream offset ?origin?*	Set the seek offset. *origin* is one of `start`, `current`, or `end`.
`eof` *stream*	Query end-of-file status.
`flush` *stream*	Write buffers of a stream.
`close` *stream*	Close an I/O stream.

Opening Files for I/O

The `open` command sets up an I/O stream to either a file or a pipeline of processes. The return value of `open` is an identifier for the I/O stream. Store the result of `open` in a variable, and use the variable like you used the `stdout`, `stdin`, and `stderr` identifiers in the examples so far. The basic syntax is:

`open` *what ?access? ?permissions?*

The *what* argument is either a file name or a pipeline specification similar to that used by the `exec` command. The *access* argument can take two forms, either a short character sequence that is compatible with the `fopen` library routine, or a list of POSIX access flags. Table 7–4 summarizes the first form, while Table 7–5 summarizes the POSIX flags. If *access* is not specified, it defaults to read. The *permissions* argument is a value used for the permission bits on a newly created file. The default permission bits are `0666`. Consult the manual page on the UNIX *chmod* command for more details about permission bits.

Example 7–5 Opening a file for writing.

```
set fileId [open /tmp/foo w 0600]
puts $fileId "Hello, foo!"
close $fileId
```

Table 7–4 Summary of the `open` access arguments.

r	Open for reading. The file must exist.
r+	Open for reading and writing. The file must exist.
w	Open for writing. Truncate if it exists. Create if it does not exist.
w+	Open for reading and writing. Truncate or create.
a	Open for writing. The file must exist. Data is appended to the file.
a+	Open for reading and writing. File must exist. Data is appended.

Table 7–5 Summary of `POSIX` flags for the access argument.

`RDONLY`	Open for reading.
`WRONLY`	Open for writing.
`RDWR`	Open for reading and writing.
`APPEND`	Open for append.
`CREAT`	Create the file if it does not exist.
`EXCL`	If `CREAT` is also specified, then the file cannot already exist.
`NOCTTY`	Prevent terminal devices from becoming the controlling terminal.
`NONBLOCK`	Do not block during the open.
`TRUNC`	Truncate the file if it exists.

(You should consult your system's manual page for the `open` system call to determine the precise effects of the `NOCTTY` and `NONBLOCK` flags.)

The following example illustrates how to use a list of POSIX access flags to open a file for reading and writing, creating it if needed, and not truncating it. This is something you cannot do with the simpler form of the access argument.

Example 7–6 Opening a file using the POSIX access flags.

```
set fileId [open /tmp/bar {RDWR CREAT}]
```

In general you should check for errors when opening files. The following example illustrates a `catch` phrase used to open files. Recall that `catch` returns 1 if it catches an error, otherwise it returns zero. It treats its second argument as the name of a variable. In the error case it puts the error message into the variable. In the normal case it puts the result of the command into the variable:

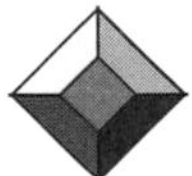

Example 7–7 A more careful use of open.

```
if [catch {open /tmp/data r} fileId] {
    puts stderr "Cannot open /tmp/data: $fileId"
} else {
    # Read and process the file, then...
    close $fileId
}
```

Opening a Process Pipeline

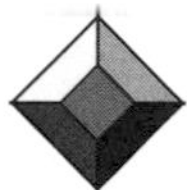

You can open a process pipeline by specifying the pipe character, |, as the first character of the first argument. The remainder of the pipeline specification is interpreted just as with the exec command, including input and output redirection. The second argument determines which end of the pipeline open returns. The following example runs the UNIX *sort* program on the password file, and it uses the split command to separate the output lines into list elements:

Example 7–8 Opening a process pipeline.

```
set input [open "|sort /etc/passwd" r]
set contents [split [read $input] \n]
close $input
```

You can open a pipeline for both read and write by specifying the r+ access mode. In this case you need to worry about buffering. After a puts the data may still be in a buffer in the Tcl library. Use the flush command to force the data out to the spawned processes before you try to read any output from the pipeline. In general, the *expect* extension, which is described in Chapter 32, provides a much more powerful way to do these kinds of things.

Reading and Writing

The standard UNIX I/O streams are already open for you. These streams are identified by stdin, stdout, and stderr, respectively. Other I/O streams are identified by the return value of the open command. There are several commands used with file identifiers.

The puts and gets Commands

The puts command writes a string and a newline to the output stream. There are a couple of details about the puts command that we have not yet used. It takes a -nonewline argument that prevents the newline character that is normally appended to the output stream. This will be used in the prompt example below. The second feature is that the stream identifier is optional, defaulting to stdout if not specified.

Example 7–9 Prompting for input.

```
puts -nonewline "Enter value: "
set answer [gets stdin]
```

The `gets` command reads a line of input, and it has two forms. In the previous example, with just a single argument, `gets` returns the line read from the specified I/O stream. It discards the trailing newline from the return value. If end-of-file is reached, an empty string is returned. You must use the `eof` command to tell the difference between a blank line and end-of-file. (`eof` returns 1 if there is end-of-file.) Given a second *varName* argument, `gets` stores the line into named variable and returns the number of bytes read. It discards the trailing newline, which is not counted. A -1 is returned if the stream has reached end of file.

Example 7–10 A read loop using `gets`.

```
while {[gets $stream line] >= 0} {
    # Process line
}
close $stream
```

The read Command

The `read` command reads blocks of data, which is often more efficient. There are two forms for `read`: you can specify the `-nonewline` argument or the *numBytes* argument, but not both. Without *numBytes*, the whole file (or what is left in the I/O stream) is read and returned. The `-nonewline` argument causes the trailing newline to be discarded. Given a byte count argument, `read` returns that amount, or less if there is not enough data in the stream. The trailing newline is not discarded in this case.

Example 7–11 A read loop using `read` and `split`.

```
foreach line [split [read $stream] \n] {
    # Process line
}
close $stream
```

For moderate-sized files it is about 10% faster to loop over the lines in a file using the read loop in the second example. In this case, `read` returns the whole file, and `split` chops the file into list elements, one for each line. For small files (less than 1K) it doesn't really matter. For large files (megabytes) you might induce paging with this approach.

Random Access I/O

The `seek` and `tell` commands provide random access to I/O streams. Each stream has a current position called the *seek offset*. Each read or write operation updates the seek offset by the number of bytes transferred. The current value of the offset is returned by the `tell` command. The `seek` command sets the seek offset by an amount, which can be positive or negative, from an origin which is either `start`, `current`, or `end`.

Closing I/O streams

The `close` command is just as important as the others because it frees operating system resources associated with the I/O stream. If you forget to close a stream it will be closed when your process exits. However, if you have a long-running program, like a Tk script, you might exhaust some operating system resources if you forget to close your I/O streams.

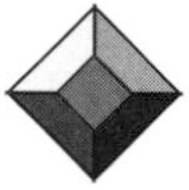

Note that the `close` command can raise an error. If the stream was a process pipeline and any of the processes wrote to their standard error stream, then Tcl believes this is an error. The error is raised when the stream to the pipeline is finally closed. Similarly, if any of the processes in the pipeline exit with a non-zero status, `close` raises an error.

The Current Directory - cd and pwd

Every UNIX process has a current directory that is used as the starting point when resolving a relative pathname (a file name that does not begin with `/`). The `pwd` command returns the current directory, and the `cd` command changes the current directory. Example 7–12 uses these commands.

Matching File Names with glob

The `glob` command expands a pattern into the set of matching file names. The general form of the glob command is:

```
glob ?flags? pattern ?pattern? ...
```

The pattern syntax is similar to the `string match` patterns:

- `*` matches zero or more characters
- `?` matches a single character
- `[abc]` matches a set of characters.
- `{a,b,c}` matches any of *a*, *b*, or *c*.
- All other characters must match themselves.

The `-nocomplain` flag causes `glob` to return an empty list if no files match the pattern. Otherwise `glob` raises an error if no files match.

The `--` flag must be used if the *pattern* begins with a `-`.

Unlike the glob matching in *csh*, the Tcl `glob` command only matches the names of existing files. In *csh*, the `{a,b}` construct can match non-existent names. In addition, the results of `glob` are not sorted. Use the `lsort` command to sort its result if you find it important.

Example 7–12 Finding a file by name.

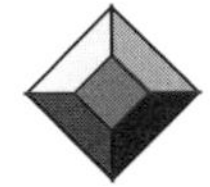

```
proc FindFile { startDir namePat } {
    set pwd [pwd]
    if [catch {cd $startDir} err] {
        puts stderr $err
        return
    }
    foreach match [glob -nocomplain -- $namePat]{
        puts stdout $startDir/$match
    }
    foreach file [glob -nocomplain *] {
        if [file isdirectory $file] {
            FindFile $startDir/$file $namePat
        }
    }
    cd $pwd
}
```

The `FindFile` procedure traverses the file system hierarchy using recursion. At each iteration it saves its current directory and then attempts to change to the next subdirectory. A `catch` guards against bogus names. The `glob` command matches file names. `FindFile` is called recursively on each subdirectory.

Expanding Tilde in File Names

The `glob` command also expands a leading tilde (~) in filenames. There are two cases:

- `~/` expands to the current user's home directory.
- `~user` expands to the home directory of `user`.

If you have a file that starts with a literal tilde you can avoid the tilde expansion by adding a leading `./` (e.g., `./~foobar`).

The exit and pid Commands

The `exit` command terminates your script. Note that `exit` causes termination of the whole UNIX process that was running the script. If you supply an integer-valued argument to `exit`, then that becomes the exit status of the process.

The `pid` command returns the process ID of the current process. This can be useful as the seed for a random number generator because it changes each time you run your script. It is also common to embed the process ID in the name of temporary files.

Environment Variables

Environment variables are a collection of string-valued variables associated with each UNIX process. The process's environment variables are available through the global array env. The name of the environment variable is the index, (e.g., env(PATH)), and the array element contains the current value of the environment variable. If assignments are made to env, they result in changes to the corresponding environment variable. Environment variables are inherited by child processes, so programs run with the exec command inherit the environment of the Tcl script. The following example prints the values of environment variables.

Example 7–13 Printing environment variable values.

```
proc printenv { args } {
    global env
    set maxl 0
    if {[llength $args] == 0} {
        set args [lsort [array names env]]
    }
    foreach x $args {
        if {[string length $x] > $maxl} {
            set maxl [string length $x]
        }
    }
    incr maxl 2
    foreach x $args {
        puts stdout [format "%*s = %s" $maxl $x $env($x)]
    }
}
printenv USER SHELL TERM
=>
USER  = welch
SHELL = /bin/csh
TERM  = tx
```

CHAPTER 8

Reflection and Debugging

This chapter describes commands that give you a view into the interpreter. The `history` command and a simple debugger are useful during development and debugging. The `info` command provides a variety of information about the internal state of the Tcl interpreter. The `time` command measures the time it takes to execute a command.

Reflection provides feedback to a script about the internal state of the interpreter. This is useful in a variety of cases, from testing to see if a variable exists to dumping the state of the interpreter. This chapter starts with a description of the `info` command that provides lots of different information about the interpreter.

Interactive command history is the second topic of the chapter. The history facility can save you some typing if you spend a lot of time entering commands interactively.

Debugging is the last topic. The old-fashioned approach of adding `puts` commands to your code is often quite useful. It takes so little time to add code and run another test that this is much less painful than if you had to wait for a long compilation every time you changed a print command. The *tkinspect* program is an inspector that lets you look into the state of a Tk application. It can hook up to any Tk application dynamically, so it proves quite useful. Don Libes has implemented a Tcl debugger that lets you set breakpoints and step through your script. This debugger is described at the end of the chapter.

The info Command

Table 8–1 summarizes the `info` command. The operations are described in more detail after the table.

Table 8–1 The `info` command.

`info args` *`procedure`*	A list of *`procedure`*'s arguments.
`info body` *`procedure`*	The commands in the body of *`procedure`*.
`info cmdcount`	The number of commands executed so far.
`info commands ?`*`pattern`*`?`	A list of all commands, or those matching *`pattern`*. Includes built-ins and Tcl procedures.
`info complete` *`string`*	True if *`string`* contains a complete Tcl command.
`info default` *`proc arg var`*	True if *`arg`* has a default parameter value in procedure *`proc`*. The default value is stored into *`var`*.
`info exists` *`variable`*	True if *`variable`* is defined.
`info globals ?`*`pattern`*`?`	A list of all global variables, or those matching *`pattorn`*.
`info level`	The stack level of the current procedure, or 0 for the global scope.
`info level` *`number`*	A list of the command and its arguments at the specified level of the stack.
`info library`	The pathname of the Tcl library directory.
`info locals ?`*`pattern`*`?`	A list of all local variables, or those matching *`pattern`*.
`info patchlevel`	The release patchlevel for Tcl.
`info procs ?`*`pattern`*`?`	A list of all Tcl procedures, or those that match *`pattern`*.
`info script`	The name of the file being processed, or NULL.
`info tclversion`	The version number of Tcl.
`info vars ?`*`pattern`*`?`	A list of all visible variables, or those matching pattern.

Variables

There are three categories of variables: local, global, and visible. Information about these categories is returned by the `locals`, `globals`, and `vars` operations, respectively. The local variables include procedure arguments as well as locally defined variables. The global variables include all variables defined at the global scope. The visible variables include locals, plus any variables made visible via `global` or `upvar` commands. Remember that a variable may not be defined yet even though a `global` command has declared it to belong to the global scope.

Perhaps the most commonly used operation is `info exists`, to test whether a variable or an array element is defined or not. An example is shown on page 30. A pattern can be specified to limit the returned list of variables to those that match the pattern. The pattern is interpreted according to the rules of the `string match` command, which is described on page 24.

Procedures

You can find out everything about a Tcl procedure with the args, body, and default operations. This is illustrated in the following ShowProc example. The puts commands use the -nonewline flag because the newlines in the procedure body, if any, are retained:

Example 8–1 Printing a procedure definition.

```
proc ShowProc {{namepat *} {file stdout}} {
    foreach proc [info procs $namepat] {
        set needspace 0
        puts -nonewline $file "proc $proc {"
        foreach arg [info args $proc] {
            if {$needspace} {
                puts -nonewline $file " "
            }
            if [info default $proc $arg value] {
                puts -nonewline $file "{$arg $value}"
            } else {
                puts -nonewline $file $arg
            }
            set needspace 1
        }
        # No newline needed because info body may return a
        # value that starts with a newline
        puts -nonewline $file "} {"
        puts -nonewline $file [info body $proc]
        puts $file "}"
    }
}
```

The info commands operation returns a list of all commands, which includes both built-in commands defined in C and Tcl procedures. There is no operation that just returns the list of built-in commands. You have to write a procedure to take the difference of two lists to get that information. A command for doing so, intersect3, is included in Extended Tcl,which is described in Chapter 32.

The Call Stack

The info level operation returns information about the Tcl evaluation stack, or *call stack*. The global level is numbered zero. A procedure called from the global level is at level one in the call stack. A procedure it calls is at level two, and so on. The info level command returns the current level number of the stack if no level number is specified.

If a positive level number is specified (e.g., info level 3) then the command returns the procedure name and argument values at that level in the call stack. If a negative level is specified, then it is relative to the current call stack. Relative level -1 is the level of the current procedure's caller, and relative-level 0 is the current procedure. The following example prints the call stack. The

CallTrace procedure avoids printing information about itself by starting at one less than the current call stack level:

Example 8–2 Getting a trace of the Tcl call stack.

```
proc CallTrace {{file stdout}} {
   puts $file "Tcl Call Trace"
   for {set x [expr [info level]-1]} {$x > 0} {incr x -1} {
      puts $file "$x: [info level $x]"
   }
}
```

Command Evaluation

The info complete operation figures out if a string is a complete Tcl command. This is useful for command interpreters that need to wait until the user has typed in a complete Tcl command before passing it to eval.

If you want to know how many Tcl commands are executed, use the info cmdcount command. This counts all commands, not just top-level commands. The counter is never reset, so you need to sample it before and after a test run if you want to know how many commands are executed during a test.

Scripts and the Library

The name of the current script file is returned with the info script command. For example, if you use the source command to read commands from a file, then info script returns the name of that file if it is called during execution of the commands in that script. This is true even if the info script command is called from a procedure that is not defined in the script.

The pathname of the Tcl library is returned by the info library command. While you could put scripts into this directory, it might be better to have a separate directory and use the script library facility described in Chapter 9. This makes it easier to deal with new releases of Tcl, and to package up your code if you want other sites to use it.

Version Numbers

Each Tcl release has a version number such as 7.4. This number is returned by the info tclversion command. If you want your script to run on a variety of Tcl releases, you may need to test the version number and take different actions in the case of incompatibilities between releases. If there are patches to the release, then a patch level is incremented. The patch level is reset to zero on each release, and it is returned by the info patchlevel command.

Tracing Variable Values

The `trace` command registers a command to be called whenever a variable is accessed, modified, or unset. This form of the command is:

```
trace variable name ops command
```

The *name* is a Tcl variable name, which can be a simple variable, an array, or an array element. If a whole array is traced, the trace is invoked when any element is used according to *ops*. The *ops* argument is one or more of the letters `r`, for read traces, `w`, for write traces, and `u`, for unset traces. The *command* is executed when one of these events occurs. It is invoked as:

```
command name1 name2 op
```

The *name1* argument is the variable or array name. The *name2* argument is the name of the array index, or null if the trace is on a simple variable. If there is an unset trace on an entire array and the array is unset, *name2* is also null. The value of the variable is not passed to the procedure. The `upvar`, `uplevel`, or `global` commands need to be used to make the variable visible in the scope of the command. These commands are described in more detail in Chapter 5.

The next example uses traces to implement a read-only variable. The value is modified before the trace procedure is called, so another variable (or some other mechanism) is needed to preserve the original value:

Example 8–3 Tracing variables.

```
set x-orig $x
trace variable x wu FixupX
proc FixupX { varName index op } {
    upvar $varName var
    global x-orig
    switch $op {
        w {set var $x-orig}
        u {unset x-orig}
    }
}
```

This example merely overrides the new value with the saved valued. Another alternative is to raise an error with the `error` command. This will cause the command that modified the variable to return the error. Another common use of `trace` is to update a user interface widget in response to a variable change. Several of the Tk widgets have this feature built into them.

If more than one trace is set on a variable, then they are invoked in the reverse order; the most recent trace is executed first. If there is a trace on an array and on an array element, then the trace on the array is invoked first. The next example uses an array trace to dynamically create array elements:

Example 8–4 Creating array elements with array traces.

```
# make sure variable is an array
set dynamic() {}
trace variable dynamic r FixupDynamic
proc FixupDynamic {name index op} {
    global dynamic;# We know this is $name
    if ![info exists dynamic($index)] {
        set dynamic($index) 0
    }
}
```

Information about traces on a variable is returned with the `vinfo` option:

```
trace vinfo dynamic
=> {r FixupDynamic}
```

A trace is deleted with the `vdelete` option, which has the same form as the `variable` option. The trace in the previous example can be removed with the following command:

```
trace vdelete dynamic r FixupDynamic
```

Interactive Command History

The Tcl shell programs keep a log of the commands that you type by using a history facility. The log is controlled and accessed via the `history` command. The history facility uses the term *event* to mean an entry in its history log. The events are just commands, and they have an event ID that is their index in the log. You can also specify an event with a negative index that counts backwards from the end of the log. Event -1 is the previous event. Table 8–2 summarizes the Tcl `history` command. In the table, *`event`* defaults to -1.

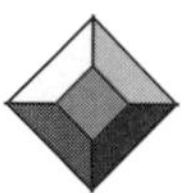

In practice you will want to take advantage of the ability to abbreviate the history options and even the name of the `history` command itself. For the command you need to type a unique prefix, and this depends on what other commands are already defined. For the options, there are unique one-letter abbreviations for all of them. For example, you could reuse the last word of the previous command with `[hist w $]`. This works because a `$` that is not followed by alphanumerics (or an open brace) is treated as a literal `$`.

Several of the history operations update the history list. They remove the actual `history` command and replace it with the command that resulted from the history operation. The `event`, `redo`, `substitute`, and `words` operations all behave in this manner. This makes perfect sense because you would rather have the actual command in the history, instead of the history command used to retrieve the command.

Table 8–2 The `history` command.

`history`	Short for `history info` with no *`count`*.
`history add command ?exec?`	Add the command to the history list. If `exec` is specified, then execute the command.
`history change` *`new`* `?`*`event`*`?`	Change the command specified by *`event`* to *`new`* in the command history.
`history event ?`*`event`*`?`	Returns the command specified by *`event`*.
`history info ?`*`count`*`?`	Returns a formatted history list of the last *`count`* commands, or of all commands.
`history keep` *`count`*	Limit the history to the last *`count`* commands.
`history nextid`	Returns the number of the next event.
`history redo ?`*`event`*`?`	Repeat the specified command.
`history substitute` *`old new`* `?`*`event`*`?`	Globally replace *`old`* with *`new`* in the command specified by *`event`*, then execute the result.
`history words` *`selector`* `?`*`event`*`?`	Return list elements from the event according to *`selector`*. List items count from zero. `$` is the last item. A range is specified as *a-b*, e.g., *1-$*.

History Syntax

Some extra syntax is supported when running interactively to make the history facility more convenient to use. Table 8–3 shows the special history syntax supported by *tclsh* and *wish*.

Table 8–3 Special `history` syntax.

`!!`	Repeat the previous command.
`!`*`n`*	Repeat command number *`n`*. If *`n`* is negative it counts backward from the current command. The previous command is event -1.
`!`*`prefix`*	Repeat the last command that begins with *`prefix`*.
`!`*`pattern`*	Repeat the last command that matches *`pattern`*.
`^`*`old`*`^`*`new`*	Globally replace *`old`* with *`new`* in the last command.

The next example shows how some of the history operations work:

Example 8–5 Interactive `history` usage.

```
% set a 5
5
% set a [expr $a+7]
12
% history
```

```
     1 set a 5
     2 set a [expr $a+7]
     3 history
% !2
19
% !!
26
% ^7^13
39
% !h
     1 set a 5
     2 set a [expr $a+7]
     3 history
     4 set a [expr $a+7]
     5 set a [expr $a+7]
     6 set a [expr $a+13]
     7 history
```

A Comparison to /bin/csh History Syntax

The history syntax shown in the previous example is simpler than the history syntax provided by the C-shell. Not all of the history operations are supported with special syntax. The substitutions (using `^old^new`) are performed globally on the previous command. This is different than the quick-history of the C-shell. Instead, it is like the `!:gs/old/new/` history command. So, for example, if the example had included `^a^b` in an attempt to set `b` to `39`, an error would have occurred because the command would have used `b` before it was defined:

```
set b [expr $b+7]
```

If you want to improve the history syntax, you will need to modify the `unknown` command, which is where it is implemented. This command is discussed in more detail in Chapter 9. Here is the code from the `unknown` command that implements the extra history syntax. The main limitation in comparison with the C-shell history syntax is that the `!` substitutions are only performed when `!` is at the beginning of the command:

Example 8–6 Implementing special history syntax.

```
# Excerpts from the standard unknown command
# uplevel is used to run the command in the right context
if {$name == "!!"} {
   return [uplevel {history redo}]
}
if [regexp {^!(.+)$} $name dummy event] {
   return [uplevel [list history redo $event]]
}
if [regexp {^\^([^^]*)\^([^^]*)\^?$} $name dummy old new] {
   return [uplevel [list history substitute $old $new]]
}
```

Debugging

The rapid turn around with Tcl coding means that it is often sufficient to add a few `puts` statements to your script to gain some insight about its behavior. This solution doesn't scale too well, however. A slight improvement is to add a `Debug` procedure that can have its output controlled better. You can log the information to a file, or turn it off completely. In a Tk application, it is simple to create a text widget to hold the contents of the log so you can view it from the application. Here is a simple `Debug` procedure. To enable it you need to set the `debug(enable)` variable. To have its output go to your terminal, set `debug(file)` to `stderr`.

Example 8–7 A Debug procedure.

```
proc Debug { string } {
    global debug
    if ![info exists debug(enabled)] {
        # Default is to do nothing
        return
    }
    puts $debug(file) $string
}
proc DebugOn {{file {}}} {
    global debug
    set debug(enabled) 1
    if {[string length $file] == 0} {
        set debug(file) stderr
    } else {
        if [catch {open $file w} fileID] {
            puts stderr "Cannot open $file: $fileID"
            set debug(file) stderr
        } else {
            puts stderr "Debug info to $file"
            set debug(file) $fileID
        }
    }
}
proc DebugOff {} {
    global debug
    if [info exists debug(enabled)] {
        unset debug(enabled)
        flush $debug(file)
        if {$debug(file) != "stderr" &&
             $debug(file) != "stdout"} {
            close $debug(file)
            unset $debug(file)
        }
    }
}
```

Don Libes' Debugger

Don Libes at the National Institute of Standards and Technology has built a Tcl debugger that lets you set breakpoints and step through your scripts interactively. He is also the author of the *expect* program that is described in Chapter 32. The debugger requires a modified Tcl shell because the debugger needs a few more built-in commands to support it. This section assumes you have it built into your shell already. The *expect* program includes the debugger, and creating a custom shell that includes the debugger is described in Chapter 32 on page 394.

The most interesting feature of the debugger is that you set breakpoints by specifying patterns that match commands. The reason for this is that Tcl doesn't keep around enough information to map from file line numbers to Tcl commands in scripts. The pattern matching is a clever alternative, and it opens up lots of possibilities.

The debugger defines several one-character command names. The commands are only defined when the debugger is active, and you should not have one-letter commands of your own so there should not be conflicts :-) The way you enter the debugger in the first place is left up to the application. The *expect* shell enters the debugger when you generate a keyboard interrupt. Example 32–2 on page 395 shows how to set this up. Table 8–4 summarizes the commands.

Table 8–4 Debugger commands.

`s ?`*`n`*`?`	Step.Goes into procedures. Step once, or *n* times.
`n ?`*`n`*`?`	Step. Skips over procedures. Step once, or *n* times.
`r`	Return from a procedure.
`b`	Set, clear or show a breakpoint.
`c`	Continue execution to next breakpoint or interrupt.
`w ?-w `*`width`*`? ?-c `*`X`*`?`	Show the call stack, limiting each line to *width* characters. `-c` 1 displays control characters as escape sequences. -c 0 displays control characters normally.
`u ?`*`level`*`?`	Move scope up the call stack one level, or to level *level*.
`d ?`*`level`*`?`	Move scope down the call stack one level, or to level *level*.
`h`	Display help information.

When you are at the debugger prompt, you are talking to your Tcl interpreter so you can issue any Tcl command. There is no need to define new commands to look at variables. Just use `set`!

The `s` and `n` command step through your script. They take an optional parameter that indicates how many steps to take before stopping again. The `r` command completes execution of the current procedure and stops right after the procedure returns.

The w command prints the call stack. Each level is proceeded by its number, with level 0 being the top of the stack. An asterisk is printed by the current scope, which you can change as described next. Each line of the stack trace can get quite long because of argument substitutions. Control the output width with the -w argument.

The u and d commands change the current scope. They move up and down the Tcl call stack, where "up" means towards the calling procedures. The very top of the stack is the global scope. You need to use these commands to easily examine variables in different scopes. They take an optional parameter that specifies what level to go to. If the level specifier begins with #, then it is an absolute level number and the current scope changes to that level. Otherwise the scope moves up or down the specified number of levels.

Breakpoints by Pattern Matching

The b command manipulates breakpoints. The location of a breakpoint is specified by a pattern. When a command that matches the pattern is executed, the breakpoint occurs. Eventually it will be possible to specify breakpoints by line number, but the Tcl interpreter doesn't keep around enough information to make that easy to do. The general form of the command to set a breakpoint is shown below:

```
b ?-re regexp? ?if condition? ?then action?
b ?-glob pattern? ?if condition? ?then action?
```

The b command supports both glob patterns and regular expressions. Patterns will be discussed later in more detail. A breakpoint can have a test associated with it. The breakpoint will only occur if the condition is met. A breakpoint can have an action, independent of a condition. The action provides a way to patch code into your script. Finally, the pattern itself is also optional, so you can have a breakpoint that is just a conditional. A breakpoint that just has an action will trigger on every command.

Here are several examples:

```
b -re ^foobar
```

This breaks whenever the foobar command is invoked. The ^ in the regular expression ensures that foobar is the first word in the command. In contrast, the next breakpoint occurs whenever foobar is about to be called from within another command. A glob pattern is used for comparison. A glob pattern has to match the whole command string, hence the asterisk at the beginning and end of the pattern:

```
b -glob {*\[foobar *}
```

The subpattern matching of the regular expression facility is supported. If you have subpatterns, the parts of the string that match are stored in the dbg(1) through dbg(9) array elements. The string that matched the whole pattern is stored in dbg(0). The following breakpoint stops when the crunch command is about to be called with its first argument greater than 1024:

```
b -re {^crunch ([0-9]+)} if {$dbg(1) > 1024}
```

If you just want to print information and keep going, you can put a `c`, `s`, `n`, or `r` command into the action associated with a breakpoint. The following breakpoint traces assignments to a variable:

```
b -re {^set a ([^ ]+)} then {
     puts "a changing from $a to $dbg(1)"
     c
}
```

The breakpoint is called before the command executes, so in this case `$a` refers to the old value, and the pattern extracts the new value. If an error occurs inside the action the error is discarded and the rest of the action is skipped.

Deleting Break Points

The b command with no arguments lists the defined breakpoints. Each breakpoint is proceeded by an ID number. To delete a breakpoint, give the breakpoint number proceeded by a minus sign:

```
b -N
```

Debugging Tk Scripts

You can use the techniques outlined so far to debug Tk scripts. There are some additional techniques, too. Instead of logging error messages to a file, you can log them to a text widget and view them from within your application. You can also use the ability to send Tcl commands between Tk applications to look at the state of your application.

The tkinspect Program

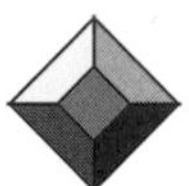

The *tkinspect* program is a Tk application that lets you look at the state of other Tk applications. It displays procedures, variables, and the Tk widget hierarchy. With *tkinspect* you can issue commands to another application in order to change variables or test out commands. This turns out to be a very useful way to debug Tk applications. It was written by Sam Shen and is available in the Tcl archives. The current FTP address for this is:

```
ftp.aud.alcatel.com:/pub/tcl/code/tkinspect-4d.tar.gz
```

The tkerror Command

When the Tk widgets encounter an error from a callback, such as the command associated with a button, they signal the error by calling the `tkerror` procedure. A default implementation displays a dialog and gives you an opportunity to view the Tcl call stack at the point of the error. You can supply your own version of `tkerror`. For example, when my *exmh* mail application gets an error it offers to send mail to me with a few words of explanation from the user and a copy of the stack trace. I get interesting bug reports from all over the world!

The tkerror command is called with one argument that is the error message. The global variable errorInfo contains the stack trace information. There is an example tkerror implementation in the on-line sources associated with this book.

Performance Tuning

The time command measures the execution time of a Tcl command. It takes an optional parameter that is a repetition count.

```
time {set a "Hello, World!"} 1000
=> 305 microseconds per iteration
```

This provides a very simple timing mechanism. A more advanced profile command is part of the Extended Tcl package, which is described on page 387. The profile command monitors the number of calls, the CPU time, and the elapsed time spent in different procedures.

Perhaps the most common performance bug in a Tcl program is the use of big lists instead of arrays. Extracting items from a list is expensive because the list must be reparsed to find each element. With a Tcl array you can access any element in constant time.

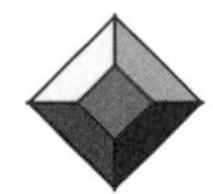

In general, iterating through large data structures is slow because Tcl parses loop bodies and procedure bodies each time it evaluates them. If you want to squeeze the last millisecond out of some Tcl code you can try some hand optimizations:

- Shorten the names of variables and commands used in the inner loops. You can use the rename command to create short names for the commands used within a tight loop.
- Move large comment blocks outside of inner loops and procedure bodies. Comments are not discarded; they are read each time a procedure or loop body is evaluated.

For reasons of good programming style you should not resort to these techniques except in extreme cases. Highly iterative code is best optimized by moving it into C code. The ideal performance solution is a compiler for Tcl. A compiler is expected, but probably not until 1996.

CHAPTER 9

Script Libraries

You can use a script library to share a collection of useful Tcl procedures among applications. The library is implemented by the `unknown` command, which also provides a few other facilities. One of its features is the automatic execution of UNIX programs during interactive use.

*L*ibraries group useful sets of Tcl procedures so they can be used by multiple applications. For example, you could use any of the code examples that come with this book by creating a script library, and then directing your application to check in that library for missing procedures. One way to structure a large application is to have a short main script and a library of support scripts. The advantage of this approach is that not all the Tcl code needs to be loaded to get the application started. Then, as new features are accessed the code that implements them can be loaded.

If you are writing Tcl code that is designed to be used in a library, you need to pay attention to some coding conventions. Because there is no formal module system in Tcl, coding conventions have to be followed to avoid conflicts between procedures and global variables used in different packages. This chapter explains a simple coding convention for large Tcl programs.

The unknown Command

The Tcl library facility is made possible by the `unknown` command. Whenever the Tcl interpreter encounters a command that it does not know about, it calls the `unknown` command with the name of the missing command. The `unknown` command is implemented in Tcl, so you are free to provide your own mechanism to handle unknown commands. This chapter describes the behavior of the default implementation of `unknown`, which can be found in the `init.tcl` file in the Tcl library. The location of the library is returned by the `info library` command. In order to bootstrap the library facility, the Tcl shells (*tclsh* and *wish*) invoke the following Tcl command:

```
source [info library]/init.tcl
```

The tclIndex File

The `unknown` command uses an index to make the search for missing commands fast. When you create a script library, you must generate the index that records what procedures are defined in the library. The `auto_mkindex` procedure creates the index, which is stored in a file named `tclIndex` that is kept in the same directory as the files that make up the script library.

Suppose all the examples from this book are in the directory `/usr/local/tcl/welchbook`. You can make the examples into a script library just by creating the `tclIndex` file:

```
auto_mkindex /usr/local/tcl/welchbook *.tcl
```

You will need to update the `tclIndex` file if you add procedures or change any of their names. A conservative approach to this is shown in the next example. It is conservative because it recreates the index if anything in the library has changed since the `tclIndex` file was last generated, whether or not the change added or removed a Tcl procedure.

Example 9–1 Maintaining a `tclIndex` file.

```
proc Library_UpdateIndex { libdir } {
	if ![file exists $libdir/tclIndex] {
		set doit 1
	} else {
		set age [file mtime $libdir/tclIndex]
		set doit 0
		# Changes to directory may mean files were deleted
		if {[file mtime $libdir] > $age} {
			set doit 1
		} else {
			# Check each file for modification
			foreach file [glob $libdir/*.tcl] {
				if {[file mtime $file] > $age} {
					set doit 1
					break
				}
			}
		}
	}
	if { $doit } {
		auto_mkindex $libdir *.tcl
	}
}
```

Using a Library: auto_path

To use a script library you must inform the unknown command where to look. It uses the auto_path variable to record a list of directories to search for unknown commands. To continue our example, you can make the procedures in the book examples available by putting this command at the beginning of your scripts:

```
lappend auto_path /usr/local/tcl/welchbook
```

This has no effect if you have not created the tclIndex file. If you wanted to be extra careful you can call Library_UpdateIndex. This will update the index if you add new things to the library.

```
lappend auto_path /usr/local/tcl/welchbook
Library_UpdateIndex /usr/local/tcl/welchbook
```

This will not work if there is no tclIndex file at all because the unknown procedure won't be able to find the implementation of Library_UpdateIndex. Once the tclIndex has been created for the first time, then this will ensure that any new procedures added to the library will be installed into tclIndex. In practice, if you want this sort of automatic update it is wise to include something like the Library_UpdateIndex file directly into your application as opposed to loading it from the library it is supposed to be maintaining.

Disabling the Library Facility: auto_noload

If you do not want the unknown procedure to try and load procedures, you can set the auto_noload variable to disable the mechanism:

```
set auto_noload anything
```

How Auto Loading Works

If you look at the contents of a tclIndex file, you will see that it defines an array named auto_index. One element of the array is defined for each procedure in the script library. The value of the array element is a command that defines the procedure. A line in the tclIndex file looks something like this:

```
set auto_index(Bind_Interface) "source $dir/bind_ui.tcl"
```

When the tclIndex file is read, the $dir gets substituted with the name of the directory that contains the tclIndex file, so the result is a source command that loads the file containing the Tcl procedure. The substitution is done with eval, so you could build a tclIndex file that contained any commands at all and count on $dir being defined properly. The next example is a simplified version of the code that reads the tclIndex file.

Example 9–2 Loading a `tclIndex` file.

```
# This is a simplified part of the auto_load command.
# Go through auto_path from back to front.
set i [expr [llength $auto_path]-1]
for {} {$i >= 0} {incr i -1} {
    set dir [lindex $auto_path $i]
    if [catch {open $dir/tclIndex} f] {
        # No index
        continue
    }
    # eval the file as a script. Because eval is
    # used instead of source, an extra round of
    # substitutions is performed and $dir get expanded
    # The real code checks for errors here.
    eval [read $f]
    close $f
}
```

Dynamic Linking C Code

The behavior of the `auto_load` facility is exploited by schemes that dynamically link object code in order to define commands that are implemented in C. Instead of sourcing a Tcl script that defines procedures, a compiled object file is dynamically linked into the Tcl shell. The Tcl `load` command initiates the linking. This is not yet a standard command because the details of dynamic linking vary considerably from system to system. One version of `load` that I have used with success on SunOS is part of the *tcl-shells* extension package. You can find it in the Tcl archive, which is discussed in Chapter 32.

Interactive Conveniences

The `unknown` command provides a few other conveniences. These are only used when you are typing commands directly. They are disabled once execution enters a procedure or if the Tcl shell is not being used interactively. The convenience features are automatic execution of programs, command history, and command abbreviation. These options are tried, in order, if a command implementation cannot be loaded from a script library.

Auto Execute

The `unknown` procedure implements a second feature: automatic execution of external programs. This makes a Tcl shell behave more like other UNIX shells that are used to execute programs. The search for external programs is done using the standard `PATH` environment variable that is used by other shells to find programs. If you want to disable the feature all together, set the `auto_noexec` variable:

```
set auto_noexec anything
```

History

The history facility described in Chapter 8 is implemented by the `unknown` procedure.

Abbreviations

If you type a unique prefix of a command, `unknown` recognizes it and executes the matching command for you. This is done after automatic program execution is attempted and history substitutions are performed.

Tcl Shell Library Environment

It may help to understand how the Tcl shells initialize their library environment. The first toehold on the environment is made when the shells are compiled. At that point the default pathname of the library directory is defined. For Tcl, this pathname is returned by the `info` command:

```
info library
```

One of the first things that a Tcl shell does is this:

```
source [info library]/init.tcl
```

The primary thing defined by `init.tcl` is the implementation of the `unknown` procedure. The Tk library pathname is defined by the `tk_library` variable. For Tk, *wish* also does this:

```
source $tk_library/tk.tcl
```

This initializes the scripts that support the Tk widgets. There are still more scripts, and they are organized as a library. So, the tk.tcl script sets up the auto_path variable so the Tk script library is accessible. It does this:

```
lappend auto_path $tk_library
```

To summarize, the bootstrap works as follows:

- The Tcl C library defines the pathname returned by the `info library` command, and this default can be overridden with the `TCL_LIBRARY` environment variable.
- The Tcl interpreter sources `[info library]/init.tcl` to define the `unknown` command that implements the bulk of the library facility.
- The Tk C library defines a pathname and stores it into `tk_library`, a Tcl variable. The default can be overridden with the `TK_LIBRARY` environment variable.
- The Tk interpreter sources `init.tcl` as above, and `$tk_library/tk.tcl`.
- The Tk initialization script appends `$tk_library` to `auto_path`.

Normally these details are taken care of by the proper installation of the Tcl and Tk software, but I find it helps to understand things when you see all the steps in the initialization process. If you have only a binary distribution of Tcl and Tk (e.g., a Linux shared library) you may need to adjust TCL_LIBRARY and TK_LIBRARY to reflect the location of the libraries on your system.

Coding Style

If you supply a library , you need to follow some simple coding conventions to make your library easier to use by other programmers. The main problem is that there is no formal module system in Tcl, so you must follow some conventions to avoid name conflicts with other library packages and the main application.

A Module Prefix for Procedure Names

The first convention is to choose an identifying prefix for the procedures in your package. For example, the preferences package in Chapter 28 uses `Pref` as its prefix. All the procedures provided by the library begin with `Pref`. This convention is extended to distinguish between private and exported procedures. An exported procedure has an underscore after its prefix, and it is acceptable to call this procedure from the main application or other library packages. Examples include `Pref_Add`, `Pref_Init`, and `Pref_Dialog`. A private procedure is meant for use only by the other procedures in the same package. Its name does not have the underscore. Examples include `PrefDialogItem` and `PrefXres`.

A Global Array for State Variables

You should use the same prefix on the global variables used by your package. You can alter the capitalization, just keep the same prefix. I capitalize procedure names and use lowercase for variables. By sticking with the same prefix you identify what variables belong to the package and you avoid conflict with other packages.

In general I try to use a single global array for a package. The array provides a convenient place to collect a set of related variables, much like a struct is used in C. For example, the preferences package uses the `pref` array to hold all its state information. It is also a good idea to keep the use of the array private. It is better coding practice to provide exported procedures than to let other modules access your data structures directly. This makes it easier to change the implementation of your package without affecting its clients.

If you do need to export a few key variables from your module, use the underscore convention to distinguish exported variables too. If you need more than one global variable, just stick with the prefix convention to avoid conflicts.

If you are disappointed by the lack of real modules in Tcl, then you should consider one of the object system extensions for Tcl. The [incr Tcl] package described in Chapter 32 provides classes that have their own scope for member functions and instance variables.

CHAPTER 10

Tk Fundamentals

This chapter introduces the basic concepts used in the Tk toolkit for the X window system. Tk adds about 35 Tcl commands that let you create and manipulate widgets in a graphical user interface.

Tk is a toolkit for window programming. It was designed for the X window system, although ports to the Macintosh and Windows environments are already underway. (Tcl has already been ported.) Tk shares many concepts with other windowing toolkits, but you do not need to know much about graphical user interfaces to get started with Tk.

Tk provides a set of Tcl commands that create and manipulate *widgets*. A widget is a window in a graphical user interface that has a particular appearance and behavior. The terms *widget* and *window* are often used interchangeably. Widget types include buttons, scrollbars, menus, and text windows. Tk also has a general purpose drawing widget called a canvas that lets you create lighter-weight items such as lines, boxes and bitmaps. The Tcl commands added by the Tk extension are summarized at the end of this chapter.

The X window system supports a hierarchy of windows, and this is also reflected by the Tk commands. To an application, the window hierarchy means that there is a primary window, and inside that window there can be a number of children windows. The children windows can contain more windows, and so on. Just as a hierarchical file system has directories that are containers for files and directories, a hierarchical window system uses windows as containers for other windows. The hierarchy affects the naming scheme used for Tk widgets as described later, and it is used to help arrange widgets on the screen.

Widgets are under the control of a *geometry manager* that controls their size and location on the screen. Until a geometry manager learns about a widget, it will not be mapped onto the screen and you will not see it. There are a few different geometry managers you can use in Tk, although this book primarily uses the *packer*. The main trick with any geometry manager is that you use *frame* widgets as containers for other widgets. One or more widgets are created and then arranged in a frame by a geometry manager. The packer is discussed in detail in Chapter 12.

A Tk-based application has an event-driven control flow, like most window system toolkits. An event is handled by associating a Tcl command to that event using the `bind` command. There are a large number of different events defined by the X protocol, including mouse and keyboard events. Tk widgets have default bindings so you do not need to program every detail yourself. Bindings are discussed in detail in Chapter 13. You can also arrange for events to occur after a specified period of time with the `after` command. The event loop is implemented by the `wish` shell, or you can provide the event loop in your own C program as described in Chapter 29.

Event bindings are grouped into global bindings, class bindings, and instance bindings. An example of a class is `Button`, which is all the button widgets. The Tk toolkit provides the default behavior for buttons as bindings on the `Button` class. You can supplement these bindings for an individual button, and define global bindings that apply to all widget classes. You can even introduce new binding groups to collect sets of bindings together. The `bindtags` command controls binding groups and their precedence.

A concept related to binding is *focus*. At any given time, one of the widgets has the input focus, and keyboard events are directed to it. There are two general approaches to focusing: give focus to the widget under the mouse, or explicitly set the focus to a particular widget. Tk provides commands to change focus so you can implement either style of focus management. To support modal dialog boxes, you can forcibly *grab* the focus away from other widgets. Chapter 18 describes focus, grabs, and dialogs.

The basic structure of a Tk script begins by creating widgets and arranging them with a geometry manager, and then binding actions to the widgets. After the interpreter processes the commands that initialize the user interface, the event loop is entered and your application begins running.

If you use *wish* interactively, it creates and displays an empty main window and gives you a command line prompt. With this interface, your keyboard commands are handled by the event loop, so you can build your Tk interface gradually. As we will see, you will be able to change virtually all aspects of your application interactively.

Hello World In Tk

Our first Tk script is very simple. It creates a button that prints "Hello, World!" to standard output when you press it. Above the button widget is a title bar that is provided by the window manager, which in this case is *twm*. There are two commands in the script: one to create the button, and one to make it visible on the display:

Example 10–1 "Hello, World!" Tk program.

```
#!/usr/local/bin/wish
button .hello -text Hello \
    -command {puts stdout "Hello, World!"}
pack .hello -padx 20 -pady 10
```

The first line identifies the interpreter for the script:

```
#!/usr/local/bin/wish
```

This special line is necessary if the script is in a file that will be used like other UNIX command files. An additional `-f` flag is required in versions of Tk before 4.0:

```
#!/usr/local/bin/wish -f
```

The pathname might be different on your system. Remember, on many UNIX systems the whole first line is limited to 32 characters, including the `#!` and the `-f`.

The `button` command creates an instance of a button:

```
button .hello -text Hello \
     -command {puts stdout "Hello, World!"}
=> .hello
```

The name of the button is `.hello`. The label on the button is `Hello`, and the command associated with the button is:

```
puts stdout "Hello, World!"
```

The `pack` command maps the button onto the screen. Some padding parameters are supplied so there is space around the button:

```
pack .hello -padx 20 -pady 10
```

If you type these two commands into `wish`, you will not see anything happen when the `button` command is given. After the `pack` command, though, you will see the empty main window shrink to be just big enough to contain the button and its padding. The behavior of the packer will be discussed further in Chapters 11 and 12.

Tk uses an object-based system for creating and naming widgets. Associated with each class of widget (e.g., `Button`) is a command that creates instances of that class of widget. As the widget is created, a new Tcl command is defined that operates on that instance of the widget. Example 10–1 creates a button named `.hello`, and we can operate on the button using its name as a command. For example, we can cause the button to highlight a few times:

```
.hello flash
```

Or, we can run the command associated with the button:

```
.hello invoke
=> Hello, World!
```

Naming Tk Widgets

The period in the name of the button instance, `.hello`, is required. Tk uses a naming system for the widgets that reflects their position in a hierarchy of widgets. The root of the hierarchy is the main window of the application, and its name is simply a dot (i.e., .). This is similar to the naming convention for directories in UNIX where the root directory is named /, and then / is used to separate components of a file name. Tk uses a dot in the same way. Each widget that is a child of the main window is named something like `.foo`. A child widget of `.foo` would be `.foo.bar`, and so on. Just as file systems have directories that are containers for files (and other directories), the Tk window hierarchy uses frame widgets that are containers for widgets (and other frames).

Each component of a Tk pathname must start with a lowercase letter or a number. Obviously, a component cannot include a period, either. Upper case reserved for class identifiers used in resource specifications. A resource name can include Tk pathname components and Tk widget classes, and case is used to distinguish them. Chapter 15 describes resources in detail.

There is one drawback to the Tk widget naming system. If your interface changes enough it can result in some widgets changing their position in the widget hierarchy. In that case they may need to change their name. You can insulate yourself from this programming nuisance by using variables to hold the names of important widgets. Use a variable reference instead of widget pathnames in case you need to change things, or if you want to reuse your code in a different interface.

Configuring Tk Widgets

Example 10–1 illustrates a style of named parameter passing that is prevalent in the Tk commands. Pairs of arguments specify the attributes of a widget. The attribute names begin with `-`, such as `-text`, and the next argument is the value of that attribute. Even the simplest Tk widget can have a dozen or more attributes that can be specified this way, and complex widgets can have 20 or more attributes. However, the beauty of Tk is that you only need to specify the attributes for which the default value is not good enough. This is illustrated by the simplicity of this `Hello, World` example.

Finally, each widget instance supports a `configure` (often abbreviated to `config`) operation that can query and change these attributes. The syntax for `config` uses the same named argument pairs used when you create the widget. For example, we can change the background color of the button to red even after it has been created and mapped onto the screen:

```
.hello config -background red
```

You can use configure to query the current value of an attribute by leaving off the value. For example:

```
.hello config -background
=> -background background Background #ffe4c4 red
```

The returned information includes the command line switch, the resource name, the class name, the default value, and the current value, which is last. The class and resource name have to do with the X resource mechanism. In most cases you just need the current value, and you can use the `cget` operation for that.

```
.hello cget -background
=> red
```

Widget attributes can be redefined any time, even the text and command that were set when the button was created. The following command changes `.hello` into a goodbye button:

```
.hello config -text Goodbye! -command exit
```

Tk Widget Attributes and X Resources

A widget attribute can be named three different ways: by its command-line option, by its name, and by its class. The command-line option is the format you use in Tcl scripts. This form is always all lowercase and prefixed with a hyphen (e.g., `-offvalue`).

The name and class have to do with X resource specifications, which are described in detail in Chapter 15. The resource name for the attribute has no leading hyphen, and it has uppercase letters at internal word boundaries (e.g., `offValue`). The resource class begins with an uppercase letter and has uppercase letters at internal word boundaries. (e.g., `OffValue`). You need to know these naming conventions if you specify widget attributes via the X resource mechanism. In addition, *the tables in this book list widget attributes by their resource name*. The command line option can be derived from the resource name by mapping it to all lowercase.

The primary advantage to using resources to specify attributes is that you do not have to litter your code with attribute specifications. With just a few resource database entries you can specify attributes for all your widgets. In addition, if attributes are specified with resources, users can provide alternate resource specifications in order to override the values supplied by the application. For attributes like colors and fonts, this feature can be important to users.

The Tk Manual Pages

This book provides summaries for all the Tk commands, the widget attributes, and the default bindings. However, for the absolute truth, you may need to read the on-line manual pages that come with Tk. They provide a complete reference source for the Tk commands. You should be able to use the UNIX *man* program to read them:

```
% man button
```

There are a large number of attributes that are common across most of the Tk widgets. These are described in a separate man page under the name `options`. Each man page begins with a `STANDARD OPTIONS` section that lists which of these standard attributes apply, but you have to look at the `options` man page for the description. (The tables in this book always list all widget attributes.)

Summary Of The Tk Commands

The following two tables list the Tcl commands added by Tk. Table 10–1 lists commands that create widgets. There are 15 different widgets in Tk, although 4 of them are variations on a button, and 5 are devoted to different flavors of text display. Table 10–2 lists commands that manipulate widgets and provide associated functions like input focus, event binding, and geometry management. The page number in the table is the primary reference for the command, and there are other references in the index.

Table 10–1 Tk widget-creation commands.

Command	Pg.	Description
`button`	145	Create a command button.
`checkbutton`	149	Create a toggle button that is linked to a Tcl variable.
`radiobutton`	149	Create one of a set of radio buttons that are linked to one variable.
`menubutton`	153	Create a button that posts a menu.
`menu`	153	Create a menu.
`canvas`	236	Create a canvas, which supports lines, boxes, bitmaps, images, arcs, text, polygons, and embedded widgets.
`label`	173	Create a read-only, one-line text label.
`entry`	188	Create a one-line text entry widget.
`message`	175	Create a read-only, multi-line text message.
`listbox`	191	Create a line-oriented, scrolling text widget.
`text`	219	Create a general purpose text widget.
`scrollbar`	180	Create a scrollbar that can be linked to another widget.
`scale`	177	Create a scale widget that adjusts the value of a variable.
`frame`	171	Create a container widget used with geometry managers.
`toplevel`	171	Create a frame that is a new top level X window.

Table 10–2 Tk widget-manipulation commands.

Command	Pg.	Description
after	267	Execute a command after a period of time elapses.
bell	184	Ring the X bell device.
bind	133	Bind a Tcl command to an X event.
bindtags	134	Create binding classes and control binding inheritance.
clipboard	263	Manipulate the X clipboard.
destroy	208	Delete a widget.
fileevent	268	Associate Tcl commands with file descriptors.
focus	203	Control the input focus.
grab	205	Steal the input focus from other widgets.
image	289	Create and manipulate images.
lower	131	Lower a window in the stacking order.
option	165	Access the Xresources database.
pack	128	Pack a widget in the display with constraints.
place	129	Place a widget in the display with positions.
raise	131	Raise a window in the stacking order.
selection	262	Manipulate the X PRIMARY selection.
send	269	Send a Tcl command to another Tk application.
tk	319	Query internal Tk state (e.g., the color model).
tkerror	86	Handler for background errors.
tkwait	206	Wait for an event.
update	208	Update the display by going through the event loop.
winfo	314	Query window state.
wm	309	Interact with the window manager.

CHAPTER 11

Tk by Example

This chapter introduces Tk through a series of short examples.

Tk provides a quick and fun way to generate user interfaces. In this chapter we will go through a series of short example programs to give you a feel for what you can do. Some details are glossed over in this chapter and considered in more detail later. In particular, the packing geometry manager is covered in Chapter 12 and event bindings are discussed in Chapter 13. The Tk widgets are discussed in more detail in later chapters.

ExecLog

Our first example provides a simple user interface to running a `UNIX` program. The interface consists of two buttons, `Run it` and `Quit`, an entry widget in which to enter a command, and a text widget in which to log the results of running the program. The script runs the program in a pipeline and uses the `fileevent` command to wait for output. This structure lets the user interface remain responsive while the program executes. You could use this to run *make*, for example, and it would save the results in the log. The complete example is given first, and then its commands are discussed in more detail.

Example 11–1 Logging the output of a UNIX program.

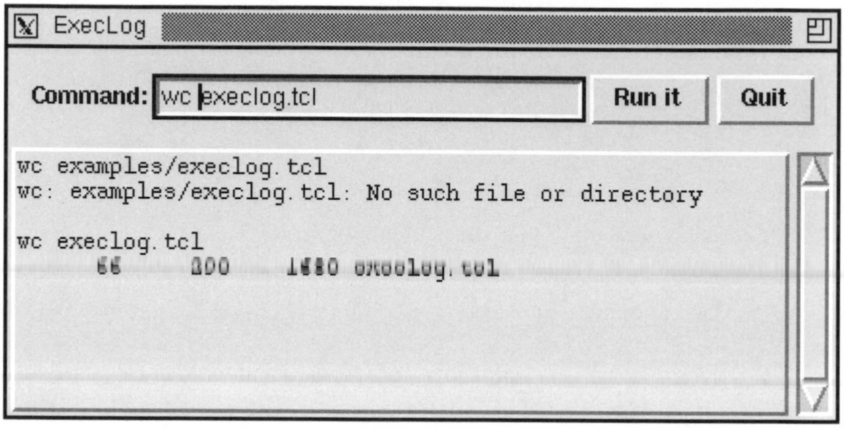

```
#!/usr/local/bin/wish -f
# execlog - run a UNIX program and log the output
# Set window title
wm title . ExecLog

# Create a frame for buttons and entry.
frame .top -borderwidth 10
pack .top -side top -fill x

# Create the command buttons.
button .top.quit -text Quit -command exit
set but [button .top.run -text "Run it" -command Run]
pack .top.quit .top.run -side right

# Create a labeled entry for the command
label .top.l -text Command: -padx 0
rntry .top.cmd -width 20 -relief sunken \
    -textvariable command
pack .top.l -side left
pack .top.cmd -side left -fill x -expand true

# Set up key binding equivalents to the buttons
bind .top.cmd <Return> Run
bind .top.cmd <Control-c> Stop
focus .top.cmd

# Create a text widget to log the output
frame .t
set log [text .t.log -width 80 -height 10 \
    -borderwidth 2 -relief raised -setgrid true \
    -yscrollcommand {.t.scroll set}]
scrollbar .t.scroll -command {.t.log yview}
pack .t.scroll -side right -fill y
pack .t.log -side left -fill both -expand true
pack .t -side top -fill both -expand true
```

```
# Run the program and arrange to read its input
proc Run {} {
    global command input log but
    if [catch {open "|$command |& cat"} input] {
        $log insert end $input\n
    } else {
        fileevent $input readable Log
        $log insert end $command\n
        $but config -text Stop -command Stop
    }
}
# Read and log output from the program
proc Log {} {
    global input log
    if [eeof $input] {
        Stop
    } else {
        gets $input line
        $log insert end $line\n
        $log see end
    }
}
# Stop the program and fix up the button
proc Stop {} {
    global input but
    catch {close $input}
    $but config -text "Run it" -command Run
}
```

Window Title

The first command sets the title that appears in the title bar implemented by the window manager. Recall that dot (i.e., `.`) is the name of the main window:

```
wm title . ExecLog
```

The `wm` command communicates with the window manager. The window manager is the program that lets you open, close, and resize windows. It implements the title bar for the window and probably some small buttons to close or resize the window. Different window managers have a distinctive look; the figure shows a *twm* title bar.

A Frame for Buttons

A frame is created to hold the widgets that appear along the top of the interface. The frame has a border to provide some space around the widgets:

```
frame .top -borderwidth 10
```

The frame is positioned in the main window. The default packing side is the top, so `-side top` is redundant here, but it is used for clarity. The `-fill x` packing option makes the frame fill out to the whole width of the main window:

```
pack .top -side top -fill x
```

Command Buttons

Two buttons are created: one to run the command, the other to quit the program. Their names, `.top.quit` and `.top.run`, imply that they are children of the `.top` frame. This affects the `pack` command, which positions widgets inside their parent by default:

```
button .top.quit -text Quit -command exit
set but [button .top.run -text "Run it" \
    -command Run]
pack .top.quit .top.run -side right
```

A Label and an Entry

The label and entry are also created as children of the top frame. The label is created with no padding in the X direction so it can be positioned right next to the entry. The size of the entry is specified in terms of characters. The `relief` attribute gives the entry some looks to set it apart visually on the display. The contents of the entry widget are associated with the Tcl variable `command`:

```
label .top.l -text Command: -padx 0
entry .top.cmd -width 20 -relief sunken \
    -textvariable command
```

The label and entry are positioned to the left inside the `.top` frame. The additional packing parameters to the entry allow it to expand is packing space and fill up that extra area with its display. The difference between packing space and display space is discussed in Chapter 12 on page 119:

```
pack .top.l -side left
pack .top.cmd -side left -fill x -expand true
```

Key Bindings and Focus

Key bindings are set up for the entry widget that provide an additional way to invoke the functions of the application. The `bind` command associates a Tcl command with an X event in a particular widget. The `<Return>` event is generated when the user presses the `Return` key on the keyboard. The `<Control-c>` event is generated when the letter `c` is typed while the `Control` key is already held down. For the events to go to the entry widget, `.top.cmd`, input focus must be given to the widget. By default, an entry widget gets the focus when you click the left mouse button in it. The explicit `focus` command is helpful for users with the focus-follows-mouse model. As soon as the mouse is over the main window the user can type into the entry:

```
bind .top.cmd <Return> Run
bind .top.cmd <Control-c> Stop
focus .top.cmd
```

A Resizable Text and Scrollbar

A text widget is created and packed into a frame with a scrollbar. The scrollbar is a separate widget in Tk, and it can be connected to a few different widgets using the same setup as is used here. The text's `yscrollcommand` updates the display of the scrollbar when the text widget is modified, and the scrollbar's `command` scrolls the associated widget when the user manipulates the scrollbar.

The `setgrid` attribute of the text widget is turned on. This has two effects. The most important is that it allows interactive resizing of the main window. By default, a Tk window is not resizable interactively, although it can always be resized under program control. The other effect of gridding is to restrict the resize so that only a whole number of lines and average sized characters can be displayed:

```
frame .t
set log [text .t.log -width 80 -height 10 \
    -borderwidth 2 -relief raised -setgrid true\
    -yscrollcommand {.t.scroll set}]
scrollbar .t.scroll -command {.t.log yview}
pack .t.scroll -side right -fill y
pack .t.log -side left -fill both -expand true
pack .t -side top -fill both -expand true
```

A side effect of creating a Tk widget is the creation of a new Tcl command that operates on that widget. The name of the Tcl command is the same as the Tk pathname of the widget. In this script, the text widget command, `.t.log`, is needed in several places. However, it is a good idea to put the Tk pathname of an important widget into a variable because that pathname can change if you reorganize your user interface. The disadvantage of this is that you must declare the variable with `global` inside procedures. The variable `log` is used for this purpose in this example to demonstrate this style.

The Run Procedure

The `Run` procedure starts the UNIX program specified in the command `entry`. That value is available in the global `command` variable because of the `textvariable` attribute of the entry. The command is run in a pipeline so that it executes in the background. The `catch` command guards against bogus commands. The variable `input` is set to an error message, or to the normal `open` return that is a file descriptor. A trick is used so that the error output of the program is captured. The program is started like this:

```
if [catch {open "|$command |& cat"} input] {
```

The leading | indicates that a pipeline is being created. If you do not use *cat* like this, then the error output from the pipeline, if any, shows up as an error message when the pipeline is closed. In this example it turns out to be awkward to distinguish between errors generated from the program and errors generated

because of the way the `Stop` procedure is implemented. Furthermore, some programs interleave output and error output, and you might want to see the error output in order instead of all at the end.

If the pipeline is opened successfully, then a callback is setup using the `fileevent` command. Whenever the pipeline generates output then the script can read data from it. The `Log` procedure is registered to be called whenever the pipeline is readable.

```
fileevent $input readable Log
```

The `command` (or the error message) is inserted into the log. This is done using the name of the text widget, which is stored in the `log` variable, as a Tcl command. The value of the command is appended to the log, and a newline is added so its output will appear on the next line.

```
$log insert end $command\n
```

The text widget's `insert` function takes two parameters: a *mark* and a string to insert at that mark. The symbolic mark `end` represents the end of the contents of the text widget.

The run button is changed into a stop button after the program begins. This avoids a cluttered interface and demonstrates the dynamic nature of a Tk interface. Again, because this button is used in a few different places in the script, its pathname has been stored in the variable `but`:

```
$but config -text Stop -command Stop
```

The Log Procedure

The `Log` procedure is invoked whenever data can be read from the pipeline, and end-of-file has been reached. This condition is checked first, and the `Stop` procedure is called to clean things up. Otherwise, one line of data is read and inserted into the log. The text widget's `see` operation is used to position the view on the text so the new line is visible to the user:

```
if [eof $input] {
   Stop
} else {
   gets $input line
   $log insert end $line\n
   $log see end
}
```

The Stop Procedure

The `Stop` procedure terminates the program by closing the pipeline. This results in a signal, `SIGPIPE`, being delivered to the program the next time it does a write to its standard output. The `close` is wrapped up with a `catch`. This suppresses the errors that can occur when the pipeline is closed prematurely on the process. Finally, the button is restored to its run state so that the user can run another command:

```
catch {close $input}
$but config -text "Run it" -command Run
```

In most cases, closing the pipeline is adequate to kill the job. If you really need more sophisticated control over another process, you should check out the *expect* Tcl extension, which is described briefly in Chapter 32 on page 390.

The Example Browser

The next example is a browser for the code examples that appear in this book. The basic idea is to provide a menu that selects the examples, and a text window to display the examples. Because there are so many examples, a cascaded menu is set up to group the examples by the chapter in which they occur:

Example 11–2 A browser for the code examples in the book.

```
#!/usr/local/bin/wish
#   Browser for the Tcl and Tk examples in the book.
#   Version 0. This gets extended by Example 22-4

# The directory containing all the tcl files
set browse(dir) /tilde/welch/doc/tclbook/examples

# Set up the main display
wm minsize . 30 5
wm title . "Tcl Example Browser, v0"

frame .menubar
pack .menubar -fill x
button .menubar.quit -text Quit -command exit
pack .menubar.quit -side right

# A label identifies the current example
label .menubar.label -textvariable browse(current)
pack .menubar.label -side right -fill x -expand true

# Look through the .tcl files for the keywords
# that group the examples.
foreach f [glob $browse(dir)/*.tcl] {
	if [catch {open $f} in] {
		puts stderr "Cannot open $f: $in"
		continue
	}
	while {[gets $in line] >= 0} {
		if [regexp -nocase {^# ([^ ]+) chapter} $line \
				x keyword] {
			lappend examples($keyword) $f
			close $in
			break
		}
	}
}
```

```
# Create the menubutton and menu
menubutton .menubar.ex -text Examples -menu .menubar.ex.m
pack .menubar.ex -side left
set m [menu .menubar.ex.m]

# Create a cascaded menu for each group of examples
set i 0
foreach key [lsort [array names examples]] {
	$m add cascade -label $key -menu $m.sub$i
	set sub [menu $m.sub$i -tearoff 0]
	incr i
	foreach item [lsort $examples($key)] {
		$sub add command -label [file tail $item] \
			-command [list Browse $item]
	}
}

# Create the text to display the example
frame .body
text .body.t -setgrid true -width 80 -height 25 \
	-yscrollcommand {.body.s set}
scrollbar .body.s -command {.body.t yview} -orient vertical
pack .body.s -side left -fill y
pack .body.t -side right -fill both -expand true
pack .body -side top -fill both -expand true
set browse(text) .body.t

# Display a specified file. The label is updated to
# reflect what is displayed, and the text is left
# in a read-only mode after the example is inserted.
proc Browse { file } {
	global browse
	set browse(current) [file tail $file]
	set t $browse(text)
	$t config -state normal
	$t delete 1.0 end
	if [catch {open $file} in] {
		$t insert end $in
	} else {
		$t insert end [read $in]
		close $in
	}
	$t config -state disabled
}
```

More About Resizing Windows

This example uses the `wm minsize` command to put a constraint on the minimum size of the window. The arguments specify the minimum width and height. These values can be interpreted in two ways. By default they are pixel values. However, if an internal widget has enabled *geometry gridding*, then the dimensions are in grid units of that widget. In this case the text widget enables gridding with its setgrid attribute, so the minimum size of the window is set so that the text window is at least 30 characters wide by five lines high:

```
wm minsize . 30 5
```

The other important side effect of setting the minimum size is that it enables interactive resizing of the window. Interactive resizing is also enabled if gridding is turned on by an interior widget, or if the maximum size is constrained with the wm maxsize command.

Managing Global State

The example uses the browse array to collect its global variables. This makes it simpler to reference the state from inside procedures because only the array needs to be declared global. As the application grows over time and new features are added, that global command won't have to be adjusted. This style also serves to emphasize what variables are important.

The example uses the array to hold the name of the example directory (dir), the Tk pathname of the text display (text), and the name of the current file (current).

Searching Through Files

The browser searches the file system to determine what it can display. It uses glob to find all the Tcl files in the example directory. Each file is read one line at a time with gets, and then regexp is used to scan for keywords. The loop is repeated here for reference:

```
foreach f [glob $browse(dir)/*.tcl] {
    if [catch {open $f} in] {
        puts stderr "Cannot open $f: $in"
        continue
    }
    while {[gets $in line] >= 0} {
        if [regexp -nocase {^# ([^ ]+) chapter} $line \
                x keyword] {
            lappend examples($keyword) $f
            close $in
            break
        }
    }
}
```

The example files contain lines like this:

```
# Canvas chapter
```

The regexp picks out the keyword Canvas with the ([^]+) part of the pattern, and this is assigned to the keyword variable. The x variable is assigned the value of the whole match, which is more than we are interested in. Once the keyword is found the file is closed and the next file is searched. At the end of the foreach loop the examples array has an element defined for each chapter keyword, and the value of each element is a list of the files that had examples for that chapter.

Cascaded Menus

The values in the examples array are used to build up a cascaded menu structure. First a menubutton is created that will post the main menu. It is associated with the main menu with its `menu` attribute. The menu must be a child of the menubutton for its display to work properly.

```
menubutton .menubar.ex -text Examples \
    -menu .menubar.ex.m
set m [menu .menubar.ex.m]
```

For each example a `cascade` menu entry is added to the main menu and the associated menu is defined. Once again, the submenu is defined as a child of the main menu. The submenu gets filled out with `command` entries that browse the file. Note the inconsistency with menu entries. Their text is defined with the `-label` option, not `-text`. Other than this they are much like buttons. Chapter 14 describes menus in more detail:

```
set i 0
foreach key [lsort [array names examples]] {
    $m add cascade -label $key -menu $m.sub$i
    set sub [menu $m.sub$i -tearoff 0]
    incr i
    foreach item [lsort $examples($key)] {
        $sub add command -label [file tail $item] \
            -command [list Browse $item]
    }
}
```

A Read-Only Text Widget

The `Browse` procedure is fairly simple. It sets `browse(current)` to be the name of the file. This changes the main label because of its `textvariable` attribute that ties it to this variable. The `state` attribute of the text widget is manipulated so that the text is read-only after the text is inserted. You have to set the `state` to `normal` before inserting the text, otherwise the `insert` has no effect. Here are a few commands from the body of `Browse`:

```
global browse
set browse(current) [file tail $file]
$t config -state normal
$t insert end [read $in]
$t config -state disabled
```

A Tcl Shell

This section demonstrates the text widget with a simple Tcl shell application. Instead of using some other terminal emulator, it provides its own terminal environment using a text widget. You can use the Tcl shell as a sandbox to try out Tcl examples. The browser can too, by sending Tcl commands to the shell. Because the shell is a separate program, the browser is insulated from crashes. The shell and the browser are hooked together in Chapter 22 on page 275.

Example 11–3 A Tcl shell in a text widget.

```
#!/usr/local/bin/wish
# Simple evaluator. It executes Tcl in its own interpreter
# and it uses up the following identifiers.
# Tk widgets:
#   .eval - the frame around the text log
# Procedures:
#   _Eval - the main eval procedure
# Variables:
#   prompt - the command line prompt
#   _t - holds the ID of the text widget

# A frame, scrollbar, and text
frame .eval
set _t [text .eval.t -width 80 -height 20 \
    -yscrollcommand {.eval.s set}]
scrollbar .eval.s -command {.eval.t yview}
pack .eval.s -side left -fill y
pack .eval.t -side right -fill both -expand true
pack .eval -fill both -expand true

# Insert the prompt and initialize the limit mark
.eval.t insert insert "Tcl eval log\n"
set prompt "tcl> "
.eval.t insert insert $prompt
.eval.t mark set limit insert
.eval.t mark gravity limit left
focus .eval.t

# Key bindings that limit input and eval things
bind .eval.t <Return> { _Eval .eval.t ; break }
bind .eval.t <Any-Key> {
    if [%W compare insert < limit] {
        %W mark set insert end
    }
}
bindtags .eval.t {.eval.t Text all}

proc _Eval { t } {
    global prompt _debug
    set command [$t get limit end]
    if [info complete $command] {
        set err [catch {uplevel #0 $command} result]
```

```
        if {$_debug} {
         puts stdout "$err: $result\n"
        }
        $t insert insert \n$result\n
        $t insert insert $prompt
        $t see insert
        $t mark set limit insert
        return
    }
}
```

Naming Issues

This example uses some odd names for variables and procedures. This is a crude attempt to limit conflicts with the commands that you will type at the shell. The comments at the beginning explain what identifiers are used by this script. With a small amount of C programming you can easily introduce multiple Tcl interpreters into a single process to avoid problems like this. The *minterps* extension provides this capability at the Tcl level, and you can find this at the Tcl archive site.

Text Marks and Bindings

The shell uses a text *mark* and some extra bindings to ensure that users only type new text into the end of the text widget. The `limit` mark keeps track of the boundary between the read-only area and the editable area. The mark is used in two ways. First, the `_Eval` procedure looks at all the text between `limit` and `end` to see if it is a complete Tcl command. If it is, it evaluates it at the global scope using `uplevel #0`. Second, the `<Any-Key>` binding checks to see where the insert point is, and bounces it to the `end` if the user tries to input text before the `limit` mark. Chapter 19 describes the text widget and its mark facility in more detail.

CHAPTER 12

The Pack Geometry Manager

This chapter explores the `pack` geometry manager that positions widgets on the screen. The `place` geometry manager is also briefly described.

Geometry managers arrange widgets on the screen. There are a few different geometry managers, and you can use different ones to control different parts of your user interface. This book primarily uses the `pack` geometry manager, which is a constraint-based system. Tk also provides the `place` geometry manager, which is discussed briefly at the end of this chapter. In addition, the `table` geometry manager is provided as part of the *BLT* extension package, which is reviewed in Chapter 32.

A geometry manager uses one widget as a parent, and it arranges multiple children (also called slaves) inside the parent. The parent is almost always a frame, but this is not strictly necessary. A widget can only be managed by one geometry manager at a time. If a widget is not managed, then it doesn't appear on your display at all.

The packer is a powerful constraint-based geometry manager. Instead of specifying in detail the placement of each window, the programmer defines some constraints about how windows should be positioned, and the packer works out the details. It is important to understand the algorithm the packer uses, otherwise the constraint-based results may not be what you expect.

This chapter explores the packer through a series of examples. The background of the main window is set to black, and the other frames are given different colors so you can identify frames and observe the effect of the different packing parameters. When consecutive examples differ by a small amount, the added command or option is printed in **`bold courier`** to highlight the addition.

Packing Toward a Side

The following example creates two frames and packs them toward the top side of the main window. The upper frame, `.one`, is not as big and the main window shows through on either side. The children are packed toward the specified side in order, so `.one` is on top. The four possible sides are: `top`, `right`, `bottom`, and `left`. The `top` side is the default.

Example 12–1 Two frames packed inside the main frame.

```
# Make the main window black
. config -bg black
# Create and pack two frames
frame .one -width 40 -height 40 -bg white
frame .two -width 100 -height 100 -bg grey50
pack .one .two -side top
```

Shrinking Frames and Pack Propagate

In the previous example the main window shrunk down to be just large enough to hold its two children. In most cases this is the desired behavior. If not, you can turn it off with the `pack propagate` command. Apply this to the parent frame, and it will not adjust its size to fit its children:

Example 12–2 Turning off geometry propagation.

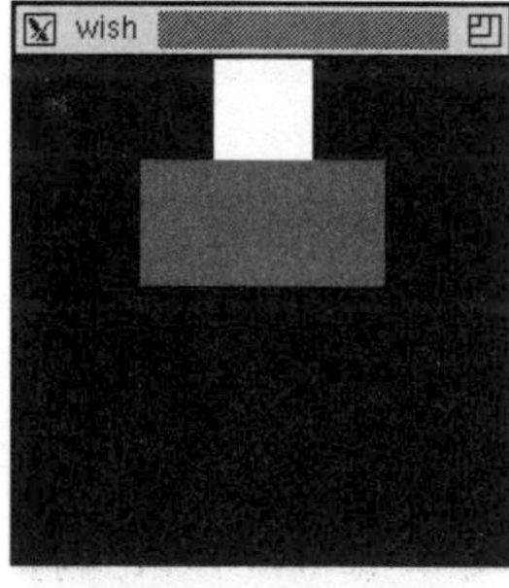


```
frame .one -width 40 -height 40 -bg white
frame .two -width 100 -height 100 -bg grey50
pack propagate . false
pack .one .two -side top
```

Horizontal and Vertical Stacking

In general you use either horizontal or vertical stacking within a frame. If you mix sides such as `left` and `top`, the effect might not be what you expect. Instead, you should introduce more frames to pack a set of widgets into a stack of a different orientation. For example, suppose we want to put a row of buttons inside the upper frame in the examples we have given so far:

Example 12–3 A horizontal stack inside a vertical stack.

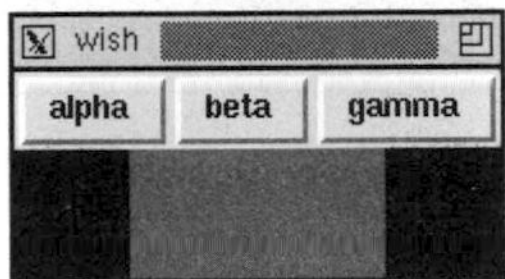


```
frame .one -bg white
frame .two -width 100 -height 50 -bg grey50
# Create a row of buttons
foreach b {alpha beta gamma} {
	button .one.$b -text $b
	pack .one.$b -side left
}
pack .one .two -side top
```

Example 12–4 Even more nesting of horizontal and vertical stacks.

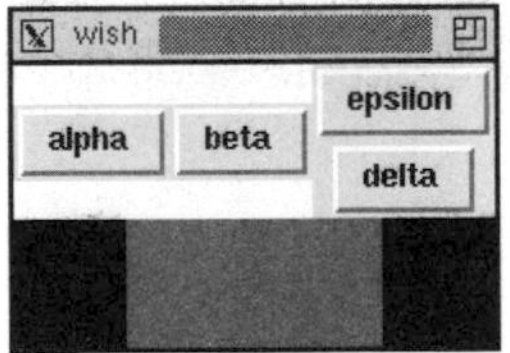


```
frame .one -bg white
frame .two -width 100 -height 50 -bg grey50
foreach b {alpha beta} {
	button .one.$b -text $b
	pack .one.$b -side left
}
# Create a frame for two more buttons
frame .one.right
foreach b {delta epsilon} {
	button .one.right.$b -text $b
	pack .one.right.$b -side bottom
}
pack .one.right -side right
pack .one .two -side top
```

You can build more complex arrangements by introducing nested frames and switching between horizontal and vertical stacking as you go. Within each frame pack all the children with either a combination of `-side left` and `-side right`, or `-side top` and `-side bottom`.

Example 12–4 replaces the `.one.gamma` button with a vertical stack of two buttons, `.one.right.delta` and `.one.right.epsilon`. These are packed toward the bottom of `.one.right`, so the first one packed is on the bottom.

The frame `.one.right` was packed to the right, and in the previous example the button `.one.gamma` was packed to the `left`. Despite the difference, they ended up in the same position relative to the other two widgets packed inside the `.one` frame. The next section explains why.

The Cavity Model

The packing algorithm is based on a *cavity model* for the available space inside a frame. For example, when the main *wish* window is created, the main frame is empty and there is an obvious space, or cavity, in which to place widgets. The primary rule about the packing cavity is: *a widget occupies one whole side of the cavity.* To demonstrate this, pack three widgets into the main frame. Put the first two on the bottom, and the third one on the right:

Example 12–5 Mixing `bottom` and `right` packing sides.

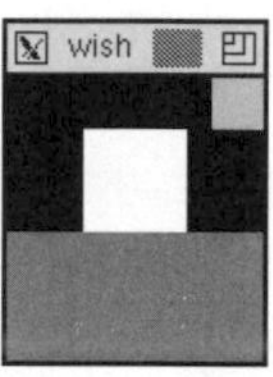


```
# pack two frames on the bottom.
frame .one -width 100 -height 50 -bg grey50
frame .two -width 40 -height 40 -bg white
pack .one .two -side bottom
# pack another frame to the right
frame .three -width 20 -height 20 -bg grey75
pack .three -side right
```

When we pack a third frame into the main window with `-side left` or `-side right`, the new frame is positioned inside the cavity, which is above the two frames already packed toward the `bottom` side. The frame does not appear to the right of the existing frames as you might have expected. This is because the `.two` frame occupies the whole `bottom` side of the packing cavity, even though its display does not fill up that side.

Can you tell where the packing cavity is after this example? It is to the left of the frame `.three`, which is the last frame packed toward the `right`, and it is above the frame `.two`., which is the last frame packed toward the `bottom`. This explains why there was no difference between the previous two examples when `.one.gamma` was packed to the `left`, but `.one.right` was packed to the `right`. At that point, packing to the left or right of the cavity had the same effect. However, it will affect what happens if another widget is packed into those two configurations. Try out the following commands after running Example 12–3 and Example 12–4 and compare the difference.*

```
button .one.omega -text omega
pack .one.omega -side right
```

Each packing parent has its own cavity, which is why introducing nested frames can help. If you use a horizontal or vertical arrangement inside any given frame, you can more easily simulate the packer's behavior in your head!

Packing Space and Display Space

The packer distinguishes between *packing* space and *display* space when it arranges the widgets. The display space is the area requested by a widget for the purposes of painting itself. The packing space is the area the packer allows for the placement of the widget. Because of geometry constraints, a widget may be allocated more (or less) packing space than it needs to display itself. The extra space, if any, is along the side of the cavity against which the widget was packed.

The -fill Option

The `-fill` packing option causes a widget to fill up the allocated packing space with its display. A widget can fill in the X or Y direction, or both. The default is not to fill, which is why the black background of the main window has shown through in the examples so far:

Example 12–6 Filling the display into extra packing space.

```
frame .one -width 100 -height 50 -bg grey50
frame .two -width 40 -height 40 -bg white
# Pack with fill enabled
pack .one .two -side bottom -fill x
frame .three -width 20 -height 20 -bg red
pack .three -side right -fill x
```

* Answer: After Example 12–3 the new button is to the right of all buttons. After Example 12–4 the new button is between `.one.beta` and `.one.right`.

This is just like the previous example, except that `-fill x` has been specified for all the frames. The `.two` frame fills, but the `.three` frame does not. This is because the fill does not expand into the packing cavity. In fact, after this example, the packing cavity is the part that shows through in black. Another way to look at this is that the `.two` frame was allocated the whole bottom side of the packing cavity, so its fill can expand the frame to occupy that space. The `.three` frame has only been allocated the right side, so a fill in the x direction will not have any effect.

Another use of fill is for a menu bar that has buttons at either end and some empty space between them. The frame that holds the buttons is packed toward the top. The buttons are packed into the left and right sides of the menu bar frame. Without fill, the menu bar shrinks to be just large enough to hold all the buttons, and the buttons are squeezed together. When fill is enabled in the X direction, the menu bar fills out the top edge of the display:

Example 12–7 Using horizontal fill in a menubar.

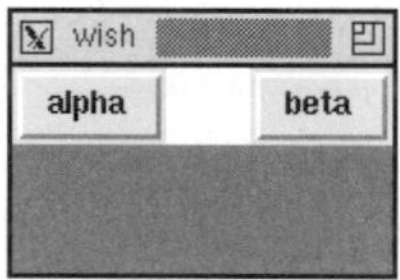


```
frame .menubar -bg white
frame .body -width 150 -height 50 -bg grey50
# Create buttons at either end of the menubar
foreach b {alpha beta} {
    button .menubar.$b -text $b
}
pack .menubar.alpha -side left
pack .menubar.beta -side right
# Let the menu bar fill along the top
pack .menubar -side top -fill x
pack .body
```

Internal Padding with -ipadx and -ipady

Another way to get more fill space is with the `-ipadx` and `-ipady` packing options that request more display space in the x and y directions, respectively. Due to other constraints the request might not be offered, but in general you can use this to give a widget more display space. The next example is just like the previous one except that some internal padding has been added:

Example 12–8 The effects of internal padding (-ipady).

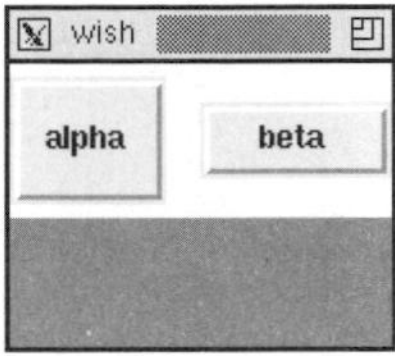


```
# Create and pack two frames
frame .menubar -bg white
frame .body -width 150 -height 50 -bg grey50
# Create buttons at either end of the menubar
foreach b {alpha beta} {
   button .menubar.$b -text $b
}
pack .menubar.alpha -side left -ipady 10
pack .menubar.beta -side right -ipadx 10
# Let the menu bar fill along the top
pack .menubar -side top -fill x -ipady 5
pack .body
```

The alpha button is taller and the beta button is wider because of the internal padding. The frame has internal padding, which reduces the space available for the packing cavity, so the .menubar frame shows through above and below the buttons.

Some widgets have attributes that result in more display space. For example, it would be hard to distinguish a frame with width 50 and no internal padding from a frame with width 40 and a -ipadx 5 packing option. The packer would give the frame 5 more pixels of display space on either side for a total width of 50.

Buttons have their own -padx and -pady options that give them more display space, too. This padding provided by the button is used to keep its text away from the edge of the button. The following example illustrates the difference. The -anchor e button option positions the text as far to the right as possible. Example 23–5 on page 283 provides another comparison of these options:

Example 12–9 Button padding vs. packer padding.

```
# Foo has internal padding from the packer
button .foo -text Foo -anchor e -padx 0 -pady 0
pack .foo -side right -ipadx 10 -ipady 10
# Bar has its own padding
button .bar -text Bar -anchor e -pady 10 -padx 10
pack .bar -side right -ipadx 0 -ipady 0
```

External Padding with -padx and -pady

The packer can provide external padding that allocates packing space that cannot be filled. The space is outside of the border that widgets use to implement their 3D reliefs. Example 23–2 on page 280 shows the different reliefs. The look of a default button is achieved with an extra frame and some padding:

Example 12–10 The look of a default button.

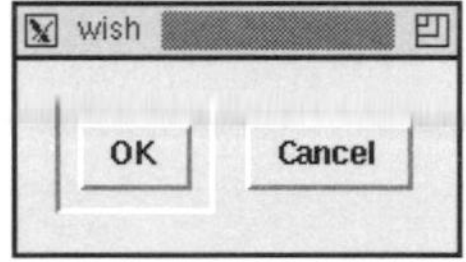


```
. config -borderwidth 10
# OK is the default button
frame .ok -borderwidth 2 -relief sunken
button .ok.b -text OK
pack .ok.b -padx 5 -pady 5
# Cancel is not
button .cancel -text Cancel
pack .ok .cancel -side left -padx 5 -pady 5
```

Even if the `.ok.b` button were packed with `-fill both`, it would look the same. The external padding provided by the packer will not be filled by the child widgets.

Expand and Resizing

The `-expand true` packing option lets a widget expand its packing space into unclaimed space in the packing cavity. Example 12–6 could use this on the small frame on top to get it to expand across the top of the display, even though it is packed to the right side. The more common case occurs when you have a resizable window. When the user makes the window larger, the widgets have to be told to take advantage of the extra space. Suppose you have a main widget like a text, listbox, or canvas that is in a frame with a scrollbar. That frame has to be told to expand into the extra space in its parent (e.g., the main window) and then the main widget (e.g., the canvas) has to be told to expand into its parent frame. Example 11–1 does this.

In nearly all cases the `-fill both` option is used along with `-expand true` so that the widget actually uses its extra packing space for its own display. The converse is not true. There are many cases where a widget should fill extra space, but not attempt to expand into the packing cavity. The examples below show the difference.

The main window can be made larger by interactive resizing, or under program control with the `wm geometry` command. By default interactive resizing is not enabled. You must use the `wm minisize` or `wm maxsize` commands which have the side effect of enabling interactive resizing. These commands place constraints on the size of the window. The `text`, `canvas`, and `listbox` widgets also have a `setgrid` attribute that, if enabled, makes the main window resizable. Chapter 25 describes geometry gridding on page 301.

Now we can investigate what happens when the window is made larger. The next example starts like Example 12–7 on page 120 but the size of the main window is increased:

Example 12–11 Resizing without the expand option.

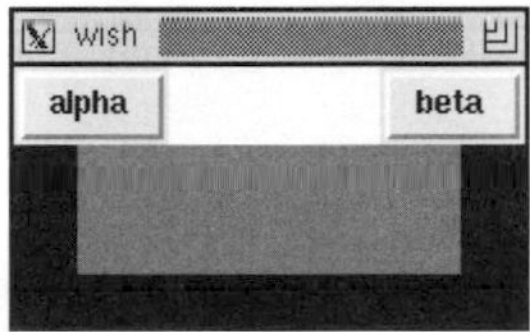


```
# Make the main window black
. config -bg black
# Create and pack two frames
frame .menubar -bg white
frame .body -width 150 -height 50 -bg grey50
# Create buttons at either end of the menubar
foreach b {alpha beta} {
   button .menubar.$b -text $b
}
pack .menubar.alpha -side left
pack .menubar.beta -side right
# Let the menu bar fill along the top
pack .menubar -side top -fill x
pack .body
# Resize the main window to be bigger
wm geometry . 200x100
# Allow interactive resizing
wm minsize . 100 50
```

The only widget that claims any of the new space is `.menubar` because of its `-fill x` packing option. The `.body` frame needs to be packed properly:

Example 12–12 Resizing with expand turned on.

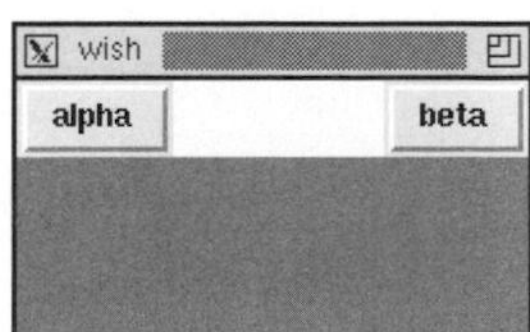


```
# Use all of Example 12-11 then repack .body
pack .body -expand true -fill both
```

If more than one widget inside the same parent is allowed to expand, then the packer shares the extra space between them proportionally. This is probably not the effect you want in the examples we have built so far. The `.menubar`, for example is not a good candidate for expansion.

Example 12–13 More than one expanding widget.

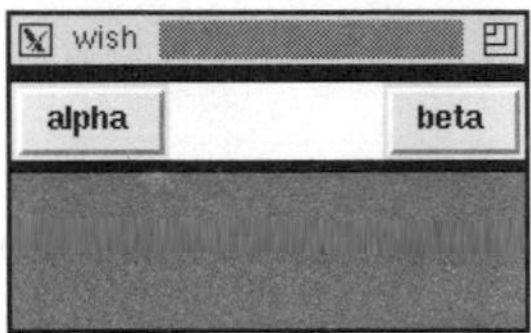


```
# Use all of Example 12-11 then repack .menubar and .body
pack .menubar -expand true -fill x
pack .body -expand true -fill both
```

Anchoring

If a widget is left with more packing space than display space, you can position it within its packing space using the `-anchor` packing option. The default is anchor position is `center`. The other options correspond to points on a compass: `n`, `ne`, `e`, `se`, `s`, `sw`, `w`, and `nw`:

Example 12–14 Setup for anchor experiments.

```
# Make the main window black
. config -bg black
# Create two frames to hold open the cavity
frame .prop -bg white -height 80 -width 20
frame .base -width 120 -height 20 -bg grey50
pack .base -side bottom
# Float a label and the prop in the cavity
label .foo -text Foo
pack .prop .foo -side right -expand true
```

The `.base` frame is packed on the bottom. Then the `.prop` frame and the `.foo` label are packed to the right with expand set but no fill. Instead of being pressed up against the right side, the expand gives each of these widgets half of the extra space in the X direction. Their default anchor of `center` results in the positions shown. The next example shows some different anchor positions:

Example 12–15 The effects of non-center anchors.

```
. config -bg black
# Create two frames to hold open the cavity
frame .prop -bg white -height 80 -width 20
frame .base -width 120 -height 20 -bg grey50
pack .base -side bottom
# Float the label and prop
# Change their position with anchors
label .foo -text Foo
pack .prop -side right -expand true -anchor sw
pack .foo -side right -expand true -anchor ne
```

The `label` has room on all sides, so each of the different anchors will position it differently. The `.prop` frame only has room in the X direction, so it can only be moved into three different positions: left, center, and right. Any of the anchors `w`, `nw`, and `sw` result in the left position. The anchors `center`, `n`, and `s` result in the center position. The anchors `e`, `se`, and `ne` result in the right position.

If you want to see all the variations, type in the following commands to animate the different packing anchors. The `update idletasks` forces any pending display operations. The `after 500` causes the script to wait for `500` milliseconds:

Example 12–16 Animating the packing anchors.

```
foreach anchor {center n ne e se s sw w nw center} {
   pack .foo .prop -anchor $anchor
   # Update the display
   update idletasks
   # Wait half a second
   after 500
}
```

Packing Order

The packer maintains an order among the children that are packed into a frame. By default, each new child is appended to the end of the packing order. The most obvious effect of the order is that the children first in the packing order are closest to the side they are packed against. You can control the packing order with the `-before` and `-after` packing options, and you can reorganize widgets after they have already been packed:

Example 12–17 Controlling the packing order.

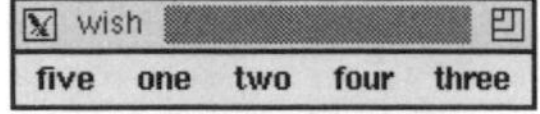


```
# Create five labels in order
foreach label {one two three four five} {
    label .$label -text $label
    pack .$label -side left -padx 5
}
# ShuffleUp moves a widget to the beginning of the order
proc ShuffleUp { parent child } {
    set first [lindex [pack slaves $parent] 0]
    pack $child -in $parent -before $first
}
# ShuffleDown moves a widget to the end of the order
proc ShuffleDown { parent child } {
    pack $child -in $parent
}
ShuffleUp . .five
ShuffleDown . .three
```

Pack Slaves and Pack Info

The `pack slaves` command returns the list of children in their packing order. The `ShuffleUp` procedure uses this to find out the first child so it can insert another child before it. The `ShuffleDown` procedure is simpler because the default is to append the child to the end of the packing order.

When a widget is repacked, then it retains all its packing parameters that have already been set. If you need to examine the current packing parameters for a widget use the `pack info` command.

```
pack info .five
=> -in . -anchor center -expand 0 -fill none -ipadx 0 \
     -ipady 0 -padx 0 -pady 0 -side left
```

Pack the Scrollbar First

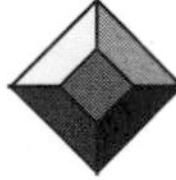

The packing order also determines what happens when the window is made too small. If the window is made small enough the packer will clip children that come later in the packing order. This is why, when you pack a scrollbar and a text widget into a frame, you should pack the scrollbar first. Otherwise, when the window is made smaller the `text` widget takes up all the space and the scrollbar is clipped.

Choosing the Parent for Packing

In nearly all of the examples in this chapter a widget is packed into its parent frame. In general, it is possible to pack a widget into any descendent of its parent. For example, the `.a.b` widget could be packed into `.a`, `.a.c` or `.a.d.e.f`. The `-in` packing option lets you specify an alternate packing parent. One motivation for this is that the frames introduced to get the arrangement right can cause cluttered names for important widgets. In Example 12–4 on page 117 the buttons have names like `.one.alpha` and `.one.right.delta`, which is not consistent. Here is an alternate implementation of the same example that simplifies the button names and gives the same result:

Example 12–18 Packing into other relatives.

```
# Create and pack two frames
frame .one -bg white
frame .two -width 100 -height 50 -bg grey50
# Create a row of buttons
foreach b {alpha beta} {
    button .$b -text $b
    pack .$b -in .one -side left
}
# Create a frame for two more buttons
frame .one.right
foreach b {delta epsilon} {
    button .$b -text $b
    pack .$b -in .one.right -side bottom
}
pack .one.right -side right
pack .one .two -side top
```

When you do this, remember that the order in which you create widgets is important. Create the frames first, then create the widgets. The X stacking order for windows will cause the later windows to obscure the windows created first. The following is a common mistake:

```
button .a -text hello
frame .b
pack .a -in .b
```

If you cannot avoid this problem scenario, then you can use the `raise` command to fix things up. Stacking order is also discussed on page 131.

```
raise .a
```

Unpacking a Widget

The `pack forget` command removes a widget from the packing order. The widget gets unmapped so it is not visible. If you unpack a parent frame, the packing structure inside it is maintained, but all the widgets inside the frame get unmapped. Unpacking a widget is useful if you want to suppress extra features of your interface. You can create all the parts of the interface, and just delay packing them in until the user requests to see them. Then you can pack and unpack them dynamically.

Packer Summary

Keep these rules in mind about the packer:

- Pack vertically (`-side top` and `-side bottom`) or horizontally (`-side left` and `-side right`) within a frame. Only rarely will a different mixture of packing directions work out the way you want. Add frames to build more complex structures.
- By default, the packer puts widgets into their parent frame, and the parent frame must be created before the children that are packed into it.
- If you put widgets into other relatives, remember to create the frames first so the frames stay underneath the widgets packed into them.
- By default, the packer ignores `-width` and `-height` attributes of frames that have widgets packed inside them. It shrinks frames to be just big enough to allow for its borderwidth and to hold the widgets inside them. Use `pack propagate` to turn off the shrink wrap behavior.
- The packer distinguishes between packing space and display space. A widget's display might not take up all the packing space allocated to it.
- The `-fill` option causes the display to fill up the packing space in the x or y directions, or both.
- The `-expand true` option causes the packing space to expand into any room in the packing cavity that is otherwise unclaimed. If more than one widget in the same frame wants to expand, then they share the extra space.
- The `-ipadx` and `-ipady` options allocate more display space inside the border, if possible.
- The `-padx` and `-pady` options allocate more packing space outside the border, if possible.

The pack Command

Table 12–1 summarizes the `pack` command. Table 12–2 summarizes the packing options for a widget. These are set with the `pack configure` command, and the current settings are returned by the `pack info` command:

Table 12–1 The `pack` command.

`pack win ?win ..? ?options?`	This is just like `pack configure`.
`pack configure win ?win ...? ?options?`	Pack one or more widgets according to the *options*, which are given in the next table.
`pack forget win ?win...?`	Unpack the specified windows.
`pack info win`	Return the packing parameters of *win*.
`pack propagate win ?bool?`	Query or set the geometry propagation of *win*, which has other widgets packed inside it.
`pack slaves win`	Return the list of widgets managed by *win*.

Table 12–2 Packing options.

`-after win`	Pack after *win* in the packing order.
`-anchor anchor`	Anchors: `center`, `n`, `ne`, `e`, `se`, `s`, `sw`, `w`, or `nw`.
`-before win`	Pack before *win* in the packing order.
`-expand boolean`	Control expansion into the unclaimed packing cavity.
`-fill style`	Control fill of packing space. Style: `x`, `y`, `both`, or `none`.
`-in win`	Pack inside *win*.
`-ipadx amount`	Horizontal internal padding, in screen units.
`-ipady amount`	Vertical internal padding, in screen units.
`-padx amount`	Horizontal external padding, in screen units.
`-pady amount`	Vertical external padding, in screen units.
`-side side`	Sides: `top`, `right`, `bottom`, or `left`.

The Place Geometry Manager

The `place` geometry manager is much simpler than the packer. You specify the exact position and size of a window, or you specify the relative position and relative size of a widget. This is useful in a few situations, but it rapidly becomes tedious if you have to position lots of windows. The following `place` command centers a window in its parent. Use this command to position dialogs that you do not want to be detached toplevel windows:

```
place $w -in $parent -relx 0.5 -rely 0.5 -anchor center
```

The `-relx` and `-rely` specify the relative X and Y position of the anchor point of the widget `$w` in `$parent`. A value of zero corresponds to the left (or top) edge of `$parent`. A value of one corresponds to the right (or bottom) edge of `$parent`. A value of `0.5` specifies the middle. The anchor point determines what point in `$w` is positioned according to the specifications. In this case the `center` anchor point is used so that the center of $w is centered in $parent. The default anchor point for windows is their upper-left hand corner (nw). The following example completely covers one window with another window:

```
place $w -in $parent -relwidth 1 -relheight 1 -x 0 -y 0
```

It is not necessary for $parent to actually be the parent widget of $w. The requirement is that $parent be the parent, or a descendent of the parent, of $w. It also has to be in the same toplevel window. This guarantees that $w is visible whenever $parent is visible. (These are the same restrictions imposed by the pack geometry manager.)

It is not necessary to position a widget inside another widget, either. The following command positions a window five pixels above a sibling widget. If $sibling is repositioned, then $w moves with it. This approach is useful when you decorate a resizable window by placing other widgets at its corners or edges. When the window is resized, the decorations automatically move into place:

```
place $w -in $sibling -relx 0.5 -y -5 -anchor s \
    -bordermode outside
```

The -bordermode outside option is specified so that any decorative border in $sibling is ignored when positioning $w. In this case the position is relative to the outside edge of $sibling. By default, the border is taken into account to make it easy to position widgets inside their parent's border.

The parent widget does not have to be a frame. You can use the first place command shown above to place a dialog in the middle of a text widget. In the third command, $sibling and $w might both be label widgets, for example.

The place Command

Table 12–3 summarizes the usage of the place command.

Table 12–3 The place command.

place *win* ?*win* ..? ?*options*?	This is just like place configure.
place configure *win* ?*win* ...? ?*options*?	Place one or more widgets according to the *options,* which are given in the next table.
place forget *win* ?*win*...?	Unmap the specified windows.
place info *win*	Return the placement parameters of *win*.
place slaves *win*	Return the list of widgets managed by *win*.

Table 12–4 summarizes the placement options for a widget. These are set with the place configure command, and the current settings are returned by the place info command.

Table 12–4 Placement options.

`-in` *win*	Place inside (or relative to) *win*.
`-anchor` *where*	Anchors: `center`, `n`, `ne`, `e`, `se`, `s`, `sw`, `w`, or `nw`. Default: `nw`.
`-x` *coord*	X position, in screen units, of the anchor point.
`-relx` *offset*	Relative X position. 0.0 is the left edge. 1.0 is the right edge.
`-y` *coord*	Y position, in screen units, of the anchor point.
`-rely` *offset*	Relative Y position. 0.0 is the top edge. 1.0 is the bottom edge.
`-width size`	Width of the window, in screen units.
`-relwidth size`	Width relative to parent's width. 1.0 is full width.
`-height size`	Height of the window, in screen units.
`-relheight size`	Height relative to the parent's height. 1.0 is full height.
`-bordermode mode`	If mode is `inside`, then size and position are inside the parent's border. If mode is `outside`, then size and position are relative to the outer edge of the parent.

Window Stacking Order

The `raise` and `lower` commands control the X window stacking order. The stacking order controls the display of windows. Windows higher in the stacking order obscure windows lower in the stacking order. By default, new windows are created at the top of the stacking order so they obscure older windows. Consider this sequence of commands:

```
button .one
frame .two
pack .one -in .two
```

If you do this, you do not see the button. The problem is that the frame is higher in the stacking order so it obscures the button. You can change the stacking order with the `raise` command:

```
raise .one .two
```

This puts `.one` just above `.two` in the stacking order. If `.two` was not specified, then `.one` would be put at the top of the stacking order.

The `lower` command has a similar form. With one argument it puts that window at the bottom of the stacking order. Otherwise it puts it just below another window in the stacking order.

You can use `raise` and `lower` on toplevel windows to control their stacking order among all other toplevel windows. For example, if a user requests a dialog that is already displayed, use `raise` to make it pop to the foreground of their cluttered X desktop.

CHAPTER 13

Binding Commands to X Events

This chapter introduces the event binding mechanism in Tk. Bindings associate a Tcl command with an event like a mouse click or a key stroke. This chapter describes the `bind` and `bindtags` commands.

Bindings associate a Tcl command with a sequence of events from the X window system. Events include key press, key release, button press, button release, mouse entering a window, mouse leaving, window changing size, window open, window close, focus in, focus out, and widget destroyed. The bindings are defined on *binding tags*, and each widget is associated with an ordered set of binding tags. The level of indirection between bindings and widgets leads to a flexible and powerful system.

The binding mechanism changed substantially between Tk 3.6 and Tk 4.0. Several sections point out the important changes.

The bind Command

The `bind` command returns information about current bindings, and defines new bindings. The general form of the command is:

```
bind bindingTag ?eventSequence? ?command?
```

The *bindingTag* is typically a widget class name (e.g., `Button`) or a widget instance name (e.g., `.buttons.foo`). Binding tags are described in more detail later. Called with a single argument, a binding tag, `bind` returns the events for which there are command bindings:

```
bind Menubutton
=> <Key-Return> <Key-space> <ButtonRelease-1>
   <B1-Motion> <Motion> <Button-1> <Leave> <Enter>
```

The events in this example are button-related events. `<Button-1>` is the event generated when the user presses the first, or left-hand, mouse button. `<B1-Motion>` is a mouse motion event modified by the first mouse button. This event is generated when the user drags the mouse with the left button pressed. The surrounding angle brackets delimit a single event, and you can define bindings for a sequence of events. The event syntax is described on page 137, and event sequences are described on page 142.

If `bind` is given an event sequence argument, it returns the Tcl command bound to that event sequence:

```
bind Menubutton <B1-Motion>
=> tkMbMotion %W down %X %Y
```

The Tcl commands in event bindings support an additional syntax for event keywords. These keywords begin with a percent sign and have one more character that identifies some attribute of the event. The keywords are replaced (i.e., substituted) with event-specific data before the Tcl command is evaluated. For example, `%W` is replaced with the widget's pathname. The `%X and %Y` keywords are replaced with the coordinates of the event relative to the screen. The `%x` and `%y` keywords are replaced with the coordinates of the event relative to the widget. The event keywords are summarized on page 143.

The `%` substitutions are performed throughout the entire command bound to an event, without regard to other quoting schemes. You must use `%%` to obtain a single percent sign. For this reason you should make your binding commands short, adding a new procedure if necessary (e.g., `tkMbMotion`), instead of littering percent signs throughout your code.

A new binding is created by specifying an event sequence and a command:

```
bind Menubutton <B1-Motion> {tkMbMotion %W down %X %Y}
```

If the first character of the binding command is `+`, the command (without the `+`) is added to the commands, if any, for that event and binding tag:

```
bind bindingTag event {+ command args}
```

To delete a binding for an event, bind the event to the null string:

```
bind bindingTag event {}
```

When a binding is triggered, the command is evaluated at the global scope. A very common mistake is to confuse the scope that is active when the `bind` command creates a binding, and the scope that is active when the binding is triggered. The same problem crops up with the commands associated with buttons, and it is discussed in more detail at the beginning of Chapter 14.

The bindtags Command

Bindings are associated with a *binding tag* that groups related bindings. Each widget is associated with an ordered set of binding tags. Bindings from each tag in the set may be triggered by an event. The result is a powerful and flexible way to manage bindings. The `bindtags` command controls the binding tags for a widget, and the ordering of a binding tag set.

The general form of the `bindtags` command is:

```
bindtags widget ?tagList?
```

The following command returns the default binding tags for a text widget:

```
bindtags .t
=> Text .t . all
```

All the Tk widgets, except toplevel, have four binding tags by default:

- The widget's class. The class for a widget is derived from the name of the command that creates it. A button widget has the class `Button`, a canvas has the class `Canvas`, and so on.
- The widget's Tk pathname (e.g., `.buttons.foo`)
- The Tk pathname of the widget's toplevel window (e.g., .). This is redundant in the case of a toplevel widget, so it is not used twice.
- The global binding tag `all`.

You can change the binding tags and their order. The *tagList* argument to `bindtags` must be a proper Tcl list. The following command reorders the binding tags for `$t` and eliminates the `.` binding tag:

```
bindtags $t [list all Text $t]
```

The order of the tag list determines the order that commands are executed if an event matches more than one binding tag in the set. The Tk widgets define their default behavior with bindings on their class. You can add additional bindings for a widget by binding events to the name of the widget. The bindings on a toplevel window can be used in dialog boxes to handle keyboard accelerators. Finally, the `all` binding tag is meant for bindings that are global to all widgets. The default bindings on `all` are used to change focus among widgets. They are described on page 208. By default there are no bindings on a toplevel, and there are no bindings on the name of a widget.

Example 13–1 Bindings on different binding tags.

```
frame .one -width 30 -height 30
frame .two -width 30 -height 30
bind Frame <Enter> {%W config -bg red}
bind Frame <Leave> {%W config -bg white}
bind .two <Any-Button> {puts "Button %b at %x %y"}
pack .one .two -side left
bind all <Control-c> {destroy %W}
bind all <Enter> {focus %W}
```

In the example, the `Frame` class has a binding to change a frame's background color when the mouse moves into the window. One of the frames, `.two`, is set up to report the location of mouse clicks.

The example defines a global handler for `<Control-c>`. Because this is a keystroke, it is important to get the focus directed at the proper widget. By default, focus is on the main window, and destroying it terminates the entire application. The global binding for `<Enter>` gives focus to a widget when you move the mouse over the widget. Specify <Any-Button> instead of <Enter> if you prefer a click-to-type focus model. Focus is described in Chapter 18 on page 203.

Using break and continue in Bindings

The break and continue commands control the progression through the set of binding tags. The break command stops the current binding and suppresses the bindings from any remaining tags in the binding set order. The continue command in a binding stops the current binding and continues with the command from the next binding tag.

Note that you cannot use the break or continue commands inside a procedure that is called by the binding. This is because the procedure mechanism will not propagate the break or continue signal. Instead, you could use the -code option to return, which is described on page 47.

Defining New Binding Tags

You introduce new binding tags just by using them in a bind or bindtags command. This is useful for grouping bindings into different sets, such as specialized bindings for different modes of an editor. One way to emulate the *vi* editor, for example, is to use two bind tags, one for insert mode and one for command mode. The user types i to enter insert mode, and they type <Escape> to enter command mode:

```
bindtags $t [list ViInsert Text $t all]
bind ViInsert <Escape> {bindtags %W {ViCmd %W all}}
bind ViCmd <Key-i> {bindtags %W {ViInsert Text %W all}}
```

The Text class bindings are used in insert mode. The command to put the widget into command mode is put on a new binding tag, ViInsert, instead of changing the default Text bindings. The bindtag command changes the mode by changing the set of binding tags for the widget. Recall that %W is replaced with the name of the widget, which is the same as $t in this example. Of course, you need to define many more bindings to fully implement all the *vi* commands.

Binding Precedence in Tk 3.6

In versions of Tk 3.6 and earlier, only one source of bindings for an event is used. If there is a binding on a widget instance for an event sequence, that binding overrides any class-specific or global bindings for that event sequence. Similarly, if there is a class-specific binding, that overrides an all binding.

There are two problems in this scheme. First, all bindings are not that useful because they are almost always overridden. Second, if you add custom behavior to a widget instance, you suppress the default bindings on the class. Even the + syntax on a binding at the instance level does not preserve the class bindings; they are still overridden. The following trick adds a new instance binding while preserving the class binding.

```
bind .list <Button-1> "[bind Listbox <Button-1>] ; Doit"
```

Event Syntax

The `bind` command uses the following syntax to describe events:

<*modifier-modifier-type-detail*>

The primary part of the description is the *type*, (e.g. `Button` or `Motion`). The *detail* is used in some events to identify keys or buttons, (.e.g. `Key-a` or `Button-1`). A *modifier* is another key or button that is already pressed when the event occurs, (e.g., `Control-Key-a` or `B2-Motion`). There can be multiple modifiers (e.g., `Control-Shift-x`). The < and > delimit a single event.

Table 13–1 briefly describes all the event types. When two event types are listed together (e.g., `ButtonPress` and `Button`) they are equivalent.

Table 13–1 Event types.

Event type	Description
`ButtonPress, Button`	A button is pressed (down).
`ButtonRelease`	A button is released (up).
`Circulate`	The stacking order of the window changed.
`Colormap`	The colormap has changed.
`Configure`	The window has changed size, position, border, or stacking order.
`Destroy`	The window has been destroyed.
`Enter`	The mouse has entered the window.
`Expose`	The window has been exposed.
`FocusIn`	The window has received focus.
`FocusOut`	The window has lost focus.
`Gravity`	The window has moved because of a change in size of its parent window.
`Keymap`	The keyboard mapping has changed.
`KeyPress, Key`	A key is pressed (down).
`KeyRelease`	A key is released (up).
`Motion`	The mouse is moving in the window.
`Leave`	The mouse is leaving the window.
`Map`	The window has been mapped (opened).
`Property`	A property on the window has been changed or deleted.
`Reparent`	A window has been reparented.
`Unmap`	The window has been unmapped (iconified).
`Visibility`	The window has changed visibility.

Keyboard Events

The `KeyPress` type is distinguished from `KeyRelease` so that you can have different bindings for each of these events. `KeyPress` can be abbreviated `Key`, and `Key` can be left off altogether if a detail is given to indicate what key. Finally, as a special case for KeyPress events, the angle brackets can also be left out. The following are all equivalent event specifications:

```
<KeyPress-a>
<Key-a>
<a>
a
```

The detail for a key is also known as the *keysym*, which is an X technical term that refers to the graphic printed on the key of the keyboard. For punctuation and non-printing characters, special keysyms are defined. Commonly encountered keysyms include (note capitalization):

```
Return, Escape, BackSpace, Tab, Up, Down, Left, Right,
comma, period, dollar, asciicircum, numbersign, exclam
```

The definitions of these keysyms are buried inside an X11 header file, and they can also be affected by a dynamic keyboard map, the X modmap. You may find the next binding useful to determine just what the keysym for a particular key is on your system:

```
bind $w <KeyPress> {puts stdout {%%K=%K %%A=%A}}
```

The `%K` keyword is replaced with the keysym from the event. The `%A` is replaced with the printing character that results from the event and any modifiers like `Shift`. The `%%` is replaced with a single percent sign. Note that these substitutions occur in spite of the curly braces used for grouping. If the user types a capital `Q` there are two `KeyPress` events, one for the `Shift` key, and one for the `q` key. The output is:

```
%K=Shift_R %A={}
%K=Q %A=Q
```

The `Shift_R` keysym indicates the right-hand shift key was pressed. The `%A` keyword is replaced with `{}` when modifier keys are pressed. You can check for this in `<KeyPress>` bindings to avoid doing anything if only a modifier key is pressed. The following can be used with a text widget. The double-quotes are necessary to force a string comparison:

```
bind $w <KeyPress> {
    if {"%A" != "{}"} {%W insert insert %A}
}
```

Detecting Modifiers in Tk 3.6

In Tk 3.6 and earlier, the `%A` keyword is substituted with an empty string instead of the literal `{}`. In addition, you must use the `Any` event modifier to allow any key sequence to match. The previous example must be changed to this if you are using Tk 3.6:

```
bind $w <Any-Key> {
    if {"%A" != ""} {%W insert insert %A}
}
```

Mouse Events

Button events also distinguish between `ButtonPress`, (or `Button`), and `ButtonRelease`. `Button` can be left off if a detail specifies a button by number. The following are equivalent:

```
<ButtonPress-1>
<Button-1>
<1>
```

Note: the event `<1>` implies a `ButtonPress` event, while the event `1` implies a `KeyPress` event. To avoid confusion, I always specify the `Key` or `Button` type.

The mouse is tracked by binding to the `Enter`, `Leave`, and `Motion` events. `Enter` and `Leave` are triggered when the mouse comes into and exits out of the widget, respectively. A `Motion` event is generated when the mouse moves within a widget.

The coordinates of the mouse event are represented by the `%x` and `%y` keywords in the binding command. The coordinates are widget-relative, with the origin at the upper-left hand corner of a widget's window. The keywords `%X` and `%Y` represent the coordinates relative to the screen:

```
bind $w <Enter>  {puts stdout "Entered %W at %x %y"}
bind $w <Leave>  {puts stdout "Left %W at %x %y"}
bind $w <Motion> {puts stdout "%W %x %y"}
```

Other Events

The `<Map>` and `<Unmap>` events are generated when a window is opened and closed, or when a widget is packed or unpacked by its geometry manager.

The `<Configure>` event is generated when the window changes size. A canvas that computes its display based on its size can bind a redisplay procedure to the `<Configure>` event, for example. The `<Configure>` event can be caused by interactive resizing. It can also be caused by a `configure` widget command that changes the size of the widget. You should not reconfigure a widget's size while processing a `<Configure>` event to avoid an indefinite sequence of these events.

The `<Destroy>` event is generated when a widget is destroyed. You can intercept requests to delete windows, too. See also the description of the `wm` command on page 312.

Chapter 18 presents some examples that use the `<FocusIn>` and `<FocusOut>` events. The remaining events in Table 13–1 have to do with dark corners of the X protocol, and they are seldom used. More information can be found on these events in the Event Reference section of the *Xlib Reference Manual* published by O'Reilly & Associates, Inc.

Modifiers

A modifier indicates that another key or button is being held down at the time of the event. Typical modifiers are the `Shift` and `Control` keys. The mouse buttons can also be used as modifiers. If an event does not specify any modifiers, the presence of a modifier key is ignored by the event dispatcher. However, if there are two possible matching events, the more accurate match will be used.

For example, consider these three bindings:

```
bind $w <KeyPress> {puts "key=%A"}
bind $w <Key-c> {puts "just a c"}
bind $w <Control-Key-c> {exit}
```

The last event is more specific than the others. Its binding will be triggered when the user types `c` with the `Control` key held down. If the user types `c` with the `Meta` key held down, the second binding will be triggered. The `Meta` key is ignored because it does not match any binding. If the user types something other than a `c`, the first binding is triggered. If the user presses the `Shift` key, then the keysym that is generated is `C`, not `c`, so the last two events do not match.

There are eight modifier keys defined by the X protocol. The `Control`, `Shift`, and `Lock` modifiers are found on nearly all keyboards. The `Meta` and `Alt` modifiers tend to vary from system to system, and they may not be defined at all. They are commonly mapped to be the same as `Mod1` or `Mod2`, and Tk will try to determine how the mappings are set. The remaining modifiers, `Mod3` through `Mod5`, are sometimes mapped to other special keys. In OpenLook environments, for example, the `Paste` function key is also mapped to be the `Mod5` modifier.

The button modifiers, `B1` through `B5`, are most commonly used with the `Motion` event to distinguish different mouse dragging operations.

The `Double` and `Triple` events match on repetitions of an event within a short period of time. These are commonly used with mouse events.*Warning*: the binding for the regular press event will match on the first press of the `Double`. Then the command bound to the `Double` event will match on the second press. Similarly, a `Double` event will match on the first two presses of a `Triple` event. Verify this by trying out the following bindings:

```
bind . <1> {puts stdout 1}
bind . <Double-1> {puts stdout 2}
bind . <Triple-1> {puts stdout 3}
```

Your bindings must take into consideration that more than one binding might match a `Double` or `Triple` event. This effect is compatible with an interface that selects an object with the first click, and then operates on the selected object with a `Double` event. In an editor, character, word, and line selection on a single, double and triple click, respectively, is a good example.*

Table 13–2 summarizes the modifiers.

---

* If you really want to disable this, you can experiment with using `after` to postpone processing of one event. The time constant in the bind implementation of `<Double>` is 500 milliseconds. At the single click event, schedule its action to occur after 600 milliseconds, and verify at that time that the `<Double>` event has not occurred.

Table 13–2 Event modifiers.

`Control`	The control key.
`Shift`	The shift key.
`Lock`	The caps-lock key.
`Meta, M`	Defined to be what ever modifier (`M1` through `M5`) is mapped to the `Meta_L` and `Meta_R` keysyms.
`Alt`	Defined to be the modifier mapped to `Alt_L` and `Alt_R`.
`Mod1, M1`	The first modifier.
`Mod2, M2, Alt`	The second modifier.
`Mod3, M3`	Another modifier.
`Mod4, M4`	Another modifier.
`Mod5, M5`	Another modifier.
`Button1, B1`	The first mouse button (left).
`Button2, B2`	The second mouse button (middle).
`Button3, B3`	The third mouse button (right).
`Button4, B4`	The fourth mouse button.
`Button5, B5`	The fifth mouse button.
`Double`	Matches double press event.
`Triple`	Matches triple press event.
`Any`	Matches any combination of modifiers.

The UNIX *xmodmap* program returns the current mappings from keys to these modifiers. The first column of its output lists the modifier. The rest of each line identifies the keysym(s) and low-level keycodes that are mapped to each modifier. The *xmodmap* program can also be used to change mappings. The following example shows the mappings on my system. Your setup may be different.

Example 13–2 Output from the UNIX *xmodmap* program.

```
xmodmap: up to 3 keys per modifier,
        (keycodes in parentheses):
shift Shift_L (0x6a), Shift_R (0x75)
lock Caps_Lock (0x7e)
control Control_L (0x53)
mod1 Meta_L (0x7f), Meta_R (0x81)
mod2 Mode_switch (0x14)
mod3 Num_Lock (0x69)
mod4 Alt_L (0x1a)
mod5 F13 (0x20), F18 (0x50), F20 (0x68)
```

Modifiers in Tk 3.6

In Tk version 3.6 and earlier, extra modifier keys prevent events from matching. If you want your bindings to be liberal about what modifiers are in effect, you must use the Any modifier. This modifier is a wild card that matches if zero or more modifiers are in effect. You can still use Any in Tk 4.0 scripts, but it has no effect.

Event Sequences

The bind command accepts a sequence of events in a specification, and most commonly this is a sequence of key events:

```
bind . a {puts stdout A}
bind . abc {puts stdout C}
```

With these bindings in effect, both bindings are executed when the user types abc. The binding for a is executed when a is pressed, even though this event is also part of a longer sequence. This is similar to the behavior with Double and Triple event modifiers. For this reason you must be careful when binding sequences. If you have a text or entry widget, you may want to reorder the binding tags so the class bindings come second. Then you can use break in the binding for the prefix to ensure that it does not do anything:

```
bindtags $w [list $w Text [winfo toplevel $w] all]
bind $w <Control-x> break
bind $w <Control-x><Control-s> {Save ; break}
bind $w <Control-x><Control-c> {Quit ; break}
```

The break ensures that the default Text binding that inserts characters does not trigger. This trick is embodied by BindSequence in the next example. If a sequence is detected, then a break binding is added for the prefix. The procedure also supports the *emacs* convention that <Meta-x> is equivalent to <Escape>x. This convention arose because Meta is not that standard across keyboards. The regexp command is used to pick out the detail from the <Meta> event.

Example 13–3 Emacs-like binding convention for Meta and Escape.

```
proc BindSequence { w seq cmd } {
    bind $w $seq $cmd
    # Double-bind Meta-key and Escape-key
    if [regexp {<Meta-(.*)>} $seq match letter] {
        bind $w <Escape><$letter> $cmd
    }
    # Make leading keystroke harmless
    if [regexp {(<.+>)<.+>} $seq match prefix] {
        bind $w $prefix break
    }
}
```

The use of `break` and `continue` in bindings is not supported in Tk 3.6 and earlier. This is because only a single binding tag can match an event. To make a prefix of a sequence harmless, bind a space to it:

```
bind $w $prefix { }
```

This installs a binding for the widget, which supresses the class binding in Tk 3.6. The space is different than a null string, `{}`. Binding to a null string deletes the current binding instead of replacing it with a harmless one.

Event Keywords

Table 13–3 describes the keyword substitutions. Remember that these substitutions occur throughout the command, regardless of other Tcl quoting conventions. Keep your binding commands short, introducing procedures if needed. For the details about various event fields, consult the *Xlib Reference Manual*. The string values for the keyword substitutions are listed after a short description of the keyword. If no string values are listed, the keyword has an integer value like a coordinate or a window ID.

Table 13–3 A summary of the event keywords.

`%%`	Use this to get a single percent sign. All events.
`%#`	The serial number for the event. All events.
`%a`	The above field from the event. `Configure` event.
`%b`	Button number. Events: `ButtonPress` and `ButtonRelease`.
`%c`	The count field. Events: `Expose` and `Map`.
`%d`	The detail field. Values: `NotifyAncestor`, `NotifyNonlinearVirtual`, `NotifyDetailNone`, `NotifyPointer`, `NotifyInferior`, `NotifyPointer-Root`, `NotifyNonlinear`, or `NotifyVirtual`. Events: `Enter`, `Leave`, `FocusIn`, and `FocusOut`.
`%f`	The focus field (0 or 1). Events: `Enter` and `Leave`.
`%h`	The height field. Events: `Configure` and `Expose`.
`%k`	The keycode field. Events: `KeyPress` and `KeyRelease`.
`%m`	The mode field. Values: `NotifyNormal`, `NotifyGrab`, `NotifyUngrab`, or `NotifyWhileGrabbed`. Events: `Enter`, `Leave`, `FocusIn`, and `FocusOut`.
`%o`	The override_redirect field. Events: `Map`, `Reparent`, and `Configure`.
`%p`	The place field. Values: `PlaceOnTop`, `PlaceOnBottom`. `Circulate` event.
`%s`	The state field. A decimal string for events: `ButtonPress`, `ButtonRelease`, `Enter`, `Leave`, `KeyPress`, `KeyRelease`, and `Motion`. Values for the `Visibility` event: `VisibilityUnobscured`, `Visibili-tyPartiallyObscured`, or `VisibilityFullyObscured`.

Table 13–3 A summary of the event keywords. (Continued)

`%t`	The time field. All events.
`%v`	The value_mask field. `Configure` event.
`%w`	The width field. Events: `Configure` and `Expose`.
`%x`	The x coordinate, widget relative. Mouse events.
`%y`	The y coordinate, widget relative. Mouse events.
`%A`	The printing character from the event, or `{}`. Events: `KeyPress` and `KeyRelease`.
`%B`	The border width. `Configure` event.
`%D`	The display field. All events.
`%E`	The send_event field. All events.
`%K`	The keysym from the event. Events: `KeyPress` and `KeyRelease`.
`%N`	The keysym as a decimal number. Events: `KeyPress` and `KeyRelease`.
`%R`	The root window ID. All events.
`%S`	The subwindow ID. All events.
`%T`	The type field. All events.
`%W`	The Tk pathname of the widget receiving the event. All events.
`%X`	The x_root field. Relative to the (virtual) root window. Events: `ButtonPress`, `ButtonRelease`, `KeyPress`, `KeyRelease`, and `Motion`.
`%Y`	The y_root field. Relative to the (virtual) root window. Events: `ButtonPress`, `ButtonRelease`, `KeyPress`, `KeyRelease`, and `Motion`.

CHAPTER 14

Buttons and Menus

Buttons and menus are the primary way that applications expose functions to users. This chapter describes how to create and manipulate buttons and menus.

A button widget is associated with a Tcl command that invokes an action in the application. The checkbutton and radiobutton widgets affect an application indirectly by controlling a Tcl variable. A menu elaborates on this concept by organizing button-like items into related sets, including cascaded menus. The menubutton widget is a special kind of button that displays a menu when you click on it.

Associating a command to a button is often quite simple, as illustrated by the Tk Hello World example:

```
button .hello -command {puts stdout "Hello, World!"}
```

This chapter describes a few useful techniques for setting up the commands in more general cases. If you use variables inside button commands, you have to understand the scoping rules that apply. This is the first topic of the chapter. Once you get scoping figured out, then the other aspects of buttons and menus are quite straight-forward.

Button Commands and Scope Issues

Perhaps the trickiest issue with button commands has to do with variable scoping. A button command is executed at the global scope, which is outside of any procedure. If you create a button while inside a procedure, then the button command executes in a different scope later. The commands used in event bindings also execute later at the global scope.

I think of this as the "now" (i.e., button definition) and "later" (i.e., button use) scope problem. For example, you may want to use the values of some variables when you define a button command, but use the value of other variables when the button command is used. When these two contexts are mixed, it can be confusing. The next example illustrates the problem. The button's command involves two variables: `x` and `val`. The global variable `x` is needed later, when the button's command executes. The local variable `val` is needed now, in order to define the command. This mixture makes things awkward:

Example 14–1 A troublesome button command.

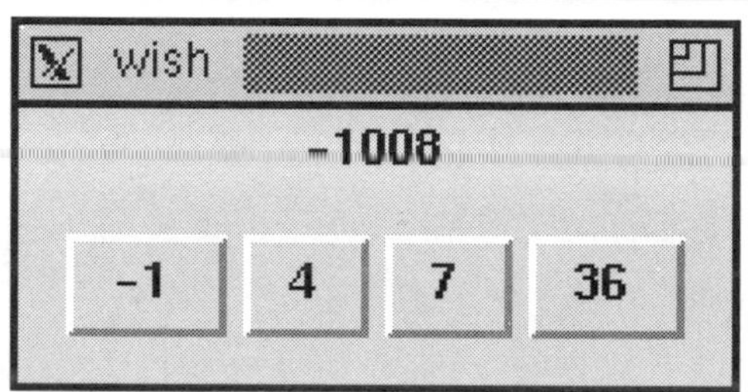


```
proc Trouble {args} {
    set b 0
    # Display the value of x, a global variable
    label .label -textvariable x
    set f [frame .buttons -borderwidth 10]
    # Create buttons that multiply x by their value
    foreach val $args {
        button $f.$b -text $val \
            -command "set x \[expr \$x * $val\]"
        pack $f.$b -side left
        incr b
    }
    pack .label $f
}
set x 1
Trouble -1 4 7 36
```

The example uses a label widget to display the current value of `x`. The `textvariable` attribute is used so that the label displays the current value of the variable, which is always a global variable. It is not necessary to have a `global` command inside `Trouble` because the value of `x` is not used there. The button's command is executed later at the global scope.

The definition of the button's command is ugly, though. The value of the loop variable `val` is needed when the button is defined, but the rest of the substitutions need to be deferred until later. The variable substitution of `$x` and the command substitution of `expr` are suppressed by quoting with backslashes:

```
set x \[expr \$x * $val\]
```

In contrast, the following command assigns a constant expression to x each time the button is clicked, and it depends on the current value of x, which is not defined the first time through the loop. Clearly, this is incorrect:

```
button $f.$b -text $val \
    -command "set x [expr $x * $val]"
```

Another incorrect approach is to quote the whole command with braces. This defers too much, preventing the value of val from being used at the correct time.

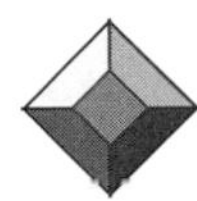

The general technique for dealing with these sorts of scoping problems is to introduce Tcl procedures for use as the button commands. The troublesome example given above can be cleaned up by introducing a little procedure to encapsulate the expression:

Example 14–2 Fixing the troublesome situation.

```
proc LessTrouble { args } {
    set b 0
    label .label -textvariable x
    set f [frame .buttons -borderwidth 10]
    foreach val $args {
        button $f.$b -text $val \
            -command "UpdateX $val"
        pack $f.$b -side left
        incr b
    }
    pack .label $f
}
proc UpdateX { val } {
    global x
    set x [expr $x * $val]
}
set x 1
LessTrouble -1 4 7 36
```

It may seem just like extra work to introduce the helper procedure, UpdateX. However, it makes the code clearer in two ways. First, you do not have to struggle with backslashes to get the button command defined correctly. Second, the code is much clearer about the function of the button. Its job is to update the global variable x.

Double quotes are used in the button command to allow $val to be substituted. Whenever you use quotes like this, you have to be aware of the possible values for the substitutions. If you are not careful, the command you create may not be parsed correctly. The safest way to generate the command is with the list procedure:

```
button $f.$b -text $val -command [list UpdateX $val]
```

Using list ensures that the command is a list of two elements, UpdateX and the value of val. This is important because UpdateX takes only a single argument. If val contained white space then the resulting command would be parsed into more words than you expected. Of course, in this case we plan to always call `LessTrouble` with a set of numbers, which do not contain white space.

The next example provides a more straight-forward application of procedures for button commands. In this case the advantage of the procedure `MaxLineLength` is that it creates a scope for the local variables used during the button action. This ensures that the local variables do not accidentally conflict with global variables used elsewhere in the program. There is also the standard advantage of a procedure, which is that you may find another use for the action in another part of your program:

Example 14–3 A button associated with a Tcl procedure.

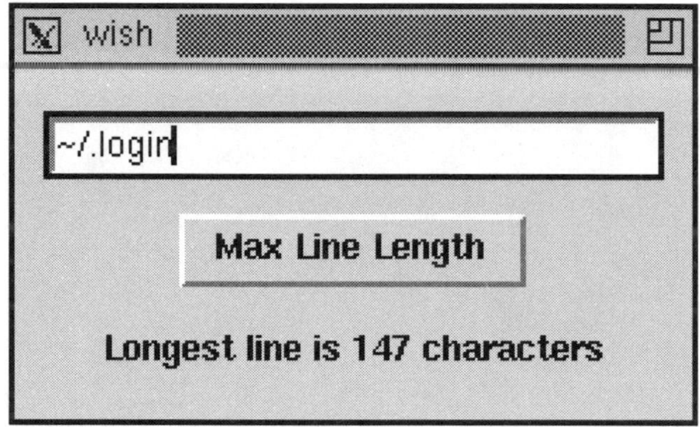


```
proc MaxLineLength { file } {
    set max 0
    if [catch {open $file} in] {
        return $in
    }
    foreach line [split [read $in] \n] {
        set len [string length $line]
        if {$len > $max} {
            set max $len
        }
    }
    return "Longest line is $max characters"
}
# Create an entry to accept the file name,
# a label to display the result
# and a button to invoke the action
. config -borderwidth 10
entry .e -width 30 -bg white -relief sunken
button .doit -text "Max Line Length" \
    -command {.label config -text [MaxLineLength [.e get]]}
label .label -text "Enter file name"
pack .e .doit .label -side top -pady 5
```

The example is centered around the MaxLineLength procedure. This opens a file and loops over the lines finding the longest one. The file open is protected with catch in case the user enters a bogus file name. In that case, the procedure returns the error message from open. Otherwise, the procedure returns a message about the longest line in the file. The local variables in, max, and len are hidden inside the scope of the procedure.

The user interface has three widgets, an entry for user input, the button, and a label to display the result. These are packed into a vertical stack, and the main window is given a border. Obviously this simple interface can be improved in several ways. There is no Quit button, for example.

All the action happens in the button command:

```
.label config -text [MaxLineLength [.e get]]
```

Braces are used when defining the button command so that the command substitutions all happen when the button is clicked. The value of the entry widget is obtained with .e get. This value is passed into MaxLineLength, and the result is configured as the text for the label. This command is still a little complex for a button command. For example, suppose you wanted to invoke the same command when the user pressed <Return> in the entry. You would end up repeating this command in the entry binding. It might be better to introduce a one-line procedure to capture this action so it is easy to bind the action to more than one user action. Here is how that might look:

```
proc Doit {} {
    .label config -text [MaxLineLength [.e get]]
}
button .doit -text "Max Line Length" -command Doit
bind .e <Return> Doit
```

Chapter 13 describes the bind command in detail, Chapter 16 describes the label widget, and Chapter 17 describes the entry widget.

Buttons Associated with Tcl Variables

The checkbutton and radiobutton widgets are associated with a global Tcl variable. When one of these buttons is clicked, a value is assigned to the Tcl variable. In addition, if the variable is assigned a value elsewhere in the program, the appearance of the checkbutton or radiobutton is updated to reflect the new value. A set of radiobuttons all share the same global variable. The set represents a choice among mutually exclusive options. In contrast, each checkbutton has its own global variable.

The ShowChoices example uses a set of radiobuttons to display a set of mutually exclusive choices in a user interface. The ShowBooleans example uses checkbutton widgets:

Example 14–4 Radiobuttons and checkbuttons.

```
proc ShowChoices { parent varname args } {
    set f [frame $parent.choices -borderwidth 5]
    set b 0
    foreach item $args {
        radiobutton $f.$b -variable $varname \
            -text $item -value $item
        pack $f.$b -side left
        incr b
    }
    pack $f -side top
}
proc ShowBooleans { parent args } {
    set f [frame $parent.choices -borderwidth 5]
    set b 0
    foreach item $args {
        checkbutton $f.$b -text $item -variable $item
        pack $f.$b -side left
        incr b
    }
    pack $f -side top
}
set choice kiwi
ShowChoices {} choice apple orange peach kiwi strawberry
set Bold 1 ; set Italic 1
ShowBooleans {} Bold Italic Underline
```

The `ShowChoices` procedure takes as arguments the parent frame, the name of a variable, and a set of possible values for that variable. If the parent frame is null, `{}`, then the interface is packed into the main window. `ShowChoices` creates a radiobutton for each value, and it puts the value into the text of the button. It also has to specify the value to assign to the variable when the button is clicked because the default value associated with a radiobutton is the empty string. Another way to define the radiobutton and get the correct value would be like this:

The `ShowBooleans` procedure is similar to `ShowChoices`. It takes a set of variable names as arguments, and it creates a checkbutton for each variable. The default values for the variable associated with a checkbutton are zero and one, which is fine for this example. If you need particular values you can specify them with the `-onvalue` and `-offvalue` options.

Radio and check buttons can have commands associated with them, just like ordinary buttons. The command is invoked after the associated Tcl variable has been updated. Remember that the Tcl variable associated with the button is defined in the global scope. For example, you could log the changes to variables as shown in the next example.

Example 14–5 A command on a radiobutton or checkbutton.

```
proc PrintByName { varname } {
    upvar #0 $varname var
    puts stdout "$varname = $var"
}
checkbutton $f.$b -text $item -variable $item \
    -command [list PrintByName $item]
radiobutton $f.$b -variable $varname \
    -text $item -value $item \
    -command [list PrintByName $varname]
```

Button Attributes

Table 14–1 lists the attributes for the button, checkbutton, menubutton, and radiobutton widgets. Unless otherwise indicated, the attributes apply to all of these widget types. Chapters 23, 24, and 25 discuss many of these attributes in more detail.

The table uses the X resource name, which has capitals at internal word boundaries. In Tcl commands the attributes are specified with a dash and all lowercase. Compare:

```
option add *Menubutton.activeBackground: red
.mb configure -activebackground red
```

The first command defines a resource database entry that covers all menubuttons and gives them a red active background. This only affects menubuttons created after the database entry is added. The second command changes an existing menubutton (`.mb`) to have a red active background. Note the difference in capitalization of `background` in the two commands. Chapter 15 explains how to use resource specifications for attributes.

Table 14–1 Resource names of attributes for all button widgets.

`activeBackground`	Background color when the mouse is over the button.
`activeForeground`	Text color when the mouse is over the button.
`anchor`	Anchor point for positioning the text.
`background`	The normal background color.
`bitmap`	A bitmap to display instead of text.
`borderWidth`	Width of the border around the button.

Table 14–1 Resource names of attributes for all button widgets. (Continued)

`command`	Tcl command to invoke when button is clicked.
`cursor`	Cursor to display when mouse is over the widget.
`disabledForeground`	Foreground (text) color when button is disabled.
`font`	Font for the text.
`foreground`	Foreground (text) color. (Also `fg`).
`height`	Height, in lines for text, or screen units for images.
`highlightColor`	Color for input focus highlight border.
`highlightThickness`	Width of highlight border.
`image`	Image to display instead of text or bitmap.
`indicatorOn`	Boolean that controls if the indicator is displayed. `checkbutton`, `menubutton`, or `radiobutton`.
`justify`	Text justification: `center`, `left`, or `right`.
`menu`	Menu posted when `menubutton` is clicked.
`offValue`	Value for Tcl variable when `checkbutton` is not selected.
`onValue`	Value for Tcl variable when `checkbutton` is selected.
`padX`	Extra space to the left and right of the button text.
`padY`	Extra space above and below the button text.
`relief`	3D relief: `flat`, `sunken`, `raised`, `groove`, or `ridge`.
`selectColor`	Color for selector. `checkbutton` or `radiobutton`.
`selectImage`	Alternate graphic image for selector. `checkbutton` or `radiobutton`.
`state`	Enabled (`normal`) or deactivated (`disabled`).
`text`	Text to display in the button.
`textVariable`	Tcl variable that has the value of the text.
`underline`	Index of text character to underline.
`value`	Value for Tcl variable when `radiobutton` is selected.
`variable`	Tcl variable associated with the button. `checkbutton` or `radiobutton`.
`width`	Width, in characters for text, or screen units for image.
`wrapLength`	Maximum character length before text is wrapped, *in screen units*.

Button Operations

Table 14–2 summarizes the operations on button widgets. In the table `$w` is a button, checkbutton, radiobutton, or menubutton, except when noted. For the most part these operations are used by the script libraries that implement the bindings for buttons. The `cget` and `configure` operations are the most commonly used.

Table 14–2 Button operations.

`$w cget` *option*	Return the value of the specified attribute.
`$w configure ?`*option*`?` `?`*value*`? ...`	Query or manipulate the configuration information for the widget.
`$w deselect`	Deselect the `radiobutton` or `checkbutton`. Set the `radiobutton` variable to the null string. Set the `checkbutton` variable to the off value.
`$w flash`	Redisplay the button several times in alternate colors.
`$w invoke`	Invoke the command associated with the button.
`$w select`	Select the `radiobutton` or `checkbutton`, setting the associated variable appropriately.

Menus and Menubuttons

A menu presents a set of button-like *menu entries* to users. A menu entry is not a full fledged Tk widget. Instead, you create a menu widget and then add entries to the menu as shown in the following examples. There are several kinds of menu entries, including command entries, check entries, and radio entries. These all behave much like the button, checkbutton, and radiobutton widgets. Separator entries are used to visually set apart entries. Cascade entries are used to post sub-menus. Tear-off entries are used to detach a menu from its menu button so that it becomes a new top-level window.

A menubutton is a special kind of button that posts (i.e., displays) a menu when you press it. If you click on a menubutton, then the menu is posted and remains posted until you click on a menu entry to select it, or click outside the menu to dismiss it. If you press and hold the menubutton, then the menu is unposted when you release the mouse. If you release the mouse over the menu it selects the menu entry that was under the mouse.

You can have a command associated with a menubutton, too. The command is invoked *before* the menu is posted, which means you can compute the menu contents when the user presses the menubutton.

Our first menu example creates a sampler of the different entry types:

Example 14–6 A menu sampler.

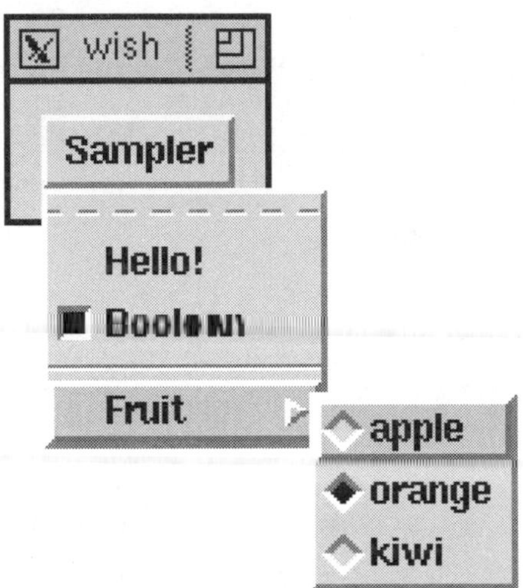


```
menubutton .mb -text Sampler -menu .mb.menu
pack .mb -padx 10 -pady 10
set m [menu .mb.menu -tearoff 1]
$m add command -label Hello! -command {puts "Hello, World!"}
$m add check -label Boolean -variable foo \
   -command {puts "foo = $foo"}
$m add separator
$m add cascade -label Fruit -menu $m.sub1
set m2 [menu $m.sub1 -tearoff 0]
$m2 add radio -label apple -variable fruit
$m2 add radio -label orange -variable fruit
$m2 add radio -label kiwi -variable fruit
```

The example creates a menubutton and two menus. The main menu `.mb.menu` is a child of the menubutton `.mb`. This relationship is necessary so the menu displays correctly when the menubutton is selected. Similarly, the cascaded submenu `.mb.menu.sub1` is a child of the main menu. The first menu entry is represented by the dashed line. This is a tear-off entry that, when selected, makes a copy of the menu in a new toplevel window. This is useful if the menu operations are invoked frequently. The `-tearoff 0` argument is used when creating the submenu to eliminate its tear-off entry.

The command, radio, and check entries are similar to the corresponding button types. The configuration options for menu entries are similar to those for buttons. The main difference is that the text string in the menu entry is defined with the `-label` option, not `-text`. Table 14–6 gives the complete set of options for menu entries.

The cascade menu entry is associated with another menu. It is distinguished by the small right arrow in the entry. When you select the entry the submenu is posted. It is possible to have several levels of cascaded menus. There is no limit to the number of levels, except that your users will complain if you nest too many menus.

Pop-up Menus

A pop-up menu is not associated with a menubutton. Instead, it is posted in response to a keystroke or other event in the application. The `tk_popup` command posts a pop-up menu:

```
tk_popup menu x y ?entry?
```

The last argument specifies the entry to activate when the menu is posted. It is an optional parameter that defaults to 1, which avoids the tear-off entry in position zero. The menu is posted at the specified X and Y coordinates in its parent widget.

Option Menus

An option menu represents a choice with a set of radio entries, and it displays the current choice in the text of the menubutton. The `tk_optionMenu` command creates a menubutton and a menu full of radio entries:

```
tk_optionMenu w varname firstValue ?value value ...?
```

The first argument is the pathname of the menubutton to create. The second is the variable name. The third is the initial value for the variable, and the rest are the other choices for the value. The menubutton displays the current choice and a small symbol, the indicator, to indicate it is a choice menu.

Keyboard Traversal

The default bindings for menus allow for keyboard selection of menu entries. The selection process is started by pressing `<Alt-x>` where *x* is the distinguishing letter for a menubutton. The `underline` attribute of a menubutton is used to highlight the appropriate letter. The `underline` value is a number that specifies a character position, and the count starts at zero. For example, a `File` menu with a highlighted `F` is created like this:

```
menubutton .menubar.file -text File -underline 0 \
    -menu .menubar.file.m
```

When the user types `<Alt-f>` over the main window, the menu is posted. The case of the highlighted letter is not important.

After a menu is posted the arrow keys change the selected entry. The `<Up>` and `<Down>` keys move within a menu, and the `<Left>` and `<Right>` keys move between adjacent menus. The bindings assume that you create your menus from left to right.

If any of the menu entries have a letter highlighted with the `-underline` option, typing that letter invokes that menu entry. For example, an `Export` entry that is invoked by typing `x` can be created like this:

```
.menubar.file.m add command -label Export -underline 1 \
    -command File_Export
```

The <space> and <Return> keys invoke the menu entry that is currently selected. The <Escape> key aborts the menu selection and removes the menu.

Manipulating Menus and Menu Entries

There are a number of operations that apply to menu entries. We have already introduced the `add` operation. The `entryconfigure` operation is similar to the `configure` operation. It accepts the same attribute-value pairs used when the menu entry was added. The `delete` operation removes a range of menu entries. The rest of the operations are used by the library scripts that implement the standard bindings for menus. Table 14–3 summarizes the complete set of menu operations. In the table, `$w` is a menu widget:

Table 14–3 Menu operations.

`$w activate` *index*	Highlight the specified entry.
`$w add` *type ?option value? ...*	Add a new menu entry of the specified type with the given values for various attributes.
`$w cget` *option*	Return the value for the configuration *option*.
`$w configure` *?option? ?value? ...*	Return the configuration information for the menu.
`$w delete` *i1 ?i2?*	Delete the menu entries from index *i1* to *i2*.
`$w entrycget` *index option*	Return the value of *option* for the specified entry.
`$w entryconfigure` *index ?option? ?value? ...*	Query or modify the configuration information for the specified menu entry.
`$w index` *index*	Return the numerical value of *index*.
`$w invoke` *index*	Invoke the command associated with the entry.
`$w post` *x y*	Display the menu at the specified coordinates.
`$w type` *index*	Return the type of the entry at *index*.
`$w unpost`	Unmap the menu.
`$w ypostion` *index*	Return the y coordinate of the top of the entry.

A menu entry is referred to by an *index*. The index can be numerical, counting from zero, or symbolic. Table 14–4 summarizes the index formats. One of the most useful indices is a pattern that matches the `label` in the menu entry. The pattern matching is done with the rules of `string match`. Using a pattern eliminates the need to keep track of the numerical indices.

Table 14–4 Menu entry index keywords

`index`	A numerical index counting from zero.
`active`	The activated entry, either because it is under the mouse or has been activated by keyboard traversal.
`last`	The last menu entry.
`none`	No entry at all.
`@ycoord`	The entry under the given Y coordinate. Use `@%y` in bindings.
`pattern`	A `string match` pattern to match the label of a menu entry.

Menu Attributes

A menu has a few global attributes, and then each menu entry has many button-like attributes that describe its appearance and behavior. Table 14–5 specifies the attributes that apply globally to the menu, unless overridden by a per-entry attribute. The table uses the X resource names, which may have a capital at interior word boundaries. In Tcl commands use all lowercase and a leading dash:

Table 14–5 Menu attribute resource names.

`activeBackground`	Background color when the mouse is over a menu entry.
`activeForeground`	Text color when the mouse is over a menu entry.
`activeBorderWidth`	Width of the raised border around active entries.
`background`	The normal background color for menu entries.
`borderWidth`	Width of the border around all the menu entries.
`cursor`	Cursor to display when mouse is over the menu.
`disabledForeground`	Foreground (text) color when menu entries are disabled.
`font`	Default font for the text.
`foreground`	Foreground color. (Also `fg`).
`postCommand`	Tcl command to run just before the menu is posted.
`selectColor`	Color for selector in check and radio type entries.
`tearOff`	True if menu should contain a tear off entry.

Table 14–6 describes the attributes for menu entries, as you would use them in a Tcl command (i.e., all lowercase with a leading dash.) The attributes for menu entries are not supported directly by the X resource database. However, Example 15–6 on page 169 describes how you can use the resource database for menu entries.

Table 14–6 Attributes for menu entries.

`-activebackground`	Background color when the mouse is over the entry.
`-activeforeground`	Foreground (text) color with mouse is over the entry.
`-accelerator`	Text to display as a reminder about keystroke binding.
`-background`	The normal background color.
`-bitmap`	A bitmap to display instead of text.
`-command`	Tcl command to invoke when entry is invoked.
`font`	Default font for the text
`-foreground`	Foreground color. (Also `fg`).
`-image`	Image to display instead of text or bitmap.
`-label`	Text to display in the menu entry.
`-justify`	Text justification: `center`, `left`, or `right`.
`-menu`	Menu posted when `cascade` entry is invoked.
`-offvalue`	Variable value when `check` entry is not selected.
`-onvalue`	Value for Tcl variable when `check` entry is selected.
`-selectcolor`	Color for selector. `check` and `radio` entries.
`-state`	The state: `normal`, `active`, or `disabled`
`-underline`	Index of text character to underline.
`-value`	Value for Tcl variable when `radiobutton` entry is selected.
`-variable`	Tcl variable associated with the `check` or `radio` entry.

A Menu by Name Package

If your application supports extensible or user-defined menus, then it can be tedious to expose all the details of the Tk menus. The examples in this section create a little package that lets users refer to menus and entries by name. In addition, the package supports keystroke accelerators for menus.

The `MenuSetup` procedure initializes the package. It creates a frame to hold the set of menu buttons, and it initializes some state variables: the frame for the menubuttons and a counter used to generate widget pathnames. All the global state for the package is kept in the array called `Menu`.

The `Menu` procedure creates a menubutton and a menu. It records the association between the text label of the menubutton and the menu that was created for it. This mapping is used throughout the rest of the package so that the client of the package can refer to the menu by its label (e.g., `File`) as opposed to the internal Tk pathname, (e.g., `.top.menubar.file.menu`).

Example 14–7 A simple menu-by-name package.

```
proc MenuSetup { menubar } {
    global Menu
    frame $menubar
    pack $menubar -side top -fill x
    set Menu(menubar) $menubar
    set Menu(uid) 0
}
proc Menu { label } {
    global Menu
    if [info exists Menu(menu,$label)] {
        error "Menu $label already defined"
    }
    # Create the menubutton and its menu
    set name $Menu(menubar).mb$Menu(uid)
    set menuName $name.menu
    incr Menu(uid)
    set mb [menubutton $name -text $label -menu $menuName]
    pack $mb -side left
    set menu [menu $menuName -tearoff 1]
    # Remember the name to menu mapping
    set Menu(menu,$label) $menu
}
```

The procedures `MenuCommand`, `MenuCheck`, `MenuRadio`, and `MenuSeparator` are simple wrappers around the basic menu commands. The only trick is that they use the `Menu` variable to map from the menu label to the Tk widget name. If the user specifies a bogus menu name, the undefined variable error is caught and a more informative error is raised instead.

Example 14–8 Adding menu entries.

```
proc MenuCommand { menuName label command } {
    global Menu
    if [catch {set Menu(menu,$menuName)} menu] {
        error "No such menu: $menuName"
    }
    $menu add command -label $label -command $command
}

proc MenuCheck { menuName label var { command {} } } {
    global Menu
    if [catch {set Menu(menu,$menuName)} menu] {
        error "No such menu: $menuName"
    }
    $menu add check -label $label -command $command \
        -variable $var
}

proc MenuRadio { menuName label var {val {}} {command {}} } {
    global Menu
    if [catch {set Menu(menu,$menuName)} menu] {
```

```
        error "No such menu: $menuName"
    }
    if {[string length $val] == 0} {
        set val $label
    }
    $menu add radio -label $label -command $command \
        -value $val -variable $var
}

proc MenuSeparator { menuName } {
    global Menu
    if [catch {set Menu(menu,$menuName)} menu] {
        error "No such menu: $menuName"
    }
    $menu add separator
}
```

Creating a cascaded menu also requires saving the mapping between the label in the cascade entry and the Tk pathname for the submenu. This package imposes a restriction that different menus, including submenus, cannot have the same label.

Example 14–9 A wrapper for cascade entries.

```
proc MenuCascade { menuName label } {
    global Menu
    if [catch {set Menu(menu,$menuName)} menu] {
        error "No such menu: $menuName"
    }
    if [info exists Menu(menu,$label)] {
        error "Menu $label already defined"
    }
    set sub $menu.sub$Menu(uid)
    incr Menu(uid)
    menu $sub -tearoff 0
    $menu add cascade -label $label -menu $sub
    set Menu(menu,$label) $sub
}
```

Creating the sampler menu with this package looks like this:

Example 14–10 Using the menu-by-name package.

```
MenuSetup
Menu Sampler
MenuCommand Sampler Hello! {puts "Hello, World!"}
MenuCheck Sampler Boolean foo {puts "foo = $foo"}
MenuSeparator Sampler
MenuCascade Sampler Fruit
MenuRadio Fruit apple fruit
MenuRadio Fruit orange fruit
MenuRadio Fruit kiwi fruit
```

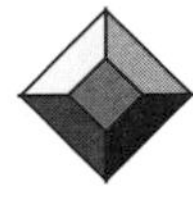

The final touch on the menu package is to support accelerators in a consistent way. A menu entry can display another column of information that is assumed to be a keystroke identifier to remind users of a binding that also invokes the menu entry. However, there is no guarantee that this string is correct, or that if the user changes the binding that the menu will be updated. The `MenuBind` procedure takes care of this:

Example 14–11 Keeping the accelerator display up-to-date.

```
proc MenuBind { what sequence menuName label } {
    global Menu
    if [catch {set Menu(menu,$menuName)} menu] {
        error "No such menu: $menuName"
    }
    if [catch {$menu index $label} index] {
        error "$label not in menu $menuName"
    }
    set command [$menu entrycget $index -command]
    bind $what $sequence $command
    $menu entryconfigure $index -accelerator $sequence
}
```

The `MenuBind` command uses the `index` operation to find out what menu entry has the given label. It updates the display of the entry using the `entryconfigure` operation, and it creates a binding using the `bind` command. This approach has the advantage of keeping the keystroke command consistent with the menu command, as well as updating the display. To try `MenuBind`, add an empty frame to the sampler example, and bind a keystroke to it and one of the menu commands, like this:

```
frame .body -width 100 -height 50
pack .body ; focus .body
MenuBind .body <space> Sampler Hello!
```

CHAPTER 15

Using X Resources

This chapter describes the use of the X resource database, and how users can define buttons and menus via resource specifications. This chapter describes the `option` command.

X supports a resource database which lets users and site administrators customize applications. The database holds specifications of widget attributes such as fonts and colors. You can control all attributes of the Tk widgets through the resource database. It can also be used as a more general database of application-specific parameter settings.

Because a Tk application can use Tcl for customization, it might not seem necessary to use the X resource mechanism. The X resource mechanism is, however, a useful tool for your Tk application. It lets users and site administrators customize applications without modifying the code.

An Introduction to X Resources

When a Tk widget is created, its attributes are set by one of three sources. It is important to note that command line specifications have priority over resource database specifications:

- The most evident source of attributes is the command line switches in the tcl command, such as the `-text quit` attribute specification for a button.
- If an attribute is not specified on the command line, then the X resource database is queried as described later.
- If there is nothing in the resource database, then a hard coded value from the widget implementation is used.

The resource database consists of a set of keys and values. Unlike many databases, however, the keys are patterns that are matched against the names of widgets and attributes. This makes it possible to specify attribute values for a large number of widgets with just a few database entries. In addition, the resource database can be shared by many applications, so users and administrators can define common attributes for their whole set of applications.

The resource database is maintained in main memory by the Tk toolkit. It is initialized from the `RESOURCE_MANAGER` property on the root window, or the `.Xdefaults` file in your home directory. Additional files can be explicitly loaded with the `option readfile` command. An application can also add individual database entries with the `option add` Tcl command. This is different than the Xt toolkit, which loads specifications from as many as five different files to allow per-user, per-site, per-application, per-machine, and per-user-per-application specifications. You can achieve the same effect in Tk, but you must do it yourself. Example 28–1 on page 330 gives a partial solution.

The pattern language for the keys is related to the naming convention for tk widgets. Recall that a widget name reflects its position in the hierarchy of windows. You can think of the resource names as extending the hierarchy one more level at the bottom to account for all the attributes of each individual widget. There is also a new level of the hierarchy at the top to specify the application by name. For example, the database could contain an entry like the following in order to define a font for the `quit` button in a frame called `.buttons`:

```
Tk.buttons.quit.font: fixed
```

The leading `Tk.` matches the default class name for `wish` applications. You could also specify a more specific application name, such as `exmh`, or an asterisk to match any application:

```
*buttons.quit.font: fixed
```

Resource keys can also specify *classes* of widgets and attributes as opposed to individual instances. The `quit` button, for example, is an instance of the `Button` class. Class names for widgets are the same as the tcl command used to create them, except for a leading capital. A class-oriented specification that would set the font for all buttons in the `.buttons` frame would be:

```
Tk.buttons.Button.font: fixed
```

Patterns let you replace one or more components of the resource name with an asterisk (`*`). For example, to set the font for all the widgets packed into the `.buttons` frame, you could use the resource name `*buttons*font`. Or, you could specify the font for all buttons with the pattern `*Button.font`. In these examples we have replaced the leading `Tk` with an asterisk as well. It is the ability to collapse several layers of the hierarchical name with a single asterisk that makes it easy to specify attributes for many widgets with just a few database entries.

The tables in this book list attributes by their resource name. The resource names use a capital letter at the internal word boundaries. For example, if the command line switch is `-offvalue`, then the corresponding resource name is `offValue`. There are also class names for attributes, which are distinguished with a leading capital (e.g., `OffValue`).

Warning: Order is Important!

The matching between a widget name and the patterns in the database can be ambiguous. It is possible that multiple patterns can match the same widget. The way this is resolved in Tk is by the ordering of database entries, with later entries taking precedence. (This is different from the Xt toolkit, in which longer matching patterns have precedence, and instance specifications have priority over class specifications.) Suppose the database contained just two entries, in this order:

```
*Text*foreground: blue
*foreground: red
```

Despite the more specific `*Text*foreground` entry, all widgets will have a red foreground, even `text` widgets. For this reason you should list your most general patterns early in your resource files, and give the more specific patterns later.

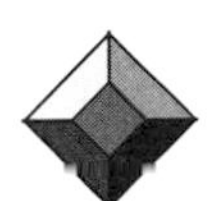

Loading Option Database Files

The `option` command manipulates the resource database. The first form of the command loads a file containing database entries:

```
option readfile filename ?priority?
```

The *priority* distinguishes different sources of resource information and gives them different priorities. Priority levels are numeric, from 0 to 100. However, symbolic names are defined for standard priorities. From lowest to highest, the standard priorities are: `widgetDefault` (20), `startupFile` (40), `userDefault` (60), and `interactive` (80). These names can be abbreviated. The default priority is `interactive`.

Example 15–1 Reading an option database file.

```
if [file exists $appdefaults] {
    if [catch {option readfile $appdefaults startup} err] {
        puts stderr "error in $appdefaults: $err"
    }
}
```

The format of the entries in the file is:

```
key: value
```

The key has the pattern format previously described. The value can be anything, and there is no need to group multi-word values with any quoting characters. In fact, quotes will be picked up as part of the value.

Comment lines are introduced by the exclamation mark (`!`).

Example 15–2 A file containing resource specifications.

```
!
! Grey color set
! Slightly modified from Ron Frederick's nv grey family
!
*background: #efefef
*foreground: black
*activeBackground: white
*activeForeground: black
*selectColor: black
*selectBackground: #bfdfff
*troughColor: #dfdfdf
*disabledforeground: #7f7f7f
```

The example resource file specifies an alternate color scheme for the Tk widget set that is based on a family of gray levels. Color highlighting shows up well against this backdrop. These colors are applied generically to all the widgets. The hexadecimal values for the colors specify two digits (eight bits) each for red, green, and blue. Chapter 24 describes the use of color in detail.

Adding Individual Database Entries

You can enter individual database entries with the `option add` Tcl command. This is appropriate to handle special cases, or if you do not want to manage a separate per-application resource specification file. The command syntax is:

```
option add pattern value ?priority?
```

The *priority* is the same as that used with `option readfile`. The *pattern* and *value* are the same as in the file entries, except that the key does not have a trailing colon when specified in an `option add` command. Some of the specifications from the last example could be added as follows:

```
option add *foreground black
option add *selectBackground #bfdfff
```

You can clear the option database:

```
option clear
```

However, the database is initialized from your `~/.Xdefaults` file, or the `RESOURCE_MANAGER` property on the root window, the next time the database is accessed.

Accessing the Database

Often it is sufficient to just set up the database and let the widget implementations use the values. However, it is also possible to record application-specific information in the database. To fetch a resource value, use `option get`:

```
option get window name class
```

The *`window`* is a Tk widget pathname. The *`name`* is a resource name. In this case, it is not a pattern or a full name. Instead, it is the resource name as specified in the tables in this book. Similarly, the *`class`* is a simple class name. It is possible to specify a null name or class. If there is no matching database entry, `option get` returns the empty string.

User-Defined Buttons

In a big application, suppose we want users to be able to define a set of their own buttons for frequently executed commands. Or, as we will describe later, perhaps users can augment the application with their own Tcl code. The following scheme, which is based on an idea from John LoVerso, lets them define buttons to invoke their own code or their favorite commands.

The user interface creates a special frame to hold the user-defined buttons, and places it appropriately. Assume the frame is created like this:

```
frame .user -class User
```

The class specification for the frame means that we can name resources for the widgets inside the frame relative to `*User`. Users specify the buttons that go in the frame via a personal file containing X resource specifications.

The first problem is that there is no means to enumerate the database, so we must create a resource that lists the names of the user defined buttons. We use the name `buttonlist`, and make an entry for `*User.buttonlist` that specifies which buttons are being defined. It is possible to use artificial resource names (e.g., `buttonlist`), but they must be relative to an existing Tk widget.

Example 15–3 Using resources to specify user-defined buttons.

```
*User.buttonlist: save search justify quit
*User.save.text: Save
*User.save.command: File_Save
*User.search.text: Search
*User.search.command: Edit_Search
*User.justify.text: Justify
*User.justify.command: Edit_Justify
*user.quit.text: Quit
*User.quit.command: File_Quit
*User.quit.background: red
```

In this example, we have listed four buttons and specified some of the attributes for each, most importantly the `text` and `command` attributes. We are assuming, of course, that the application manual publishes a set of commands that users can invoke safely. In this simple example the commands are all one word, but there is no problem with multi-word commands. There is no interpretation done of the value, so it can include references to Tcl variables and nested command calls. The following code uses these resource specifications to define the buttons.

Example 15–4 `ButtonResources` defines buttons based on resources.

```
proc ButtonResources { f class } {
    frame $f -class $class -borderwidth 2
    pack $f -side top -fill x
    foreach b [option get $f buttonlist {}] {
        if [catch {button $f.$b}] {
            button $f.$b -font fixed
        }
        pack $f.$b -side right
    }
}
```

The `catch` phrase is introduced to handle a common problem with fonts and widget creation. If the user's resources specify a bogus or missing font, then the widget creation command will fail. The `catch` phrase guards against this case by falling back to the `fixed` font, which is guaranteed to exist by the X server.

The following example assumes the resource specifications from Example 15–2 are in the file `button.resources`. It creates the user-defined buttons in the `.users` frame.

Example 15–5 Using `ButtonResources`.

```
option readfile button.resources
ButtonResources .user User
```

User Defined Menus

User-defined menus can be set up with a similar scheme. However, it is more complex because there are no resources for specific menu entries. We must use more artificial resources to emulate this. We use `menulist` to name the set of menus. Then, for each of these, we define an `entrylist` resource. Finally, for each entry we define a few more resources. The name of the entry has to be combined with some type information, which leads to the following convention:

- `l_`*`entry`* is the label for the entry.
- `t_`*`entry`* is the type of the entry.
- `c_`*`entry`* is the command associated with the entry.
- `v_`*`entry`* is the variable associated with the entry.
- `m_`*`entry`* is the menu associated with the entry.

Example 15–6 Specifying menu entries via resources.

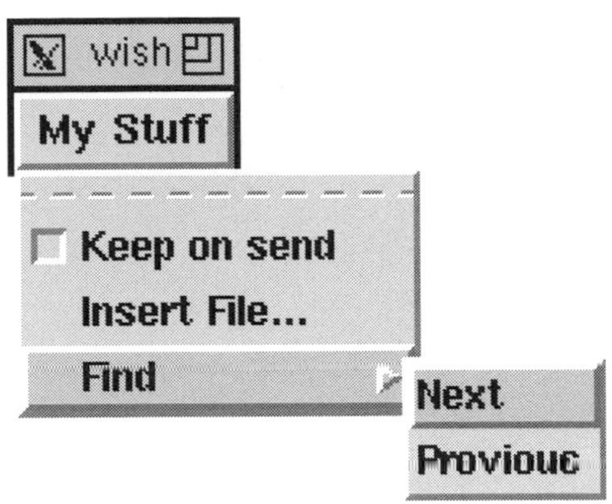


```
*User.menulist: stuff
*User.stuff.text: My stuff
*User.stuff.m.entrylist: keep insert find
*User.stuff.m.l_keep: Keep on send
*User.stuff.m.t_keep: check
*User.stuff.m.v_keep: checkvar
*User.stuff.m.l_insert: Insert File...
*User.stuff.m.c_insert: InsertFileDialog
*User.stuff.m.l_find: Find
*User.stuff.m.t_find: cascade
*User.stuff.m.m_find: find
*User.stuff.m.find.entrylist: next prev
*User.stuff.m.find.tearoff: 0
*User.stuff.m.find.l_next: Next
*User.stuff.m.find.c_next: Find_Next
*User.stuff.m.find.l_prev: Previous
*User.stuff.m.find.c_prev: Find_Previous
```

In the example, `.user.stuff` is a Tk menubutton. It has a menu as its child, `.user.stuff.m`, where the menu is `.m` is set by convention. You will see this later in the code for `MenuResources`. The `entrylist` for the menu is similar in spirit to the `buttonlist` resource. For each entry, however, we have to be a little creative with the next level of resource names. The following does not work:

```
*User.stuff.m.keep.label: Keep on send
```

The problem is that Tk does not directly support resources for menu entries, so it assumes `.stuff.m.keep` is a widget pathname, but it is not. You can add the resource, but you cannot retrieve it with `option get`. Instead, we must combine the attribute information (i.e., label) with the name of the entry:

```
*User.stuff.m.l_keep: Keep on send
```

You must do something similar if you want to define resources for items on a canvas, too, because that is not supported directly by Tk. The code to support menu definition by resources shown in the next example:

Example 15–7 Defining menus from resource specifications.

```
proc MenuResources { f class } {
    set f [frame $f -class User]
    pack $f -side top
    foreach b [option get $f menulist {}] {
        set cmd [list menubutton $f.$b -menu $f.$b.m \
                -relief raised]
        if [catch $cmd t] {
            eval $cmd {-font fixed}
        }
        if [catch {menu $f.$b.m}] {
            menu $f.$b.m -font fixed
        }
        pack $f.$b -side left
        MenuButtonInner $f.$b.m
    }
}
proc MenuButtonInner { menu } {
    foreach e [option get $menu entrylist {}] {
        set l [option get $menu l_$e {}]
        set c [option get $menu c_$e {}]
        set v [option get $menu v_$e {}]
        switch -- [option get $menu t_$e {}] {
            check {
                $menu add checkbutton -label $l -command $c \
                    -variable $v
            }
            radio {
                $menu add radiobutton -label $l -command $c \
                    -variable $v
            }
            separator {
                $menu add separator
            }
            cascade {
                set sub [option get $menu m_$e {}]
                if {string length $sub] != 0} {
                    set submenu [menu $menu.$sub]
                    $menu add cascade -label $l -command $c \
                         -menu $submenu
                    MenuButtonInner $submenu
                }
            }
            default {
                $menu add command -label $l -command $c
            }
        }
    }
}
```

CHAPTER 16

Simple Tk Widgets

This chapter describes several simple Tk widgets: the `frame`, `label`, `message`, `scale`, and `scrollbar`. In general, these widgets require minimal setup to be useful in your application. The `bell` command rings the X display bell.

This chapter describes five simple widgets and the `bell` command.

- The `frame` is a building block for widget layout.
- The `label` provides a line of read-only text.
- The `message` provides a read-only block of text that gets formatted onto several lines.
- The `scale` is a slider-like widget used to set a numeric value.
- The `scrollbar` is used to control other widgets.
- The `bell` command rings the X display bell.

Chapter 23, 24, and 25 go into more detail about some of the generic widget attributes shared by the widgets presented in this chapter. The examples in this chapter use the default widget attributes in most cases.

Frames and Toplevel Windows

Frames have been introduced before for use with the geometry managers. There is not much to a frame, except for its background color and border. You can also specify a colormap and visual type for a frame. Chapter 24 describes visual types and colormaps on page 287.

A toplevel widget is like a frame, except that it is created as a new main window. That is, it is not positioned inside the main window of the application. This is useful for dialog boxes, for example. A toplevel has the same attributes as a frame, with the addition of a `screen` option that lets you put the toplevel on any X display. The value of the `screen` option has the following format:

host:*display*.*screenNum*

For example, I have one X server on my workstation `corvina` that controls two screens. My two screens are named `corvina:0.0` and `corvina:0.1`. If the *screenNum* specifier is left off, it defaults to `0`.

Attributes for Frames and Toplevels

Table 16–1 lists the attributes for the frame and toplevel widgets. The attributes are named according to their X resource name, which includes a capital letter at internal word boundaries. When you specify an attribute in a Tcl command when creating or reconfiguring a widget, however, you specify the attribute with a dash and all lowercase letters. Chapter 15 explains how to use resource specifications for attributes. Chapters 23, 24, and 25 discuss many of these attributes in more detail.

Table 16–1 Frame and toplevel attribute resource names.

`background`	Background color (also `bg`).
`borderWidth`	Extra space around the edge of the label.
`class`	X resource class and binding class name.
`colormap`	The value is `new` or the name of a window.
`cursor`	Cursor to display when mouse is over the label.
`height`	Height, in screen units.
`highlightColor`	Color for input focus highlight.
`highlightThickness`	Thickness of focus highlight rectangle.
`relief`	3D relief: `flat`, `sunken`, `raised`, `groove`, or `ridge`.
`screen`	An X display specification. (toplevel only, and this cannot be specified in the resource database.)
`visual`	Type: `staticgrey`, `greyscale`, `staticcolor`, `pseudocolor`, `directcolor`, or `truecolor`.
`width`	Width, in screen units.

You cannot change the `class`, `colormap`, `visual`, or `screen` attributes after the frame or toplevel has been created. These settings are so fundamental that you need to destroy the frame and start over if you must change them.

The Label Widget

The label widget provides a read-only text label, and it has attributes that let you control the position of the label within the display space. Most commonly, however, you just need to specify the text for the label:

```
label .version -text "MyApp v1.0"
```

The text can be specified indirectly by using a Tcl variable to hold the text. In this case the label is updated whenever the value of the Tcl variable changes. The variable is used from the global scope, even if there happens to be a local variable by the same name when you create the widget inside a procedure:

```
set version "MyApp v1.0"
label .version -textvariable version
```

You can change the appearance of a label dynamically by using the `configure` widget operation. If you change the text or font of a label you are liable to change the size of the widget, and this causes the packer to shuffle window positions. You can avoid this by specifying a width for the label that is large enough to hold all the strings you plan to display in it. The width is specified in characters, not screen coordinates:

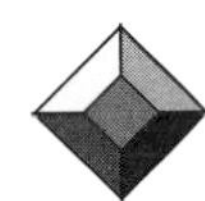

Example 16–1 A label that displays different strings.

```
proc FixedWidthLabel { name values } {
    # name is a widget name to be created
    # values is a list of strings
    set maxWidth 0
    foreach value $values {
        if {[string length $value] > $maxWidth} {
            set maxWidth [string length $value]
        }
    }
    # Use -anchor w to left-justify short strings
    label $name -width $maxWidth -anchor w \
        -text [lindex $values 0]
    return $name
}
```

The `FixedWidthLabel` example is used to create a label with a width big enough to hold a set of different strings. It uses the `-anchor w` attribute to left justify strings that are shorter than the maximum. You can change the text for the label later by using the `configure` widget operation, which can be abbreviated to `config`:

```
FixedWidthLabel .status {OK Busy Error}
.status config -text Busy
```

A label can display a bitmap or image instead of a text string. For a discussion of using bitmaps, see Chapter 24 and the section on *Bitmaps and Images*.

Label Attributes

Table 16–2 lists the widget attributes for the label widget. The attributes are named according to their X resource name, which includes a capital letter at internal word boundaries. When you specify an attribute as an option in a Tcl command when creating or reconfiguring a widget, however, you specify the attribute with a dash and all lowercase letters. Chapter 15 explains how to use resource specifications for attributes. Chapters 23, 24, and 25 discuss many of these attributes in more detail.

Table 16–2 Label attribute resource names.

`anchor`	Relative position of the label within its packing space.
`background`	Background color (also `bg`).
`bitmap`	Name of a bitmap to display instead of a text string.
`borderWidth`	Extra space around the edge of the label.
`cursor`	Cursor to display when mouse is over the label.
`font`	Font for the label's text.
`foreground`	Foreground color. (Also `fg`).
`height`	In screen units for bitmaps, in lines for text.
`highlightColor`	Color for input focus highlight.
`highlightThickness`	Thickness of focus highlight rectangle.
`image`	Specifies image to display instead of bitmap or text.
`justify`	Text justification: `left`, `right`, or `center`.
`padX`	Extra space to the left and right of the label.
`padY`	Extra space above and below the label.
`relief`	3D relief: `flat`, `sunken`, `raised`, `groove`, or `ridge`.
`text`	Text to display.
`textVariable`	Name of Tcl variable. Its value is displayed.
`underline`	Index of character to underline.
`width`	Width. In characters for text labels.
`wrapLength`	Length at which text is wrapped *in screen units*.

Label Width and Wrap Length

When a label is displaying text, its `width` attribute is interpreted as a number of characters. The label is made wide enough to hold this number of averaged width characters in the label's font. However, if the label is holding a bitmap or an image, then the `width` is in pixels or another screen unit.

The `wrapLength` attribute determines when a label's text is wrapped onto multiple lines. *The wrap length is always screen units.* If you need to compute a `wrapLenth` based on the font metrics (instead of guessing) then you must use a `text` widget with the same font. Chapter 19 describes the `text` widget operations that return size information for characters.

The Message Widget

The message widget displays a long text string by formatting it onto several lines. It is designed for use in dialog boxes. It can format the text into a box of a given width, in screen units, or a given *aspect ratio*. The aspect ratio is defined to be the ratio of the width to the height, times 100. The default is 150, which means the text will be one and a half times as wide as it is high:

Example 16–2 The message widget formats long lines of text.

```
message .msg -justify center -text "This is a very long text\
    line that will be broken into many lines by the\
    message widget"
pack .msg
```

This example creates a message widget with one long line of text. Backslashes are used to continue the text string without embedding any newlines. (You can also just type a long line into your script.) Note that backslash-newline collapses white space after the newline into a single space.

One disadvantage of a message widget is that, by default, you cannot select the text it displays. Chapter 21 describes how to define custom selection handlers, so you could define one that returned the message string.

A newline in the string forces a line break in the message display. You can retain exact control over the formatting by putting newlines into your string and specifying a very large aspect ratio. In the next example, grouping with double quotes is used to continue the string over more than one line. The newline character between the quotes is included in the string, and it causes a line break:

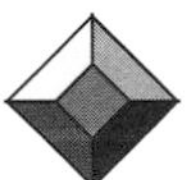

Example 16–3 Controlling the text layout in a message widget.

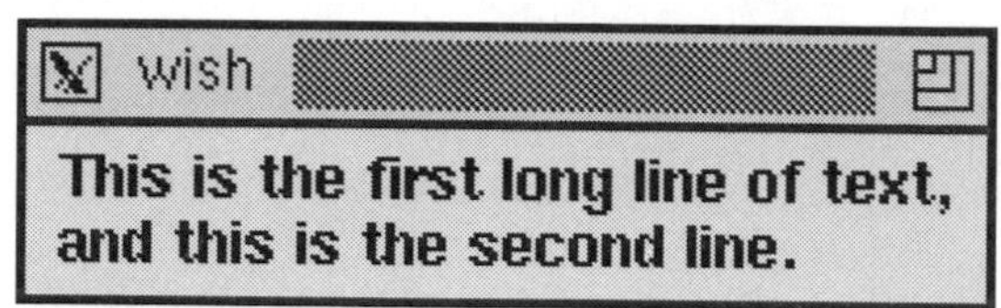


```
message .msg -aspect 1000 -justify left -text \
"This is the first long line of text,
and this is the second line."
pack .msg
```

Message Attributes

Table 16–3 lists the attributes for the message widget. The table list the X resource name, which has capitals at internal word boundaries. In Tcl commands these options are specified with a dash and all lowercase:

Table 16–3 Message attribute resource names.

`anchor`	Relative position of the text within its packing space.
`aspect`	100 * width / height. Default 150.
`background`	Background color (also `bg`).
`borderWidth`	Extra space around the edge of the text.
`cursor`	Cursor to display when mouse is over the widget.
`font`	Font for the message's text.
`foreground`	Foreground color. (Also `fg`).
`highlightColor`	Color for input focus highlight.
`highlightThickness`	Thickness of focus highlight rectangle.
`justify`	Justification: `left`, `center`, or `right`.
`padX`	Extra space to the left and right of the text.
`padY`	Extra space above and below the text.
`relief`	3D relief: `flat`, `sunken`, `raised`, `groove`, or `ridge`.
`text`	Text to display.
`textVariable`	Name of Tcl variable. Its value is displayed.
`width`	Width, in screen units.

Arranging Labels and Messages

Both the label and message widgets have attributes that control the position of their text in much the same way that the packer controls the position of widgets within a frame. These attributes are `padX`, `padY`, `anchor` and `borderWidth`. The `anchor` takes effect when the size of the widget is larger than the space needed to display its text. This happens when you specify the `-width` attribute or if you pack the widget with fill enabled and there is extra room. See Chapter 23 and the section on *Padding and Anchors* for more details.

The Scale Widget

The scale widget displays a *slider* in a *trough*. The trough represents a range of numeric values, and the slider position represents the current value. The scale can have an associated label, and it can display its current value next to the slider. The value of the scale can be used in three different ways:

- Explicitly get and set the value with widget commands.
- Associate the scale with a Tcl variable. The variable is kept in sync with the value of the scale, and changing the variable affects the scale.
- Register a Tcl command to be executed after the scale value changes. You specify the initial part of the Tcl command, and the scale implementation adds the current value as another argument to the command.

Example 16–4 A scale widget.

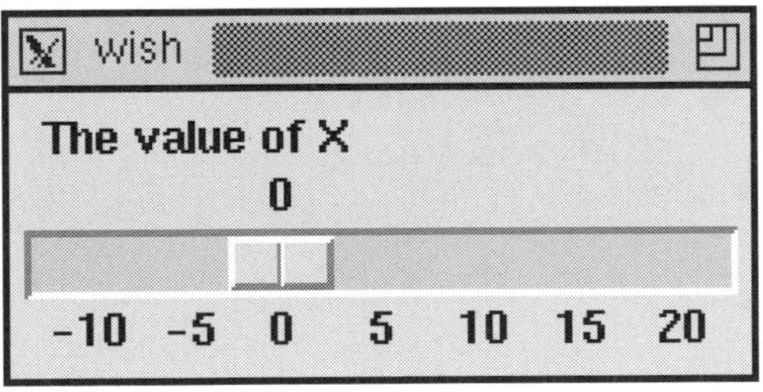


```
scale .scale -from -10 -to 20 -length 200 -variable x \
   -orient horizontal -label "The value of X" \
   -tickinterval 5 -showvalue true
pack .scale
```

The example shows a scale for a variable that ranges in value from -10 to +20. The variable `x` is defined at the global scope. The `tickinterval` option results in the labels across the bottom, and the `showvalue` option causes the current value to be displayed. The `length` of the scale is in screen units (i.e. pixels).

Scale Bindings

Table 16–4 lists the bindings for scale widgets. You must direct focus to a scale explicitly for the key bindings like <Up> and <Down> to take effect.

Table 16–4 Scale bindings.

<Button-1>	Clicking on the trough moves the slider by one unit of resolution towards the mouse click.
<Control-Button-1>	Clicking on the trough moves the slider all the way to the end of the trough towards the mouse click.
<Left> <Up>	Move the slider towards the left (top) by one unit.
<Control-Left> <Control-Up>	Move the slider towards the left (top) by the value of the bigIncrement attribute.
<Right> <Down>	Move the slider towards the right (bottom) one unit.
<Control-Right> <Control-Down>	Move the slider towards the right (bottom) by the value of the bigIncrement attribute.
<Home>	Move the slider all the way to the left (top).
<End>	Move the slider all the way to the right (bottom).

Scale Attributes

Table 16–5 lists the scale widget attributes. The table uses the X resource name, which has capitals at internal word boundaries. In Tcl commands the attributes are specified with a dash and all lowercase.

Table 16–5 Scale attribute resource names.

activeBackground	Background color when the mouse is over the slider.
background	The background color. (Also bg in commands.)
bigIncrement	Coarse grain slider adjustment value.
borderWidth	Extra space around the edge of the text.
command	Command to invoke when the value changes. The current value is appended as another argument
cursor	Cursor to display when mouse is over the widget.
digits	Number of significant digits in scale value.
from	Minimum value. The left or top end of the scale.
font	Font for the label.
foreground	Foreground color. (Also fg).
highlightColor	Color for input focus highlight.

Table 16–5 Scale attribute resource names. (Continued)

`highlightThickness`	Thickness of focus highlight rectangle.
`label`	A string to display with the scale.
`length`	The length, in screen units, of the long axis of the scale.
`orient`	`horizontal` or `vertical`.
`relief`	3D relief: `flat`, `sunken`, `raised`, `groove`, `ridge`.
`repeatDelay`	Delay before keyboard auto-repeat starts. Auto-repeat is used when pressing `<Button-1>` on the trough.
`repeatInterval`	Time period between auto-repeat events.
`resolution`	The value is rounded to a multiple of this value.
`showValue`	If true, value is displayed next to the slider.
`sliderLength`	The length, in screen units, of the slider.
`state`	`normal`, `active`, or `disabled`.
`tickInterval`	Spacing between tick marks. Zero means no marks.
`to`	Maximum value. Right or bottom end of the scale.
`troughColor`	The color of the bar on which the slider sits.
`variable`	Name of Tcl variable. Changes to the scale widget are reflected in the Tcl variable value, and changes in the Tcl variable are reflected in the scale display.
`width`	Width of the trough, or slider bar.

Programming Scales

The scale operations are primarily used by the default bindings and you do not need to program the scale directly. Table 16–6 lists the operations supported by the scale. In the table, `$w` is a scale widget.

Table 16–6 Scale operations.

`$w cget` *`option`*	Return the value of the configuration option.
`$w configure ...`	Query or modify the widget configuration.
`$w coords ?`*`value`*`?`	Returns the coordinates of the point in the trough that corresponds to *`value`*, or the scale's value.
`$w get ?x y?`	Return the value of the scale, or the value that corresponds to the position given by *x* and *`y`*.
`$w identify` *`x y`*	Returns `trough1`, `slider`, or `trough2` to indicate what is under the position given by *x* and *`y`*.
`$w set` *`value`*	Set the value of the scale.

The Scrollbar Widget

A scrollbar controls the display of another widget. The Tk widgets designed to work with scrollbars are: entry, listbox, text, and canvas. There is a simple protocol between the scrollbar and these widgets. While this section explains the protocol, you don't need to know the details to use a scrollbar. All you need to know is how to set things up, and then these widgets take care of themselves.

A scrollbar is made up of five components: `arrow1`, `trough1`, `slider`, `trough2`, and `arrow2`. The arrows are on either end, with `arrow1` being the arrow to the left for horizontal scrollbars, or the arrow on top for vertical scrollbars. The slider represents the relative position of the information displayed in the associated widget, and the size of the slider represents the relative amount of the information displayed. The two trough regions are the areas between the slider and the arrows. If the slider covers all of the trough area, you can see all the information in the associated widget.

The protocol between the scrollbar and its associated widget (or widgets) is initialized by registering a command with each of the widgets. The scrollbar has a `command` attribute that scrolls the associated widget. The `xview` and `yview` operations of the scrollable widgets are designed for this. These operations require parameters that indicate how to adjust their view, and the scrollbar adds these parameters when it calls the command. The command to create a scrollbar for a text widget looks something like this:

```
scrollbar .scroll -command {.text yview} -orient vertical
```

The scrollable widgets have `xscrollcommand` and/or `yscrollcommand` attributes that they use to update the display of the scrollbar. The scrollbar's `set` operation is designed for this callback. Additional parameters are appended to these commands that indicate how much information is visible in the widget and the relative position of that information. The command below sets up the other half of the relationship between the scrollbar and the text widget.

```
text .text -yscrollcommand {.scroll set}
```

The protocol works like this. When the user manipulates the scrollbar, it calls its registered `command` with some parameters that indicate what the user said to do. The associated widget responds to this command (e.g., its `xview` operation) by changing its display. After the widget changes its display, it calls the scrollbar by using its registered `xscrollcommand` or `yscrollcommand` (e.g., the `set` operation) with some parameters that indicate the new relative size and position of the display. The scrollbar updates its appearance to reflect this information. The protocol supports widgets that change their display by themselves, such as by dragging them with `<B2-Motion>` events or simply by adding more information. When this happens, the scrollbar will be updated correctly, even though it did not cause the display change.

Example 16–5 A text widget and two scrollbars.

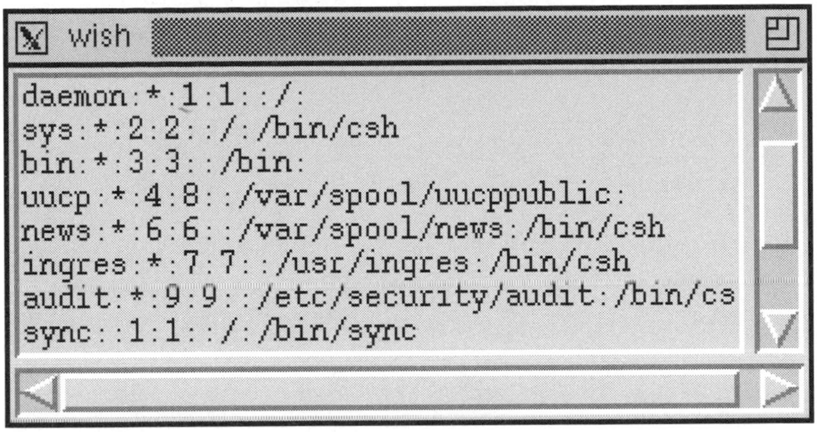

```
wish
daemon:*:1:1::/:
sys:*:2:2::/:/bin/csh
bin:*:3:3::/bin:
uucp:*:4:8::/var/spool/uucppublic:
news:*:6:6::/var/spool/news:/bin/csh
ingres:*:7:7::/usr/ingres:/bin/csh
audit:*:9:9::/etc/security/audit:/bin/cs
sync::1:1::/:/bin/sync
```

```
proc ScrolledText { f width height } {
	frame $f
	# The setgrid setting allows the window to be resized.
	text $f.text -width $width -height $height \
		-setgrid true -wrap none \
		-xscrollcommand [list $f.xscroll set] \
		-yscrollcommand [list $f.yscroll set]
	scrollbar $f.xscroll -orient horizontal \
		-command [list $f.text xview]
	scrollbar $f.yscroll -orient vertical \
		-command [list $f.text yview]
	pack $f.xscroll -side bottom -fill x
	pack $f.yscroll -side right -fill y
	# The fill and expand are needed when resizing.
	pack $f.text -side left -fill both -expand true
	pack $f -side top -fill both -expand true
	return $f.text
}
set t [ScrolledText .f 40 8]
set in [open /etc/passwd]
$t insert end [read $in]
close $in
```

The example associates a text widget with two scrollbars. It reads and inserts the password file into the text widget. There is not enough room to display all the text, and the scrollbars indicate how much text is visible. Chapter 19 describes the text widget in more detail.

The `list` command constructs the `-command` and `-xscrollcommand` values. Even though one could use double-quotes here, you should make a habit of using `list` when constructing values that are used later as Tcl commands.

Scrollbar Bindings

Table 16–7 lists the default bindings for scrollbars. Button 1 and button 2 of the mouse have the same bindings. You must direct focus to a scrollbar explicitly for the key bindings like `<Up>` and `<Down>` to take effect.

Table 16–7 Scrollbar bindings.

`<Button-1> <Button-2>`	Clicking on the arrows scrolls by one unit. Clicking on the trough moves by one screenful.
`<B1-Motion> <B2-Motion>`	Dragging the slider scrolls dynamically.
`<Control-Button-1>` `<Control-Button-2>`	Clicking on the trough or arrow scrolls all the way to the beginning (end) of the widget.
`<Up> <Down>`	Scroll up (down) by one unit.
`<Control-Up>` `<Control-Down>`	Scroll up (down) by one screenful.
`<Left> <Right>`	Scroll left (right) by one unit.
`<Control-Left>` `<Control-Right>`	Scroll left (right) by one screenful.
`<Prior> <Next>`	Scroll back (forward) by one screenful.
`<Home>`	Scroll all the way to the left (top).
`<End>`	Scroll all the way to the right (bottom).

Scrollbar Attributes

Table 16–8 lists the scrollbar attributes. The table uses the X resource name for the attribute, which has capitals at internal word boundaries. In Tcl commands the attributes are specified with a dash and all lowercase.

Table 16–8 Scrollbar attribute resource names.

`activeBackground`	Color when the mouse is over the slider or arrows.
`activeRelief`	Relief of slider and arrows when mouse is over them.
`background`	The background color. (Also `bg` in commands.)
`borderWidth`	Extra space around the edge of the scrollbar.
`command`	Prefix of the command to invoke when the scrollbar changes. Typically this is a `xview` or `yview` operation.
`cursor`	Cursor to display when mouse is over the widget.
`highlightColor`	Color for input focus highlight.
`highlightThickness`	Thickness of focus highlight rectangle.

Table 16–8 Scrollbar attribute resource names. (Continued)

`jump`	If true, dragging the elevator does not scroll dynamically. Instead, the display jumps to the new position.
`orient`	Orientation: `horizontal` or `vertical`.
`repeatDelay`	Milliseconds before auto-repeat starts. Auto-repeat is used when pressing `<Button-1>` on the trough or arrows.
`repeatInterval`	Milliseconds between auto-repeat events.
`troughColor`	The color of the bar on which the slider sits.
`width`	Width of the narrow dimension of the scrollbar.

There is no `length` attribute for a scrollbar. Instead, a scrollbar is designed to be packed next to another widget with a fill option that lets the `scrollbar` display grow to the right size. The relief of the scrollbar cannot be changed from `raised`. Only the relief of the active element can be set. The `background` color is used for the slider, the arrows, and the border. The slider and arrows are displayed in the `activeBackground` color when the mouse is over them. The trough is always displayed in the `troughColor`.

Programming Scrollbars

The scrollbar operations are primarily used by the default bindings. Table 16–9 lists the operations supported by the scrollbar. In the table, `$w` is a scrollbar widget.

Table 16–9 Scrollbar operations.

`$w activate` *`?element?`*	Query or set the active element, which can be `arrow1`, `arrow2`, or `slider`.
`$w cget` *`option`*	Return the value of the configuration option.
`$w configure ...`	Query or modify the widget configuration.
`$w fraction` *`x y`*	Return a number between 0 and 1 that indicates the relative location of the point in the trough.
`$s get`	Return *`first`* and *`last`* from the set operation.
`$w identify` *`x y`*	Returns `arrow1`, `trough1`, `slider`, `trough2`, or arrow2, to indicate what is under the point.
`$w set` *`first last`*	Set the scrollbar parameters. *`first`* is the relative position of the top (left) of the display. *`last`* is the relative position of the bottom (right) of the display.

The Tk 3.6 protocol

The protocol between the scrollbar and its associated widget changed in Tk 4.0. The scrollbar is backward compatible. The Tk 3.6 protocol had four parameters in the `set` operation: *totalUnits*, *windowUnits*, *firstUnit*, and *lastUnit*. If a scrollbar is updated with this form of a `set` command, then the `get` operation also changes to return this information. When the scrollbar makes the callback to the other widget (e.g., an `xview` or `yview` operation), it passes a single extra parameter that specifies what *unit* to display at the top (left) of the associated widget. The Tk widgets' `xview` and `yview` operations are also backward compatible with this interface.

The bell Command

The `bell` command rings the X display bell. The bell is associated with the display; even if you are executing your program on a remote machine, the bell is heard by the user. If your application has windows on multiple displays, you can direct the bell to the display of a particular window with the `-displayof` option. The syntax for the `bell` command is given below:

```
bell ?-displayof window?
```

If you want to control the bell's duration, pitch, or volume, you need to use the *xset* program. The volume is in percent of a maximum, e.g. 50. In practice, many keyboard bells only support a variable duration; the pitch and volume are fixed. The arguments of *xset* that controll the bell are shown below.

```
exec xset b ?volume? ?hertz? ?milliseconds?
```

The `b` argument by itself resets the bell to the default parameters. You can turn the bell off with `-b`, or you can use the `on` or `off` arguments.

```
exec xset -b
exec xset b ?on? ?off?
```

CHAPTER 17

Entry and Listbox Widgets

The entry widget provides a single line of text for use as a data entry field. The listbox provides a scrollable list of text lines.

Listbox and entry widgets are specialized text widgets. They provide a subset of the functionality of the general purpose text widget. They are more complex than the simple widgets presented in the previous chapter. You are more likely to program behavior for these widgets, especially the listbox.

The Entry Widget

The entry widget provides a one-line type-in area. It is commonly used in dialog boxes when values need to be filled in, or as a simple command entry widget. The entry widget supports editing, scrolling, and selections, which make it more complex than label or message widgets. Fortunately, the default settings for an entry widget make it usable right away. You click with the left button to set the insert point, and then type in text. Text is selected by dragging out a selection with the left button. The entry can be scrolled horizontally by dragging with the middle mouse button.

A Labeled Entry

One common use of an entry widget is to associate a label with it, and a command to execute when `<Return>` is pressed in the entry. This is implemented in the following example:

Example 17–1 A command entry.

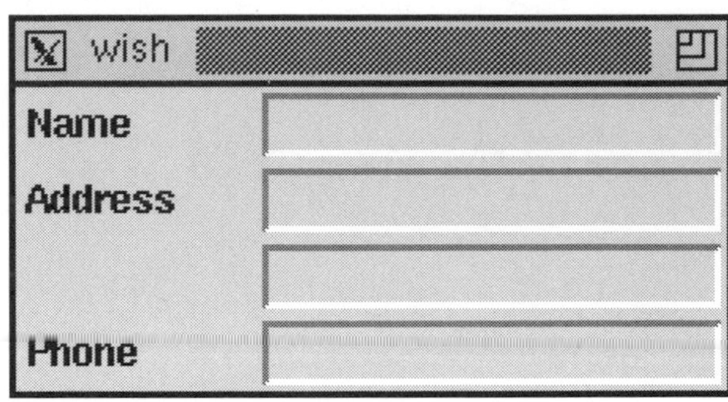


```
proc CommandEntry { name label width command args } {
    frame $name
    label $name.label -text $label -width $width -anchor w
    eval {entry $name.entry -relief sunken} $args
    pack $name.label -side left
    pack $name.entry -side right -fill x -expand true
    bind $name.entry <Return> $command
    return $name.entry
}
CommandEntry .name Name 10 UpdateAddress -textvar addr(name)
CommandEntry .address1 Address 10 UpdateAddress \
    -textvar addr(line1)
CommandEntry .address2 "" 10 UpdateAddress \
    -textvar addr(line2)
CommandEntry .phone Phone 10 UpdateAddress \
    -textvar addr(phone)
pack .name .address1 .address2 .phone
```

`CommandEntry` creates a frame to hold the label and the entry widget. The `label` and `width` arguments apply to the label. The explicit `width` and the `-anchor w` line up the labels if you have more than one `CommandEntry`. The label is packed first so it does not get clipped if the frame is made too small. The entry is packed so it fills up any extra space. The `args` parameter is used to pass extra parameters along to the entry widget. This requires the use of `eval` as discussed in Chapter 6 on page 59. The Tcl command is bound to the `<Return>` keystroke. Finally, the pathname of the entry widget is returned in case the caller needs it.

The example includes four sample calls to `CommandEntry` and the `pack` command used to arrange them. The `-relief sunken` for the entry widget sets them apart visually, and you can see the effect of the `-anchor w` on the labels. The `-textvar` attribute associates a Tcl variable with the entries, and in this case array elements are specified. The `UpdateAddress` procedure, which is not shown, can get the current values of the entry widgets through the global array `addr`.

Table 17–1 gives the bindings for entry widgets. When the table lists two sequences, they are equivalent. The table does not list all the right arrow key bindings; there are corresponding bindings for the left and right arrow keys.

Table 17–1 Entry bindings.

`<Button-1>`	Set the insert point and start a selection.
`<B1-Motion>`	Drag out a selection.
`<Double-Button-1>`	Select a word.
`<Triple-Button-1>`	Select all text in the entry.
`<Shift-B1-Motion>`	Adjust the ends of the selection.
`<Control-Button-1>`	Set insert point, leaving selection as is.
`<Button-2>`	Paste selection at the insert cursor.
`<B2-Motion>`	Scroll horizontally.
`<Left> <Control-b>`	Move insert cursor one character left. Start selection.
`<Shift-Left>`	Move cursor left and extend selection.
`<Control-Left>`	Move cursor left one word. Start selection.
`<Meta-b>`	Same as `<Control-Left>`.
`<Control-Shift-Left>`	Move cursor left one word and extend the selection.
`<Right> <Control-f>`	Move right one character.
`<Meta-f> <Control-Right>`	Move right one word.
`<Home> <Control-a>`	Move cursor to beginning of entry.
`<Shift-Home>`	Move cursor to beginning and extend the selection.
`<End> <Control-e>`	Move cursor to end of entry.
`<Shift-End>`	Move cursor to end and extend the selection.
`<Select> <Control-Space>`	Anchor the selection at the insert cursor.
`<Shift-Select>` `<Control-Shift-Space>`	Adjust the selection to the insert cursor.
`<Control-slash>`	Select all the text in the entry.
`<Control-backslash>`	Clear the selection in the entry.
`<Delete>`	Delete the selection or delete next character.
`<Backspace> <Control-h>`	Delete the selection or delete previous character.
`<Control-d>`	Delete next character.
`<Meta-d>`	Delete next word.
`<Control-k>`	Delete to the end of the entry.
`<Control-w>`	Delete previous word.
`<Control-x>`	Delete the section, if it exists.
`<Control-t>`	Transpose characters.

The middle mouse button (<Button-2>) is overloaded with two functions. If you click and release the middle button, the selection is inserted at the insert cursor. The location of the middle click does not matter. If you press and hold the middle button, you can scroll the contents of the entry by dragging the mouse to the left or right.

Entry Attributes

Table 17–2 lists the entry widget attributes. The table lists the X resource name, which has capitals at internal word boundaries. In Tcl commands these options are specified with a dash and all lowercase.

Table 17–2 Entry attribute resource names.

`background`	Background color (also `bg`).
`borderWidth`	Extra space around the edge of the text (also `bd`).
`cursor`	Cursor to display when mouse is over the widget.
`exportSelection`	If true, then the selected text is exported via the X selection mechanism.
`font`	Font for the text.
`foreground`	Foreground color. (Also `fg`).
`highlightColor`	Color for input focus highlight.
`highlightThickness`	Thickness of focus highlight rectangle.
`insertBackground`	Background for area covered by insert cursor.
`insertBorderWidth`	Width of cursor border. Non-zero for 3D effect.
`insertOffTime`	Time, in milliseconds the insert cursor blinks off.
`insertOnTime`	Time, in milliseconds the insert cursor blinks on.
`insertWidth`	Width of insert cursor. Default is 2.
`justify`	Text justification: `left`, `right`, `center`.
`relief`	3D relief: `flat`, `sunken`, `raised`, `groove`, or `ridge`.
`selectBackground`	Background color of selection.
`selectForeground`	Foreground color of selection.
`selectBorderWidth`	Width of selection border. Non-zero for 3D effect.
`show`	If false, asterisk (*) are displayed instead of contents.
`state`	State: `disabled` (read-only) or `normal`.
`textVariable`	Name of Tcl variable.
`width`	Width, in characters.
`xScrollCommand`	Connects entry to a scrollbar.

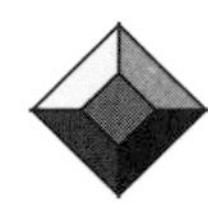

Perhaps the most useful attribute of an entry widget is the `textVariable` attribute. Use this to mirror the contents of the entry widget in a Tcl variable and your scripts will be simpler. Changes to the entry widget are reflected in the Tcl variable value, and changes in the Tcl variable are reflected in the entry contents.

An entry widget has several attributes that control the appearance of the selection and the insert cursor, such as `selectBackground` and `insertWidth`. The `exportSelection` attribute controls whether or not the selected text in the entry can be pasted into other applications. The `show` attribute is useful for entries that accept passwords or other sensitive information. Instead of displaying text, asterisks are displayed if `show` is `false`. The `state` attribute determines if the contents of an entry can be modified. Set the `state` to `disabled` to prevent modification, and set it to `normal` to allow modification.

```
.name.entry config -state disabled ;# read-only
.name.entry config -state normal   ;# editable
```

Programming Entry Widgets

The default bindings for entry widgets are fairly good. However, you can completely control the entry with a set of widget operations for inserting, deleting, selecting, and scrolling. The operations involve addressing character positions called *indices*. The indices count from zero. The entry defines some symbolic indices such as `end`. The index corresponding to an X coordinate is specified with `@`*`xcoord`*, such as `@26`. Table 17–3 lists the formats for indices.

Table 17–3 Entry indices.

`0`	Index of the first character.
`anchor`	The index of the anchor point of the selection.
`end`	Index just after the last character.
`number`	Index a character, counting from zero.
`insert`	The character right after the insertion cursor.
`sel.first`	The first character in the selection.
`sel.last`	The character just after the last character in the selection.
`@`*`xcoord`*	The character under the specified X coordinate.

Table 17–4 summarizes the operations on entry widgets. In the table, `$w` is an entry widget:

Table 17–4 Entry operations.

`$w cget` *`option`*	Return the value of the configuration option.
`$w configure ...`	Query or modify the widget configuration.
`$w delete` *`first ?last?`*	Delete the characters from *`first`* to *`last`*, not including the character at *`last`*. The character at *`first`* is deleted if *`last`* is not specified.
`$w get`	Return the string in the entry.
`$w icursor` *`index`*	Move the insert cursor.
`$w index` *`index`*	Return the numerical index corresponding to *`index`*.
`$w insert` *`index string`*	Insert the *`string`* at the given *`index`*.
`$w scan mark` *`x`*	Start a scroll operation. *x* is a screen coordinate.
`$w scan dragto` *`x`*	Scroll from previous mark position.
`$w select adjust` *`index`*	Move the boundary of an existing selection.
`$w select clear`	Clear the selection.
`$w select from` *`index`*	Set the anchor position for the selection.
`$w select present`	Returns 1 if there is a selection in the entry.
`$w select range` *`start end`*	Select the characters from *`start`* to the one just before *`end`*.
`$w select to` *`index`*	Extend a selection.
`$w xview`	Return the offset and span of visible contents. These are both real numbers between 0 and 1.0.
`$w xview` *`index`*	Shift the display so the character at `index` is at the left edge of the display.
`$w xview moveto` *`fraction`*	Shift the display so that *`fraction`* of the contents are off the left edge of the display.
`$w xview scroll` *`num what`*	Scroll the contents by the specified number of *`what`*, which can be `units` or `pages`.

For example, the binding for `<Button-1>` includes the following commands:

```
%W icursor @%x
%W select from @%x
if {%W cget -state] == "normal"} {focus %W}
```

Recall that the `%` triggers substitutions in binding commands, and that `%W` is replaced with the widget pathname and `%x` is replaced with the X coordinate of the mouse event. Chapter 13 describes bindings and these substitutions in detail. These commands set the insert point to the point of the mouse click by using the `@%x` index, which will be turned into something like `@17` when the binding is invoked. The binding also starts a selection. If the entry is not in the disabled state, then keyboard focus is given to the entry so that it gets `KeyPress` events.

If you are displaying long strings in an entry, you can use the following command to keep the end of the string in view. The command requests that all the string be off screen to the left, but the widget implementation fills up the display; the scrolling is limited so that the tail of the string is visible:

```
$entry xview moveto 1
```

The Listbox Widget

The listbox widget displays a set of text lines in a scrollable display. The basic text unit is a line. There are operations to insert, select, and delete lines, but there are no operations to modify the characters in a line. As such, the listbox is suitable for displaying a set of choices, such as in a file selection dialog, but it is not right for a general purpose text editor. The text widget described in the next chapter is designed for general text display and editing.

A listbox is almost always associated with a scrollbar, even though you can also scroll by dragging with the middle mouse button. Example 17–2 associates two scrollbars with a listbox. Example 27–4 on page 324 associates two listboxes with one scrollbar.

Example 17–2 A listbox with two scrollbars.

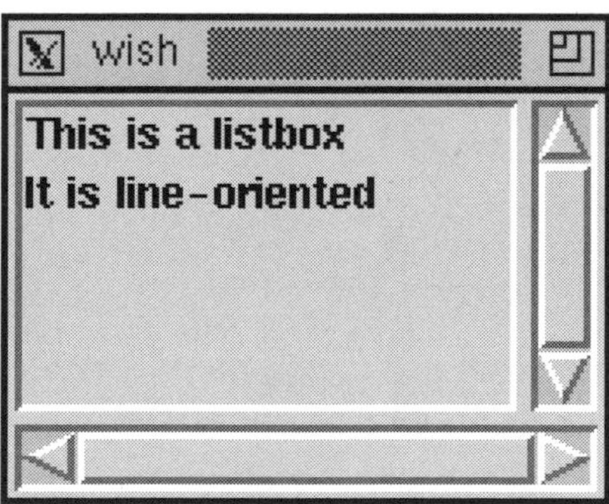


```
proc ScrolledListbox { parent args } {
    # Create listbox attached to scrollbars, pass thru $args
    frame $parent
    eval {listbox $parent.list \
        -yscrollcommand [list $parent.sy set] \
        -xscrollcommand [list $parent.sx set]} $args
    # Create scrollbars attached to the listbox
    scrollbar $parent.sx -orient horizontal \
        -command [list $parent.list xview]
    scrollbar $parent.sy -orient vertical \
```

```
        -command [list $parent.list yview]
    # Arrange them in the parent frame
    pack $parent.sx -side bottom -fill x
    pack $parent.sy -side right -fill y
    # Pack to allow for resizing
    pack $parent.list -side left -fill both -expand true
    return $parent.list
}
ScrolledListbox .f -width 20 -height 5 -setgrid true
pack .f -fill both -expand true
.f.list insert end "This is a listbox"
.f.list insert end "It is line-oriented"
```

The `ScrolledListbox` procedure uses the `eval` and `$args` technique described in Chapter 6 to pass through extra arguments to the listbox. The example specifies the `width`, `height`, and `setgrid` values for the listbox. The main window becomes resizable as a side effect of gridding the listbox. Chapter 25 describes gridding and geometry in more detail.

The listbox has two scrolling commands associated with it, one each for the X and Y directions. These commands set the parameters of the scrollbar with its `set` command. Chapter 16 describes scrollbars in detail. The `list` command constructs the `command`, `xscrollcommand`, and `yscrollcommand` values so that `$parent` gets expanded and the commands have the right form. While you could use double-quotes instead of `list` here, make a habit of using `list` when constructing Tcl commands.

The packing commands arrange three widgets on three different sides of the parent frame. This is one of the few cases where a mixture of horizontal and vertical packing within the same frame works. However, the arrangement causes the bottom scrollbar to extend past the listbox a little bit. If you want to line up the bottom scrollbar with the listbox, you must introduce a little frame to space things out, and then another frame to hold this spacer and one of the scrollbars. The second version of `ScrolledListbox` presented below achieves this:

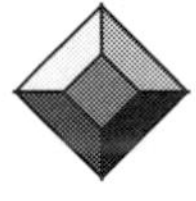

Example 17–3 A listbox with scrollbars and better alignment.

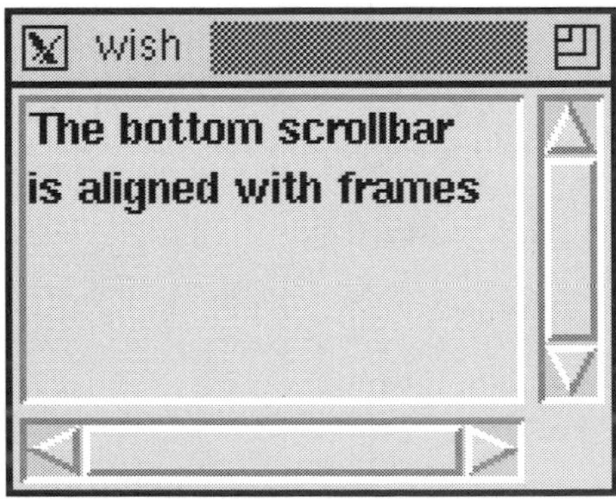

```
proc ScrolledListbox2 { parent args } {
    # Create listbox attached to scrollbars, pass thru $args
    frame $parent
    eval {listbox $parent.list \
        -yscrollcommand [list $parent.sy set] \
        -xscrollcommand [list $parent.sx set]} $args
    scrollbar $parent.sy -orient vertical \
        -command [list $parent.list yview]
    # Create extra frame to hold pad and horizontal scrollbar
    frame $parent.bottom
    scrollbar $parent.sx -orient horizontal \
        -command [list $parent.list xview]
    # Create padding based on the scrollbar width and border
    set pad [expr [$parent.sy cget -width] + 2* \
        ([$parent.sy cget -bd] + \
         [$parent.sy cget -highlightthickness])]
    frame $parent.pad -width $pad -height $pad
    # Arrange everything in the parent frame
    pack $parent.bottom -side bottom -fill x
    pack $parent.pad -in $parent.bottom -side right
    pack $parent.sx -in $parent.bottom -side bottom -fill x
    pack $parent.sy -side right -fill y
    pack $parent.list -side left -fill both -expand true
    return $parent.list
}
ScrolledListbox2 .f -width 20 -height 5 -setgrid true
pack .f -expand true -fill both
.f.list insert end \
    "The bottom scrollbar" "is aligned with frames"
```

The packing parameters are subtle in `ScrolledListbox2`. The bottom scrollbar of the previous example is replaced by a frame, `$parent.bottom`, that contains the horizontal scrollbar and another frame for padding. It is packed with the same parameters that the horizontal scrollbar was packed with before: `-side bottom -fill x`. The padding frame and the horizontal scrollbar are packed inside that using the `-in` packing option. Here we see another case of mixing horizontal and vertical packing, with the pad to the right and the scrollbar to the bottom:

```
pack $parent.sx -in $parent.bottom -side bottom -fill x
```

The combination of `-side bottom` and `-fill x` enables the scrollbar to fill out the whole bottom side of the virtual packing cavity. Another way to pack the horizontal scrollbar is given below. The `-expand true` is required, otherwise the `-side left` squeezes down the scrollbar to a minimum size.

```
pack $parent.sx -in $parent.bottom -side left -fill x \
    -expand true
```

Programming Listboxes

The listbox operations use indices to reference lines in the listbox. The lines are numbered starting at zero. Keyword indices are also used for some special lines. The listbox keeps track of an *active* element, which is displayed with underlined text. There is also a selection *anchor* that is used when adjusting selections. Table 17–5 summarizes the keywords used for indices.

Table 17–5 Listbox indices

`0`	Index of the first line.
`active`	The index of the activated line.
`anchor`	The index of the anchor point of the selection.
`end`	Index of the last line.
`number`	Index a line, counting from zero.
`@x,y`	The line closest to the specified X and Y coordinate.

Table 17–6 presents the operations for programming a listbox. In the table, `$w` is a listbox widget. Most of the operations have to do with the selection, and these operations are already programmed by the default bindings for the `Listbox` widget class:

Table 17–6 Listbox operations.

`$w activate` *`index`*	Activate the specified line.
`$w bbox` *`index`*	Return the bounding box of the text in the specified line in the form: *`xoff yoff width height`*.
`$w cget` *`option`*	Return the value of the configuration option.
`$w configure ...`	Query or modify the widget configuration.
`$w curselection`	Return a list of indices of the selected lines.
`$w delete` *`first ?last?`*	Delete the lines from *`first`* to *`last`*, including the line at *`last`*. The line at *`first`* is deleted if *`last`* is not given.
`$w get` *`first ?last?`*	Return the lines from *`first`* to *`last`* as a list.
`$w index` *`index`*	Return the numerical index corresponding to *`index`*.
`$w insert` *`index ?string string string ...?`*	Insert the *`string`* items before the line at *`index`*. If *`index`* is `end`, then append the items.
`$w nearest` *`y`*	Return the index of the line closest to the widget-relative Y coordinate.
`$w scan mark` *`x y`*	Start a scroll operation. *x* and *y* are widget-relative screen coordinates.
`$w scan dragto` *`x y`*	Scroll from previous mark position.

Table 17–6 Listbox operations. (Continued)

`$w see` *index*	Adjust the display so the line at *index* is visible.
`$w selection anchor` *index*	Anchor the selection at the specified line.
`$w selection clear` *start ?end?*	Clear the selection.
`$w selection includes` *index*	Returns 1 if the line at *index* is in the selection.
`$w selection set` *start ?end?*	Select the lines from *start* to *end*.
`$w xview`	Return the offset and span of visible contents. These are both real numbers between 0 and 1.
`$w xview` *index*	Shift the display so the character at *index* is at the left edge of the display.
`$w xview moveto` *fraction*	Shift the display so that *fraction* of the contents are off the left edge of the display.
`$w xview scroll` *num what*	Scroll the contents horizontally by the specified number of *what*, which can be `units` or `pages`.
`$w yview`	Return the offset and span of visible contents. These are both real numbers between 0 and 1.
`$w yview` *index*	Shift the display so the line at *index* is at the top edge of the display.
`$w yview moveto` *fraction*	Shift the display so that *fraction* of the contents are off the top of the display.
`$w yview scroll` *num what*	Scroll the contents vertically by the specified number of *what*, which can be `units` or `pages`.

The most common programming task for a listbox is to insert text. If your data is in a list, you can loop through the list and insert each element at the end:

```
foreach item $list {
    $listbox insert end $item
}
```

You can do the same thing by using `eval` to concatenate the list onto a single `insert` command:

```
eval {$listbox insert end} $list
```

It is also common to react to mouse clicks on a listbox. The `nearest` operation finds the listbox entry that is closest to a mouse event. If the mouse is clicked beyond the last element, the index of the last element is returned:

```
set index [$list nearest $y]
```

The following example displays two listboxes. When the user clicks on an item in the first listbox, it is copied into the second listbox. When an item in the second listbox is selected, it is removed.

Example 17–4 Choosing items from a listbox.

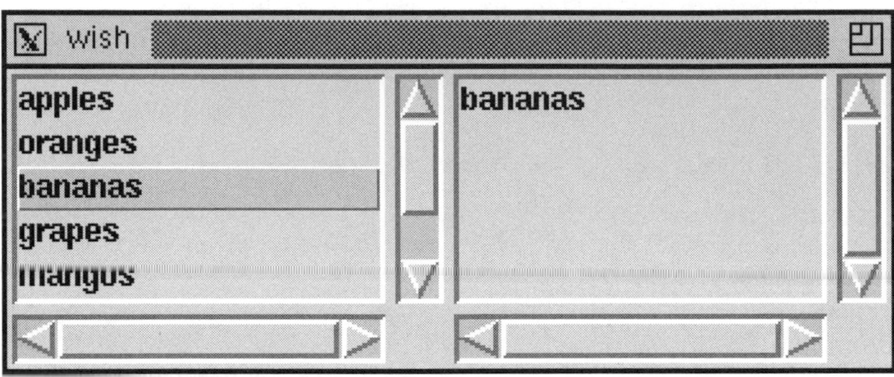


```
proc ListSelect { parent choices } {
    # Create two lists side by side
    frame $parent
    ScrolledListbox2 $parent.choices -width 20 -height 5 \
        -setgrid true
    ScrolledListbox2 $parent.picked -width 20 -height 5 \
        -setgrid true
    # The setgrid allows interactive resizing, so the
    # pack parameters need expand and fill.
    pack $parent.choices $parent.picked -side left \
        -expand true -fill both

    # Selecting in choices moves items into picked
    bind $parent.choices.list <ButtonPress-1> \
        {ListSelectStart %W %y}
    bind $parent.choices.list <B1-Motion> \
        {ListSelectExtend %W %y}
    bind $parent.choices.list <ButtonRelease-1> \
        [list ListSelectEnd %W %y $parent.picked.list]

    # Selecting in picked deletes items
    bind $parent.picked.list <ButtonPress-1> \
        {ListSelectStart %W %y}
    bind $parent.picked.list <B1-Motion> \
        {ListSelectExtend %W %y}
    bind $parent.picked.list <ButtonRelease-1> \
        {ListDeleteEnd %W %y}

    # Insert all the choices
    eval {$parent.choices.list insert 0} $choices
}

proc ListSelectStart { w y } {
    $w select anchor [$w nearest $y]
}
proc ListSelectExtend { w y } {
    $w select set anchor [$w nearest $y]
```

```
}
proc ListSelectEnd {src y dst} {
    $src select set anchor [$src nearest $y]
    foreach i [$src curselection] {
        $dst insert end [$src get $i]
    }
}
proc ListDeleteEnd {w y} {
    $w select set anchor [$w nearest $y]
    foreach i [lsort -decreasing [$w curselection]] {
        $w delete $i
    }
}
ListSelect .f {apples oranges bananas \
               grapes mangos peaches pears}
pack .f -expand true -fill both
```

The `ListSelect` procedure creates two lists using `ScrolledListbox2`. Bindings are created to move items from `$parent.choices` to `$parent.picked`, and to delete items from `$parent.picked`. Consider the `<ButtonRelease-1>` binding for `$parent.choices`:

```
bind $parent.choices.list <ButtonRelease-1> \
    [list ListSelectEnd %W %y $parent.picked.list]
```

The `list` command is used to construct the Tcl command because we need to expand the value of `$parent` at the time the binding is created. The command will be evaluated later at the global scope, and `parent` will not be defined after the `ListSelect` procedure returns. Or, worse yet, an existing global variable named `parent` will be used, which is unlikely to be correct!

Short procedures are used to implement the binding command, even though two of them are just one line. This style has two advantages. First, it confines the `%` substitutions done by `bind` to a single command. Second, if there are any temporary variables, such as the loop counter `i`, they are hidden within the scope of the procedure.

The `ListSelectEnd` procedure extends the current selection to the listbox item under the given Y coordinate. It gets the list of all the selected items, and loops over this list to insert them into the other list. The `ListDeleteEnd` procedure is similar. However, it sorts the selection indices in reverse order. It deletes items from the bottom up so the indices remain valid throughout the process.

Listbox Bindings

A listbox has an *active* element and it may have one or more *selected* elements. The active element is highlighted with an underline, and the selected elements are highlighted with a different color. There are a large number of key bindings for listboxes. You must set the input focus to the listbox for the key bindings to work. Chapter 18 describes focus. There are four selection modes for a listbox, and the bindings vary depending what mode the listbox is in. Table 17–7 lists the four possible `selectMode` settings:

Table 17–7 The values for the `selectMode` of a listbox.

`single`	A single element can be selected.
`browse`	A single element can be selected, and the selection can be dragged with the mouse. This is the default.
`multiple`	More than one element can be selected by toggling the selection state of items, but you only select or deselect one line at a time.
`extended`	More than one element can be selected by dragging out a selection with the shift or control keys.

Browse Select Mode

In `browse` selection mode, `<Button-1>` selects the item under the mouse and dragging with the mouse moves the selection, too. Table 17–8 gives the bindings for `browse` mode.

Table 17–8 Bindings for `browse` selection mode.

`<Button-1>`	Select the item under the mouse. This becomes the active element, too.
`<B1-Motion>`	Same as `<Button-1>`, the selection moves with the mouse.
`<Shift-Button-1>`	Activate the item under the mouse. The selection is not changed.
`<Key-Up> <Key-Down>`	Move the active item up (down) one line, and select it.
`<Control-Home>`	Activate and select the first element of the listbox.
`<Control-End>`	Activate and select the last element of the listbox.
`<space> <Select> <Control-slash>`	Select the active element.

Single Select Mode

In `single` selection mode, `<Button-1>` selects the item under the mouse, but dragging the mouse does not change the selection. When you release the mouse, the item under that point is activated. Table 17–9 specifies the bindings for `single` mode:

Table 17–9 Bindings for `single` selection mode.

`<ButtonPress-1>`	Select the item under the mouse.
`<ButtonRelease-1>`	Activate the item under the mouse.
`<Shift-Button-1>`	Activate the item under the mouse. The selection is not changed.

Table 17–9 Bindings for `single` selection mode. (Continued)

`<Key-Up> <Key-Down>`	Move the active item up (down) one line. The selection is not changed.
`<Control-Home>`	Activate and select the first element of the listbox.
`<Control-End>`	Activate and select the last element of the listbox.
`<space> <Select> <Control-slash>`	Select the active element.
`<Control-backslash>`	Clear the selection.

Extended Select Mode

In `extended` selection mode multiple items are selected by dragging out a selection with the first mouse button. Hold down the `Shift` key to adjust the ends of the selection. Use the `Control` key to make a disjoint selection. The `Control` key works in a toggle fashion, changing the selection state of the item under the mouse. If this starts a new part of the selection, then dragging the mouse extends the new part of the selection. If the toggle action cleared the selected item, then dragging the mouse continues to clear the selection. The extended mode is quite intuitive once you try it. Table 17–10 specifies the complete set of bindings for `extended` mode:

Table 17–10 Bindings for `extended` selection mode.

`<Button-1>`	Select the item under the mouse. This becomes the anchor point for adjusting the selection.
`<B1-Motion>`	Sweep out a selection from the anchor point.
`<ButtonRelease-1>`	Activate the item under the mouse.
`<Shift-Button-1>`	Adjust the selection from the anchor item to the item under the mouse.
`<Shift-B1-Motion>`	Continue to adjust the selection from the anchor.
`<Control-Button-1>`	Toggle the selection state of the item under the mouse, and make this the anchor point.
`<Control-B1-Motion>`	Set the selection state of the items from the anchor point to the item under the mouse to be the same as the selection state of the anchor point.
`<Key-Up> <Key-Down>`	Move the active item up (down) one line, and start a new selection with this item as the anchor point.
`<Shift-Up> <Shift-Down>`	Move the active element up (down) and extend the selection to include this element.
`<Control-Home>`	Activate and select the first element of the listbox.
`<Control-Shift-Home>`	Extend the selection to the first element.

Table 17–10 Bindings for `extended` selection mode. (Continued)

<Control-End>	Activate and select the last element of the listbox.
<Control-Shift-End>	Extend the selection to the last element.
<space> <Select>	Select the active element.
<Escape>	Cancel the previous selection action.
<Control-slash>	Select everything in the listbox.
<Control-backslash>	Clear the selection.

Multiple Select Mode

In `multiple` selection mode you can select more than one item, but you can only add or remove one item at a time. Dragging the mouse does not sweep out a selection. If you click on a selected item it is deselected. Table 17–11 specifies the complete set of bindings for `multiple` selection mode.

Table 17–11 Bindings for `multiple` selection mode.

<Button-1>	Select the item under the mouse.
<ButtonRelease-1>	Activate the item under the mouse.
<Key-Up> <Key-Down>	Move the active item up (down) one line, and start a new selection with this item as the anchor point.
<Shift-Up> <Shift-Down>	Move the active element up (down).
<Control-Home>	Activate and select the first element of the listbox.
<Control-Shift-Home>	Activate the first element of the listbox.
<Control-End>	Activate and select the last element of the listbox.
<Control-Shift-End>	Activate the last element of the listbox.
<space> <Select>	Select the active element.
<Control-slash>	Select everything in the listbox.
<Control-backslash>	Clear the selection.

Scroll Bindings

There are a number of bindings that scroll the display of the listbox. As well as the standard middle-drag scrolling, there are some additional key bindings for scrolling. Table 17–12 summarizes the the scroll-related bindings:

Table 17–12 Listbox scroll bindings.

<Button-2>	Mark the start of a scroll operation.
<B2-Motion>	Scroll vertically *and* horizontally.

Table 17–12 Listbox scroll bindings.

`<Left> <Right>`	Scroll horizontally by one character.
`<Control-Left> <Control-Right>` `<Control-Prior> <Control-Next>`	Scroll horizontally by one screen width.
`<Prior> <Next>`	Scroll vertically by one screen height.
`<Home> <End>`	Scroll to left and right edges of the screen, respectively.

Listbox Attributes

Table 17–13 lists the listbox widget attributes. The table uses the X resource name for the attribute, which has capitals at internal word boundaries. In Tcl commands these options are specified with a dash and all lowercase:

Table 17–13 Listbox attribute resource names.

`background`	Background color (also `bg`).
`borderWidth`	Extra space around the edge of the text.
`cursor`	Cursor to display when mouse is over the widget.
`exportSelection`	If `true`, then the selected text is exported via the X selection mechanism.
`font`	Font for the text.
`foreground`	Foreground color. (Also `fg`).
`height`	Number of lines in the listbox.
`highlightColor`	Color for input focus highlight.
`highlightThickness`	Thickness of focus highlight rectangle.
`relief`	3D relief: `flat`, `sunken`, `raised`, `groove`, or `ridge`.
`selectBackground`	Background color of selection.
`selectForeground`	Foreground color of selection.
`selectBorderWidth`	Width of selection border. Non-zero for 3D effect.
`selectMode`	Mode: `browse`, `single`, `extended`, or `multiple`.
`setGrid`	Boolean. Set gridding attribute.
`width`	Width, in average character sizes.
`xScrollCommand`	Connects listbox to a horizontal scrollbar.
`yScrollCommand`	Connects listbox to a vertical scrollbar.

Geometry Gridding

The `setGrid` attribute affects interactive resizing of the window containing the listbox. By default, a window can be resized to any size. If gridding is turned on, however, the size is restricted so that a whole number of listbox lines and a whole number of average-width characters is displayed. In addition, gridding affects the user feedback during an interactive resize, assuming the window manager displays the current size of the window in numeric terms. Without gridding the size is reported in pixel dimensions. When gridding is turned on, then the size is reported in grided units (e.g., `20x10`).

CHAPTER 18

Focus, Grabs, and Dialogs

Input focus directs keyboard events to different widgets. The grab mechanism lets a widget capture the input focus. Dialog boxes are the classic example of a user interface object that uses grabs. This chapter describes the `focus`, `grab`, and `tkwait` commands.

Dialog boxes are a common feature in a user interface. The application needs some user response before it can continue. A dialog box displays some information and some controls, and the user must interact with it before the application can continue. To implement this, the application grabs the input focus so the user can only interact with the dialog box. This chapter describes focus and grabs, and finishes with some examples of dialog boxes.

Input Focus

The X window system directs keyboard events to the top level window that currently has the input focus. The application, in turn, directs the keyboard events to one of the widgets within that toplevel window. The `focus` command sets focus to a particular widget. Tk remembers what widget has focus within a toplevel window, and automatically gives focus to that widget when the window manager gives focus to a toplevel window.

Two focus models are used: focus-follows-mouse, and click-to-type. In the first, moving the mouse into a toplevel window gives the application focus. In the second, the user must click on a window to give it the focus, and thereafter the position of the mouse is not important. Within a toplevel window, Tk uses the click-to-type model by default. Text and entry widgets set focus to themselves when you click on them with the left mouse button.

You can get the focus-follows-mouse model by calling the `tk_focusFollowsMouse` procedure. However, in many cases you will find that an explicit focus model is actually more convenient for users. Carefully positioning the mouse over a small widget can be tedious.

You can change focus among widgets with keyboard commands, too. The creation order of widgets determines a traversal order for focus that is used by the `tk_focusNext` and `tk_focusPrev` procedures. There are global bindings for `<Tab>` and `<Shift-Tab>` that call these procedures:

```
bind all <Tab> {tk_focusNext %W}
bind all <Shift-Tab> {tk_focusPrev %W}
```

The focus Command

Table 18–1 summarizes the `focus` command. The focus implementation supports multiple displays with a separate focus window on each display. The `-displayof` option can be used to query the focus on a particular display. The `-lastfor` option finds out what widget last had the focus within the same toplevel as another window. Tk will restore focus to that window if the widget that has the focus is destroyed. The toplevel widget gets the focus if no widget claims it.

Table 18–1 The `focus` command.

`focus`	Return the widget that currently has the focus on the display of the application's main window.
`focus` *`window`*	Set the focus to *`window`*.
`focus -displayof` *`win`*	Return the focus widget on the same display as *`win`*.
`focus -lastfor` *`win`*	Return the name of the last widget to have the focus in the same toplevel as *`win`*.

Focus Follows Mouse

To implement the focus-follows-mouse model you need to track the `<Enter>` and `<Leave>` events that are generated when the mouse moves in and out of widgets. The `tk_focusFollowsMouse` procedure sets up this binding (the real binding is slightly more complicated as shown later):

```
bind all <Enter> {focus %W}
```

It might be better to set up this binding only for those widget classes for which it makes sense to get the input focus. The next example does this. The focus detail (`%d`) is checked by the code in order to filter out extraneous focus events generated by X. This trick is borrowed from `tk_focusFollowsMouse`. (The Xlib reference manual discourages you from attempting to understand the details of its focus mechanism. After reading it, it is understandable. The following code seems plausible.)

Example 18–1 Setting focus-follows-mouse input focus model.

```
proc FocusFollowsMouse {} {
    foreach class {Button Checkbutton Radiobutton Menubutton\
                Menu Canvas Entry Listbox Text} {
            bind $class <Enter> {
                if {("%d" == "NotifyAncestor") ||
                    ("%d" == "NotifyNonlinear") ||
                    ("%d" == "NotifyInferior")} {
                    focus %W
                }
            }
        }
    }
}
```

Click to Type

To implement the click-to-type focus model you need to set up a binding on the button events. The `<Any-Button>` event works nicely.

```
bind all <Any-Button> {focus %W}
```

Again, it might be better to restrict this binding to those classes for which it makes sense. The previous example can be modified easily to account for this.

Hybrid Models

You can develop hybrid models that are natural for users. If you have a dialog or form-like window with several entry widgets, then it can be tedious for the user to position the mouse over the various entries to direct focus. Instead, click-to-type as well as keyboard shortcuts like `<Tab>` or `<Return>` may be easier for the user, even if they use focus-follows-mouse with their window manager.

Grabbing the Focus

An input *grab* overrides the normal focus mechanism. For example, a dialog box can grab the focus so that the user cannot interact with other windows in the application. The typical scenario is that the application is performing some task but it needs user input. The grab restricts the user's actions so it cannot drive the application into an inconsistent state. A *global grab* prevents the user from interacting with other applications, too, even the window manager. Tk menus use a global grab, for example, which is how they unpost themselves no matter where you click the mouse. When an application prompts for a password a global grab is also a good idea. This prevents the user from accidentally typing their password into a random window. Table 18–2 summarizes the `grab` command.

In most cases you only need to use the `grab` and `grab release` commands. Note that the `grab set` command is equivalent to the `grab` command. The next section includes examples that use the `grab` command.

Table 18–2 The `grab` command.

`grab ?-global? window`	Set a grab to a particular window.
`grab current ?window?`	Query the grabs on the display of *window*, or on all displays if *window* is omitted.
`grab release window`	Release a grab on *window*.
`grab set ?-global? win`	Set a grab to a particular window.
`grab status window`	Returns `none`, `local`, or `global`.

Dialogs

The tkwait Command

This section presents a number of different examples of dialogs. In nearly all cases the `tkwait` command is used to wait for the dialog to complete. This command waits for something to happen, and while waiting it allows events to be processed. When using `tkwait`, control the keyboard focus with `grab` so the user can only interact with the dialog. The sequence of `focus`, `grab`, `tkwait`, and `grab release` is fairly common. Table 18–3 summarizes the `tkwait` command.

Table 18–3 The `tkwait` command.

`tkwait variable varname`	Wait for the global variable *varname* to be set.
`tkwait visibility win`	Wait for the window *win* to become visible.
`tkwait window win`	Wait for the window *win* to be destroyed.

The variable specified in the `tkwait variable` command is a global variable. Remember this if you use procedures to modify the variable. They must declare it global or the `tkwait` command will not notice the assignments.

The `tkwait visibility` waits for the visibility state of the window to change. Most commonly this is used to wait for a newly created window to become visible. For example, if you have any sort of animation in a complex dialog, you must wait until the dialog is displayed before starting the animation.

Prompter Dialog

The `GetValue` dialog gets a value from the user, returning the value entered, or the empty string if the user cancels the operation. The `tkwait variable` command waits for the dialog to complete. Anything that changes the `prompt(ok)` variable will cause the `tkwait` command to return and complete the dialog. The variable is set if the user presses the `OK` or `Cancel` buttons, of if they press `<Return>` or `<Control-c>` in the entry widget.

Example 18–2 A simple dialog.

```
proc GetValue { prompt } {
   global prompt
   set f [toplevel .prompt -borderwidth 10]
   message $f.msg -text $prompt
   entry $f.entry -textvariable prompt(result)
   set b [frame $f.buttons -bd 10]
   pack $f.msg $f.entry $f.buttons -side top -fill x
   button $b.ok -text OK -command {set prompt(ok) 1} \
      -underline 0
   button $b.cancel -text Cancel \
      -command {set prompt(ok) 0} -underline 0

   # Set up bindings for shortcuts. The .prompt
   # bindtag is first to handle dialog bindings before
   # the Alt sequences add characters to the entry
   foreach w [list $f.entry $b.ok $b.cancel] {
      bindtags $w [list .prompt [winfo class $w] $w all]
   }
   bind .prompt <Alt-o> "focus $b.ok ; break"
   bind .prompt <Alt-c> "focus $b.cancel ; break"
   bind .prompt <Alt-Key> break
   bind .prompt <Return> {set prompt(ok) 1}
   bind .prompt <Control-c> {set prompt(ok) 0}
   focus $f.entry
   grab $f
   tkwait variable prompt(ok)
   grab release $f
   destroy $f
   if {$prompt(ok)} {
      return $prompt(result)
   } else {
      return {}
   }
}
GetValue "Please enter a name"
```

Keyboard Shortcuts and Focus

Users appreciate shortcuts. Once they have set focus on the entry widget in the dialog, it is convenient if they can use special key bindings to complete the dialog. Otherwise they need to take their hands off the keyboard and use the mouse.

The global `all` binding tag has bindings for `<Tab>` and `<Shift-Tab>` that cycle the focus among widgets that have key bindings. The `all` bindings use the order that widgets are created to decide what widget gets the focus next. The Tk widgets, even buttons and scrollbars, have bindings that support keyboard interaction. A `<space>` invokes the command associated with a button, if the button has the input focus. The Tk widgets highlight themselves when they have the focus, so the user has some notion of what is going on.

The example defines bindings for `<Return>` and `<Control-c>` that invoke the `Ok` and `Cancel` buttons, respectively. It also defines `<Alt-o>` and `<Alt-c>` bindings that shift focus to the buttons. The `underline` attribute for the buttons highlights the character in the `Alt` sequence.

All the bindings are put onto the `.prompt` binding tag, and the order of the binding tags is changed with `bindtag` so this binding tag is first. The accelerator bindings override all other bindings by including a `break` command. Otherwise, the `Entry` class bindings insert the accelerator keystroke. For example, the following binding prevents undefined `Alt` sequences from inserting characers:

```
bind .prompt <Alt-Key> break
```

Destroying Widgets

The `destroy` command deletes one or more widgets. If the widget has children, all the children are destroyed, too. The example deletes the dialog with a single `destroy` operation on the toplevel window. Chapter 26 describes a protocol on page 312 to handle destroy events that come from the window manager. You wait for a window to be deleted with the `tkwait window` command. This provides an alternate way to synchronize things when using dialogs.

Animation with the update Command

Suppose you want to entertain your user while your application is busy. By default, the user interface hangs until your processing completes. Even if you change a label or entry widget in the middle of processing, the updates to that widget are batched until an idle moment. The user does not see your feedback, and the window is not refreshed if it gets obscured and uncovered. The solution is to use the `update` command that forces Tk to go through its event loop and update the display.

The next example shows a `Feedback` procedure that displays status messages. A read-only entry widget displays the messages, and the `update` command ensures the user sees each new message:

Example 18–3 A feedback procedure.

```
proc Feedback { message } {
    global feedback
    # An entry widget is used because it won't change size
    # based on the message length, and it can be scrolled
    set e $feedback(entry)
    $e config -state normal
    $e delete 0 end
    $e insert 0 $message
    # Leave the entry in a read-only state
    $e config -state disabled
    # Force a display update
    update idletasks
}
```

The Tk widgets update their display at idle moments, which basically means after everything else is taken care of. This lets them collapse updates into one interaction with the X server, and it improves the batching effects that are part of the X protocol. A call to `update idletasks` causes any pending display updates to be processed. Chapter 30 describes the Tk event loop in more detail.

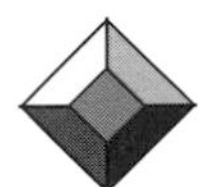

The safest way to use `update` is with its `idletasks` option. If you use the `update` command with no options, then all events are processed. In particular, user input events are processed. If you are not careful, it can have unexpected effects because another thread of execution is launched into your Tcl interpreter. The current thread is suspended and any callbacks that result from input events are executed. It is usually better to use the `tkwait` command if you need to process input because it pauses the main application at a well defined point.

File Selection Dialog

This section presents a file selection dialog. The dialog displays the current directory, and has an entry widget in which to enter a name. It uses a listbox to display the contents of the current directory. There is an `OK` and a `Cancel` button. These buttons set a variable and the dialog finishes, returning the selected pathname or an empty string.

The dialog supports file name completion. The user types part of a name and then presses `<space>`. The matching name is displayed in the entry. If more than one name matches, the common prefix is displayed in the entry, and all the matching names are displayed in the listbox.

The `tkwait` command is used in two ways in this dialog. First, `tkwait visibility` is used so we can delay listing the directory until the listbox is visible. A special message is displayed there during the listing, which can take some time for larger directories. This ensures that the dialog appears quickly so the user knows what is going on. After this, `tkwait variable` waits for the user interaction to complete.

Example 18–4 A file selection dialog.

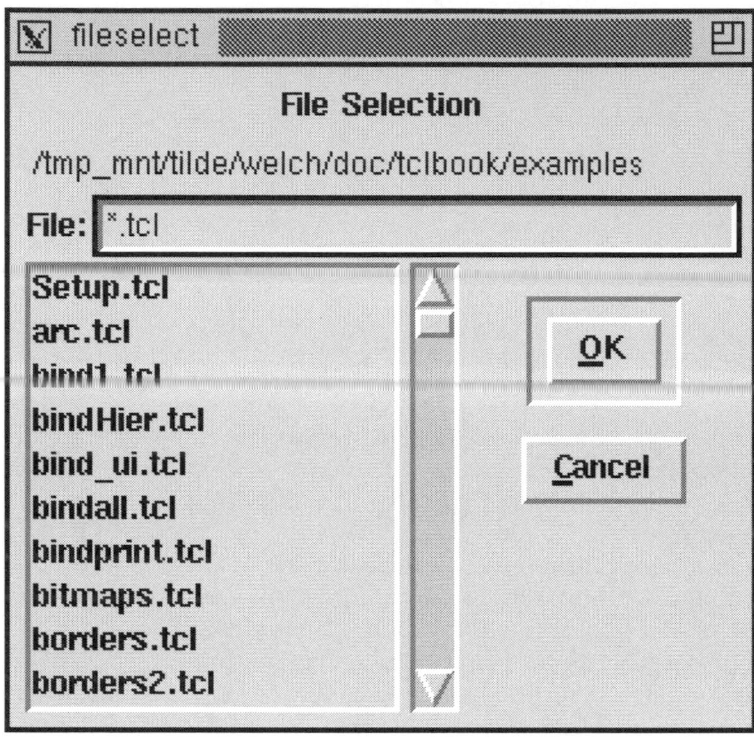


```
# fileselect returns the selected pathname, or {}
# mustExist forces the dialog to find an existing file.
proc fileselect {{why "File Selection"}
                {default {}} {mustExist 1} } {
    global fileselect

    set t [toplevel .fileselect -bd 4 -class Fileselect]
    fileselectResources

    message $t.msg -aspect 1000 -text $why
    pack $t.msg -side top -fill x

    # Create a read-only entry for the durrent directory
    set fileselect(dirEnt) [entry $t.dir -width 15 \
        -relief flat -state disabled]
    pack $t.dir -side top -fill x

    # Create an entry for the pathname
    # The value is kept in fileselect(path)
    frame $t.top
    set e [entry $t.top.path \
        -textvariable fileselect(path)]
    pack $t.top -side top -fill x
    # The label on the entry is defined with an X resource
```

```
    label $t.top.l -padx 0
    pack $t.top.l -side left
    pack $t.top.path -side right -fill x -expand true

    # Create a listbox to hold the directory contents
    set lb [listbox $t.list \
        -yscrollcommand [list $t.scroll set]]
    scrollbar $t.scroll -command [list $lb yview]

    # Create the OK and Cancel buttons
    # The button text is defined with an X resource
    # The OK button has a rim to indicate it is the default
    frame $t.buttons -bd 10
    frame $t.buttons.ok -bd 2 -relief sunken
    set ok [button $t.buttons.ok.b \
        -command fileselectOK]
    set can [button $t.buttons.cancel \
        -command fileselectCancel]

    # Pack the list, scrollbar, and button box
    # in a horizontal stack below the upper widgets
    pack $t.list -side left -fill both -expand true
    pack $t.scroll -side left -fill y
    pack $t.buttons -side left -fill both
    pack $t.buttons.ok $t.buttons.cancel \
        -side top -padx 10 -pady 5
    pack $t.buttons.ok.b -padx 4 -pady 4

    fileselectBindings $t $e $lb $ok $can

    # Initialize variables and list the directory
    if {[string length $default] == 0} {
        set fileselect(path) {}
        set dir [pwd]
    } else {
        set fileselect(path) [file tail $default]
        set dir [file dirname $default]
    }
    set fileselect(dir) {}
    set fileselect(done) 0
    set fileselect(mustExist) $mustExist

    # Wait for the listbox to be visible so
    # we can provide feedback during the listing
    tkwait visibility .fileselect.list
    fileselectList $dir

    tkwait variable fileselect(done)
    destroy $t
    return $fileselect(path)
}
```

Specifying Attributes with X Resources

Example 18–4 does not directly specify a few important widget attributes such as the text on the buttons. Instead, the attributes are specified indirectly by adding entries to the X resource database. The resources have a low priority level, `startup`, so users can override them with entries in their `~/.Xdefaults` file. The `option add` commands can be part of a procedure as show here, or they can be outside a procedure in the same file that defines the `fileselect` procedure. In that case the resource database will be updated at the time the `fileselect` procedure is defined.

Example 18–5 Specifying attributes with X resources.

```
proc fileselectResources {} {
    # The "startup" priority lets users override these
    # path is used to enter the file name
    option add *Fileselect*path.relief      sunken  startup
    option add *Fileselect*path.background  white   startup
    option add *Fileselect*path.foreground  black   startup
    # Text for the label on pathname entry
    option add *Fileselect*l.text           File:   startup
    # Text for the OK and Cancel buttons
    option add *Fileselect*ok*text          OK      startup
    option add *Fileselect*ok*underline     0       startup
    option add *Fileselect*cancel.text      Cancel  startup
    option add *Fileselect*cancel.underline 0       startup
    # Size of the listbox
    option add *Fileselect*list.width       20      startup
    option add *Fileselect*list.height      10      startup
}
```

Example 18–4 creates a toplevel window that has a class of `Fileselect`, so all the resource names in Example 18–5 start with that class. The last component of the resource name is a widget attribute (e.g., `background`). The middle part of the resource name corresponds to the widget pathname. If a resource name has an asterisk (`*`) between components, it can match multiple levels of a widget pathname. For example, the `OK` button is `.fileselect.buttons.ok.b`, and its `text` attribute is specified by `*Fileselect*ok*text`. Chapter 15 explains the `option add` command and the correspondence between the resource names and widget names in more detail.

Mouse and Key Bindings

The `fileselectBindings` procedure sets key bindings to allow keyboard selection. Once the correct pathname is entered, a `<Return>` is equivalent to pressing the `OK` button. `<Control-c>` is equivalent to pressing the `Cancel` button. A `<space>` does file name completion, which is discussed in more detail later. A `<Tab>` changes focus to the listbox so that its bindings can be used for selection. When focus is in the listbox, the arrow keys move the selection up and down, and a `<space>` copies the current name into the entry.

Example 18–6 Event bindings for the dialog.

```
proc fileselectBindings { t e lb ok can } {
    # t - toplevel
    # e - name entry
    # lb - listbox
    # ok - OK button
    # can - Cancel button

    # Elimate the all binding tag because we
    # do our own focus management
    foreach w [list $e $lb $ok $can] {
        bindtags $w [list $t [winfo class $w] $w]
    }
    # Dialog-global cancel binding
    bind $t <Control-c> fileselectCancel

    # Entry bindings
    bind $e <Return> fileselectOK
    bind $e <space> fileselectComplete

    # A single click, or <space>, puts the name in the entry
    # A double-click, or <Return>, selects the name
    bind $lb <space> "fileselectTake %W ; focus $e"
    bind $lb <Button-1> \
        "fileselectClick %W %y ; focus $e"
    bind $lb <Return> "fileselectTake %W ; fileselectOK"
    bind $lb <Double-Button-1> \
        "fileselectClick %W %y ; fileselectOK"

    # Focus management.
    bind $e <Tab> "focus $lb ; $lb select set 0"
    bind $lb <Tab> "focus $e"

    # Button focus. Extract the underlined letter
    # from the button label to use as the focus key.
    foreach but [list $ok $can] {
        set char [string tolower [string index \
            [$but cget -text] [$but cget -underline]]]
        bind $t <Alt-$char> "focus $but ; break"
    }
    bind $ok <Tab> "focus $can"
    bind $can <Tab> "focus $ok"

    # Set up for type in
    focus $e
}
```

The default `all` bindings to change focus are not used. Instead, the focus changes among widgets are implemented explicitly. (You may prefer the standard `all` bindings to what is shown here.) A `<Tab>` cycles focus between the entry and the listbox. `Alt` key sequences change focus to the buttons. The `Alt` bindings are complicated to define because the text for the button is specified indirectly.

The current value is queried to determine the appropriate accelerator key. Once focus is on a button, <space> invokes the button.

Listing the Directory

Example 18–7 Listing a directory for `fileselect`.

```
proc fileselectList { dir {files {}} } {
   global fileselect

   # Update the directory display
   set e $fileselect(dirEnt)
   $e config -state normal
   $e delete 0 end
   $e insert 0 $dir
   $e config -state disabled
   # scroll to view the tail end
   $e xview moveto 1

   set fileselect(dir) $dir
   .fileselect.list delete 0 end
   # Check for bogus names
   if ![file isdirectory $dir] {
      .fileselect.list insert 0 "Bad Directory"
      return
   }
   # Give the user some feedback
   .fileselect.list insert 0 Listing...
   update idletasks

   .fileselect.list delete 0
   if {[string length $files] == 0} {
      # List the directory and add an
      # entry for the parent directory
      set files [glob -nocomplain $fileselect(dir)/*]
      .fileselect.list insert end ../
   }

   # Sort the directories to the front
   set dirs {}
   set others {}
   foreach f [lsort $files] {
      if [file isdirectory $f] {
         lappend dirs [file tail $f]/
      } else {
         lappend others [file tail $f]
      }
   }
   foreach f [concat $dirs $others] {
      .fileselect.list insert end $f
   }
}
```

The `fileselectList` procedure does three things: update the directory name, provide some feedback, and list the directory. The entry widget that holds the parent directory is kept read-only, so it has to be reconfigured when it is updated. Then the entry's `xview moveto` operation ensures that the tail end of the pathname is visible. An argument of `1` is specified, which tries to scroll all of the pathname off screen to the left, but the widget implementation limits the scrolling so the end of the pathname is visible.

Before the directory is listed the listbox is cleared and a message is put into it. The `update idletasks` command forces Tk to do all its pending screen updates so the user sees the message while she waits for the directory listing.

The example uses `file dirname` to extract the directory part of a pathname, and `file tail` to extract the last component of a pathname. The `glob` command does the directory listing. It also has the nice property of expanding pathnames that begin with a tilde (`~`), which stands for your home directory. The slow part is the `file isdirectory` test on each pathname to decide if the trailing `/` should be appended. This requires a file system `stat` system call, which can be expensive. The directories are sorted into the beginning of the list.

Accepting a Name

When the user selects a name, there are several possible cases:

- The name matches an existing file in the current directory.
- The name matches a sub-directory.
- The parent directory is named.
- The name is a file name pattern, such as `*.tcl`.
- The name is a new absolute pathname.
- The name does not match anything.

The first two cases are straight-forward. In the case of the parent directory, the ".." component and the previous component are explicitly removed from the pathname. Even though `/a/b/c/..` is equivalent to `/a/b`, the later form is preferred. Otherwise the pathname becomes cluttered with ".." components.

The `glob` command is used to detect the other cases. The `fileselectOK` procedure is called recursively if a pattern matches a single name. The `fileselectList` procedure is used if a directory is named, or if a pattern matches multiple names. Otherwise, `filenameComplete` does file name completion.

The main variables are the current directory, `fileselect(dir)`, and the current name, `fileselect(path)`. These are updated before each recursive call depending on what the user enters or selects in the listbox. The code is shown in the following example:

Example 18–8 Accepting a file name.

```
proc fileselectOK {} {
    global fileselect
    # Trim ../ (the parent) out of the pathname
    if {[regsub {^../?} $fileselect(path) {} newpath] != 0} {
        set fileselect(path) $newpath
        set fileselect(dir) [file dirname $fileselect(dir)]
        fileselectOK
        return
    }
    # Assume path is relative to current directory
    set path [string trimright \
            $fileselect(dir)/$fileselect(path) /]
    if [file isdirectory $path] {
        set fileselect(path) {}
        fileselectList $path
        return
    }
    if [file exists $path] {
        set fileselect(path) $path
        set fileselect(done) 1
        return
    }
    # Neither a file or a directory.
    # See if glob will find something
    if [catch {glob $path} files] {
        # No, perhaps the user typed a new
        # absolute pathname
        if [catch {glob $fileselect(path)} path] {
            # Nothing good - attempt completion
            fileselectComplete
            return
        } else {
            # OK - try again
            set fileselect(dir) \
                [file dirname $fileselect(path)]
            set fileselect(path) \
                [file tail $fileselect(path)]
            fileselectOK
            return
        }
    } else {
        # Ok, select the file or list them.
        if {[llength [split $files]] == 1} {
            set fileselect(path) $files
            fileselectOK
        } else {
            set fileselect(dir) \
                [file dirname [lindex $files 0]]
            fileselectList $fileselect(dir) $files
        }
    }
}
```

Easy Stuff

If the user presses Cancel or <Control-c>, the result variable is cleared and the fileselect(done) variable is set to end the dialog. The fileselectCancel procedure does this.

Users can select something from the listbox in two ways. If they click on an item, the listbox nearest operation finds which one. If they have shifted focus to the listbox with <Tab> and then press <space>, the listbox curselection operation finds what is selected. These two operations return a listbox index, so the listbox get operation gets the actual value:

Example 18–9 Simple support routines.

```
proc fileselectCancel {} {
    global fileselect
    set fileselect(done) 1
    set fileselect(path) {}
}

proc fileselectClick { lb y } {
    # Take the item the user clicked on
    global fileselect
    set fileselect(path) [$lb get [$lb nearest $y]]
}
proc fileselectTake { lb } {
    # Take the currently selected list item
    global fileselect
    set fileselect(path) [$lb get [$lb curselection]]
}
```

File Name Completion

File name completion tries to match what the user has typed against existing files. It is more complex than using glob to match files because the common prefix of the matching names is filled in for the user. In addition, the matching names are listed in the listbox. The search for the matching prefix is crude, but effective. The prefix begins as the string that the user types. The first matching name from the glob is used as the source for the rest of the prefix. The prefix is lengthened by one until it fails to match all the names in the list.

Example 18–10 File name completion.

```
proc fileselectComplete {} {
    global fileselect

    # Do file name completion
    # Nuke the space that triggered this call
    set fileselect(path) [string trim $fileselect(path) \t\ ]

    # Figure out what directory we are looking at
```

```
    # dir is the directory
    # tail is the partial name
    if {[string match /* $fileselect(path)]} {
        set dir [file dirname $fileselect(path)]
        set tail [file tail $fileselect(path)]
    } elseif [string match ~* $fileselect(path)] {
        if [catch {file dirname $fileselect(path)} dir] {
            return    ;# Bad user
        }
        set tail [file tail $fileselect(path)]
    } else {
        set path $fileselect(dir)/$fileselect(path)
        set dir [file dirname $path]
        set tail [file tail $path]
    }
    # See what files are there
    set files [glob -nocomplain $dir/$tail*]
    if {[llength [split $files]] == 1} {
        # Matched a single file
        set fileselect(dir) $dir
        set fileselect(path) [file tail $files]
    } else {
        if {[llength [split $files]] > 1} {
            # Find the longest common prefix
            set l [expr [string length $tail]-1]
            set miss 0
            # Remember that files has absolute paths
            set file1 [file tail [lindex $files 0]]
            while {!$miss} {
                incr l
                if {$l == [string length $file1]} {
                    # file1 is a prefix of all others
                    break
                }
                set new [string range $file1 0 $l]
                foreach f $files {
                    if ![string match $new* [file tail $f]] {
                        set miss 1
                        incr l -1
                        break
                    }
                }
            }
            set fileselect(path) [string range $file1 0 $l]
        }
        fileselectList $dir $files
    }
}
```

CHAPTER 19

The Text Widget

Tk text widget is a general purpose editable text widget with features for line spacing, justification, tags, marks, and embedded windows.

The Tk text widget is versatile, simple to use for basic text display and manipulation, and has many advanced features to support sophisticated applications. The line spacing and justification can be controlled on a line-by-line basis. Fonts, sizes, and colors are controlled with *tags* that apply to ranges of text. Edit operations use positional *marks* that keep track of locations in text, even as text is inserted and deleted.

Text Indices

The characters in a text widget are addressed by their line number and the character position within the line. Lines are numbered starting at one, while characters are numbered starting at zero. The numbering for lines was chosen to be compatible with other programs that number lines starting at one, like compilers that generate line-oriented error messages. Here are some examples of text indices:

`1.0`	The first character.
`1.1`	The second character on the first line.
`1.end`	The character just before the newline on line one.

There are also symbolic indices. The `insert` index is the position at which new characters are normally inserted when the user types in characters. You can define new indices called *marks*, too, as described later. Table 19–1 summarizes the various forms for a text index.

Table 19–1 Text indices.

`line.char`	Lines count from 1. Characters count from 0.
`@x,y`	The character under the specified position.
`current`	The character currently under the mouse.
`end`	Just after the very last character.
`insert`	The position right after the insert cursor.
`mark`	Just after the named `mark`.
`tag.first`	The first character in the range tagged with `tag`
`tag.last`	Just after the last character tagged with `tag`.
`window`	The position of the embedded `window`.

Inserting and Deleting Text

You add text with the `insert` operation. The general form is (`$t` is a text widget):

```
$t insert index string ?tags?
```

The index can be any of the forms listed in the table, or it can be an index expression as described in a moment. The tags, if any, are added to the newly inserted text. Tags are described in detail later. The most common index at which to insert text is the `insert` index, which is where the insert cursor is displayed. You must include a newline character explicitly to force a line break.

```
$t insert insert "Hello, World\n"
```

The `delete` operation takes one or two indices. If only one index is given, the character at that position is deleted. If there are two indices, all the characters up to the second index are deleted. The character at the second index is not deleted. For example, you can delete the first line with this command:

```
$t delete 1.0 2.0
```

Index Arithmatic

The text widget supports a simple sort of arithmetic on indices. You can specify "the end of the line with this index" and "three characters before this index", and so on. This is done by grouping a modifying expression with the index. For example, the `insert` index can be modified like this:

```
"insert lineend"
"insert -3 chars"
```

The interpretation of indices and their modifiers is designed to operate well with the `delete` and `addtag` operations of the `text` widget. These operations apply to a range of text defined by two indices. The second index refers to the character just after the end of the range. For example, the following command deletes the word containing the insert cursor:

```
$t delete "insert wordstart" "insert wordend"
```

If you want to delete a whole line, including the trailing newline, you need to use a "`lineend +1 char`" modifier. Otherwise the newline remains and you are left with a blank line. If you supply several modifiers to an index, they are applied in left to right order:

```
$t delete "insert linestart" "insert lineend +1 char"
```

Table 19–2 summarizes the set of index modifiers.

Table 19–2 Index modifiers for text widgets.

`+ count chars`	*count* characters past the index.
`- count chars`	*count* characters before the index.
`+ count lines`	*count* lines past the index, retaining character position.
`- count lines`	*count* lines past the index, retaining character position.
`linestart`	The beginning of the line.
`lineend`	The end of the line (just before the newline character).
`wordstart`	The first character of a word.
`wordend`	Just after the last character of a word.

Text Marks

A mark is a symbolic name for a position between two characters. Marks have the property that when text is inserted or deleted they retain their logical position, not their numerical index position. Even if you delete the text surrounding a mark it remains intact. Marks are created with the `mark set` operation, and must be explicitly deleted with the `mark unset` operation. Once defined, a mark can be used in operations that require indices. The following commands define a mark at the beginning of the line containing the insert cursor, and delete from there up to the end of the line:

```
$t mark set foobar "insert wordstart"
$t delete foobar "foobar lineend"
$t mark unset foobar
```

When a mark is defined, it is set to be just before the character specified by the index expression. In the previous example, this is just before the first character of the word where the insert cursor is. When a mark is used in an operation that requires an index it refers to the character just after the mark. So, in many ways the mark seems associated with the character right after it, except that the mark remains even if that character is deleted.

You can use almost any string for the name of a mark. However, do not use pure numbers, and do not include spaces, plus (+) or minus (-). These characters are used in the mark arithmetic and will cause problems if you put them into mark names. The `mark names` operation returns a list of all defined marks.

The `insert` mark defines where the insert cursor is displayed. The `insert` mark is treated specially: you cannot remove it with the `mark unset` operation. Attempting to do so does not raise an error, though, so the following is a quick way to unset all marks:

```
eval {$t mark unset} [$t mark names]
```

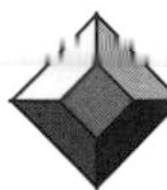

Each mark has a *gravity* that determines what happens when characters are inserted at the mark. The default gravity is `right`, which means that the mark sticks to the character that is to its right. Inserting text at a mark with `right` gravity causes the mark to be pushed along so it is always after the inserted text. With `left` gravity the mark stays with the character to its left, so inserted text goes after the mark and the mark does not move. In versions of Tk before 4.0, marks only had right gravity, which made some uses of marks awkward. The `mark gravity` operation is used to query and modify the gravity of a mark:

```
$t mark gravity foobar
=> right
$t mark gravity foobar left
```

Text Tags

A tag is a symbolic name for a range of characters. You can use almost any string for the name of a tag. However, do not use pure numbers, and do not include spaces, plus (+) or minus (-). These characters are used in the mark arithmetic and will cause problems if you use them in tag names.

A tag has attributes that affect the display of text that is tagged with it. These attributes include fonts, colors, line spacing and justification. A tag can have event bindings so you can create hypertext. You can use a tag for your own reasons, too. The text widget operations described later include operations to find out what tags are defined and where they are applied.

A tag is added to a range with the `tag add` operation. The following command applies the tag `everywhere` to all the text in the widget:

```
$t tag add everywhere 1.0 end
```

You can add one or more tags when text is inserted, too:

```
$t insert insert "new text" someTag someOtherTag
```

If you do not specify tags when text is inserted, then the text picks up any tags that are present on the characters on both sides of the insertion point. (Before Tk 4.0, tags from the left hand character were picked up.) If you specify tags in the `insert` operation, only those tags are applied to the text.

A tag is removed from a range of text with the `tag remove` operation. However, even if there is no text labeled with a tag, its attribute settings are remembered. All information about a tag can be removed with the `tag delete` operation:

```
$t tag remove everywhere 3.0 6.end
$t tag delete everywhere
```

Tag Attributes

The attributes for a tag are defined with the `tag configure` operation. Table 19–3 specifies the complete set of attributes for tags. For example, a tag for blue text is defined with the following command:

```
$t tag configure blue -foreground blue
```

Table 19–3 Attributes for text tags.

`-background` *color*	The background color for text.
`-bgstipple` *bitmap*	A stipple pattern for the background color.
`-borderwidth` *pixels*	The width for 3D border effects.
`-fgstipple` *bitmap*	A stipple pattern for the foreground color.
`-font` *font*	The font for the text.
`-foreground` *color*	The foreground color for text.
`-justify` *how*	Justification: left, right, or center.
`-lmargin1` *pixels*	Normal left indent for a line.
`-lmargin2` *pixels*	Indent for the part of a line that gets wrapped.
`-offset` *pixels*	Baseline offset. Positive for superscripts.
`-relief` *what*	Relief: flat, raised, sunken, ridge, or groove
`-rmargin` *pixels*	Right hand margin.
`-spacing1` *pixels*	Additional space above a line.
`-spacing2` *pixels*	Additional space above wrapped part of line.
`-spacing3` *pixels*	Additional space below a line.
`-underline` *boolean*	If true, the text is underlined.

The `-relief` and `-borderwidth` attributes go together. If you only specify a relief, there is no visible effect. The default relief is `flat`, too, so if you specify a border width without a relief you won't see any effect either.

The stipple attributes require a bitmap argument. Bitmaps and colors are explained in more detail in Chapter 24. For example, to "grey out" text you could use a foreground stipple of `gray50`:

```
$t tag configure disabled -fgstipple gray50
```

You can set up the appearance (and bindings) for tags once in your application, even before you have labeled any text with the tags. The attributes are retained until you explicitly delete the tag. If you are going to use the same appearance over and over again then it is more efficient to do the setup once so that Tk can retain the graphics context.

On the other hand, if you change the configuration of a tag, any text with that tag will be redisplayed with the new attributes. Similarly, if you change a binding on a tag, all tagged characters are affected immediately.

The next example defines a few tags for character styles you might see in an editor. The example is over-simplified. In practice you would want to parameterize the font family and the size for the fonts:

Example 19–1 Tag configurations for basic character styles.

```
proc TextStyles { t } {
    $t tag configure bold -font *-times-bold-r-*-12-*
    $t tag configure italic -font *-times-medium-i-*-12-*
    $t tag configure fixed -font fixed
    $t tag configure underline -underline true
    $t tag configure super -offset 6 \
        -font *-helvetica-medium-r-*-8-*
    $t tag configure sub -offset -6 \
        -font *-helvetica-medium-r-*-8-*
}
```

Mixing Attributes from Different Tags

A character can be labeled with more than one tag. For example, one tag could determine the font, another could determine the background color, and so on. If different tags try to supply the same attribute, a priority ordering is taken into account. The latest tag added to a range of text has the highest priority. The ordering of tags can be controlled explicitly with the `tag raise` and `tag lower` commands.

You can achieve interesting effects by composing attributes from different tags. In a mail reader, for example, the listing of messages in a mail folder can use one color to indicate messages that are marked for delete, and it can use another color for messages that are marked to be moved into another folder. The tags might be defined like this:

```
$t tag configure deleted -background grey75
$t tag configure moved -background yellow
```

These tags conflict, but they are never used on the same message. However, a selection could be indicated with an underline, for example:

```
$t tag configure select -underline true
```

You can add and remove the `select` tag to indicate what messages have been selected, and the underline is independent of the background color determined by the `moved` or `deleted` tag.

Line Spacing and Justification

The spacing and justification for text has several attributes. The situation is complicated by wrapped text lines. The text widget distinguishes between the first *display line* and the remaining display lines for a given text line. For example, if a line in the text widget has 80 characters but the window is only wide enough for 30, then the line may be wrapped onto three display lines. See Table 19–7 on page 234 for a description of the text widget's `wrap` attribute that controls this behavior.

Spacing is controlled with three attributes, and there are global spacing attributes as well as per-tag spacing attributes. The `-spacing1` attribute adds space above the first display line, while `-spacing2` adds space above the subsequent display lines that exist because of wrapping. The `-spacing3` attribute adds space below the last display line, which could be the same as the first display line if the line is not wrapped.

The margin settings also distinguish between the first and remaining display lines. The `-lmargin1` attribute specifies the indent for the first display line, while the `-lmargin2` attribute specifies the indent for the rest of the display lines, if any. There is only a single attribute, `-rmargin`, for the right indent. These margin attributes are only tag attributes. The closest thing for the text widget as a whole is the `-padx` attribute, but this adds an equal amount of spacing on both sides:

Example 19–2 Line spacing and justification in the text widget.

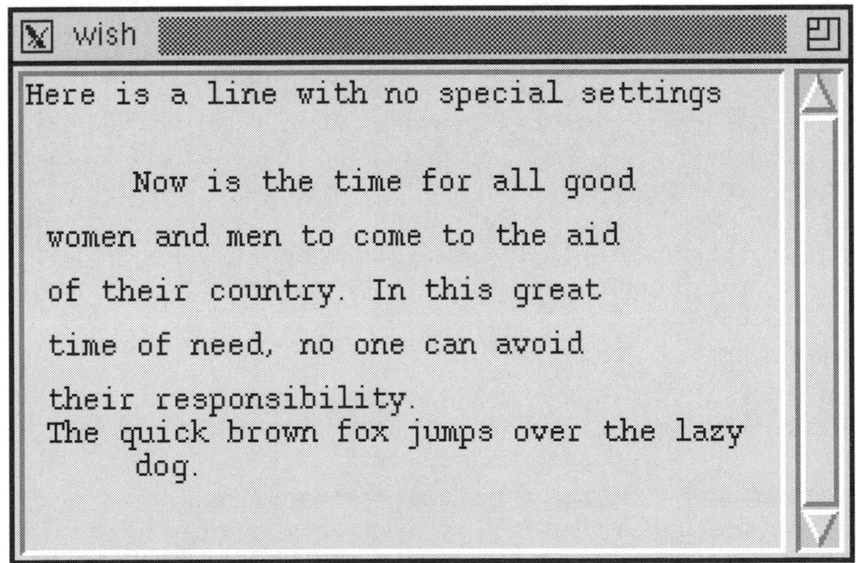

```
proc TextExample { f } {
    frame $f
    pack $f -side top -fill both -expand true
    set t [text $f.t -setgrid true -wrap word \
        -width 42 -height 14 \
        -yscrollcommand "$f.sy set"]
    scrollbar $f.sy -orient vert -command "$f.t yview"
    pack $f.sy -side right -fill y
    pack $f.t -side left -fill both -expand true

    $t tag configure para -spacing1 0.25i -spacing2 0.1i \
        -lmargin1 0.5i -lmargin2 0.1i -rmargin 0.5i
    $t tag configure hang -lmargin1 0.1i -lmargin2 0.5i

    $t insert end "Here is a line with no special settings\n"
    $t insert end "Now is the time for all good women and men
to come to the aid of their country. In this great time of
need, no one can avoid their responsibility.\n"
    $t insert end "The quick brown fox jumps over the lazy
dog."

    $t tag add para 2.0 2.end
    $t tag add hang 3.0 3.end
}
```

The example defines two tags, `para` and `hang`, that have different spacing and margins. The `-spacing1` setting for `para` causes the white space after the first line. The `-spacing2` setting causes the white space between the wrapped portions of the second paragraph. The `hang` tag has no spacing attributes so the last paragraph starts right below the previous paragraph. You can also see the difference between the `-lmargin1` and `-lmargin2` settings.

The newline characters are inserted explicitly. Each newline character defines a new line for the purposes of indexing, but not necessarily for display, as this example shows. In the third line there is no newline. This means that if more text is inserted at the `end` mark, it will be on the same logical line.

The values for the spacing and margin parameters are in screen units. Because different fonts are different sizes, you may need to compute the spacings as a function of the character sizes. The `bbox` operation returns the bounding box for a given character:

```
$t insert 1.0 "ABCDE"
$t bbox 1.0
=> 3 3 7 13
set height [lindex [$t bbox 1.0] 3]
=> 13
```

Text justification is limited to three styles: `left`, `right` or `center`. There is no setting that causes the text to line up on both margins, which would have to be achieved by introducing variable spacing between words.

The Selection

The selection is implemented with a predefined tag named `sel`. If the application tags characters with `sel`, those characters are added to the selection. This is done as part of the default bindings on the text widget.

The `exportSelection` attribute of a text widget controls whether or not selected text is exported by the X selection mechanism. By default the selection is exported. In this case, when another widget or application asserts ownership of the selection then the `sel` tag is removed from any characters that are tagged with it. Chapter 21 describes the X selection mechanism in more detail.

You cannot delete the `sel` tag with the `tag delete` operation. However, it is not an error to do so. You can delete all the tags on the text widget with the following command:

```
eval {$t tag delete} [$t tag names]
```

Tag Bindings

You can associate a tag with bindings so when the user clicks on different areas of the text display, different things happen. The syntax for the `tag bind` command is similar to that of the main Tk `bind` command. You can both query and set the bindings for a tag. Chapter 13 describes the `bind` command and the syntax for events in detail.

The only events supported by the `tag bind` command are `Enter`, `Leave`, `ButtonPress`, `Motion`, and `KeyPress`. `ButtonPress` and `KeyPress` can be shorted to `Button` and `Key` as in the regular `bind` command. The `Enter` and `Leave` events are triggered when the mouse moves in and out of characters with a tag, which is different than when the mouse moves in and out of the window.

If a character has multiple tags, then the bindings associated with all the tags will be invoked, in the order from lowest priority tag to highest priority tag. After all the tag bindings have run, the binding associated with the main widget is run, if any. The `continue` and `break` commands work inside tag bindings in a similar fashion as they work with regular command bindings. See Chapter 13 for the details.

Example 19–3 defines a text button that has a highlighted relief and an action associated with it. The example generates a new tag name so that each text button is unique. The relief and background are set for the tag to set it apart visually. The `tk colormodel` command is used to find out if the display supports color before adding a colored background to the tag. On a black and white display, the button is displayed in reverse video (i.e., white on black.) The command is bound to `<Button-1>`, which is the same as `<ButtonPress-1>`.

The cursor is changed when the mouse is over the tagged area by binding to the `<Enter>` and `<Leave>` events. Upon leaving the tagged area, the cursor is restored. Another tag is used to remember the previous setting for the cursor. You could also use a global variable, but it is often useful to decorate the text with tags for your own purposes.

Example 19–3 An active text button.

```
proc TextButton { t start end command } {
	global textbutton
	if ![info exists textbutton(uid)] {
		set textbutton(uid) 0
	} else {
		incr textbutton(uid)
	}
	set tag button$textbutton(uid)
	$t tag configure $tag -relief raised -borderwidth 2
	if {[tk colormodel $t] == "color"} {
		$t tag configure $tag -background thistle
	} else {
		$t tag configure $tag -background [$t cget -fg]
		$t tag configure $tag -foreground [$t cget -bg]
	}
	# Bind the command to the tag
	$t tag bind $tag <Button-1> $command
	$t tag add $tag $start $end
	# use another tag to remember the cursor
	$t tag add cursor=[$t cget -cursor] $start $end
	$t tag bind $tag <Enter> {%W config -cursor tcross}
	$t tag bind $tag <Leave> {TextButtonFixCursor %W}
}
proc TextButtonFixCursor {t} {
	regexp {cursor=([^ ]*)} [%W tag names] x cursor
	$t config -cursor $cursor
}
```

To behave even more like a button the action should trigger upon `<Button-Release-1>`, and the appearance should change upon `<ButtonPress-1>`. If this is important to you, you can always embed a real Tk button. Embedding widgets is described in the next section.

Embedded Widgets

The text widget can display one or more other widgets as well as text. You can include a picture, for example, by constructing it in a canvas and then inserting the canvas into the text widget. An embedded widget takes up one character in terms of indices. You can address the widget by its index position or by the Tk pathname of the widget.

For example, suppose `$t` names a text widget. The following commands create a button and insert it into the text widget. The button behaves normally, and in this case it invokes the `Help` command when the user clicks on it:

```
button $t.help -bitmap questhead -command Help
$t window create end -window $t.help
```

By default an embedded widget is centered vertically on its text line. You can adjust this with the `-align` option to the `window create` command. The possible alignments are `top`, `center`, `baseline`, or `bottom`:

`top`	Top of widget lines up with top of text line.
`center`	Center of widget lines up with center of text line.
`baseline`	Bottom of widget lines up with text baseline.
`bottom`	Bottom of widget lines up with bottom of text line.

You can postpone the creation of the embedded widget by specifying a Tcl command that creates the window, instead of specifying the `-window` option. The delayed creation is useful if you have lots of widgets embedded in your text. In this case the Tcl command is evaluated just before the text widget needs to display the widget. In other words, when the user scrolls the text so the widget would appear, the Tcl command is run to create the widget:

Example 19–4 Delayed creation of embedded widgets.

```
$t window create end -create [list MakeGoBack $t]
proc MakeGoBack { t } {
   button $t.goback -text "Go to Line 1" \
      -command [list $t see 1.0]
}
```

The `MakeGoBack` procedure is introduced to eliminate potential quoting problems. If you need to execute more than one Tcl command to create the widget or if the embedded button has a complex command, the quoting can quickly get out of hand.

Table 19–4 gives the complete set of options for creating embedded widgets. You can change these later with the `window configure` operation. For example:

```
$t window configure $t.goback -align bottom
```

Table 19–4 Options to the `window create` operation.

Option	Description
`-align` *where*	Alignment: `top`, `center`, `bottom`, or `baseline`.
`-create` *command*	Tcl command to create the widget.
`-padx` *pixels*	Padding on either side of the widget.
`-pady` *pixels*	Padding above and below the widget.
`-stretch` *boolean*	If true, the widget is stretched vertically to match the spacing of the text line.
`-window` *pathname*	Tk pathname of the widget to embed.

You can specify the window to reconfigure with either the index where the window is located, or by its pathname. If you plan on identifying a window by its position, it may help to define a mark at the position of the window. Note that `end` is not useful for identifying an embedded window because the text widget treats `end` specially. You can insert a window at `end`, but `end` is always updated to be after the last item in the widget. Thus `end` will never name the position of an existing window.

Text Bindings

There is an extensive set of default bindings for text widgets. In general, the commands that move the insertion cursor also clear the selection. Often you can hold the Shift key down to extend the selection, or hold the Control key down to move the insertion cursor without affecting the selection. Table 19–5 lists the default bindings for the text widget:

Table 19–5 Bindings for the text widget.

`<Any-Key>`	Insert normal printing characters.
`<Button-1>`	Set the insert point, clear the selection, set focus.
`<Control-Button-1>`	Set the insert point without affecting the selection.
`<B1-Motion>`	Sweep out a selection from the insert point.
`<Double-Button-1>`	Select the word under the mouse.
`<Triple-Button-1>`	Select the line under the mouse.
`<Shift-Button-1>`	Adjust the end of selection closest to the mouse.
`<Shift-B1-Motion>`	Continue to adjust the selection.
`<Button-2>`	Paste the selection, or set the scrolling anchor.
`<B2-Motion>`	Scroll the window.
`<Key-Left> <Control-b>`	Move the cursor left one character. Clear selection.
`<Shift-Left>`	Move the cursor and extend the selection.
`<Control-Left>`	Move the cursor by words. Clear the selection.
`<Control-Shift-Left>`	Move the cursor by words. Extend the selection.
`<Key-Right> <Control-f>`	All `Right` bindings are analogous to `Left` bindings.
`<Meta-b> <Meta-f>`	Same as `<Control-Left>` and `<Control-Right>`.
`<Key-Up> <Control-p>`	Move the cursor up one line. Clear the selection.
`<Shift-Up>`	Move the cursor up one line. Extend the selection.

Table 19–5 Bindings for the text widget. (Continued)

`<Control-Up>`	Move the cursor up by paragraphs, which are a group of lines separated by a blank line.
`<Control-Shift-Up>`	Move the cursor up by paragraph. Extend selection.
`<Key-Down> <Control-n>`	All `Down` bindings are analogous to `Up` bindings.
`<Next> <Prior>`	Move the cursor by one screen. Clear the selection.
`<Shift-Next>` `<Shift-Prior>`	Move the cursor by one screen. Extend the selection.
`<Home> <Control-a>`	Move the cursor to line start. Clear the selection.
`<Shift-Home>`	Move the cursor to line start. Extend the selection.
`<End> <Control-e>`	Move the cursor to line end. Clear the selection.
`<Shift-End>`	Move the cursor to line end. Extend the selection.
`<Control-Home>` `<Meta-less>`	Move the cursor to the beginning of text. Clear the selection.
`<Control-End>` `<Meta-greater>`	Move the cursor to the end of text. Clear the selection.
`<Select>` `<Control-space>`	Set the selection anchor to the position of the cursor.
`<Shift-Select>` `<Control-Shift-space>`	Adjust the selection to the position of the cursor.
`<Control-slash>`	Select everything in the text widget.
`<Control-backslash>`	Clear the selection.
`<Delete>`	Delete the selection, if any. Otherwise delete the character to the right of the cursor.
`<BackSpace> <Control-h>`	Delete the selection, if any. Otherwise delete the character to the left of the cursor.
`<Control-d>`	Delete character to the right of the cursor.
`<Meta-d>`	Delete word to the right of the cursor.
`<Control-k>`	Delete from cursor to end of the line. If you are at the end of line, delete the newline character.
`<Control-o>`	Insert a newline but do not advance the cursor.
`<Control-w>`	Delete the word to the left of the cursor.
`<Control-x>`	Deletes the selection, if any.
`<Control-t>`	Transpose the characters on either side of the cursor.

Text Operations

Table 19–6 describes the text widget operations, including some that are not discussed in this chapter. In the table, `$t` is a text widget:

Table 19–6 Operations for the text widget.

`$t bbox` *`index`*	Return the bounding box of the character at *`index`*. Four numbers are returned: *`x y width height`*.
`$t cget` *`option`*	Return the value of the configuration option.
`$t compare` *`i1 op i2`*	Perform index comparison. *`ix`* and *`i2`* are indexes. *`op`* is one of: `< <= == >= > !=`
`$t configure ...`	Query or set configuration options.
`$t debug` *`boolean`*	Enable consistency checking for B-tree code.
`$t delete` *`i1 ?i2?`*	Delete from *`i1`* up to, but not including *`i2`*. Just delete the character at *`i1`* if *`i2`* is not specified.
`$t dlineinfo` *`index`*	Return the bounding box, in pixels, of the display for the line containing index. Five numbers are returned, *`x y width height baseline`*.
`$t get` *`i1 ?i2?`*	Return the text from *`i1`* to *`i2`*, or just the character at *`i1`* if *`i2`* is not specified.
`$t index` *`index`*	Return the numerical value of *`index`*.
`$t insert` *`index chars ?tags?`*	Insert *`chars`* at the specified *`index`*. If *`tags`* are specified they are added to the new characters.
`$t mark gravity` *`name ?direction?`*	Query or assign a gravity direction to the mark *`name`*. *`direction`*, if specified, is `left` or `right`.
`$t mark names`	Return a list of defined marks.
`$t mark set` *`name index`*	Define a mark *`name`* at the given *`index`*.
`$t mark unset` *`name1 ?name2 ...?`*	Delete the named mark, or marks.
`$t scan mark` *`x y`*	Anchor a scrolling operation.
`$t scan dragto` *`x y`*	Scroll based on a new position.
`$t search` *`?switches? pattern index ?varName?`*	Search for text starting at index. The index of the start of the match is returned. The number of characters in the match is stored in `varName`. Switches are: `-forw, -back, -exact, -regexp, -nowrap, --`
`$t see` *`index`*	Position the display to view *`index`*.
`$t tag add` *`name i1 ?i2?`*	Add the tag to *`i1`* through, but not including *`i2`*, or just the character at i1 if *`i2`* is not given.

Table 19–6 Operations for the text widget. (Continued)

`$t tag bind` *name ?sequence? ?script?*	Query or define bindings for the tag *name*.
`$t tag cget` *name option*	Return the value of *option* for tag *name*.
`$t tag delete` *tag1 ?tag2 ...?*	Delete information for the named tags.
`$t tag lower` *tag ?before?*	Lower the priority of *tag* to the lowest priority or to just below tag *below*.
`$t tag names` *?index?*	Return the names of the tags at the specified *index*, or in the whole widget, sorted from lowest to highest priority.
`$t tag nextrange` *tag i1 ?i2?*	Return a list of two indices that are the next range of text with tag that starts at or after *i1* and before index *i2*, or the end.
`$t tag raise` *tag ?above?*	Raise the priority of *tag* to the highest priority, or to just above the priority of tag *above*.
`$t tag ranges` *tag*	Return a list describing all the ranges of tag.
`$t tag remove` *tag i1 ?i2?*	Remove tag from the range *i1* up to, but not including *i2*, or just at *i1* if *i2* is not specified.
`$t window config` *win ...*	Query or modify the configuration of the embedded window. *win* is a Tk pathname or an index.
`$t window create` *ix ?option value ...?*	Create an embedded window at *ix*. The configuration options depend on the type of the window.
`$t xview`	Return two fractions between zero and one that describe the amount of text off screen to the left and the amount of text displayed.
`$t xview moveto` *fraction*	Position the text so *fraction* of the text is off screen to the left.
`$t xview scroll` *num what*	Scroll *num* of *what*, which is *units* or *pages*.
`$t yview`	Return two fractions between zero and one that describe the amount of text off screen towards the beginning and the amount of text displayed.
`$t yview moveto` *fraction*	Position the text so *fraction* of the text is off screen towards the beginning.
`$t yview scroll` *num what*	Scroll *num* of *what*, which is *units* or *pages*.
`$t yview ?-pickplace?` *ix*	Obsoleted by the `see` operation, which is similar.
`$t yview` *number*	Position line *number* at the top of the screen. Obsoleted by the `yview moveto` operation.

Text Attributes

Table 19–7 lists the attributes for the text widget. The table uses the X resource name, which has capitals at internal word boundaries. In Tcl commands the attributes are specified with a dash and all lowercase:

Table 19–7 Text attribute resource names.

background	Background color (also bg).
borderWidth	Extra space around the edge of the text.
cursor	Cursor to display when mouse is over the widget.
font	Default font for the text.
foreground	Foreground color. (Also fg)
highlightColor	Color for input focus highlight border.
highlightThickness	Width of highlight border.
insertBackground	Color for the insert cursor.
insertBorderWidth	Size of 3D border for insert cursor.
insertOffTime	Milliseconds insert cursor blinks off.
insertOnTime	Milliseconds insert cursor blinks on.
insertWidth	Width of the insert cursor.
padX	Extra space to the left and right of the text.
padY	Extra space above and below the text.
relief	3D relief: flat, sunken, raised, groove, or ridge.
selectBackground	Background color of selected text.
selectForeground	Foreground color of selected text.
selectBorderWidth	Size of 3D border for selection highlight.
setGrid	Enable/disable geometry gridding.
spacing1	Extra space above each unwrapped line.
spacing2	Space between parts of a line that have wrapped.
spacing3	Extra space below an unwrapped line.
state	Editable (normal) or read-only (disabled).
width	Width, in characters, of the text display.
wrap	Line wrap mode: none, char, or word.
xScrollCommand	Tcl command prefix for horizontal scrolling.
yScrollCommand	Tcl command prefix for vertical scrolling.

CHAPTER 20

The Canvas Widget

This canvas widget provides a general-purpose display that you can program to display a variety of objects including arcs, images, lines, ovals, polygons, rectangles, text, and embedded windows.

Canvas widgets display objects such as lines and images, and each object can be programmed to respond to user input, or be animated under program control. The objects can be labeled with *tags*, and the tags can be configured with display attributes and event bindings. This chapter describes several pre-defined canvas object types. Chapter 30 outlines the C programming interface for creating new canvas objects.

Canvas Coordinates

The coordinate space of the canvas has 0, 0 at the top left corner. Larger X coordinates are to the right, and larger Y coordinates are downward. The position and possibly the size of a canvas object is determined by a set of coordinates. Different objects are characterized by different numbers of coordinates. For example, text objects have two coordinates, *x1 y1*, that specify their anchor point. A line can have many pairs of coordinates that specify the endpoints of its segments. The coordinates are set when the object is created, and they can be updated later with the `coords` operation. By default coordinates are in pixels. Append a coordinate with one of the following letters to change the units:

```
c    centimeters
i    inch
m    millimeters
p    printer points (1/72 inches)
```

The `width` and `height` attributes of the canvas determine its viewable area. The `scrollRegion` attribute of the canvas determines the boundaries of the canvas. Its value is four numbers that specify the upper left and lower right coordinates of the canvas. If you do not specify a scroll region, it defaults to the size of the viewable area. The following example creates a canvas and connects it to two scrollbars to provide horizontal and vertical scrolling.

Example 20–1 A large scrollable canvas.

```
proc ScrolledCanvas { c width height region } {
    frame $c
    canvas $c.canvas -width $width -height $height \
        -scrollregion $region \
        -xscrollcommand [list $c.xscroll set] \
        -yscrollcommand [list $c.yscroll set]
    scrollbar $c.xscroll -orient horizontal \
        -command [list $c.canvas xview]
    scrollbar $c.yscroll -orient vertical \
        -command [list $c.canvas yview]
    pack $c.xscroll -side bottom -fill x
    pack $c.yscroll -side right -fill y
    pack $c.canvas -side left -fill both -expand true
    pack $c -side top -fill both -expand true
    return $c.canvas
}
ScrolledCanvas .c 300 200 {0 0 1000 400}
=> .c.canvas
```

Hello, World!

The next example creates an object that you can drag around with the mouse:

Example 20–2 The canvas "Hello, World!" example.

```
proc CanvasHello {} {
    canvas .c -width 400 -height 100
    pack .c
    # Create a text object on the canvas
    .c create text 50 50 -text "Hello, World!" -tag movable
    # Bind actions to objects with the movable tag
    .c bind movable <Button-1> {CanvasMark %x %y %W}
    .c bind movable <B1-Motion> {CanvasDrag %x %y %W}
}
proc CanvasMark { x y w } {
    global canvas
    # Remember the object and its location
    set canvas($w,obj) [$w find closest $x $y]
    set canvas($w,x) $x
    set canvas($w,y) $y
}
```

```
proc CanvasDrag { x y w } {
    # Move the current object
    global canvas
    set dx [expr $x - $canvas($w,x)]
    set dy [expr $y - $canvas($w,y)]
    $w move $canvas($w,obj) $dx $dy
    set canvas($w,x) $x
    set canvas($w,y) $y
}
```

The example creates a `text` object and gives it a *tag* named `movable`. Tags are discussed later in this chapter. The first argument after `create` specifies the type, and the remaining arguments depend on the type of object being created. Each canvas object requires some coordinates, optionally followed by attribute value pairs. The complete set of attributes for canvas objects are presented later in this chapter. A `text` object needs two coordinates for its location:

```
.c create text 50 50 -text "Hello, World!" -tag movable
```

The `create` operation returns an ID for the object being created, which would have been 1 in this case. However, the code manipulates the canvas objects by specifying a tag instead of an object ID. A tag is a more general handle on canvas objects. Many objects can have the same tag, and an object can have more than one tag. A tag can be (almost) any string; avoid spaces and pure numbers. Nearly all the canvas operations operate on either tags or object IDs.

The example defines behavior for objects with the `movable` tag. The pathname of the canvas (`%W`) is passed to `CanvasMark` and `CanvasDrag` so these procedures could be used on different canvases. The `%x` and `%y` keywords get substituted with the X and Y coordinate of the event:

```
.c bind movable <Button-1> {CanvasMark %x %y %W}
.c bind movable <B1-Motion> {CanvasDrag %x %y %W}
```

The `CanvasMark` and `CanvasDrag` procedures let you drag the object around the canvas. Because it is applied to any object with the `movable` tag, the `Mark` procedure must first find the object that was clicked on. It uses the `find` operation:

```
set canvas($w,obj) [$w find closest $x $y]
```

The actual moving is done in `Drag` with the `move` operation:

```
$w move $canvas($w,obj) $dx $dy
```

Try creating a few other object types and dragging them around, too:

```
.c create rect 10 10 30 30 -fill red -tag movable
.c create line 1 1 40 40 90 60 -width 2 -tag movable
.c create poly 1 1 40 40 90 60 -fill blue -tag movable
```

The example may seem a little cluttered by the general use of the global array `canvas` and its indices that are parameterized by the canvas pathname. However, if you get into this coding habit early, then you will find it easy to write re-usable code.

The Min Max Scale Example

This section presents an example that constructs a scale-like object with two sliders. The sliders represent the minimum and maximum values for some parameter. Clearly, the minimum cannot be greater than the maximum, and vice versa. The example creates three rectangles on the canvas. One rectangle forms the long axis of the slider. The other two rectangles are markers that represent the values. Two text objects float below the markers to give the current values of the minimum and maximum:

Example 20–3 A min max scale canvas example

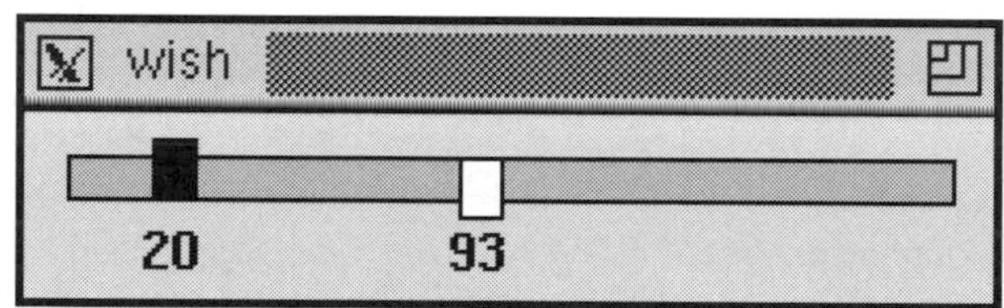


```
proc Scale2 {w min max {width {}} } {
    global scale2
    if {$width == {}} {
        # Set the long dimension, in pixels
        set width [expr $max - $min]
    }
    # Save parameters
    set scale2($w,scale) [expr ($max-$min)/$width.0]
    set scale2($w,min) $min;# Current minimum
    set scale2($w,max) $max
    set scale2($w,Min) $min;# Lower bound to the scale
    set scale2($w,Max) $max
    set scale2($w,L) 10
    set scale2($w,R) [expr $width+10]

    # Build from 0 to 100, then scale and move it later.
    # Distance between left edges of boxes is 100.
    # The box is 10 wide, therefore the slider is 110 long.
    # The left box sticks up, and the right one hangs down.
    canvas $w
    $w create rect 0 0 110 10 -fill grey -tag slider
    $w create rect 0 -4 10 10 -fill black -tag {left lbox}
    $w create rect 100 0 110 14 -fill red -tag {right rbox}
    $w create text 5 16 -anchor n -text $min -tag {left lnum}
    $w create text 105 16 -anchor n -text $max \
        -tag {right rnum} -fill red

    # Stretch/shrink the slider to the right length
    set scale [expr ($width+10) / 110.0]
    $w scale slider 0 0 $scale 1.0
    # move the right box and text to match new length
    set nx [lindex [$w coords slider] 2]
    $w move right [expr $nx-110] 0
```

```
        # Move everything into view
        $w move all 10 10

        # Make the canvas fit comfortably around the image
        set bbox [$w bbox all]
        set height [expr [lindex $bbox 3]+4]
        $w config -height $height -width [expr $width+30]

        # Bind drag actions
        $w bind left  <Button-1> {Scale2Mark %W %x lbox}
        $w bind right <Button-1> {Scale2Mark %W %x rbox}
        $w bind left  <B1-Motion> {Scale2Drag %W %x lbox}
        $w bind right <B1-Motion> {Scale2Drag %W %x rbox}
}
```

The slider is constructed with absolute coordinates, and then it is scaled to the desired width. The alternative is to compute the coordinates based on the desired width. I found it clearer to use numbers when creating the initial layout as opposed to using `expr` or introducing more variables. The `scale` operation streches the slider bar to the correct length. The `scale` operation takes a reference point, which in our case is (0, 0), and independent scale factors for the X and Y dimensions. The scale factor is computed from the `width` parameter, taking into account the extra length added (10) so that the distance between the left edge of the boxes is `$width`:

```
set scale [expr ($width+10) / 110.0]
$w scale slider 0 0 $scale 1.0
```

The `move` operation repositions the right box and right hanging text. If the marker boxes are scaled, their shape gets distorted. The `coords` operation returns a list of four numbers: *x1 y1 x2 y2*. The distance to move is just the difference between the new right coordinate and the value used when constructing the slider initially. The box and text share the same tag, `right`, so they are both moved with a single `move` operation:

```
set nx [lindex [$w coords slider] 2]
$w move right [expr $nx-110] 0
```

After the slider is constructed it is shifted away from (0, 0), which is the upper-left corner of the canvas. The `bbox` operation returns four coordinates: *x1 y1 x2 y2*, that define the bounding box of the items with the given tag. In the example, *y1* is zero, so *y2* gives us the height of the image. The information returned by `bbox` can be off by a few pixels, and the example needs a few more pixels of height to avoid clipping the text. The width is computed based on the extra length added for the marker box, the 10 pixels the whole image was shifted, and 10 more for the same amount of space on the right side:

```
set bbox [$w bbox all]
set height [expr [lindex $bbox 3]+4]
$w config -height $height -width [expr $width+30]
```

Bindings are defined for the box and hanging text. The general tags `left` and `right` are used for the bindings. This means you can drag either the box or the text to move the slider. The pathname of the canvas is passed into these procedures so you could have more than one double slider in your interface:

```
$w bind left  <Button-1> {Scale2Mark %W %x lbox}
$w bind right <Button-1> {Scale2Mark %W %x rbox}
$w bind left  <B1-Motion> {Scale2Drag %W %x lbox}
$w bind right <B1-Motion> {Scale2Drag %W %x rbox}
```

Example 20–4 Moving the markers for the min max scale.

```
proc Scale2Mark { w x what } {
    global scale2
    # Remember the anchor point for the drag
    set scale2($w,$what) $x
}
proc Scale2Drag { w x what } {
    global scale2

    # Compute delta and update anchor point
    set x1 $scale2($w,$what)
    set scale2($w,$what) $x
    set dx [expr $x - $x1]

    # Find out where the boxes are currently
    set rx [lindex [$w coords rbox] 0]
    set lx [lindex [$w coords lbox] 0]

    if {$what == "lbox"} {
        # Constrain the movement to be between the
        # left edge and the right marker.
        if {$lx + $dx > $rx} {
            set dx [expr $rx - $lx]
            set scale2($w,$what) $rx
        } elseif {$lx + $dx < $scale2($w,L)} {
            set dx [expr $scale2($w,L) - $lx]
            set scale2($w,$what) $scale2($w,L)
        }
        $w move left $dx 0

        # Update the minimum value and the hanging text
        set lx [lindex [$w coords lbox] 0]
        set scale2($w,min) [expr int($scale2($w,Min) + \
            ($lx-$scale2($w,L)) * $scale2($w,scale))]
        $w itemconfigure lnum -text $scale2($w,min)
    } else {
        # Constrain the movement to be between the
        # right edge and the left marker
        if {$rx + $dx < $lx} {
            set dx [expr $lx - $rx]
            set scale2($w,$what) $lx
        } elseif {$rx + $dx > $scale2($w,R)} {
            set dx [expr $scale2($w,R) - $rx]
            set scale2($w,$what) $scale2($w,R)
        }
```

```
        $w move right $dx 0

        # Update the maximum value and the hanging text
        set rx [lindex [$w coords right] 0]
        set scale2($w,max) [expr int($scale2($w,Min) + \
            ($rx-$scale2($w,L)) * $scale2($w,scale))]
        $w itemconfigure rnum -text $scale2($w,max)
    }
}
proc Scale2Value {w} {
    global scale2
    # Return the current values of the double slider
    return [list $scale2($w,min) $scale2($w,max)]
}
```

The Scale2Mark procedure initializes an anchor position, scale2($w,$-what), and Scale2Drag uses this to detect how far the mouse has moved. The change in position, dx, is constrained so that the markers cannot move outside their bounds. The anchor is updated if a constraint was used, and this means the marker will not move until the mouse is moved back over the marker. (Try commenting out the assignments to scale2($w,$what) inside the if statement.) After the marker and hanging text are moved, the value of the associated parameter is computed based on the parameters of the scale. The Scale2Value procedure to queries the current values of the double slider.

Many of the canvas operations take an argument that identifies objects. The value can be a tag name, or it can be the numerical object identifier returned by the create operation. You have the option of saving the numerical identifier in a variable, or assigning a symbolic identifier with a tag.

The canvas tag facility is very useful. The example uses the all tag to move all the items, and to find out the bounding box of the image. The left box and the left hanging text both have the left tag. They can be moved together, and they share the same bindings. Similarly, the right tag is shared by the right box and the right hanging text. Each item has its own unique tag so it can be manipulated individually, too. Those tags are slider, lbox, lnum, rbox, and rnum.

The next several sections describe the built-in object types for canvases.

Arc Items

An arc is a section of an oval. The dimensions of the oval are determined by four coordinates that are its bounding box. The arc is then determined by two angles, the start angle and the extent. The region of the oval can be filled or unfilled, and there are three different ways to define the fill region. The pieslice style connects the arc with the center point of the oval. The chord style connects the two endpoints of the arc. The arc style just fills the arc itself and there is no outline.

Example 20–5 Canvas arc items.

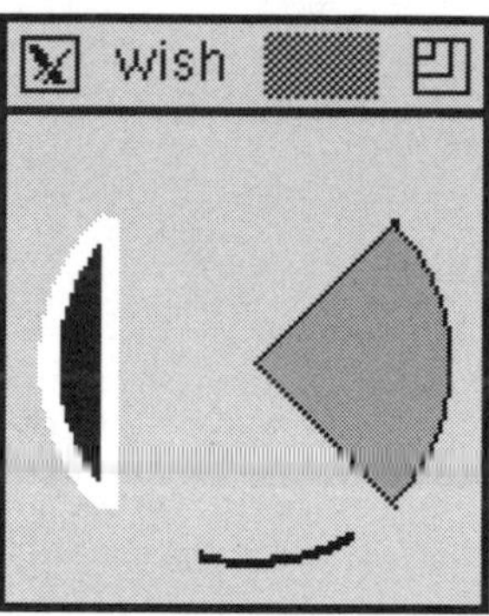


```
# $c is a canvas
$c create arc 10 10 100 100 -start 45 -extent -90 \
   -style pieslice -fill orange -outline black
$c create arc 10 10 100 100 -start 135 -extent 90 \
   -style chord -fill blue -outline white -width 4
$c create arc 10 10 100 100 -start 255 -extent 45 \
   -style arc -fill black -width 2
```

Table 20–1 specifies the complete set of `arc` attributes.

Table 20–1 Arc attributes.

`-extent` *degrees*	The length of the arc in the counter-clockwise direction.
`-fill` *color*	The color of the interior of the arc region.
`-outline` *color*	The color of the arc itself.
`-start` *degrees*	The starting angle of the arc.
`-stipple` *bitmap*	A stipple pattern for the fill.
`-style` *style*	`pieslice`, `chord`, `arc`
`-tags` *tagList*	List of tags for the arc item.
`-width` *num*	Width, in canvas coordinates, of the arc and outline.

Bitmap Items

A bitmap is a simple graphic with a foreground and background color. One-bit per pixel is used to choose between the foreground and the background. If you do not specify a background color, the background bits are clear and the canvas background shows through. A canvas `bitmap` item is positioned with two coordinates and an anchor position. Its size is determined by the bitmap data. The `bitmap` itself is specified with a symbolic name or by the name of a file that contains its definition. If the name begins with an `@` it indicates a file name. The bitmaps built into wish are shown in the example below. Chapter 30 outlines the C interface for registering bitmaps under a name.

Example 20–6 Canvas `bitmap` items.

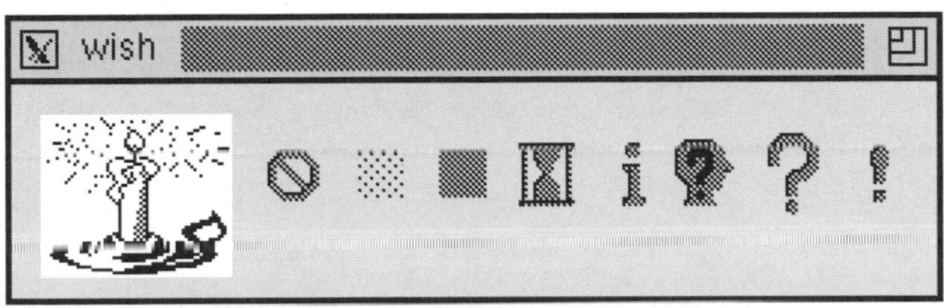


```
# $c is a canvas
set o [$c create bitmap 10 10 -bitmap @candle.xbm -anchor nw\
    -background white -foreground blue]
set x [lindex [$c bbox $o] 2];# Right edge of bitmap
foreach builtin {error gray25 gray50 hourglass \
                info questhead question warning} {
    incr x 20
    set o [$c create bitmap $x 30 -bitmap $builtin -anchor c]
    set x [lindex [$c bbox $o] 2]
}
```

Table 20–2 specifies the complete set of `bitmap` attributes.

Table 20–2 Bitmap attributes.

`-anchor` *`position`*	Anchor: `c`, `n`, `ne`, `e`, `se`, `s`, `sw`, `w`, or `nw`.
`-background` *`color`*	The background color (for zero bits).
`-bitmap` *`name`*	A built in bitmap.
`-bitmap @`*`filename`*	A bitmap defined by a file.
`-foreground` *`color`*	The foreground color (for one bits).
`-tags` *`tagList`*	List of tags for the bitmap item.

Image Items

The canvas `image` objects use the general image mechanism of Tk. You must first define an image using the `image` command, which is described in Chapter 24 in the section *Bitmaps and Images*. Once you have defined an image, all you need to specify for the canvas is its position, anchor point, and any tags. The size and color information is set when the image is defined. If an image is redefined, anything displaying that image automatically gets updated.

Example 20–7 Canvas `image` items.

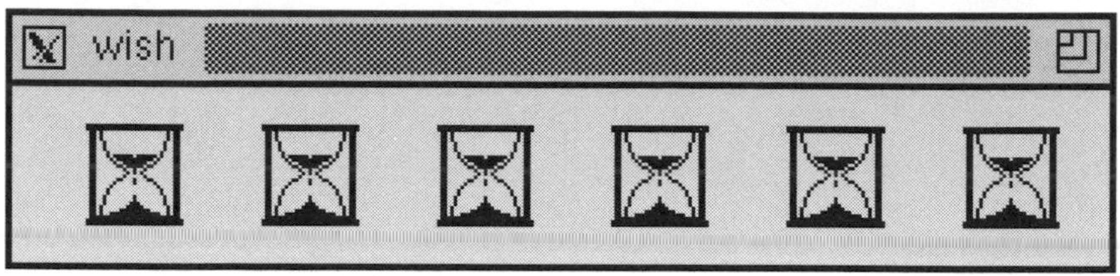


```
image create bitmap hourglass2 \
    -file hourglass.bitmap -maskfile hourglass.mask \
    -background white -foreground blue]
for {set x 20} {$x < 300} {incr x 20} {
    $c create image $x 10 -image hourglass2 -anchor nw
    incr x [image width hourglass2]
}
```

Table 20–3 specifies the attributes for canvas `image` items.

Table 20–3 Image attributes.

`-anchor` *position*	Anchor: c, n, ne, e, se, s, sw, w, or nw.
`-image` *name*	The name of an image.
`-tags` *tagList*	List of tags for the image item.

Line Items

A line has two or more sets of coordinates, where each set of coordinates defines an endpoint of a line segment. The segments can be joined in several different styles, and the whole line can be drawn with a spline fit as opposed to straight-line segments. The next example draws a line in two steps. In the first pass, single-segment lines are drawn. When the stroke completes, these are replaced with a single line segment that is drawn with a spline curve.

Example 20–8 A canvas stroke drawing example.

```
proc StrokeInit {} {
    canvas .c ; pack .c
    bind .c <Button-1> {StrokeBegin %W %x %y}
    bind .c <B1-Motion> {Stroke %W %x %y}
    bind .c <ButtonRelease-1> {StrokeEnd %W %x %y}
}
proc StrokeBegin { w x y } {
```

```
		global stroke
		catch {unset stroke}
		set stroke(N) 0
		set stroke(0) [list $x $y]
	}
	proc Stroke { w x y } {
		global stroke
		set last $stroke($stroke(N))
		incr stroke(N)
		set stroke($stroke(N)) [list $x $y]
		eval {$w create line} $last {$x $y -tag segments}
	}
	proc StrokeEnd { w x y } {
		global stroke
		set points {}
		for {set i 0} {$i <= $stroke(N)} {incr i} {
			append points $stroke($i) " "
		}
		$w delete segments
		eval {$w create line} $points \
			{-tag line -joinstyle round -smooth true -arrow last}
	}
```

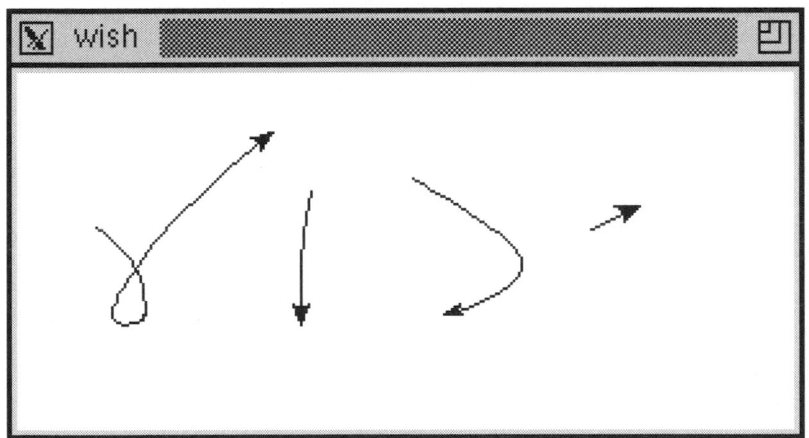

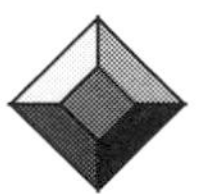

The example uses the `stroke` array to hold the points of the line as it builds up the stroke. At the end of the stroke it assembles the points into a list. The `eval` command concatenates this list of points onto the `create line` command. Recall that `eval` uses `concat` if it gets multiple arguments. The other parts of the `create line` command are protected by braces so they get evaluated only once. Chapter 6 describes this trick in more detail.

The arrow attribute adds an arrow head to the end of the stroke. If you try this example you will notice that the arrow is not always aimed as you expect. This is because there are often many points generated close together as you release the mouse button. In fact, the X and Y coordinates seen by `StrokeEnd` are always the same as those seen by the last `Stroke` call. If you add this duplicate point to the end of the list of points, no arrowhead is drawn at all. In practice you might want to make `Stroke` filter out points that are too close together.

Table 20–4 specifies the complete set of line attributes. The `capstyle` affects the way the ends of the line are drawn. The `joinstyle` affects the way line segments are joined together.

Table 20–4 Line attributes.

`-arrow` *`where`*	Arrow location: `none`, `first`, `last`, or `both`.
`-arrowshape` *`{a b c}`*	Three parameters that describe the shape of the arrow. `c` is the width and `b` is the overall length. `a` is the length of the part that touches the line (e.g., `8 10 3`).
`-capstyle` *`what`*	Line ends: `butt`, `projecting`, or `round`.
`-fill` *`color`*	The color of the line.
`-joinstyle` *`what`*	Line joints: `bevel`, `miter`, or `round`.
`-smooth` *`boolean`*	If `true`, a spline curve is drawn.
`-splinesteps` *`num`*	Number of line segments that approximate the spline.
`-stipple` *`bitmap`*	Stipple pattern for line fill.
`-tags` *`tagList`*	Set of tags for the line item.
`-width` *`width`*	Width of the line, in screen units.

Oval Items

An `oval` is defined by two sets of coordinates that define its bounding box. If the box is square, a circle is drawn. You can set the color of the interior of the oval as well as the outline of the oval. A sampler of ovals is shown in the next example.

Example 20–9 Canvas `oval` items.

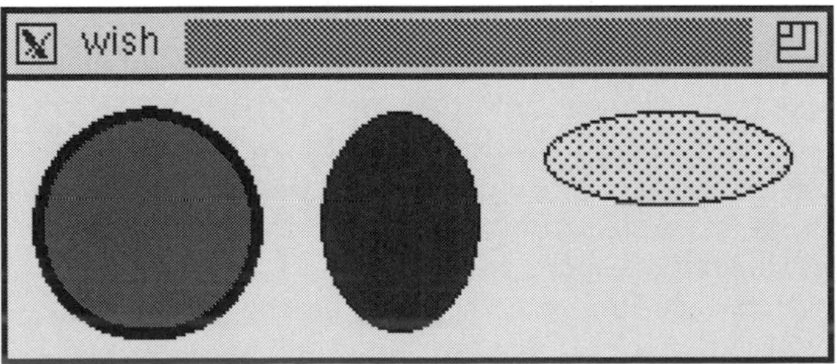

```
$c create oval 10 10 80 80 -fill red -width 4
$c create oval 100 10 150 80 -fill blue -width 0
$c create oval 170 10 250 40 -fill black -stipple gray25.
```

The various artifacts on the ovals are a function of the quality of your X server. Different X servers draw circles better and faster than others. Table 20–5 specifies the complete set of `oval` attributes.

Table 20–5 Oval attributes.

`-fill` *`color`*	The color of the interior of the oval.
`-outline` *`color`*	The color for the outline of the oval.
`-stipple` *`bitmap`*	Stipple pattern for oval fill.
`-tags` *`tagList`*	Set of tags for the oval item.
`-width` *`width`*	The thickness of the outline.

Polygon Items

A `polygon` is a closed shape specified by sets of points, one for each vertex of the polygon. The vertices can be connected with smooth or straight lines. There is no outline option for a polygon. You can get an outline by drawing a line with the same coordinates, although you will need to duplicate the starting point at the end of the list of coordinates for the line.

Example 20–10 Canvas `polygon` items.

```
$c create poly 20 -40 40 -20 40 20 20 40 -20 40 \
    -40 20 -40 -20 -20 -40 -fill red
$c create line 20 -40 40 -20 40 20 20 40 -20 40 \
    -40 20 -40 -20 -20 -40 20 -40 -fill white -width 5
$c create text 0 0 -text STOP -fill white
$c move all 50 50
```

Table 20–6 specifies the complete set of `polygon` attributes.

Table 20–6 Polygon attributes.

`-fill` *color*	The color of the polygon.
`-smooth` *boolean*	If `true`, a spline curve is drawn around the points.
`-splinesteps` *num*	Number of line segments that approximate the spline.
`-stipple` *bitmap*	Stipple pattern for polygon fill.
`-tags` *tagList*	Set of tags for the line item.

Rectangle Items

A `rectangle` is specified with two coordinates that are its opposite corners. A rectangle can have a fill color and an outline color. If you do not specify a fill, then the background of the canvas (or other objects) show through. If you stipple the fill, the background also shows through the clear bits of the stipple pattern. You must use a second rectange if you want the stippled fill to completely hide what is behind it. The following example drags out a box as the user drags the mouse. All it requires is remembering the last rectangle drawn so it can be deleted when the next box is drawn:

Example 20–11 Dragging out a box.

```
proc BoxInit {} {
    canvas .c -bg white ; pack .c
    bind .c <Button-1> {BoxBegin %W %x %y}
    bind .c <B1-Motion> {BoxDrag %W %x %y}
}
proc BoxBegin { w x y } {
    global box
    set box(anchor) [list $x $y]
    catch {unset box(last)}
}
proc BoxDrag { w x y } {
    global box
    catch {$w delete $box(last)}
    set box(last) [eval {$w create rect} $box(anchor) \
        {$x $y -tag box}]
}
```

The example uses `box(anchor)` to record the start of the box. This is a list with two elements. The `eval` command is used so that this list can be spliced into the `create rect` command. Table 20–7 specifies the complete set of rectangle attributes:

Table 20–7 Rectangle attributes.

`-fill` *color*	The color of the interior of the rectangle.
`-outline` *color*	The color for the outline of the rectangle.
`-stipple` *bitmap*	Stipple pattern for rectangle fill.
`-tags` *tagList*	Set of tags for the rectangle item.
`-width` *width*	The thickness of the outline.

Text Items

The canvas `text` item provides yet another way to display and edit text. It supports selection, editing, and can extend onto multiple lines. The position of a `text` item is specified by one set of coordinates and an anchor position. The size of the text is determined by the number of lines and the length of each line. A new line is started if there is a newline in the text string. If a width is specified, in screen units, then any line that is longer than this is wrapped onto multiple lines. The wrap occurs before a space character.

The editing and selection operations for `text` items use indices to specify positions within a given text item. These are very similar to those used in the entry widget. Table 20–8 summarizes the indices for canvas `text` items.

Table 20–8 Indices for canvas `text` items.

`0`	Index of the first character.
`end`	Index just past the last character.
`number`	Index a character, counting from zero.
`insert`	The character right after the insertion cursor.
`sel.first`	The first character in the selection.
`sel.last`	The last character in the selection.
`@`*x*,*y*	The character under the specified X and Y coordinate.

There are several canvas operations that manipulate text items. These are similar to some of the operations of the entry widget, except that they are parameterized by the tag or ID of the canvas object being manipulated. If the tag refers to more than one object, then the operations apply to the first object in the display list that supports an insert cursor. The display list is described on page 254. Table 20–9 summarizes the operations on `text` items. In the table `$t` is a text item or tag and `$c` is a canvas.

Table 20–9 Canvas operations that apply to `text` items.

`$c dchars $t` *`first ?last?`*	Delete the characters from *`first`* through *`last`*, or just the character at *`first`*.
`$c focus ?$t?`	Set input focus to the specified item, or return the id of the item with the focus if not it is given.
`$c icursor $t` *`index`*	Set the insert cursor to just before *`index`*.
`$c index $t index`	Return the numerical value of *`index`*.
`$c insert $t` *`index string`*	Insert the string just before *`index`*.
`$c select adjust $t` *`index`*	Move the boundary of an existing selection.
`$c select clear`	Clear the selection.
`$c select from $t` *`index`*	Start a selection.
`$c select item`	Returns the id of the selected item, if any.
`$c select to $t` *`index`*	Extend the selection to the specified *`index`*.

There are no default bindings for canvas `text` items. The following example sets up some rudimentary bindings for canvas text items. The `<Button-1>` and `<Button-2>` bindings are on the canvas as a whole. The rest of the bindings are on items with the `text` tag. The bindings try to be careful about introducing temporary variables because they execute at the global scope. This is a hint that it might be better to create a procedure for each binding.

The `<Button-1>` binding uses the canvas `find overlapping` operation to see if a text object has been clicked. This must be used because `find closest` finds an object no matter how far away it is.

The `<Button-2>` binding does one of two things. It pastes the selection into the canvas item that has the focus. If no item has the focus, then a new text item is created with the selection as its value.

Example 20–12 Simple edit bindings for canvas `text` items.

```
proc CanvasEditBind { c } {
	bind $c <Button-1> {
		focus %W
		if {[%W find overlapping [expr %x-2] [expr %y-2] \
				[expr %x+2] [expr %y+2]] == {}} {
			%W focus {}
		}
	}
	$c bind text <Button-1> {
		%W focus current
		%W icursor current @%x,%y
		%W select from current @%x,%y
	}
	$c bind text <B1-Motion> {
		%W select to current @%x,%y
```

```
    }
    $c bind text <Delete> {
        if {[%W select item] != {}} {
            %W dchars [%W select item] sel.first sel.last
        } elseif {[%W focus] != {}} {
            %W dchars [%W focus] insert
        }
    }
    $c bind text <Control-d> {
        if {[%W focus] != {}} {
            %W dchars [%W focus] insert
        }
    }
    $c bind text <Control-h> {
        if {[%W select item] != {}} {
            %W dchars [%W select item] sel.first sel.last
        } elseif {[%W focus] != {}} {
            set _t [%W focus]
            %W icursor $_t [expr [%W index $_t insert]-1]
            %W dchars $_t insert
            unset _t
        }
    }
    $c bind text <BackSpace> [$c bind text <Control-h>]

    $c bind text <Control-Delete> {
        %W delete current
    }
    $c bind text <Return> {
        %W insert current insert \n
    }
    $c bind text <Any-Key> {
        %W insert current insert %A
    }
    bind $c <Button-2> {
        if {[catch {selection get} _s] == 0} {
            if {[%W focus] != {}} {
                %W insert [%W focus] insert $_s
            } else {
                %W create text %x %y -text $_s -anchor nw \
                    -tag text
            }
            unset _s
        }
    }
    $c bind text <Key-Right> {
        %W icursor current [expr [%W index current insert]+1]
    }
    $c bind text <Control-f> [$c bind text <Key-Right>]
    $c bind text <Key-Left> {
        %W icursor current [expr [%W index current insert]-1]
    }
    $c bind text <Control-b> [$c bind text <Key-Left>]
}
```

Table 20–10 specifies the complete set of attributes for `text` items. Note that there are no foreground and background attributes. Instead, the fill color specifies the color for the text. It is possible to stipple the text as well.

Table 20–10 Text attributes

`-anchor` *`position`*	Anchor: `c`, `n`, `ne`, `e`, `se`, `s`, `sw`, `w`, or `nw`.
`-fill` *`color`*	The foreground color for the text.
`-font` *`font`*	The font for the text.
`-justify` *`how`*	Justification: `left`, `right`, or `center`.
`-stipple` *`bitmap`*	Stipple pattern for the text fill.
`-tags` *`tagList`*	Set of tags for the rectangle item.
`-text` *`string`*	The string to display.
`-width` *`width`*	The thickness of the outline.

Window Items

A `window` item lets you position other Tk widgets on a canvas. The position is specified by one set of coordinates and an anchor position. You can also specify the width and height, or you can let the widget determine its own size. The following example uses a canvas to provide a scrolling surface for a large set of labeled entries. A frame is created and a set of labeled entry widgets are packed into it. This main frame is put onto the canvas as a single window item. This way we let the packer take care of arranging all the labeled entries. The size of the canvas is set up so that a whole number of labeled entries are displayed. The scroll region and scroll increment are set up so that clicking on the scrollbar arrows brings one new labeled entry completely into view.

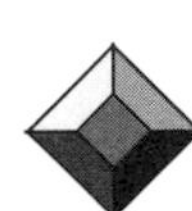

Example 20–13 Using a canvas to scroll a set of widgets.

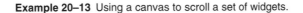

```
proc Example { top title labels } {
	# Create a resizable toplevel window
	toplevel $top
	wm minsize $top 200 100
	wm title $top $title

	# Create a frame for buttons,
	# Only Dismiss does anything useful
	set f [frame $top.buttons -bd 4]
	button $f.quit -text Dismiss -command "destroy $top"
	button $f.save -text Save
	button $f.reset -text Reset
	pack $f.quit $f.save $f.reset -side right
	pack $f -side top -fill x
```

```
    # Create a scrollable canvas
    frame $top.c
    canvas $top.c.canvas -width 10 -height 10 \
        -yscrollcommand [list $top.c.yscroll set]
    scrollbar $top.c.yscroll -orient vertical \
        -command [list $top.c.canvas yview]
    pack $top.c.yscroll -side right -fill y
    pack $top.c.canvas -side left -fill both -expand true
    pack $top.c -side top -fill both -expand true

    SetOfLabeledEntries $top.c$top.canvas $labels
}
proc SetOfLabeledEntries { canvas labels } {
    # Create one frame to hold everything
    # and position it on the canvas
    set f [frame $canvas.f -bd 0]
    $canvas create window 0 0 -anchor nw -window $f

    # Find out how big the labels are
    set max 0
    foreach label $labels {
        set len [string length $label]
        if {$len > $max} {
            set max $len
        }
    }
    # Create and pack the labeled entries
    set i 0
    foreach label $labels {
        frame $f.$i
        label $f.$i.label -text $label -width $max
        entry $f.$i.entry
        pack $f.$i.label -side left
        pack $f.$i.entry -side right -fill x
        pack $f.$i -side top -fill x
        incr i
    }
    set child [lindex [pack slaves $f] 0]

    # Wait for the window to become visible and then
    # set up the scroll region and increment based on
    # the size of the frame and the subframes

    tkwait visibility $child
    set incr [winfo height $child]
    set width [winfo width $f]
    set height [winfo height $f]
    $canvas config -scrollregion "0 0 $width $height"
    $canvas config -yscrollincrement $incr
    if {$height > 4 * $incr} {
        set height [expr 4 * $incr]
    }
    $canvas config -width $width -height $height
}
```

```
Example .top "An example" {
    alpha beta gamma delta epsilon zeta eta theta iota kappa
    lambda mu nu xi omicron pi rho sigma tau upsilon
    phi chi psi omega}
```

The `tkwait visibility` command is important to the example. It causes the script to suspend execution until the toplevel window, `$top`, is displayed on the screen. The `tkwait` is necessary so the right information gets returned by the `winfo width` and `winfo height` commands. By waiting for a subframe of the main frame, `$child`, we ensure that the packer has gone through all its processing to position the interior frames. The canvas's scroll region is set to be just large enough to hold the complete frame. The scroll increment is set to the height of one of the subframes. Each click on the scrollbar arrows brings one new subframe completely into view.

Canvas Operations

Table 20–11 summarizes the operations on canvas widgets. In the table, `$t` represents a tag that identifies one or more canvas objects, or it represents the numerical ID of a single canvas object. In some cases an operation only operates on a single object. If a tag identifies several objects, the first object in the display list is operated on.

The canvas display list refers to the global order among canvas objects. New objects are put at the end of the display list. Objects later in the display list obscure objects earlier in the list. The term *above* refers to objects later in the display list.

Table 20–9 describes several of the canvas operations that only apply to `text` objects. They are: `dchars`, `focus`, `index`, `icursor`, `insert`, and `select`. Table 20–11 does not repeat those operations. In the table, `$c` is a text item or tag and `$c` is a canvas.

Table 20–11 Operations on a `canvas` widget.

`$c addtag` *`tag`* `above $t`	Add *`tag`* to the item just above `$t` in the display list.
`$c addtag` *`tag`* `all`	Add *`tag`* to all objects in the canvas.
`$c addtag` *`tag`* `below $t`	Add *`tag`* to the item just below `$t` in the display list.
`$c addtag` *`tag`* `closest` *`x y ?halo? ?start?`*	Add *`tag`* to the item closest to the *`x y`* position. If more than one object is the same distance away, or if more than one object is within halo pixels, then the last one in the display list (uppermost) is returned. If *`start`* is specified, the closest object after *`start`* in the display list is returned.

Table 20–11 Operations on a `canvas` widget. (Continued)

`$c addtag` *`tag`* `enclosed` *`x1 y1 x2 y2`*	Add *`tag`* to the items completely enclosed in the specified region. *x1* <= *x2*, *y1* <= *y2*.
`$c addtag` *`tag`* `withtag $t`	Add *`tag`* to the items identified by `$t`.
`$c bbox $t ?`*`tag tag`* `...?`	Return the bounding box of the items identified by the tag(s) in the form *`x1 y1 x2 y2`*
`$c bind $t` *`?sequence? ?command?`*	Set or query the bindings of canvas items.
`$c canvasx` *`screenx ?grid?`*	Map from the X screen coordinate *`screenx`* to the X coordinate in canvas space, rounded to multi ples of *`grid`* if specified.
`$c canvasy` *`screeny ?grid?`*	Map from screen Y to canvas Y.
`$c cget` *`option`*	Return the value of *`option`* for the canvas.
`$c configure ...`	Query or update the attributes of the canvas.
`$c coords $t ?`*`x1 y1`* `...?`	Query or modify the coordinates of the item.
`$c create type x y ?x2 y2? ?opt value ...?`	Create a canvas object of the specified *`type`* at the specified coordinates.
`$c delete $t ?tag ...?`	Delete the item(s) specified by the tag(s) or IDs.
`$c dtag $t ?`*`deltag`*`?`	Remove the specified tags from the items identified by `$t`. If *`deltag`* is omitted, it defaults to `$t`.
`$c find` *`addtagSearch`* `...`	Return the IDs of the tags that match the search specification: `above`, `all`, `below`, `closest`, `enclosed`, and `withtag`, as for the `addtag`.
`$c gettags $t`	Return the tags associated with the first item identified by `$t`.
`$c itemconfigure $t ...`	Query or reconfigure item `$t`.
`$c lower $t` *`?belowThis?`*	Move the items identified by `$t` to the beginning of the display list, or just before *`belowThis`*.
`$c move $t dx dy`	Move `$t` by the specified amount.
`$c postscript ...`	Generate postscript. See the next section.
`$c raise $t ?`*`aboveThis`*`?`	Move the items identified by `$t` to the end of the display list, or just after *`aboveThis`*.
`$c scale $t` *`x0 y0 xS yS`*	Scale the coordinates of the items identified by `$t`. The distance between *`x0`* and a given X coordinate changes by a factor of *`xS`*. Similarly for Y.
`$c scan mark` *`x y`*	Set a mark for a scrolling operation.
`$c scan dragto x y`	Scroll the canvas from the previous mark.
`$c type $t`	Return the type of the first item identified by `$t`.

Table 20–11 Operations on a `canvas` widget. (Continued)

`$c xview` *index*	Position the canvas so that *index* (in scroll increments) is at the left edge of the screen.
`$c yview` *index*	Position the canvas so that *index* (in scroll increments) is at the top edge of the screen.

Generating Postscript

The `postscript` operation generates postscript based on the contents of a canvas. Table 20–12 summarizes all the options for generating postscript.

Table 20–12 Canvas postscript options.

`-colormap` *varName*	The index of *varName* is a named color, and the contents of each element is the postscript code to generate the RGB values for that color.
`-colormode` *mode*	*mode* is one of: `color`, `grey`, or `mono`.
`-file` *name*	The file in which to write the postscript. If not specified, the postscript is returned as the result of the command.
`-fontmap` *varName*	The index of *varName* is an X font name. Each element contains a list of two items, a postscript font name and a point size.
`-height` *size*	Height of the area to print.
`-pageanchor` *anchor*	Anchor: `c`, `n`, `ne`, `e`, `se`, `s`, `sw`, `w`, or `nw`.
`-pageheight` *size*	Height of image on the output. A floating point number followed by `c` (centimeters) `i` (inches) `m` (millimeters) `p` (printer points).
`-pagewidth` *size*	Width of image on the output.
`-pagex` *position*	The output X coordinate of the anchor point.
`-pagey` *position*	The output Y coordinate of the anchor point.
`-rotate` *boolean*	If true, rotate so that X axis is the long direction of the page (landscape orientation).
`-width` *size*	Size of the area to print.
`-x` *position*	Canvas X coordinate of left edge of the image.
`-y` *position*	Canvas Y coordinate of top edge of the image.

You control what region of the canvas is printed with the `-width`, `-height`, `-x` and `-y` options. You control the size and location of this in the output with the `-pageanchor`, `-pagex`, `-pagey`, `-pagewidth`, and `-pageheight` options. The postscript is written to the file named by the `-file` option, or it is returned as the value of the postscript canvas operation.

You control fonts with a mapping from X screen fonts to postscript fonts. Define an array where the index is the name of the X font and the contents are the name and pointsize of a postscript font.

The next example positions a number of text objects with different fonts onto a canvas. For each different X font used, it records a mapping to a postscript font. The example has a fairly simple font mapping, and in fact the canvas would have probably guessed the same font mapping itself. If you use more exotic screen fonts you may need to help the canvas widget with an explicit font map.

The example positions the output at the upper-left corner of the printed page by using the `-pagex`, `-pagey` and `-pageanchor` options. Recall that postscript has its origin at the lower left corner of the page.

Example 20–14 Generating postscript from a canvas.

```
proc Setup {} {
    global fontMap
    canvas .c
    pack .c -fill both -expand true
    set x 10
    set y 10
    set last [.c create text $x $y -text "Font sampler" \
        -font fixed -anchor nw]

    # Create several strings in different fonts and sizes

    foreach family {times courier helvetica} {
        set weight bold
        switch -- $family {
            times { set fill blue; set psfont Times}
            courier { set fill green; set psfont Courier }
            helvetica { set fill red; set psfont Helvetica }
        }
        foreach size {10 14 24} {
            set y [expr 4+[lindex [.c bbox $last] 3]]

            # Guard against missing fonts
            if {[catch {.c create text $x $y \
                    -text $family-$weight-$size \
                    -anchor nw -fill $fill \
                    -font -*-$family-$weight-*-*-*-$size-*} \
            it] == 0} {
                set fontMap(-*-$family-$weight-*-*-*-$size-*)\
                    [list $psfont $size]
                set last $it
            }
        }
    }
    set fontMap(fixed) [list Courier 12]
}
proc Postscript { c file } {
```

```
    global fontMap
    # Tweak the output color
    set colorMap(blue) {0.1 0.1 0.9 setrgbcolor}
    set colorMap(green) {0.0 0.9 0.1 setrgbcolor}
    # Position the text at the upper-left corner of
    # an 8.5 by 11 inch sheet of paper
    $c postscript -fontmap fontMap -colormap colorMap \
        -file $file \
        -pagex 0.i -pagey 11.i -pageanchor nw
}
```

Canvas Attributes

Table 20–13 lists the attributes for the `canvas` widget. The table uses the X resource name, which has capitals at internal word boundaries. In Tcl commands the attributes are specified with a dash and all lowercase.

Table 20–13 Canvas attribute resource names.

`background`	The normal background color.
`borderWidth`	The width of the border around the canvas.
`closeEnough`	Distance from mouse to an overlapping object.
`confine`	Boolean. True constrains view to the scroll region.
`cursor`	Cursor to display when mouse is over the widget.
`height`	Height, in screen units, of canvas display.
`highlightColor`	Color for input focus highlight border.
`highlightThickness`	Width of highlight border.
`insertBackground`	Background for area covered by insert cursor.
`insertBorderwidth`	Width of cursor border. Non-zero for 3D effect.
`insertOffTime`	Time, in milliseconds the insert cursor blinks off.
`insertOnTime`	Time, in milliseconds the insert cursor blinks on.
`insertWidth`	Width of insert cursor. Default is 2.
`relief`	3D relief: `flat`, `sunken`, `raised`, `groove`, or `ridge`.
`scrollIncrement`	The minimum scrolling distance.
`scrollRegion`	Left, top, right, and bottom coordinates of the `canvas`.
`selectBackground`	Background color of selection.
`selectForeground`	Foreground color of selection.
`selectBorderWidth`	Widget of selection border. Non-zero for 3D effect.

Table 20–13 Canvas attribute resource names. (Continued)

`width`	Width, in characters for text, or screen units for image.
`xScrollCommand`	Tcl command prefix for horizontal scrolling.
`xScrollIncrement`	Distance for one scrolling unit in the X direction.
`yScrollCommand`	Tcl command prefix for vertical scrolling.
`yScrollIncrement`	Distance for one scrolling unit in the Y direction.

The scroll region of a canvas defines the boundaries of the canvas coordinate space. It is specified as four coordinates, *x1 y1 x2 y2* where (*x1, y1*) is the top-left corner and (*x2, y2*) is the lower right corner. If the `confine` attribute is true, then the canvas cannot be scrolled outside this region. It is OK to position canvas objects partially or totally off the scroll region, they just may not be visible. The scroll increment attributes determine how much the canvas is scrolled when the user clicks on the arrows in the scrollbar.

The `closeEnough` attribute indicates how far away a position can be from an object and still be considered to overlap it. This applies to the `overlapping` search criteria.

Hints

Screen Coordinates vs. Canvas Coordinates

The `canvasx` and `canvasy` operations map from a screen coordinate to a canvas coordinate. If the scroll region is larger than the the display area, then you need to use these operations to map from the X and Y in an event (i.e., `%x` and `%y`) and the canvas coordinates. The typical use is:

```
set id [$c find closest [$c canvasx %x] [$c canvasy %y]]
```

Large Coordinate Spaces

Coordinates for canvas items are stored internally as floating point numbers, so the values returned by the `coords` operation will be floating point numbers. If you have a very large canvas, you may need to adjust the precision with which you see coordinates by setting the `tcl_precision` variable. This is an issue if you query coordinates, perform a computation on them, and then update the coordinates.

Scaling and Rotation

The `scale` operation scales the coordinates of one or more canvas items. It is not possible to scale the whole coordinate space. The main problem with this is that you can lose precision when scaling and unscaling objects because their internal coordinates are actually changed by the scale operation. For simple cases this is not a problem, but in extreme cases it can show up.

The canvas does not support rotation.

X Resources

There is no resource database support built into the canvas and its items. You can, however, define resources and query them yourself. For example, you could define:

```
*Canvas.foreground:   blue
```

This would have no effect by default. However, your code could look for this resource with `option get`, and specify this color directly for the `-fill` attribute of your objects:

```
set fg [option get $c foreground {}]
$c create rect 0 0 10 10 -fill $fg
```

The main reason to take this approach is to let your users customize the appearance of canvas objects without changing your code.

Objects with Many Points

The canvas implementation seems well optimized to handle lots of canvas objects. However, if an object like a line or a polygon has many points that define it, the implementation ends up scanning through these points linearly. This can adversely affect the time it takes to process mouse events in the area of the canvas containing such an item. Apparently any object in the vicinity of a mouse click is scanned to see if the mouse has hit it so that any bindings can be fired.

Selecting Canvas Items

Chapter 21 has an example on page 264 that implements cut and paste of canvas objects. The example exchanges the logical description of canvas objects with the X selection mechanism.

CHAPTER 21

Selections and the Clipboard

Cut and paste allows information exchange between applications, and it is built upon the X selection mechanism. Most applications use the `PRIMARY` selection. The `CLIPBOARD` selection is a special-purpose selection mechanism that the OpenLook tools use. This chapter describes the `selection` and `clipboard` commands.

X handles selections in a general way, including a provision for different selections, different data types, and different formats for the data. For the most part you can ignore these details because they are handled by the Tk widgets. However, you can also control the selection explicitly. This chapter describes how.

There are two Tcl commands that deal with selections. The `selection` command is a general purpose command that can set and get different selections. By default it manipulates the `PRIMARY` selection. The `clipboard` command stores data for later retrieval using the `CLIPBOARD` selection. The next example implements a robust paste operation by checking for both of these selections:

Example 21–1 Paste the `PRIMARY` or `CLIPBOARD` selection.

```
proc Paste { t } {
    if [catch {selection get} sel] {
        if [catch {selection get -selection CLIPBOARD} sel] {
            # no selection or clipboard data
            return
        }
    }
    $t insert insert $sel
}
```

The selection Command

The basic model for selections is that there is an owner for a selection, and other applications request the value of the selection from that owner. The X server keeps track of ownership, and applications are informed when some other application takes away ownership. Several of the Tk widgets implement selections and take care of asserting ownership and returning its value. The `selection get` command returns the value of the current selection, or raises an error if the selection does not exist. The error conditions are checked in the previous example.

For many purposes the selection handling that is built into the Tk widgets is adequate. If you want more control over selection ownership, you can provide a handler for selection requests. The last section of this chapter presents an example of this.

A selection can have a type. The default is STRING. The type is different than the name of the selection (e.g., PRIMARY or CLIPBOARD). Each type can have a format, and the default is also STRING. Ordinarily these defaults are fine. If you are dealing with non-Tk applications, however, you may need to ask for their selections by the right type (e.g., FILE_NAME). Other formats include ATOM and INTEGER. An ATOM is a name that is registered with the X server and identified by number. It is probably not a good idea to use non-STRING types and formats because it limits what other applications can use the information. The details about selection types and formats are specified in the *Inter-Client Communication Conventions Manual* (ICCCM).

All of the selection operations take an optional parameter that specifies what selection is being manipulated. This defaults to PRIMARY. Some of the operations take a pair of parameters that specify what X display the selection is on. The value for this is a Tk pathname of a window, and the selection on that window's display is manipulated. The default is to manipulate the selection on the display of the main window. Table 21–1 summarizes the `selection` command:

Table 21–1 The `selection` command.

`selection clear ?-displayof win? ?-selection sel?`	Clear the specified selection.
`selection get ?displayof win? ?-selection sel? ?-type type?`	Return the specified selection. Type defaults to STRING.
`selection handle ?-selection sel? ?-type type? ?-format format? window command`	Define *command* to be the handler for selection requests when *window* owns the selection.
`selection own ?-displayof window? ?-selection sel?`	Return the Tk pathname of the window that owns the selection, if it is in this application.
`selection own ?-command command? ?-selection sel? window`	Assert that *window* owns the *sel* selection. The *command* is called when ownership of the selection is taken away from *window*.

The clipboard Command

The `clipboard` command installs values into the `CLIPBOARD` selection. The `CLIPBOARD` is meant for values that have been recently or temporarily deleted. The `selection` command retrieves values from the `CLIPBOARD` selection. For example, the `Paste` function in Example 21–1 inserts from the `CLIPBOARD` if there is no `PRIMARY` selection. Table 21–2 summarizes the `clipboard` command:

Table 21–2 The `clipboard` command.

`clipboard clear ?-displayof` *`win`*`?`	Clear the `CLIPBOARD` selection.
`clipboard append ?-displayof` *`win`*`? ?-format` *`format`*`? ?-type` *`type`*`?` *`data`*	Append *`data`* to the `CLIPBOARD` with the specified *`type`* and *`format`*, which both default to `STRING`.

Interoperation with OpenLook

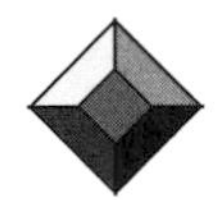

The `CLIPBOARD` is necessary to interoperate correctly with OpenLook. When the user presses the `Copy` or `Cut` function keys in an OpenLook application, a value is copied into the `CLIPBOARD`. A `Paste` inserts the contents of the `CLIPBOARD`; the contents of the `PRIMARY` selection are ignored.

In contrast, toolkits like Tk and Xt that use the `PRIMARY` selection do not need a `Copy` step. Instead, dragging out a selection with the mouse automatically asserts ownership of the `PRIMARY` selection, and paste inserts the value of the `PRIMARY` selection.

Selection Handlers

The `selection handle` command registers a Tcl command to handle selection requests. The command is called to return the value of the selection to a requesting application. If the selection value is large, the command might be called several times to return the selection in pieces. The command gets two parameters that indicate the offset within the selection to start returning data, and the maximum number of bytes to return. If the command returns fewer than that many bytes, the selection request is assumed to be completed. Otherwise the command is called again to get the rest of the data, and the offset parameter is adjusted accordingly.

You can also get a callback when you lose ownership of the selection. At that time it is appropriate to unhighlight the selected object in your interface. The `selection own` command sets ownership and registers a callback for when you lose ownership.

A Canvas Selection Handler

The following example illustrates a selection handler for a canvas widget. A description of the selected object is returned in such a way that the requester can create an identical object. The example lacks highlighting for the selected object, but otherwise provides full cut, copy and paste functionality:

Example 21–2 A selection handler for canvas widgets.

```
proc SetupCanvasSelect { c } {
    # Create a canvas with a couple of objects
    canvas $c
    pack $c
    $c create rect 10 10 50 50 -fill red -tag object
    $c create poly 100 100 100 30 140 50 -fill orange \
        -tag object
    # Set up cut and paste bindings
    $c bind object <1> [list CanvasSelect $c %x %y]
    $c bind object <3> [list CanvasCut $c %x %y]
    bind $c <2> [list CanvasPaste $c %x %y]
    # Register the handler for selection requests
    selection handle $c [list CanvasSelectHandle $c]
}

proc CanvasSelect { w x y } {
    # Select an item on the canvas.
    # This should highlight the object somehow, but doesn't
    global canvas
    set id [$w find closest $x $y]
    set canvas(select,$w) $id
    # Claim ownership of the PRIMARY selection
    selection own -command [list CanvasSelectLose $w] $w
}

proc CanvasCut { w x y } {
    # Delete an object from the canvas, saving its
    # description into the CLIPBOARD selection
    global canvas
    set id [$w find closest $x $y]
    # Clear the selection so Paste gets the clipboard
    selection clear
    clipboard clear
    clipboard append [CanvasDescription $w $id]
    $w delete $id
}

proc CanvasSelectHandle { w offset maxbytes } {
    # Handle a selection request
    global canvas
    if ![info exists canvas(select,$w)] {
        error "No selected item"
    }
    set id $canvas(select,$w)
    # Return the requested chunk of data.
```

```
	return [string range [CanvasDescription $w $id] \
		$offset [expr $offset+$maxbytes]]
}
proc CanvasDescription { w id } {
	# Generate a description of the object that can
	# be used to recreate it later.
	set type [$w type $id]
	set coords [$w coords $id]
	set config {}
	# Bundle up non-default configuration settings
	foreach conf [$w itemconfigure $id] {
		# itemconfigure returns a list like
		# -fill {} {} {} red
		set default [lindex $conf 3]
		set value [lindex $conf 4]
		if {[string compare $default $value] != 0} {
			append config [list [lindex $conf 0] $value] " "
		}
	}
	return [concat CanvasObject $type $coords $config]
}

proc CanvasSelectLose { w } {
	# Some other app has claimed the selection
	global canvas
	unset canvas(select,$w)
}

proc CanvasPaste { w x y } {
	# Paste the selection, from either the
	# PRIMARY or CLIPBOARD selections
	if [catch {selection get} sel] {
		if [catch {selection get -selection CLIPBOARD} sel] {
			# no selection or clipboard data
			return
		}
	}
	if [regexp {^CanvasObject} $sel] {
		if [catch {eval {$w create} [lrange $sel 1 end]} id] {
			return;
		}
		# look at the first coordinate to see where to
		# move the object. Element 1 is the type, the
		# next two are the first coordinate
		set x1 [lindex $sel 2]
		set y1 [lindex $sel 3]
		$w move $id [expr $x-$x1] [expr $y-$y1]
	}
}
```

C H A P T E R 22

Callbacks and Handlers

This chapter describes the `send` command that invokes Tcl commands in other applications, the `after` command that causes Tcl commands to occur at a time in the future, and the `fileevent` command that registers a command to occur in response to file input/output (I/O).

Callbacks and interprocess communication provide powerful mechanisms for structuring your application. The `send` command lets Tk applications send each other Tcl commands and cooperate in very flexible ways. A large application can be structured as a set of smaller tools that cooperate instead of one large monolith. This encourages reuse, and it exploits your workstation's multiprogramming capabilities. Within a single application you can use the `after` command to cause events to occur at a specified time in the future. This is useful for periodic tasks and animations. The `fileevent` command lets your application do I/O processing in the background and respond as needed when I/O events occur. Together, all of these mechanisms support flexible and powerful applications.

The after Command

The `after` command sets up commands to happen in the future. In its simplest form it just pauses the application for a specified time, in milliseconds. During this time the application processes no events. This behavior is different than the `tkwait` command that does allow event processing. The example below waits for half a second:

```
after 500
```

The `after` command can register a Tcl command to occur after a period of time, in milliseconds. The `after` command behaves like `eval`; if you give it extra arguments it concatenates them to form a single command. If your argument structure is important, use `list` to build the command. The following example always works, no matter what the value of `myvariable` is:

```
after 500 [list puts $myvariable]
```

The return value of `after` is an identifier for the registered command. You can cancel this command with the `after cancel` operation. You specify either the identifier returned from `after`, or the command string. In the latter case the event that matches the command string exactly is canceled.

Table 22–1 summarizes the `after` command:

Table 22–1 The `after` command.

`after` *`milliseconds`*	Pause for *`milliseconds`*.
`after` *`ms arg ?arg ...?`*	Concatenate the *`args`* into a command and execute it after *`ms`* milliseconds. Immediately returns an ID.
`after cancel` *`id`*	Cancel the command registered under *`id`*.
`after cancel` *`command`*	Cancel the registered *`command`*.

The fileevent Command

The `fileevent` command registers a procedure that is called when an I/O stream is ready for read or write events. For example, you can open a pipeline for reading, and then process the data from the pipeline using a command registered with `fileevent`. The advantage of this approach is that your application can do other things, like update the user interface, while waiting for data from the pipeline. If you use a Tcl extension like Tcl-DP that lets you open network I/O streams, then you can also use `fileevent` to register procedures to handle data from those I/O streams. You can use `fileevent` on `stdin` and `stdout`, too.

The command registered with `fileevent` uses the regular Tcl commands to read or write data on the I/O stream. For example, if the pipeline generates line-oriented output, you can use `gets` to read a line of input. If you try and read more data than is available, your application will hang waiting for more input. For this reason you should read one line in your fileevent handler, assuming the data is line-oriented. If you know the pipeline will generate data in fixed-sized blocks, then you can use the `read` command to read one block.

Currently there is no support for non-blocking writes, so there is a chance that writing too much data on a writable I/O stream will block your process.

You should check for end-of-file in your read handler because it will be called when end-of-file occurs. It is safe to close the stream inside the handler. Closing the stream automatically unregisters the handler.

There can be at most one read handler and one write handler for an I/O stream. If you register a handler and one is already registered, then the old registration is removed. If you call `fileevent` without a command argument it returns the currently registered command, or null if there is none. If you register the null string, it deletes the current file handler.

The following example shows a read event handler. Example 11–1 on page 104 also uses `fileevent` to read from a pipeline. A pipeline is opened for reading and its command executes in the background. The `Reader` command is invoked when data is available on the pipe. The end-of-file condition is checked, and then a single line of input is read and processed:

Example 22–1 A read event file handler.

```
set pipe [open "|some command"]
fileevent $pipe readable [list Reader $pipe]
proc Reader { pipe } {
    if [eof $pipe] {
        catch {close $pipe}
        return
    }
    gets $pipe line
    # Process one line
}
```

Table 22–2 summarizes the `fileevent` command.

Table 22–2 The `fileevent` command.

`fileevent` *`fileId`* `readable` ?*`command`*?	Query or register *`command`* to be called when *`fileId`* is readable.
`fileevent` *`fileId`* `writable` ?*`command`*?	Query or register *`command`* to be called when *`fileId`* is writable.

The send Command

The `send` command invokes a Tcl command in another application. This provides a general way for scripts to cooperate. The general form of the command is:

`send` *`options interp arg ?arg...?`*

The `send` command behaves like `eval`; if you give it extra arguments it concatenates them to form a single command. If your argument structure is important, use `list` to build the command. Table 22–3 lists the options to `send`:

Table 22–3 Options to the `send` command.

`-async`	Do not wait for the remote command to complete.
`-displayof` *`window`*	Send to the application on the same display as *`window`*.
`--`	Delimits options from the *`interp`* argument. Useful if the *`interp`* begins with a dash.

The *interp* argument is the name of the other application. An application defines its own name when it creates its main window. The *wish* shell uses as its name the last component of the filename of the script. For example, when *wish* interprets `/usr/local/bin/exmh` it sets its application name to `exmh`. However, if another instance of the `exmh` application is already running, *wish* chooses the name `exmh #2`, and so on. If *wish* is not executing from a file, its name is just `wish`. You may have noticed `wish #2` or `wish #3` in your window title bars, and this reflects the fact that multiple *wish* applications are running on your display. If your application crashes it can forget to unregister its name. The *tkinspect* program has a facility to clean up these old registrations.

A script can find out its own name, so you can pass names around or put them into files in order to set up communications. The `tk appname` command queries or changes the application name:

```
set myname [tk appname]
tk appname aNewName
```

In Tk 3.6 and earlier, you have to use the `winfo name` command to get the name of the application:

```
set myname [winfo name .]
```

Send and X Authority

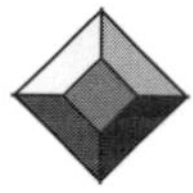

The `send` command relies on the X authority mechanism for authorization. A command is rejected by the target interpreter if you do not have X authority set up. There are two ways around this problem. First, you can disable the access check by compiling the `tkSend.c` file with the `-DTK_NO_SECURITY` compile flag. If you must worry about malicious programs that send your programs commands, then you should not do this.

The second option is to start your X server with its `-auth` flag, which initializes the X authority mechanism. The details vary depending on your X server. The general picture is that you generate a pseudo-random string and store it into a file, which is usually named `~/.Xauthority` and must be readable only by your account. The `-auth` flag specifies the name of this file to the X server. Each X application reads this file and sends the contents to the X server when opening the connection to the server. If the contents match what the server read when it started, then the connection is allowed. The system is slightly more complicated than described here. The file actually contains a sequence of records to support multiple displays and client hosts. Consult your local X guru or the documentation for the details particular to your system.

Note: Tk also requires that the *xhost* list be empty. This is the old, not-so-secure authentication mechanism in X. The *xhost* program should report "all hosts being restricted".

The Sender Script

The following example is a general purpose script that reads input and then sends it to another application. You can put this at the end of a pipeline to get a loopback effect to the main application, although you can also use `fileevent` for similar effects. One advantage of `send` over `fileevent` is that the sender and receiver can be more independent. A logging application, for example, can come and go independently of the applications that log error messages:

Example 22–2 The sender application.

```
#!/usr/local/bin/wish
# sender takes up to four arguments:
# 1) the name of the application to send to.
# 2) a command prefix.
# 3) the name of another application to notify
#    after the end of the data.
# 4) the command to use in the notification.

# Hide the unneeded window
wm withdraw .
# Process command line arguments
if {$argc == 0} {
    puts stderr "Usage: send name ?cmd? ?uiName? ?uiCmd?"
    exit 1
} else {
    set app [lindex $argv 0]
}
if {$argc > 1} {
    set cmd [lindex $argv 1]
} else {
    set cmd Send_Insert
}
if {$argc > 2} {
    set ui [lindex $argv 2]
    set uiCmd Send_Done
}
if {$argc > 3} {
    set uiCmd [lindex $argv 3]
}
# Read input and send it to the logger
while {[gets stdin input] >= 0} {
    # Ignore errors with the logger
    catch {send $app [concat $cmd [list $input\n]]}
}
# Notify the controller, if any
if [info exists ui] {
    if [catch {send $ui $uiCmd} msg] {
        puts stderr "send.tcl could not notify $ui\n$msg"
    }
}
# This is necessary to force wish to exit.
exit
```

The *sender* application supports communication with two processes. It sends all its input to a primary "logging" application. When the input finishes, it can send a notification message to another "controller" application. The logger and the controller could be the same application. An example that sets up this three way relationship is detailed later.

Consider the `send` command used in the example:

```
send $app [concat $cmd [list $input\n]]
```

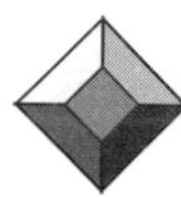

The combination of `concat` and `list` is tricky. The `list` command quotes the value of the input line. This quoted value is then appended to the command so it appears as a single extra argument. Without the quoting by `list`, the value of the input line will affect the way the remote interpreter parses the command. Consider these alternatives:

```
send $app [list $cmd $input]
```

This form is safe, except that it limits `$cmd` to a single word. If `cmd` contains a value like the ones given below, the remote interpreter will not parse it correctly. It will treat the whole multi-word value as the name of a command:

```
.log insert end
.log see end ; .log insert end
```

This is the most common wrong answer:

```
send $app $cmd $input
```

The `send` command concatenates `$cmd` and `$input` together, and the result will be parsed again by the remote interpreter. The success or failure of the remote command depends on the value of the input data. If the input included Tcl syntax like $ or [ ], errors or other unexpected behavior would result.

Using Sender

The following example is taken from a control panel that runs jobs in the background and uses *sender* to send their output to an editor for logging. When the job finishes, the control panel is notified.

The editor is *mxedit*, a Tcl-based editor. It defines its application name to be `mxedit` *`pathname`*, where pathname is the name of the file being edited. That name is passed to *sender* as the name of the logging application. The control panel passes its own name as the name of the controller. It uses `tk appname` to find out its own name.

Example 22–3 is similar to the `ExecLog` application from Example 11–1 on page 104. Instead of creating a text widget for a log, this version forks the *mxedit* program to serve as the logging application. The command is run in a pipeline. Instead of reading the pipeline itself, the control panel lets the *sender* program send the output to the editor. The editor's `mxInsert` command is used to insert text into its buffer. When the process completes, *sender* notifies the control panel.

Example 22–3 Using the sender application.

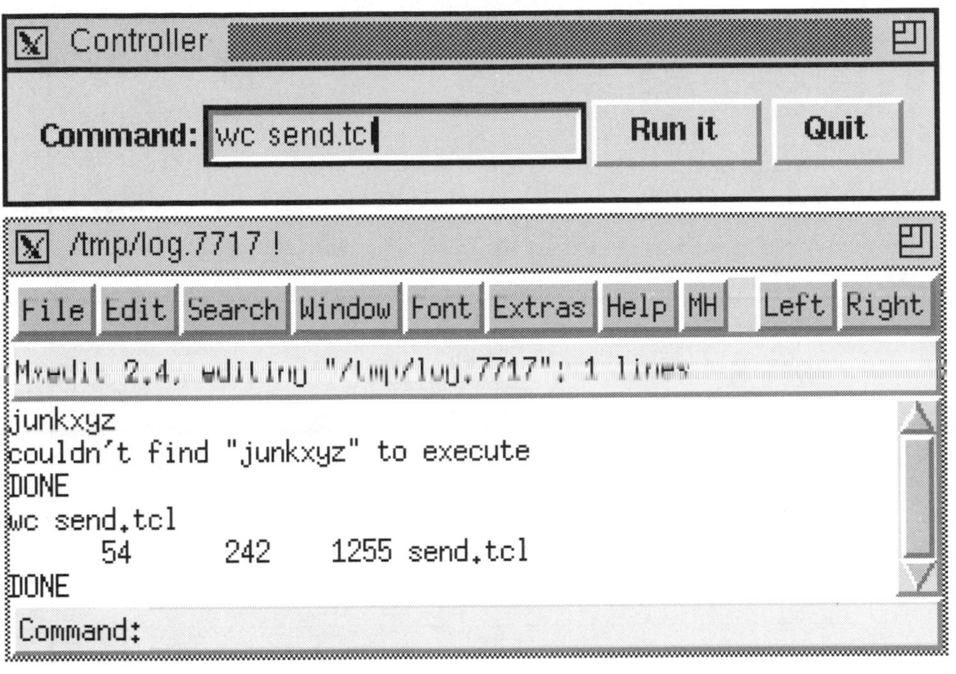


```
#!/usr/local/bin/wish
wm title . Controller
# Create a frame for buttons and entry.
frame .top -borderwidth 10
pack .top -side top -fill x
# Create the command buttons.
button .top.quit -text Quit -command exit
set but [button .top.run -text "Run it" -command Run \
    -width 6]
pack .top.quit .top.run -side right

# Create a labeled entry for the command
label .top.l -text Command: -padx 0
entry .top.cmd -width 20 -relief sunken \
    -textvariable command
pack .top.l -side left
pack .top.cmd -side left -fill x -expand true

# Set up key binding equivalents to the buttons
bind .top.cmd <Return> Run
bind .top.cmd <Control-c> Stop
focus .top.cmd

# Fork an editor to log the output.
exec mxedit /tmp/log.[pid] &
set sendCmd [list /usr/local/bin/send.tcl \
        "mxedit /tmp/log.[pid]" mxInsert [tk appname]]
```

```
# Run the program and arrange to log its input via sender
proc Run {} {
	global command job sendCmd but
	set cmd [concat exec $command |& $sendCmd &]
	send "mxedit /tmp/log.[pid]" [list mxInsert $command\n]
	if [catch {eval $cmd} job] {
		send "mxedit /tmp/log.[pid]" [list mxInsert $job\n]
	} else {
		$but config -text Stop -command Stop
	}
}
# Stop the program and fix up the button
proc Stop {} {
	global job but
	# job contains multiple pids
	catch {eval {exec kill} $job}
	send "mxedit /tmp/log.[pid]" [list mxInsert ABORT\n]
	$but config -text "Run it" -command Run
}
# Handle the callback from sender
proc Send_Done {} {
	global but
	send "mxedit /tmp/log.[pid]" [list mxInsert DONE\n]
	$but config -text "Run it" -command Run
}
```

The formation of the command to execute *sender* is done in two parts. First, the `sendCmd` variable is set up with the right arguments to *sender* (i.e., `send.tcl`). This includes the result of `tk appname`, which returns the name of the controller application. Once again, it is crucial to use `list` so that spaces in the names of the interpreters are quoted properly. In the second step the user's command (e.g., *make*) is concatenated into a pipeline command, and `eval` interprets the carefully constructed command.

The return from `exec` is a list of process IDs, one for each process in the pipeline. This leads to another use of `eval` to construct a `kill` command that lists each process ID as separate arguments.

The example always uses `list` to construct the command used in a `send`. In this case it is necessary to preserve the newline character that is appended to the string being inserted. Another approach would be to use curly braces. In that case the `\n` would be converted to a newline character by the remote interpreter. However, this doesn't work when the command or error message is being sent. In these cases the variable needs to be expanded, so `list` is used in all cases for consistency.

Communicating Processes

Chapter 11 presented two examples, a browser for the examples in this book, and a simple shell in which to try out Tcl commands. The two examples shown below hook these two applications together using the `send` command. The first example adds a `Load` button to the browser that tells the shell to source the current file. The browser starts up the shell, if necessary:

Example 22–4 Hooking the browser to an `eval` server.

```
# Add this to Example 11-2
button .menubar.load -text Load -command Load
pack .menubar.load -side right

# Start up the eval.tcl script.
proc StartEvalServer {} {
	global browse
	# Start the shell and pass it our name.
	exec eval.tcl [tk appname] &
	# Wait for eval.tcl to send us its name
	tkwait variable browse(evalInterp)
}
proc Load {} {
	global browse
	if {[lsearch [winfo interps] eval.tcl] < 0} {
		StartEvalServer
	}
	if [catch {send $browse(evalInterp) {info vars}} err] {
		# It probably died - restart it.
		StartEvalServer
	}
	# Send the command asynchronously. The two
	# list commands foil the concat done by send and
	# the uplevel in _EvalServe
	send -async $browse(evalInterp) \
		[list _EvalServe [list source $browse(current)]]
}
```

The number of lists created before the `send` command may seem excessive, but they are all necessary. The `send` command concatenates its arguments, so instead of letting it do that, we pass it a single list. Similarly, `_EvalServe` expects a single argument that is a valid command, so `list` is used to construct that.

We must add two things to Example 11–3 to support these additions to the browser. First, when the tcl shell starts up it needs to send the browser its application name. The browser passes its own name on the command line that starts the shell, so the shell knows how to talk to the browser. Second, an `_EvalServe` procedure is added. It accepts a remote command, inserts it in the text widget, and evaluates it. The results, or errors, are added to the text widget.

Example 22–5 Making the shell into an `eval` server.

```
# Add this to the beginning of Example 11-3
if {$argc > 0} {
   # Check in with the browser
   send [lindex $argv 0] \
      [list set browse(evalInterp) [tk appname]]
}

# Add this after _Eval
proc _EvalServe { command } {
   global prompt

   set t .eval.t
   $t insert insert $command\n

   set err [catch {uplevel #0 $command} result]
   $t insert insert \n$result\n
   $t insert insert $prompt
   $t see insert
   $t mark set limit insert
}
```

CHAPTER 23

Tk Widget Attributes

Each Tk widget has a number of attributes that affect its appearance and behavior. This chapter describes attributes in general, and covers some of the size and appearance-related attributes. The next two chapters cover the attributes associated with colors, images, and text.

This chapter describes some of the attributes that are in common among many Tk widgets. A widget always provides a default value for its attributes, so you can avoid specifying most of them. If you want to fine-tune things, however, you'll need to know about all the widget attributes.

Configuring Attributes

You specify attributes for Tk widgets when you create them. You can also change them dynamically at any time after that. In both cases the syntax is similar, using pairs of arguments. The first item in the pair identifies the attribute, the second provides the value. For example, a button can be created like this:

```
button .doit -text Doit -command DoSomething
```

The name of the button is `.doit`, and two attributes are specified, the `text` and the `command`. You can change the `.doit` button later with the `configure` widget operation:

```
.doit configure -text Stop -command StopIt
```

The current configuration of a widget can be queried with another form of the `configure` operation. If you just supply an attribute, the settings associated with that attribute are returned:

```
.doit configure -text
=> -text text Text { } Stop
```

This command returns several pieces of information: the command line switch, the resource name, the resource class, the default value, and the current value. In most cases you want the current value, which comes last. One way to get this value is with `lindex`:

```
lindex [.doit configure -text] 4
```

Tk 4.0 has a `cget` widget command that makes life easier:

```
.doit cget -text
=> Stop
```

You can also configure widget attributes indirectly by using the X resource database. An advantage of using the resource database is that users can reconfigure your application without touching the code. Otherwise, if you specify attribute values explicitly in the code, they cannot be overridden by resource settings. This is especially important for attributes like fonts and colors.

The tables in this chapter list the attributes by their X resource name, which may have a capital letter at an internal word boundary (e.g., `activeBackground`). When you specify attributes in a Tcl command, use all lowercase instead, plus a leading dash. Compare:

```
option add *Button.activeBackground red
$button configure -activebackground red
```

The first command defines a resource that affects all buttons created after that point, and the second command changes an existing button. Command line settings override resource database specifications. Chapter 15 describes the use of X resources in detail.

Size

Table 23–1 summarizes the attributes used to specify the size for widgets:

Table 23–1 Size attribute resource names.

`aspect`	The aspect ratio of a `message` widget, which is 100 times the ratio of width divided by height.
`height`	Height, in text lines or screen units. Widgets: `button`, `canvas`, `checkbutton`, `frame`, `label`, `listbox`, `menubutton`, `radiobutton`, `text`, and `toplevel`.
`length`	The long dimension of a `scale`.
`orient`	Orientation for long and narrow widgets: `horizontal` or `vertical`. Widgets: `scale` and `scrollbar`.
`width`	Width, in characters or screen units. Widgets: `button`, `canvas`, `checkbutton`, `entry`, `frame`, `label`, `listbox`, `menubutton`, `message`, `radiobutton`, `scale`, `scrollbar`, `text`, or `toplevel`.

Most widgets have a `width` and `height` attribute that specifies their desired size, although there are some special cases. In all cases, the geometry manager for a widget might modify the size to some degree. The commands described on page 311 return the current size of a widget.

Most of the text-related widgets interpret their sizes in units of characters for width and lines for height. All other widgets, including the `message` widget, interpret their dimensions in screen units. Screen units are pixels by default, although you can suffix the dimension with a unit specifier:

```
c    centimeters
i    inch
m    millimeters
p    printer points (1/72 inches)
```

Scales and scrollbars can have two orientations as specified by the `orient` attribute, so width and height are somewhat ambiguous. These widgets do not support a `height` attribute, and they interpret their `width` attribute to mean the size of their narrow dimension. The `scale` has a `length` attribute that determines its long dimension. Scrollbars do not even have a `length`. Instead, a `scrollbar` is assumed to be packed next to the widget it controls, and the `fill` packing attribute is used to extend the scrollbar to match the length of its adjacent widget. Example 16–5 shows how to pack scrollbars with another widget.

The `message` widget displays a fixed string on multiple lines, and it uses one of two attributes to constrain its size: its `aspect` or its `width`. The aspect ratio is defined to be 100*width/height, and it formats its text to honor this constraint. However, if a `width` is specified, it just uses that and uses as many lines (i.e., as much height) as needed. Example 16–2 and Example 16–3 show how message widgets display text.

It is somewhat unfortunate that text-oriented widgets only take character- and line-oriented dimensions. These sizes change with the font used, and if you want a precise size you might be frustrated. One trick is to put each widget, such as a label, in its own frame. Specify the size you want for the frame, and then pack the label and turn off size propagation. For example:

Example 23–1 Equal-sized labels.

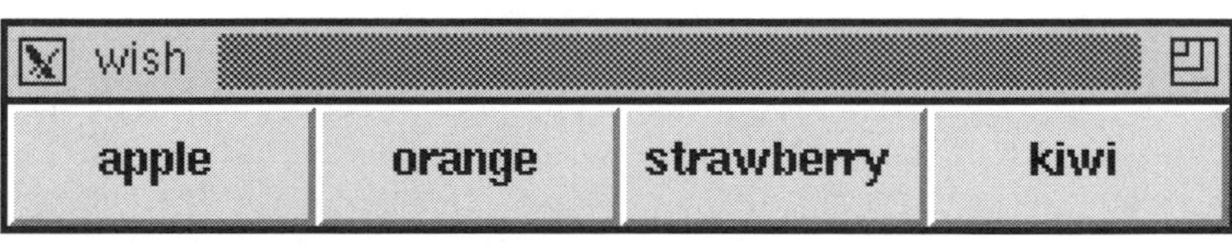


```
proc EqualSizedLabels { parent width height strings args } {
    set l 0
    foreach s $strings {
        frame $parent.$l -width $width -height $height
        pack propagate $parent.$l false
        pack $parent.$l -side left
```

```
        eval {label $parent.$l.l -text $s} $args
        pack $parent.$l.l -fill both -expand true
        incr l
    }
}
frame .f ; pack .f
EqualSizedLabels .f 1i 1c {apple orange strawberry kiwi} \
    -relief raised
```

The frames `$parent.$l` are all created with the same size. The `pack propagate` command prevents these frames from changing size when the labels are packed into them later. The labels are packed with `fill` and `expand` turned on so they fill up the fixed-sized frames around them.

Borders and Relief

The three dimensional appearance of widgets is determined by two attributes: `borderWidth` and `relief`. The `borderWidth` adds extra space around the edge of a widget's display, and this area can be displayed in a number of ways according to the `relief` attribute. The following example illustrates the different reliefs:

Example 23–2 3D relief sampler.

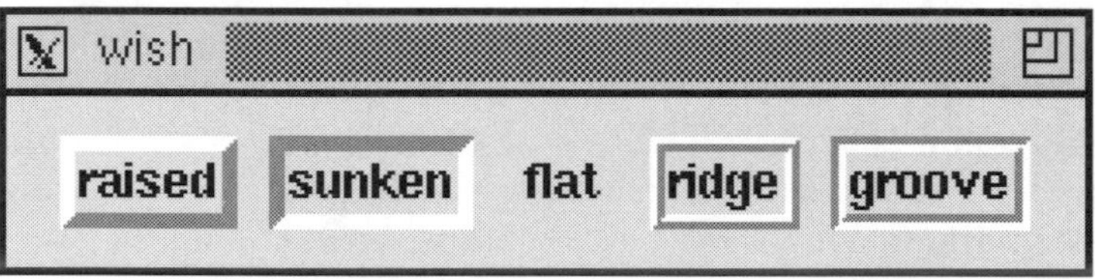


```
frame .f -borderwidth 10
pack .f
foreach relief {raised sunken flat ridge groove} {
    label .f.$relief -text $relief -relief $relief -bd 4
    pack .f.$relief -side left -padx 4
}
```

The `activeBorderWidth` attribute is a special case for menus. It defines the border width for the menu entries. The relief of a menu is not configurable. It probably is not worth adjusting the menu border width attributes because the default looks OK.

The `activeRelief` applies to the elements of a scrollbar (the elevator and two arrows) when the mouse is over them. In this case there is no corresponding border width to play with, and changing the `activeRelief` does not look good. Table 23–2 lists the attributes for borders and relief.

Table 23–2 Border and relief attribute resource names.

`borderWidth`	The width of the border around a widget, in screen units. Widgets: `button`, `canvas`, `checkbutton`, `entry`, `frame`, `label`, `listbox`, `menu`, `menubutton`, `message`, `radiobutton`, `scale`, `scrollbar`, `text`, or `toplevel`.
`bd`	Short for borderWidth. Tcl commands only.
`relief`	The appearance of the border: Values: `flat`, `raised`, `sunken`, `ridge`, or `groove`. Widgets: `button`, `canvas`, `checkbutton`, `entry`, `frame`, `label`, `listbox`, `menubutton`, `message`, `radiobutton`, `scale`, `scrollbar`, `text`, or `toplevel`.
`activeBorderWidth`	The borderwidth for `menu` entries.
`activeRelief`	The relief for a active `scrollbar` elements.

The Focus Highlight

Each widget can have a focus highlight indicating which widget currently has the input focus. This is a thin rectangle around each widget that is displayed in the normal background color by default. When the widget gets the input focus, the highlight rectangle is displayed in an alternate color. The addition of the highlight adds a small amount of space outside the border described in the previous section. The attributes in Table 23–3 control the width and color of this rectangle. If the widget is zero, no highlight is displayed.

By default, only the widgets that normally expect input focus have a nonzero width highlight border. This includes the `text`, `entry`, and `listbox` widgets. It also includes the `button` and `menu` widgets because there is a set of keyboard traversal bindings that focus input on these widgets, too.

Table 23–3 Highlight attribute resource names.

`highlightColor`	The color of the highlight when the widget has focus.
`highlightThickness`	The width of the highlight border.

Padding and Anchors

Table 23–4 lists padding and anchor attributes that are similar in spirit to some packing attributes described in Chapter 12. However, they are distinct from the packing attributes, and this section explains how they work together with the packer.

The padding attributes for a widget define space that is never occupied by the display of the widget's contents. For example, if you create a `label` with the following attributes and pack it into a frame by itself, you will see the text is still centered, despite the `anchor` attribute.

Table 23–4 Layout attribute resource names.

`anchor`	The anchor position of the widget. Values: `n`, `ne`, `e`, `se`, `s`, `sw`, `w`, `nw`, or `center`. Widgets: `button`, `checkbutton`, `label`, `menubutton`, `message`, or `radiobutton`.
`padX, padY`	Padding space in the X or Y direction, in screen units. Widgets: `button`, `checkbutton`, `label`, `menubutton`, `message`, `radiobutton`, or `text`.

Example 23–3 Padding provided by labels and buttons.

```
label .foo -text Foo -padx 20 -anchor e
pack .foo
```

The `anchor` attribute only affects the display if there is extra room for another reason. One way to get extra room is to specify a `width` attribute that is longer than the text. The following label has right-justified text. You can see the default `padx` value for labels, which is one pixel:

Example 23–4 Anchoring text in a label or button.

```
label .foo -text Foo -width 10 -anchor e
pack .foo
```

Another way to get extra display space is with the `-ipadx` and `-ipady` packing parameters. The example in the next section illustrates this effect. Chapter 12 has several more examples of the packing parameters.

Putting it all Together

The number of different attributes that contribute to the size and appearance can be confusing. The example in this section uses a label to demonstrate the difference among size, borders, padding, and the highlight. Padding can come from the geometry manager, and it can come from widget attributes:

Example 23–5 Borders and padding.

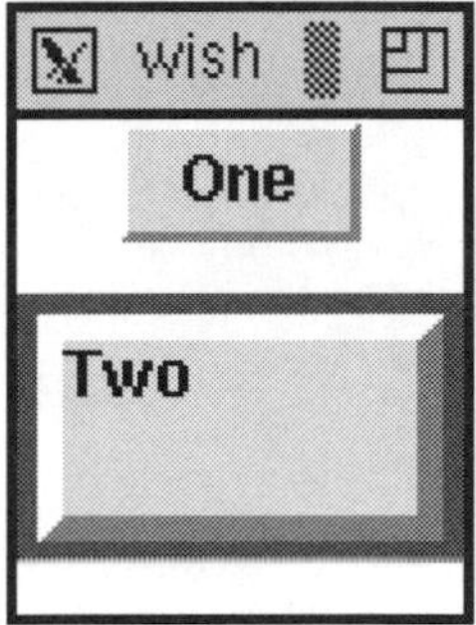


```
frame .f -bg white
label .f.one -text One -relief raised
pack .f.one -side top
label .f.two -text Two \
    -highlightthickness 4 -highlightcolor red \
    -borderwidth 5 -relief raised \
    -padx 0 -pady 0 \
    -width 10 -anchor w
pack .f.two -side top -pady 10 -ipady 10 -fill both
focus .f.two
pack .f
```

The first label in the example uses a raised relief so you can see the default two-pixel border. There is no highlight on a label by default. There is internal padding so that the text is spaced away from the edge of the label. The second label adds a highlight rectangle by specifying a non-zero thickness. Widgets like buttons, entries, listboxes, and text have a highlight rectangle by default. The second label's padding attributes are reduced to zero. The anchor positions the text right next to the border in the upper left (`nw`) corner. However, note the effect of the padding provided by the packer. There is both external and internal padding in the Y direction. The external padding (from `pack -pady`) results in unfilled space. The internal packing (`pack -ipady`) is used by the label for its display. This is different than the label's own `-pady` attribute, which keeps the text away from the top edge of the widget.

CHAPTER 24

Color, Images, and Cursors

This chapter describes the color attributes shared by the Tk widgets. Images and bitmaps can be displayed instead of text by several widgets. This chapter describes commands that create and manipulate images. The cursor attribute controls the shape and color of the mouse cursor when it is over a particular widget. This chapter includes a figure that shows all the cursors in the X cursor font.

Color is one of the most fun things to play with in a user interface. However, this chapter makes no attempt to improve your taste in color choices; it just describes the attributes that affect color. Because color choices are often personal, it is a good idea to specify them via X resources so your users can change them easily. For example, Tk does not have a reverse video mode. However, with a couple resource specifications you can convert a monochrome display into reverse video. The definitions are given in the next example. The `Foreground` and `Background` class names are used, and the various foreground and background colors (e.g., `activeBackground`) have the correct resource class so these settings work:

Example 24–1 Resources for reverse video.

```
proc ReverseVideo {} {
    option add *Foreground white
    option add *Background black
}
```

This chapter describes images, too. The image facility in Tk lets you create an image and then have other Tk widgets display it. The same image can be displayed by many different widgets (or multiple times on a canvas). If you redefine an image, its display is updated in whatever widgets are displaying it.

The last topic of the chapter is cursors. All widgets can control what the mouse cursor looks like when it is over them. In addition, the widgets that support text input define another cursor, the insert cursor. Its appearance is controlled with a few related attributes.

Colors

Table 24–1 lists the resource names for color attributes. The table indicates what widgets use the different color attributes. Remember to use all lowercase and a leading dash when specifying attributes in a Tcl command.

Table 24–1 Color attribute resource names.

`background`	The normal background color. Widgets: `button`, `canvas`, `checkbutton`, `entry`, `frame`, `label`, `listbox`, `menu`, `menubutton`, `message`, `radiobutton`, `scale`, `scrollbar`, `text`, and `toplevel`.
`bg`	Short for background. Command line only.
`foreground`	The normal foreground color. Widgets: `button`, `checkbutton`, `entry`, `label`, `listbox`, `menu`, `menubutton`, `message`, `radiobutton`, `scale`, and `text`.
`fg`	Short for foreground. Command line only.
`activeBackground`	The background when a mouse button will take an action. Widgets: `button`, `checkbutton`, `menu`, `menubutton`, `radiobutton`, `scale`, and `scrollbar`.
`activeForeground`	The foreground when the mouse is over an active widget Widgets: `button`, `checkbutton`, `menu`, `menubutton`, and `radiobutton`.
`disabledForeground`	The foreground when a widget is disabled. Widgets: `button`, `checkbutton`, `menu`, `menubutton`, and `radiobutton`.
`highlightColor`	The color for input focus highlight. Widgets: `button`, `canvas`, `checkbutton`, `entry`, `frame`, `label`, `menubutton`, `radiobutton`, `scale`, `scrollbar`, `text`, and `toplevel`.
`insertBackground`	The color of the insert cursor. Widgets: `canvas`, `entry`, and `text`.
`selectBackground`	The background of selected items. Widgets: `canvas`, `entry`, `listbox`, and `text`.
`selectColor`	The color of the selector indicator. Widgets: `checkbutton`, and `radiobutton`.
`selectForeground`	The foreground of selected text. Widgets: `canvas`, `entry`, `listbox`, and `text`.
`troughColor`	The trough part of scales and scrollbars.

The `foreground` color is used to draw an element, while the `background` color is used for the blank area behind the element. Text, for example, is painted with the foreground color. There are several variations on foreground and background that reflect different states for widgets or items they are displaying.

Color values are specified in two ways: symbolically (e.g., `red`), or by hexadecimal numbers (e.g., `#ff0000`). The leading `#` distinguishes the hexadecimal representation from the symbolic one. The number is divided into three equal sized fields that give the red, green, and blue values, respectively. The fields can specify 4, 8, 12, or 16 bits of a color:

```
#RGB           4 bits per color
#RRGGBB        8 bits per color
#RRRGGGBBB     12 bits per color
#RRRRGGGGBBBB  16 bits per color
```

If you specify more resolution than is supported by the X server, the low order bits of each field are discarded. The different display types supported by X are described in the next section. Each field ranges from 0, which means no color, to a maximum, which is all ones in binary, or all `f` in hex, that means full color saturation. For example, pure red can be specified four ways:

```
#f00 #ff0000 #fff000000 #ffff00000000
```

The symbolic color names understood by the X server may vary from system to system. You can hunt around for a file named `rgb.txt` in the X directory structure to find a listing of them. Or, run the *xcolors* program that comes with the standard X distribution.

The `winfo rgb` command maps from a color name (or value) to three numbers that are its red, green, and blue values. You can use this to compute variations on a color. The `ColorDarken` procedure shown below uses the `winfo rgb` command to get the red, green, and blue components of the input color. It reduces these amounts by five percent, and reconstructs the color specification using the `format` command.

Example 24–2 Computing a darker color.

```
proc ColorDarken { color } {
    set rgb [winfo rgb $color]
    return [format "#%03x%03x%03x" \
        [expr round([lindex $rgb 0] * 0.95)] \
        [expr round([lindex $rgb 1] * 0.95)] \
        [expr round([lindex $rgb 2] * 0.95)]]
}
```

Colormaps and Visuals

For the most part Tk manages the color resources of the display for you. However, if your application uses a lot of colors you may need to control the display with the `Visual` and `Colormap` attributes described in this section. Competition from other applications can cause color allocations to fail, and this causes Tk to switch into monochrome mode (i.e., black and white).

Each pixel on the screen is represented by one or more bits of memory. There are a number of ways to map from a value stored at a pixel to the color that appears on the screen at that pixel. The mapping is a function of the number of bits at each pixel, which is called the *depth* of the display, and the style of interpretation, or *visual class*. The six visual classes defined by X are listed in the following table. Some of the visuals use a *colormap* that maps from the value stored at a pixel to a value used by the hardware to generate a color. A colormap enables a compact encoding for a much richer color. For example, a 256 entry colormap can be indexed with 8 bits, but it may contain 24 bits of color information. The UNIX *xdpyinfo* program reports the different visual classes supported by your display. Table 24–2 lists the visual classes:

Table 24–2 Visual classes for X displays.

`staticgrey`	Greyscale with a fixed colormap defined by the X server.
`greyscale`	Greyscale with a writable colormap.
`staticcolor`	Color with a fixed colormap defined by the X server.
`pseudocolor`	Color values determined by single writable colormap.
`truecolor`	Color values determined by three colormaps defined by the X server: one each for red, green, and blue.
`directcolor`	Color values determined by three writable colormaps: one each for red, green, and blue.

The frame and toplevel widgets support a `colormap` and `visual` attribute that gives you control over these features of the X display. Again, in a Tcl command specify these attributes in all lowercase with a leading dash. Unlike other attributes, these cannot be changed after the widget is created. The value of the `visual` attribute has two parts, a visual type and the desired depth of the display. The following example requests a greyscale visual with a depth of 4 bits per pixel.

```
toplevel .grey -visual "greyscale 4"
```

By default a widget inherits the colormap and visual from its parent widget. The value of the `colormap` attribute can be the keyword `new`, in which case the frame or toplevel gets a new private colormap, or it can be the name of another widget, in which case the frame or toplevel shares the colormap of that widget. When sharing colormaps, the other widget must be on the same screen and using the same visual class.

Bitmaps and Images

The label and all the button widgets have an `image` attribute that specifies a graphic image to display. Using an image takes two steps. In the first step the image is created via the `image create` command. This command returns an identifier for the image, and it is this identifier that is passed to widgets as the value of their image attribute.

Example 24–3 Specifying an image for a widget.

```
set im [image create bitmap \
    -file glyph.bitmap -maskfile glyph.mask \
    -background white -foreground blue]
button .foo -image $im
```

There are three things that can be displayed by labels and all the buttons: text, bitmaps, and images. If more than one of these attributes are specified, then the image has priority over the bitmap, and the bitmap has priority over the text. You can remove the image or bitmap attribute by specifying a null string for its value:

```
.foo config -image {}
```

The image Command

Table 24–3 summarizes the `image` command.

Table 24–3 Summary of the `image` command.

`image create` *type* *?name? ?options?*	Create an image of the specified type. If name is not specified, one is made up. The remaining arguments depend on the type of image being created.
`image delete` *name*	Delete the named image.
`image height` *name*	Return the height of the image, in pixels.
`image names`	Return the list of defined images.
`image type` *name*	Return the type of the named image.
`image types`	Return the list of possible image types.
`image width` *name*	Return the width of the image, in pixels.

The exact set of options for `image create` depend on the image type. There are two built-in image types: `bitmap` and `photo`. Chapter 30 describes the C interface for defining new image types.

Bitmap Images

A `bitmap` image has a main image and an optional mask image. The main image is drawn in the foreground color. The mask image is drawn in the background color, unless the corresponding bit is set in the main image. The remaining bits are "clear" and the widget's normal background color shows through. Table 24–4 lists the options supported by the `bitmap` image type:

Table 24–4 Bitmap image options.

`-background` *color*	The background color. (*no* `-bg` *equivalent)*
`-data` *string*	The contents of the bitmap as a string.
`-file` *name*	The name of the file containing a bitmap definition.
`-foreground` *color*	The foreground color. (*no* `-fg` *equivalent)*
`-maskdata` *string*	The contents of the mask as a string.
`-maskfile` *name*	The name of the file containing the mask data.

The bitmap definition files are stylized C structure definitions that the X server parses. The files usually have a `.xbm` file name extension. These are generated by bitmap editors such as `bitmap` program, which comes with the standard X distribution. The `-file` and `-maskfile` options name a file that contains such a definition. The `-data` and `-maskdata` options specify a string in the same format as the contents of one of those files.

The bitmap Attribute

The label and all the button widgets also support a `bitmap` attribute, which is a special case of an image. This attribute is a little more convenient than the image attribute because the extra step of creating an image is not required. However, there is some power and flexibility with the `image` command, such as the ability to reconfigure a named image (e.g., for animation) that is not possible with a bitmap.

Example 24–4 Specifying a bitmap for a widget.

```
button .foo -bitmap @glyph.xbm -fg blue
```

The `@` syntax for the bitmap attribute signals that a file containing the bitmap is being specified. It is also possible to name built-in bitmaps. The predefined bitmaps are shown in the next figure along with their symbolic name. Chapter 30 describes the C interface for defining built in bitmaps.

Example 24–5 The built-in bitmaps.

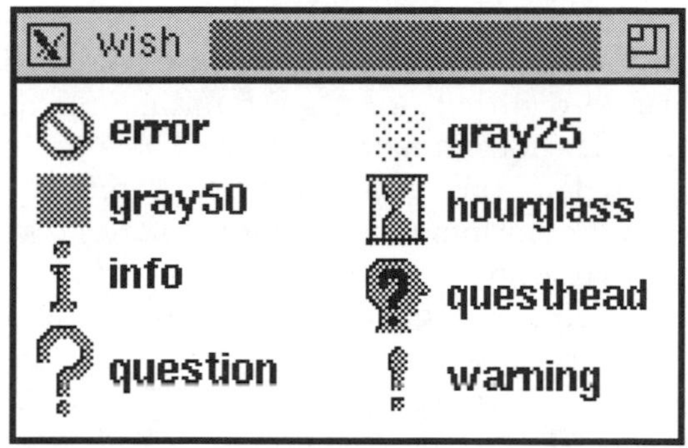


```
frame .f -bd 4; frame .g -bd 4 ; pack .f .g -side left
set parent .f ; set next .g
foreach name {error gray25 gray50 hourglass \
             info questhead question warning} {
    frame $parent.$name
    label $parent.$name.l -text $name -width 9 -anchor w
    label $parent.$name.b -bitmap $name
    pack $parent.$name.l -side right
    pack $parent.$name.b -side top
    pack $parent.$name -side top -expand true -fill x
    set tmp $parent ; set parent $next ; set next $tmp
}
```

Photo Images

The `photo` image type was contributed to Tk by Paul Mackerras. It displays full color images and can do dithering and gamma correction. Table 24–5 lists the attributes for photo images. These are specified in the `image create photo` command.

Table 24–5 Photo image attributes.

`-format` *format*	Specifies the data format for the file or data string.
`-data` *string*	The contents of the photo as a string.
`-file` *name*	The name of the file containing a photo definition.
`-gamma` *value*	A gamma correction factor, which must be greater than zero. A value greater than one brightens an image.
`-height` *value*	The height, in screen units.
`-width` *value*	The width of the image, in screen units.
`-palette` *spec*	The number of shades of gray or color for the image.

The `format` indicates what format the data is in. The `photo` image supports different image formats, although the only format supported by Tk 4.0 is the PPM format. There is a C interface to define new photo formats. Normally you do not need to specify the format because the photo implementation will try all format handlers until it find one that accepts the data. An explicit format limits what handlers are tried. The format name is treated as a prefix that is compared against the names of handlers. Case is not significant in the format name.

The `palette` setting determines how many colors or graylevels are used with rendering an image. If a single number is specified, the image is rendered in greyscale with that many shades of gray. For full color, three numbers separated by slashes specify the number of shades of red, green, and blue, respectively. The more shades you specify the more room you take up in your colormap. The photo widget will switch to a private colormap if necessary. Multiply the number of red, green, and blue shades to determine how many different colors you use. If you have an 8-bit display, there are only 256 colors available. Reasonable palette settings that do not hog the colormap include `5/5/4` and `6/6/5`. You can use fewer shades of blue because the human eye is less sensitive to blue.

After you create an image you can operate. Table 24–6 lists the image instance operations. In the table, `$p` is a photo image handle returned by the `image create photo` command.

Table 24–6 Photo image operations.

`$p blank`	Clear the image. It becomes transparent.
`$p cget` *`option`*	Return the configuration attribute *`option`*.
`$p configure ...`	Reconfigure the photo image attributes.
`$p copy` *`source options`*	Copy another image. Table 24–7 lists the copy options.
`$p get` *`x y`*	Return the pixel value at position *x y*.
`$p put` *`data`* `?-to` *`x1 y1 x2 y2`*`?`	Insert *`data`* into the image. *`data`* is a list of rows, where each row is a list of colors.
`$p read` *`file options`*	Load an image from a file. Table 24–8 lists the read options.
`$p redither`	Reapply the dithering algorithm to the image.
`$p write file options`	Save the image to *`file`* accoring to *`options`*. Table 24–9 lists the write options.

Table 24–7 lists the options available when you copy data from one image to another. The regions involved in the copy are specified by the upper-left and lower-right corners. If the lower-right corner of the source is not specified, then it defaults to the lower-right corner of the image. If the lower-right corner of the destination is not specified, then the size is determined by the area of the source. Otherwise, the source image may be cropped or replicated to fill the destination.

Table 24–7 Copy options for photo images.

`-from` *x1 y1 ?x2 y2?*	Specifies the location and area in the source image. If *x2* and *y2* are not given, they are set to the bottom-right corner.
`-to` *x1 y1 ?x2 y2?*	Specifies the location and area in the destination. If *x2* and *y2* are not given, the size is determined by the source. The source may be cropped or tiled to fill the destination.
`-shrink`	Shrink the destination so its bottom right corner matches the bottom right corner of the data copied in. This has no effect if the `width` and `height` have been set for the image.
`-zoom` *x ?y?*	Magnify the source so each source pixel becomes a block of *x* by *y* pixels. *y* defaults to *x* if it is not specified.
`-decimate` *x ?y?*	Reduce the source by taking every *x*'th pixel in the X direction and every *y*'th pixel in the Y direction. *y* defaults to *x*.

Table 24–8 lists the read options, and Table 24–9 lists the write options. The format option is more important for writing, because the first format found is used. With reading, the format is determined automatically. If there are multiple image types that can read the same data, you may specify a read format.

Table 24–8 Read options for photo images.

`-format` *format*	Specifies the format of the data. By default, the format is determined automatically.
`-from` *x1 y1 ?x2 y2?*	Specifies a subregion of the source data. If *x2* and *y2* are not given, the size is determined by the data.
`-to` *x1 y1*	Specifies the top-left corner of the new data.
`-shrink`	Shrink the destination so its bottom right corner matches the bottom right corner of the data read in. This has no efect if the width and height have been set for the image.

Table 24–9 Write options for photo images.

`-format` *format*	Specifies the format of the data.
`-from` *x1 y1 ?x2 y2?*	Specifies a subregion of the data to save. If *x2* and *y2* are not given, they are set to the lower-right corner.

The Mouse Cursor

The `cursor` attribute defines the mouse cursor. This attribute can take a number of forms. The simplest is a symbolic name for one of the glyphs in the X cursor font. A foreground and background color for the cursor can be specified.

Example 24–6 The X cursor font.

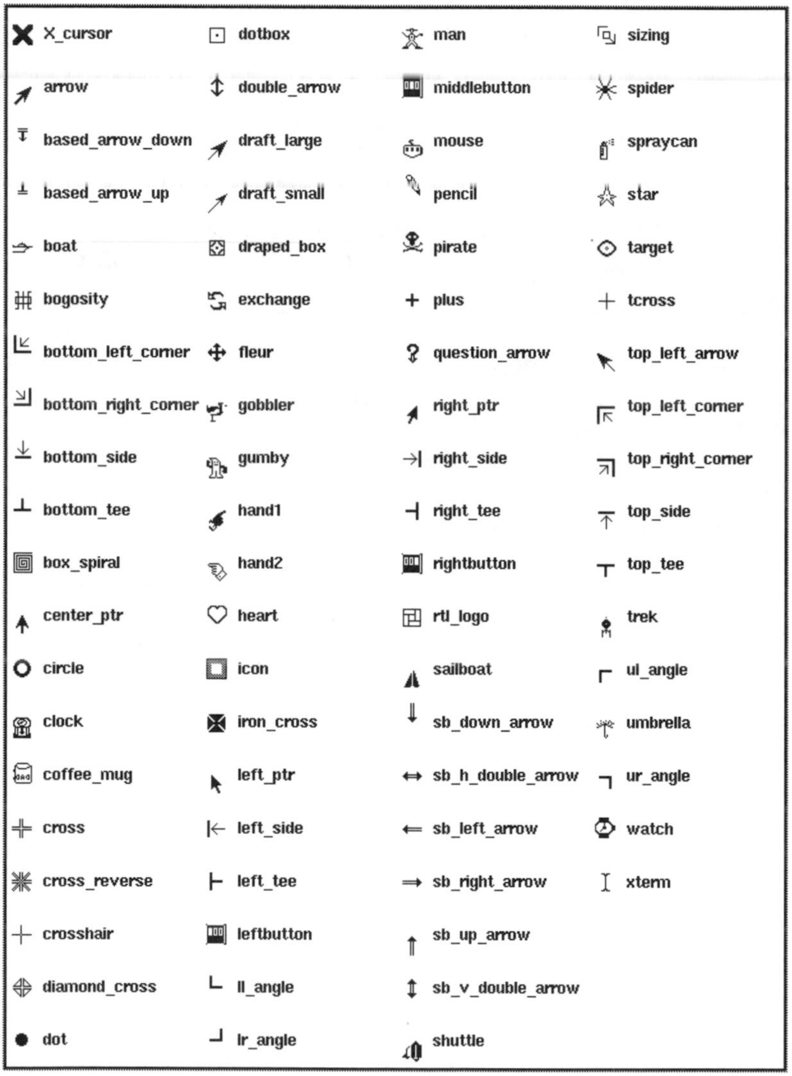

X_cursor	dotbox	man	sizing
arrow	double_arrow	middlebutton	spider
based_arrow_down	draft_large	mouse	spraycan
based_arrow_up	draft_small	pencil	star
boat	draped_box	pirate	target
bogosity	exchange	plus	tcross
bottom_left_corner	fleur	question_arrow	top_left_arrow
bottom_right_corner	gobbler	right_ptr	top_left_corner
bottom_side	gumby	right_side	top_right_corner
bottom_tee	hand1	right_tee	top_side
box_spiral	hand2	rightbutton	top_tee
center_ptr	heart	rtl_logo	trek
circle	icon	sailboat	ul_angle
clock	iron_cross	sb_down_arrow	umbrella
coffee_mug	left_ptr	sb_h_double_arrow	ur_angle
cross	left_side	sb_left_arrow	watch
cross_reverse	left_tee	sb_right_arrow	xterm
crosshair	leftbutton	sb_up_arrow	
diamond_cross	ll_angle	sb_v_double_arrow	
dot	lr_angle	shuttle	

Here are some example cursor specifications:

```
$w config -cursor watch                ;# stop-watch cursor
$w config -cursor {gumby blue}         ;# blue gumby
$w config -cursor {X_cursor red white}  ;# red X on white
```

The other form for the cursor attribute specifies a file that contains the definition of the cursor bitmap. If two file names are specified, then the second specifies the cursor mask that determines what bits of the background get covered up. Bitmap editing programs like *idraw* and *iconedit* can be used to generate these files. Here are some example cursor specification using files. You need to specify a foreground color, and if you specify a mask file then you also need to specify a background color:

```
$w config -cursor "@timer.xbm black"
$w config -cursor "@timer.xbm timer.mask black red"
```

The Text Insert Cursor

The text, entry, and canvas widgets have a second cursor to mark the text insertion point. The text insert cursor is described by a set of attributes. These attributes can make the insert cursor vary from a thin vertical line to a large rectangle with its own relief. Table 24–10 lists these attributes. The default insert cursor is a two-pixel wide vertical line. You may not like the look of a wide insert cursor. The cursor is centered between two characters, so a wide one does not look the same as the block cursors found in many terminal emulators. Instead of occupying the space of a single character, it partially overlaps the two characters on either side:

Table 24–10 Cursor attribute resource names.

`cursor`	The mouse cursor. See text for sample formats. Widgets: `button`, `canvas`, `checkbutton`, `entry`, `frame`, `label`, `listbox`, `menu`, `menubutton`, `message`, `radiobutton`, `scale`, `scrollbar`, `text`, or `toplevel`.
`insertBackground`	Color for the text insert cursor. Widgets: `canvas`, `entry`, and `text`.
`insertBorderWidth`	Width for three dimensional appearance. Widgets: `canvas`, `entry`, and `text`.
`insertOffTime`	Milliseconds the cursor blinks off. Widgets: `canvas`, `entry`, and `text`.
`insertOnTime`	Milliseconds the cursor blinks on. Widgets: `canvas`, `entry`, and `text`.
`insertWidth`	Width of the text insert cursor, in screen units. Widgets: `canvas`, `entry`, and `text`.

CHAPTER 25

Fonts and Text Attributes

This chapter describes the naming convention for X fonts. The examples show how to trap errors from missing fonts. This chapter describes other text-related attributes such as justification, anchoring, and geometry gridding.

Fonts describe how characters look on the screen. They can cause trouble because the set of installed fonts can vary from system to system. This chapter describes the font naming convention and the pattern matching done on font names. If you use many different fonts in your application, you should specify them in the most general way so the chances of the font name matching an installed font is increased.

After fonts are described, the chapter explains a few of the widget attributes that relate to fonts. This includes justification, anchors, and geometry gridding.

Fonts

Fonts are specified with X font names. The font names are specified with the `-font` attribute when creating or reconfiguring a widget.

```
label .foo -text "Foo" -font fixed
```

This label command creates a label widget with the `fixed` font. `fixed` is an example of a short font name. Other short names might include `6x12`, `9x15`, or `times12`. However, these aliases are site-dependent. In fact, all font names are site dependent because different fonts may be installed on different systems. The only font guaranteed to exist is named `fixed`.

The more general form of a font name has several components that describe various attributes of the font. Each component is separated by a dash, and asterisk (`*`) is used for unspecified components. Short font names are just aliases for these more complete specifications. Here is an example:

```
-*-times-medium-r-normal-*-18-*-*-*-*-*-iso8859-1
```

The components of font names are listed in Table 25–1 in the order in which they occur in the font specification. The table gives the possible values for the components. If there is an ellipsis (...) then there are more possibilities, too.

Table 25–1 X Font specification components.

Component:	Possible values:
foundry	`adobe xerox linotype misc ...`
family	`times helvetica lucida courier symbol ...`
weight	`bold medium demibold demi normal book light`
slant	`i r o`
swidth	`normal sans narrow semicondensed`
adstyle	`sans`
pixels	`8 10 12 14 18 24 36 48 72 144 ...`
points	`0 80 100 120 140 180 240 360 480 720 ...`
resx	`0 72 75 100`
resy	`0 72 75 100`
space	`p m c`
avgWidth	`73 94 124 ...`
registry	`iso8859 xerox dec adobe jisx0208.1983 ...`
encoding	`1 fontspecific dectech symbol dingbats`

The most common attributes chosen for a font are its family, weight, slant, and size. The family determines the basic look, such as `courier` or helvetica. The weight is usually **bold** or medium. The slant component is a bit cryptic, but `i` means *italic*, `r` means roman (i.e., normal), and `o` means *oblique*. A given font family might have an italic version, or an oblique version, but not both. Similarly, not all weights are offered by all font families. Size can be specified in pixels (i.e., screen pixels) or points. Points are meant to be independent of the screen resolution. On a 75dpi font, there are about 10 points per pixel. Again, not all font sizes are available in all fonts.

It is generally a good idea to specify just a few key components and use `*` for the remaining components. The X server attempts to match the font specification with its set of installed fonts, but it fails if there is a specific component that it cannot match. If the first or last character of the font name is an asterisk, then that can match multiple components. The following selects a 12 pixel times font:

```
*times-medium-r-*-*-12*
```

Two useful UNIX programs that deal with X fonts are *xlsfonts* and *xfontsel*. These are part of the standard X11 distribution. *xlsfonts* simply lists the available fonts that match a given font name. It uses the same pattern matching that the server does. Because asterisk is special to most UNIX shells, you need to quote the font name argument if you run *xslfonts* from your shell. *xfontsel* has a graphical user interface and displays the font that matches a given font name.

Unfortunately, if a font is missing, neither Tk nor the X server attempt to substitute another font, not even `fixed`. The `FindFont` routine looks around for an existing font. It falls back to `fixed` if nothing else matches:

Example 25–1 `FindFont` matches an existing font.

```
proc FindFont { w {sizes 14} {weight medium} {slant r}} {
    foreach family {times courier helvetica} {
        foreach size $sizes {
            if {[catch {$w config -font \
                -*-$family-$weight-$slant-*-*-$size-*}] == 0} {
                return -*-$family-$weight-$slant-*-*-$size-*
            }
        }
    }
    $w config -font fixed
    return fixed
}
```

The `FindFont` proc takes the name of a widget, `w`, as an argument, plus some optional font characteristics. All five kinds of text widgets take a `-font` attribute specification, so you can use this routine on any of them. The `sizes` argument is a set of pixel sizes for the font (not points). The routine is written so you can supply a choice of sizes, but it fixes the set of families it uses and allows only a single weight and slant. Another approach is to loop through a set of more explicit font names, with `fixed` being your last choice. The font that works is returned by the procedure so that the search results can be saved and reused later. This is important because opening a font for the first time is a fairly heavyweight operation, and a failed font lookup is also expensive.

Another approach to the font problem is to create a wrapper around the Tk widget creation routines. While you are at it you can switch some attributes to positional arguments if you find you are always specifying them:

Example 25–2 Handling missing font errors.

```
proc Button { name text command args } {
    set cmd [list button $name -text $text -command $command]
    if [catch {concat $cmd $args} w] {
        puts stderr "Button (warning) $w"
        # Delete the font specified in args, if any
        set ix [lsearch $args -font]
        if {$ix >= 0} {
            set args [lreplace $args $ix [expr $ix+1]]
```

```
        }
        # This font overrides the resource database
        eval $cmd $args {-font fixed}
    }
    return $name
}
```

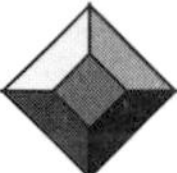

The Button procedure creates a button and always takes a text and command argument. Note that list is used to carefully construct the prefix of the Tcl command so that the values of text and command are preserved. Other arguments are passed through with args. The procedure falls back to the fixed font if the button command fails. It is careful to eliminate the font specified in args, if it exists. The explicit font overrides any setting from the resource database or the Tk defaults. Of course, it might fail for some more legitimate reason, but that is allowed to happen in the backup case. The next example provides a generic wrapper that can be used when creating any widget:

Example 25–3 FontWidget protects against font errors.

```
proc FontWidget { args } {
    if [ccatch $args w] {
        # Delete the font specified in args, if any
        set ix [lsearch $args -font]
        if {$ix >= 0} {
            set args [lreplace $args $ix [expr $ix+1]]
        }
        # This font overrides the resource database
        set w [eval $args {-font fixed}]
    }
    return $w
}
FontWidget button .foo -text Foo -font garbage
```

Text Layout

Table 25–2 summarizes two simple text layout attributes, justify and wrapLength. The text widget introduces several more layout-related attributes, and Chapter 19 describes those in detail. The two attributes described in this section apply to the various button widgets, the label, entry, and message widgets. Those widgets are described in Chapters 14, 16, and 17. The justify attribute causes text to be centered, left-justified, or right justified. The default justification is center for all the widgets in the table, except for the entry widget, which is left-justified by default.

The wrapLength attribute specifies how long a line of text is before it is wrapped onto another line. It is used to create multi-line buttons and labels. This attribute is specified in screen units, however, not string length. It is probably easier to achieve the desired line breaks by inserting newlines into the text for the button or label and specifying a wrapLength of 0, which is the default.

Table 25–2 Layout attribute resource names

`justify`	Text line justification. Values: `left`, `center`, or `right`. Widgets: `button`, `checkbutton`, `entry`, `label`, `menubutton`, `message`, and `radiobutton`.
`wrapLength`	Maximum line length for text, in screen units. `Widgets`: `button`, `checkbutton`, `label`, `menubutton`, and `radiobutton`.

Gridding, Resizing, and Geometry

The text, listbox, and canvas widgets support geometry gridding. This is an alternate interpretation of the main window geometry that is in terms of grid units, typically characters, as opposed to pixels. The `setGrid` attribute is a boolean that indicates if gridding should be turn on. The widget implementation takes care of defining a grid size that matches its character size.

When a widget is gridded, its size is constrained to have a whole number of grid units displayed. In other words, the height will be constrained to show a whole number of text lines, and the width will be constrained to show a whole number of average width characters. This affects interactive resizing by users, as well as the various window manger commands (`wm`) that relate to geometry. When gridding is turned on, the geometry argument (e.g., `24x80`) is interpreted as grid units, otherwise it is interpreted as pixels. The window manager geometry commands are summarized in Table 26–1 on page 311.

An important side-effect of gridding is that it enables the user to do interactive resizing. Setting the mininum size or maximum size of a window also enables resizing. Otherwise, Tk windows are only resizable under program control. Try the following example with and without the `-setgrid` flag, and with and without the `wm minsize` command, which sets the minimum size of the window. The `ScrolledListbox` procedure is defined on page 191.

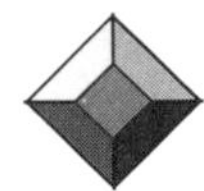

Example 25–4 A gridded, resizable listbox.

```
wm minsize . 20 20
button .quit -text Quit -command exit
pack .quit -side top -anchor e
frame .f
pack .f -side top -fill both -expand true
ScrolledListbox .f -width 10 -height 5 -setgrid true
```

Selection Attributes

Table 25–3 lists the selection-related attributes. The `exportSelection` attribute controls if the selection is exported for cut and paste to other widgets. The colors for selected text are set with `selectForeground` and `selectBackground`. The selection is drawn in a raised relief, and the `selectBorderWidth` attribute affects the 3D appearance. Choose a border width of zero to get a flat relief.

Table 25–3 Selection attribute resource names.

`exportSelection`	Enable X selection. Widgets: `entry`, `canvas`, `listbox`, and `text`.
`selectForeground`	Foreground of selected text.
`selectBackground`	Background of selected text.
`selectBorderWidth`	Width of 3D raised border for selection highlight.

A Font Selection Application

This chapter concludes with an application that lets you browse the fonts available in your system. This is modeled after the *xfontsel* program. It displays a set of menus, one for each component of a font name. You can select different values for the components, although the complete space of font possibilities is not defined. You might choose components that result in an invalid font name. The tool also lets you browse the list of available fonts, so you can find out what is offered. This is what the interface looks like:

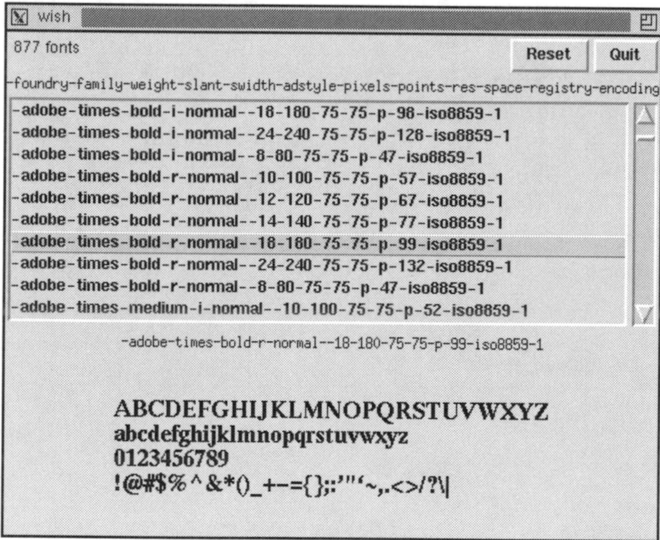

Setup and Widget Layout

The application uses the `font` global variable for its state. It creates a status line and a few buttons at the top. Underneath that is a set of menus, one for each font component. The next example creates the layout of the buttons and the menus. The menu buttons have no padding or border width so their text appears as one continuous string.

Example 25–5 A font selection application.

```
#!/usr/local/bin/wish
# The menus are big, so position the window
# near the upper-left corner of the display
wm geometry . +30+30

# Create a frame and buttons along the top
frame .buttons
pack .buttons -side top -fill x
button .buttons.quit -text Quit -command exit
button .buttons.reset -text Reset -command Reset
pack .buttons.quit .buttons.reset -side right

# An entry widget is used for status messages
entry .buttons.e -textvar status -relief flat
pack .buttons.e -side top -fill x
proc Status { string } {
	global status
	set status $string
	update idletasks
}
# So we can see status messages
tkwait visibility .buttons.e

# Set up the menus. There is one for each
# component of a font name, except that the two resolutions
# are combined and the avgWidth is suppressed.
frame .menubar
set font(comps) {foundry family weight slant swidth \
	adstyle pixels points res res2 \
	space avgWidth registry encoding}
foreach x $font(comps) {
	# font(component) lists all possible component values
	# font(cur,component) keeps the current component values
	set font(cur,$x) *
	set font($x) {}
	# Trim out the second resolution and the average width
	if {$x == "res2" || $x == "avgWidth"} {
		continue
	}
	# The border and highlight thickness are set to 0 so the
	# button texts run together into one long string.
	menubutton .menubar.$x -menu .menubar.$x.m -text -$x \
		-padx 0 -bd 0 -font fixed \
		-highlightthickness 0
	menu .menubar.$x.m
	pack .menubar.$x -side left
	# Create the initial wild card entry for the component
	.menubar.$x.m add radio -label * \
		-variable font(cur,$x) \
		-value * \
		-command [list DoFont]
}
```

Tracing Variables

The menus for two components are left out. The two resolutions are virtually always the same, so one is enough. The `avgWidth` component varies wildly, and user probably won't choose a font based on it. Variable traces are used to fix up the values associated with these components. The second resolution is tied to the first resolution. The `avgWidth` always returns *, which matches anything. The points are set to 10 times the pixels if the pixels are set. However, if that is not right, which sometimes happens, then the user can set the points explicitly.

Example 25–6 Using variable traces to fix things up.

```
# Use traces to patch up the suppressed font(comps)
trace variable font(cur,res2) r TraceRes2
proc TraceRes2 { args } {
    global font
    set font(cur,res2) $font(cur,res)
}
trace variable font(cur,avgWidth) r TraceWidth
proc TraceWidth { args } {
    global font
    set font(cur,avgWidth) *
}
# Mostly, but not always, the points are 10x the pixels
trace variable font(cur,pixels) w TracePixels
proc TracePixels { args } {
    global font
    catch {
     # Might not be a number
     set font(cur,points) [expr 10*$font(cur,pixels)]
    }
}
```

Listing Available Fonts

The application displays a listbox with all the possible font names in it. If you click on a font name its font is displayed. The set of possible font names is obtained by running the *xlsfonts* program.

Example 25–7 Listing available fonts.

```
# Create a listbox to hold all the font names
frame .body
set font(list) [listbox .body.list \
    -setgrid true -selectmode browse \
    -yscrollcommand {.body.scroll set}]
scrollbar .body.scroll -command {.body.list yview}
pack .body.scroll -side right -fill y
pack .body.list -side left -fill both -expand true

# Clicking on an item displays the font
```

```
bind $font(list) <ButtonRelease-1> [list SelectFont
$font(list) %y]

# Use the xlsfonts program to generate a
# list of all fonts known to the server.
Status "Listing fonts..."
if [catch {open "|xlsfonts *"} in] {
    puts stderr "xlsfonts failed $in"
    exit 1
}
```

Keeping Track of Fonts

Example 25–8 Determining possible font components.

```
set font(num) 0
set numAliases 0
set font(N) 0
while {[gets $in line] >= 0} {
    $font(list) insert end $line
    # fonts(all,$i) is the master list of existing fonts
    # This is used to avoid potentially expensive
    # searches for fonts on the server, and to
    # highlight the matching font in the listbox
    # when a pattern is specified.
    set font(all,$font(N)) $line
    incr font(N)

    set parts [split $line -]
    if {[llength $parts] < 14} {
        # Aliases do not have the full information
        lappend aliases $line
        incr numAliases
    } else {
        incr font(num)
        # Chop up the font name and record the
        # unique font(comps) in the font array.
        # The leading - in font names means that
        # parts has a leading null element and we
        # start at element 1 (not zero).
        set i 1
        foreach x $font(comps) {
            set value [lindex $parts $i]
            incr i
            if {[lsearch $font($x) $value] < 0} {
                # Missing this entry, so add it
                lappend font($x) $value
            }
        }
    }
}
```

The program uses a simple data structure based on the list of available fonts. For each font component, all possible values are recorded. These values are used to create the menus.

Creating the Menus

Menus are created so the user can select different font components. Radio button entries are used so that the current selection is highlighted. The special case for the two suppressed components crops up here. We let the variable traces fix up those values.

Example 25–9 Creating the radiobutton menu entries.

```
# Fill out the menus
foreach x $font(comps) {
    if {$x == "res2" || $x == "avgWidth"} {
     continue
    }
    foreach value [lsort $font($x)] {
        if {[string length $value] == 0} {
            set label (nil)
        } else {
            set label $value
        }
        .menubar.$x.m add radio -label $label \
            -variable font(cur,$x) \
            -value $value \
            -command DoFont
    }
}
Status "Found $font(num) fonts and $numAliases aliases"
```

The Font Sampler Display

Below the menu is a label that holds the current font name. Below that is a message widget that displays a sample of the font. One of two messages are displayed, depending on if the font is matched or not.

Example 25–10 Setting up the label and message widgets.

```
# This label displays the current font
label .font -textvar font(current) -bd 5 -font fixed

# A message displays a string in the font.
set font(msg) [message .font(msg) -aspect 1000 \
                -borderwidth 10]
set font(sampler) "
ABCDEFGHIJKLMNOPQRSTUVWXYZ
abcdefghijklmnopqrstuvwxyz
0123456789
```

```
!@#$%^&*()_+-=[]{};:'''~,.<>/?\\|
"
set font(errormsg) "

(No matching font)


"
# font Now pack the main display
pack .menubar -side top -fill x
pack .body -side top -fill both -expand true
pack .font $font(msg) -side top
```

Selecting a Font

The next example has the core procedures of the example. The DoFont procedure is triggered by changing a radiobutton menu entry. It rebuilds the font name and calls SetFont. The SetFont procedure searches the list of all fonts for a match. This prevents expensive searches by the X server, and it allows the application to highlight the matching font in the listbox. The SelectFont procedure is triggered by a selection in the listbox. It also constructs a font name and calls SetFont. Finally, Reset restores the font name to the match-all pattern.

Example 25–11 The font selection procedures.

```
proc DoFont { } {
    global font
    set font(current) {}
    foreach x $font(comps) {
        append font(current) -$font(cur,$x)
    }
    SetFont
}
proc SelectFont { list y } {
    # Extract a font name from the listbox
    global font
    set ix [$font(list) nearest $y]
    set font(current) [$font(list) get $ix]
    set parts [split $font(current) -]
    if {[llength $parts] < 14} {
        foreach x $font(comps) {
            set font(cur,$x) {}
        }
    } else {
        set i 1
        foreach x $font(comps) {
            set value [lindex $parts $i]
            incr i
            set font(cur,$x) $value
        }
    }
    SetFont
```

```
}
proc SetFont {} {
    global font
    # Generate a regular expression from the font pattern
    regsub -all -- {<nil>} $font(current) {} font(current)
    regsub -all -- {\*} $font(current) {[^-]*} pattern
    for {set n 0} {$n < $font(N)} {incr n} {
        if [regexp -- $pattern $font(all,$n)] {
            $font(msg) config -font $font(current) \
                -text $font(sampler)
            catch {$font(list) select clear \
                [$font(list) curselection]}
            $font(list) select set $n
            $font(list) see $n
            return
        }
    }
    $font(msg) config -text $font(errormsg)
}

proc Reset {} {
    global font
    foreach x $font(comps) {
        set font(cur,$x) *
    }
    DoFont
    Status "$font(num) fonts"
}

Reset
```

CHAPTER 26

Window Managers and Window Information

A window manager is a special application that controls the size and location of other applications' windows. The wm command provides an interface to the window manager. The winfo command returns information about windows.

Management of toplevel windows is done by a distinguished application called the *window manager*. The window manager controls the position of toplevel windows, provides a way to resize windows, open and close them, and implements a border and decorative title for windows. The window manager contributes to the general look and feel of the X display, but there is no requirement that the look and feel of the window manager be the same as that used in an application. The wm command interacts with the window manager so the application can control its size, position, and iconified state.

If you need to fine tune your display you may need some detailed information about widgets. The winfo command returns all sorts of information about windows, including interior widgets, not just toplevel windows.

The wm Command

The wm command has about 20 operations that interact with the window manager. The general form of the commands is:

```
wm operation win ?args?
```

In all cases the *win* argument must be for a toplevel window. Otherwise, an error is raised. In many cases the operation either sets or queries a value. If a new value is not specified, then the current settings are returned. For example, this first command returns the current window geometry, and the next command defines a new geometry:

```
wm geometry .
=> 300x200+327+20
wm geometry . 400x200+0+0
```

The operations can be grouped into four main categories:

- Size, placement and decoration of windows.
- Icons.
- Long-term session state.
- Miscellaneous.

Size, Placement, and Decoration

Each window has a title that appears in the title bar that the window manager places above the window. In a *wish* script, the default title of the main window is the last component of the file name of the script. You can use the `wm title` command to change the title of the window. The title can also appear in the icon for your window, unless you specify another name with `wm iconname`.

```
wm title . "My Application"
```

You can use the `wm geometry` command to adjust the position or size of your main windows. A geometry specification has the general form *W*x*H*+*X*+*Y*, where *W* is the width, *H* is the height, and *X* and *Y* specify the location of the upper-left corner of the window. The location `+0+0` is the upper-left corner of the display. You can specify a negative *X* or *Y* to position the bottom (right) side of the window relative to the bottom (right) side of the display. For example, `+0-0` is the lower left corner, and `-100-100` is offset from the lower-right corner by 100 pixels in the X and Y direction. If you do not specify a geometry, then the current geometry is returned.

A window can have a gridded geometry, which means that the geometry is in terms of some unit other than pixels. For example, the text and listbox widgets can set a grid based on the size of the characters they display. They have a `setgrid` attribute that turns on gridding. You can also define a grid with the `wm grid` command, and you can use that command to determine the current grid size. The next example sets up gridded geometry for a canvas.

Example 26–1 Gridded geometry for a canvas.

```
canvas .c -width 300 -height 150
pack .c -fill both -expand true
wm geometry
=> 300x200+678+477
wm grid . 30 15 10 10
wm geometry .
=> 30x20+678+477
```

An important side effect of gridding is that it enables interactive resizing of windows. By default, Tk windows are not resizable except by program control.

You can constrain the minimum size, maximum size, and the aspect ratio of a toplevel window. The aspect ratio is the width divided by the height. The constraint is applied when the user resizes the window interactively. The `minsize`, `maxsize`, and `aspect` operations apply these constraints. As with gridding, a side effect of setting one of these constraints is to allow interactive resizing.

Some window managers insist on having the user position windows. The `sizefrom` and `positionfrom` operations let you pretend that the user specified the size and position in order to work around this restriction.

Table 26–1 summarizes the `wm` commands that deal with size, decorations, placement:

Table 26–1 Size, placement and decoration window manager operations.

`wm aspect` *`win ?a b c d?`*	Constrain *win*'s ratio of width to height to be between (*a/b* and *c/d*).
`wm geometry` *`win ?geometry?`*	Query or set the geometry of *win*.
`wm grid` *`win ?w h dx dy?`*	Query or set the grid size. *w* and *h* are the base size, in grid units. *dx* and *dy* are the size, in pixels, of a grid unit.
`wm group` *`win ?leader?`*	Query or set the group leader (a toplevel widget) for win. The window manager may unmap all the group at once.
`wm maxsize` *`win ?width height?`*	Constrain the maximum size of *win*.
`wm minsize` *`win ?width height?`*	Constrain the minimum size of *win*.
`wm positionfrom` *`win ?who?`*	Query or set *who* to be `program` or `user`.
`wm sizefrom` *`win ?who?`*	Query or set *who* to be `program` or `user`.
`wm title` *`win ?string?`*	Query or set the window title to *string*.

Icons

When you close a window the window manager unmaps the window and replaces it with an icon. You can open and close the window yourself with the `deiconify` and `iconify` operations, respectively. Use the `withdraw` operation to unmap the window without replacing it with an icon. The `state` operation returns the current state, which is one of `normal`, `iconified`, or `withdrawn`. If you withdraw a window, you can restore it with `deiconify`.

You can set the attributes of the icon with the `iconname`, `iconposition`, `iconbitmap`, and `iconmask` operations. The icon's mask is used to get irregularly shaped icons. Chapter 24 describes how masks and bitmaps are defined. In the case of an icon, it is most likely that you have the definition in a file, so your command will look like this:

```
wm iconbitmap . @myfilename
```

Table 26–2 summarizes the `wm` operations that have to do with icons:

Table 26–2 Window manager commands for icons.

`wm deiconify` *win*	Open the window *win*.
`wm iconbitmap` *win ?bitmap?*	Query or define the bitmap for the icon.
`wm iconify` *win*	Close the window *win*.
`wm iconmask` *win ?mask?*	Query or define the mask for the icon.
`wm iconname` *win ?name?*	Query or set the name on the icon.
`wm iconposition` *win ?x y?*	Query or set the location of the icon.
`wm iconwindow` *win ?window?*	Query or specify an alternate window to display when in the iconified state.
`wm state` *win*	Returns `normal`, `iconic`, or `withdrawn`.
`wm withdraw` *win*	Unmap the window and forget about it. No icon is displayed.

Session State

Some window managers support the notion of a *session* that lasts between runs of the window system. A session is implemented by saving state about the applications that are running, and using this information to restart the applications when the window system is restarted. This section also describes how you can intercept requests to quit your application so you can stop cleanly.

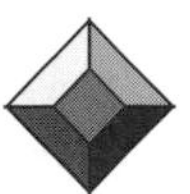

An easy way to participate in the session protocol is to save the command used to start your application. The `wm command` operation does this. The *wish* shell saves this information, so it is just a matter of registering it with the window manager. `argv0` is the command, and `argv` is the command line arguments:

```
wm command . "$argv0 $argv"
```

If your application is typically run on a different host than the one with the display (like in an Xterminal environment), then you also need to record what host to run the application on. Use the `wm client` operation for this. You might need to use *hostname* instead of *uname* on your system:

```
wm client . [exec uname -n]
```

The window manager usually provides a way to quit applications. If you have any special processing that must take place when the user quits, you need to intercept the quit action. Use the `wm protocol` operation to register a command that handles the `WM_DELETE_WINDOW` message from the window manager. The command must eventually call `exit` to actually stop your application:

```
wm protocol . WM_DELETE_WINDOW Quit
```

Other window manager messages that you can intercept are `WM_SAVE_YOURSELF` and `WM_TAKE_FOCUS`. The first is called by some session managers when shutting down. The latter is used in the active focus model. Tk (and this book) assumes a passive focus model where the window manager assigns focus to a toplevel window.

Table 26–3 describes the session-related window manager operations.

Table 26–3 Session-related window manager operations.

`wm client` *`win`* `?`*`name`*`?`	Record the hostname in the `WM_CLIENT_MACHINE` property.
`wm command` *`win`* `?`*`command`*`?`	Record the startup command in the `WM_COMMAND` property.
`wm protocol` *`win`* `?`*`name`*`?` `?`*`command`*`?`	Register a *`command`* to handle the protocol request *`name`*, which can be: `WM_DELETE_WINDOW`, `WM_SAVE_YOURSELF`, or `WM_TAKE_FOCUS`.

Miscellaneous

A window manager works by reparenting an application's window so it is a child of the window that forms the border and decorative title bar. The `wm frame` operation returns the window ID of the new parent, or the ID of the window itself if it has not been reparented. The `winfo id` command returns the ID of a window. The `wm overrideredirect` operation can set a bit that overrides the reparenting. This means that no title or border will be drawn around the window, and you cannot control the window through the window manager.

The `wm group` operation collects groups of windows so the window manager can open and close them together. Not all window managers implement this. One window, typically the main window, is chosen as the leader. The other members of the group are iconified when it is iconified.

The `wm transient` operation informs the window manager that this is a temporary window and there is no need to decorate it with the border and decorative title bar. This is used, for example, on pop-up menus, but in that case it is handled by the menu implementation.

Table 26–4 lists the remaining window manager operations:

Table 26–4 Miscellaneous window manager operations.

`wm focusmodel` *`win`* `?`*`what`*`?`	Set or query the focus model: `active` or `passive`. (Tk assumes the `passive` model.)
`wm frame` *`win`*	Return the ID of the parent of *`win`* if it has been reparented, otherwise return the ID of *`win`* itself.
`wm group` *`win`* `?`*`leader`*`?`	Assign *`win`* to the group headed by *`leader`*.
`wm overrideredirect` *`win`* `?`*`boolean`*`?`	Set or query the override redirect bit that suppresses reparenting by the window manager.
`wm transient` *`win`* `?`*`leader`*`?`	Query or mark a window as a transient window working for *`leader`*, another widget.

The winfo Command

The `winfo` command has just over 40 operations that return information about a widget or the display. The operations fall into the following categories:

- Sending commands between applications.
- Family relationships.
- Size.
- Location.
- Virtual root coordinates.
- Atoms and IDs.
- Colormaps and visuals.

Sending Commands Between Applications

Each Tk application has a name that is used when sending commands between applications using the `send` command. The list of Tk applications is returned by the `interps` operation. The `tk appname` is used to get the name of the application, and that command can also be used to set the application name. In Tk 3.6 and earlier, you had to use `winfo name .` to get the name of the application.

Example 26–2 Telling other applications what your name is.

```
foreach app [winfo interps] {
   catch {send $app [list Iam [tk appname]]}
}
```

The example shows how your application might connect up with several existing applications. It contacts each registered Tk interpreter and sends a short command that contains the applications own name as a parameter. The other application can use that name to communicate back.

Table 26–5 summarizes these commands:

Table 26–5 `send` command information.

`tk appname ?newname?`	Query or set the name used with `send`.
`winfo name .`	Also returns the name used for `send`, for backward compatibility with Tk 3.6 and earlier.
`winfo name pathname`	Return the last component of *pathname*.
`winfo ?-displayof win? interps`	Return the list of registered Tk applications on the same display as *win*.

Family Relationships

The Tk widgets are arranged in a hierarchy, and you can use the `winfo` command to find out about the structure of the hierarchy. The `winfo children` operation returns the children of a window, and the `winfo parent` operation returns the parent. The parent of the main window is null (i.e., an empty string).

A widget is also a member of a class, which is used for bindings and as a key into the X resource database. The `winfo class` operation returns this information. You can test for the existence of a window with `window exists`, and whether or not a window is mapped onto the screen with `winfo ismapped`.

The `winfo manager` operation tells you what geometry manager is controlling the placement of the window. This returns the name geometry manager command. Examples include `pack`, `place`, `canvas`, and `text`. The last two indicate the widget is imbedded into a canvas or text widget.

Table 26–6 summarizes these `winfo` operations:

Table 26–6 Window hierarchy information.

`winfo children` *`win`*	Return the list of children widgets of *`win`*.
`winfo class` *`win`*	Return the resource class of *`win`*.
`winfo exists` *`win`*	Returns 1 if *`win`* exists.
`winfo ismapped` *`win`*	Returns 1 if *`win`* is mapped onto the screen.
`winfo manager` *`win`*	The geometry manager: `pack`, `place`, `canvas`, or `text`.
`winfo parent` *`win`*	Returns the parent widget of *`win`*.

Size

The `winfo width` and `winfo height` operations return the width and height of a window, respectively. However, a window's size is not set until a geometry manager maps a window onto the display. Initially a window starts out with a width and height of 1. You can use `tkwait visibility` to wait for a window to be mapped before asking its width or height.

Alternatively, you can ask for the requested width and height of a window. Use `winfo reqwidth` and `winfo reqheight` for this information. The requested size may not be accurate, however, because the geometry manager may allocate more of less space, and the user may resize the window.

The `winfo geometry` operation returns the size and position of the window in the standard geometry format: *`W`*`x`*`H`*`+`*`X`*`+`*`Y`*. In this case the X and Y offsets are relative to the parent widget, or relative to the root window in the case of the main window.

You can find out how big the display is, too. The `winfo screenwidth` and winfo `screenheight operations` return this information in pixels. The `winfo screenmmwidth` and `winfo screenmmheight` return this information in millimeters.

You can convert between pixels and screen distances with the `winfo pixels` and `winfo fpixels` operations. Given a number of screen units such as `10m`, `3c`, or `72p`, these return the corresponding number of pixels. The first form rounds to a whole number, while the second form returns a floating point number. Chapter 23 explains screen units on page 278. For example:

```
set pixelsToInch [winfo pixels . 2.54c]
```

Table 26–7 summarizes these operations:

Table 26–7 Window size information.

`winfo fpixels` *`win num`*	Convert *num*, in screen units, to pixels. Returns a floating point number.
`winfo geometry` *`win`*	Return the geometry of *`win`*, in pixels and relative to the parent in the form *`W`*`x`*`H`*`+`*`X`*`+`*`Y`*
`winfo height` *`win`*	Return the height of *`win`*, in pixels.
`winfo pixels` *`win num`*	Convert num to a whole number of pixels.
`winfo reqheight` *`win`*	Return the requested height of *`win`*, in pixels.
`winfo reqwidth` *`win`*	Return the requested width of *`win`*, in pixels.
`winfo screenheight` *`win`*	Return the height of the screen, in pixels.
`winfo screenmmheight` *`win`*	Return the height of the screen, in millimeters.
`winfo screenmmwidth` *`win`*	Return the width of the screen, in millimeters.
`winfo screenwidth` *`win`*	Return the width of the screen, in pixels.
`winfo width` *`win`*	Return the width of *`win`*, in pixels.

Location

The `winfo x` and `winfo y` operations return the position of the upper left corner of a window relative to its parent widget. In the case of the main window, this is its location on the screen. The `winfo rootx` and `winfo rooty` return the screen location of the upper left corner of a widget, even if it is not a toplevel window.

The `winfo containing` operation returns the pathname of the window that contains a point on the screen. This is useful in implementing menus and drag and drop applications.

The `winfo toplevel` operation returns the pathname of the toplevel window that contains a widget. If the window is itself a `toplevel`, then this operation returns its pathname.

The `winfo screen` operation returns the display identifier for the screen of the window. This value is useful in the `selection` command.

Table 26–8 summarizes these operations:

Table 26–8 Window location information.

`winfo containing ?-displayof win? win x y`	Return the pathname of the window at *x* and *y*.
`winfo rootx win`	Return the X screen position of *win*.
`winfo rooty win`	Return the Y screen position of *win*.
`winfo screen win`	Return the display identifier of *win*'s screen.
`winfo toplevel win`	Return the pathname of the toplevel that contains *win*.
`winfo x win`	Return the X position of *win* in its parent.
`winfo y win`	Return the Y position of *win* in its parent.

Virtual Root Window

Some window managers use a virtual root window to give the user a larger virtual screen. At any given time only a portion of the virtual screen is visible, and the user can change the view on the virtual screen to bring different applications into view. In this case, the `winfo x` and `winfo y` operations return the coordinates of a main window in the virtual root window (i.e., not the screen).

The `winfo vrootheight` and `winfo vrootwidth` operations return the size of the virtual root window. If there is no virtual root window, then these just return the size of the screen.

The `winfo vrootx` and `winfo vrooty` are used to map from the coordinates in the virtual root window to screen-relative coordinates. These operations return 0 if there is no virtual root window. Otherwise they return a negative number. If you add this number to the value returned by `winfo x` or `winfo y`, it gives the screen-relative coordinate of the window.

Table 26–9 summarizes these operations:

Table 26–9 Virtual root window information.

`winfo vrootheight win`	Return the height of the virtual root window for *win*.
`winfo vrootwidth win`	Return the width of the virtual root window for *win*.
`winfo vrootx win`	Return the X position of *win* in the virtual root.
`winfo vrooty win`	Return the Y position of *win* in the virtual root.

Atoms and IDs

An *atom* is an X technical term for an identifier that is registered with the X server. Applications map names into atoms, and the X server assigns each atom a 32-bit identifier that can be passed between applications. One of the few places this is used in Tk is when the selection mechanism is used to interface with different toolkits. In some cases the selection is returned as atoms, which appear as 32-bit integers. The `winfo atomname` operation converts that number into an atom (i.e., a string), and the `winfo atom` registers a string with the X server and returns the 32-bit identifier as a hexadecimal string.

Each widget has an ID from the X server. The `winfo id` command returns this identifier. The `winfo pathname` operation returns the Tk pathname of the widget that has a given ID, but only if the window is part of the same application. Table 26–10 summarizes these operations:

Table 26–10 Atom and window ID information.

`winfo atom` *name*	Returns the 32-bit identifier for the atom *name*.
`winfo atomname` *id*	Returns the atom that corresponds to the 32-bit ID.
`winfo id` *win*	Returns the X window ID of *win*.
`winfo pathname` *id*	Returns the Tk pathname of the window with *id*, or null.

Colormaps and Visuals

Table 26–11 summarizes operations that return information about colormaps and visual classes, which are described in Chapter 24:

Table 26–11 Colormap and visual class information.

`winfo cells` *win*	Returns the number of colormap cells in *win*'s visual.
`winfo depth` *win*	Return the number of bits per pixel for *win*.
`winfo rgb` *win color*	Return the red, green, and blue values for *color*.
`winfo screencells` *win*	Returns the number of colormap cells in the default visual.
`winfo screendepth` *win*	Returns the number of bits per pixel in the screen's default visual.
`winfo visual` *win*	Returns the visual class of win.
`winfo visualsavailable` *win*	Returns a list of pairs that specify the visual type and bits per pixel of the available visual classes.

The `winfo depth` returns the number of bits used to represent the color in each pixel. The `winfo cells` command returns the number of colormap entries used by the visual class of a window. These two values are generally related. A window with eight bits per pixel usually has 256 colormap cells. The `winfo screendepth` and `winfo screencells` return this information for the default visual class.

The `winfo visualsavailable` command returns a list of the visual classes and screen depths that are available. For example, a display with eight bits per pixel might report the following visual classes are available:

```
winfo visualsavailable .
=> {staticgray 8} {grayscale 8} {staticcolor 8} \
    {pseudocolor 8}
```

The `winfo visual` operation returns the visual class of a window, and the `winfo screenvisual` returns the default visual class of the screen.

The `winfo rgb` operation converts from a color name or value to the red, green, and blue components of that color. Three decimal values are returned. Example 24–2 on page 287 uses this command to compute a slightly darker version of the same color.

The tk Command

The `tk` command provides a few miscellaneous entry points into the Tk library. The first form is used to set or query the application name used with the Tk send command. If you define a new name and it is already in use by another application, (perhaps another instance of yourself) then a number is appended to the name (e.g., `#2`, `#3`, and so on).

```
tk appname ?name?
```

The other form of the `tk` command is used to query and set the *colormodel* of the application. The colormodel is either `monochrome` or `color`, and it determines what default colors are chosen by the Tk widgets. You should test the color model yourself before setting up colors in your application. Note that when a color allocation fails, Tk automatically changes the colormodel to `monochrome` (i.e., black and white.) You can force it back into color mode with another call to `tk colormodel`. This form of the command is shown below.

```
tk colormodel window ?what?
```

CHAPTER 27

A User Interface to Bindings

This chapter presents a user interface to view and edit bindings.

A good way to learn about how a widget works is to examine the bindings that are defined for it. This chapter presents a user interface that lets you browse and change bindings for a widget or a class of widgets.

The interface uses a pair of listboxes to display the events and their associated commands. An entry widget is used to enter the name of a widget or a class. There are a few command buttons that let the user add a new binding, edit an existing binding, save the bindings to a file, and dismiss the dialog. Here is what the display looks like:

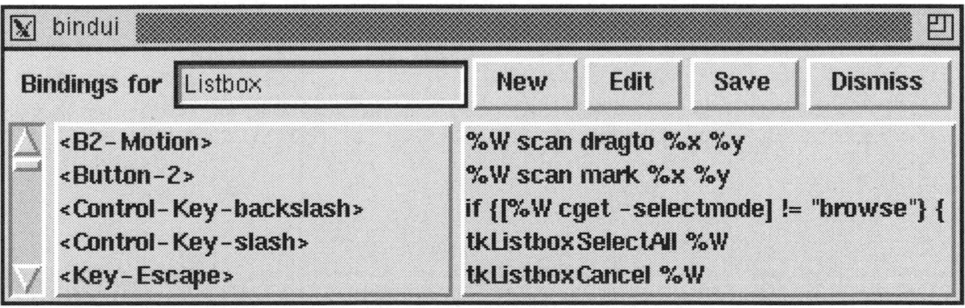

Example 27–1 A user interface to widget bindings.

```
proc Bind_Interface { w } {
    # Our state
    global bind
    set bind(class) $w

    # Set a class used for resource specifications
    set frame [toplevel .bindui -class Bindui]
    # Default relief
    option add *Bindui*Entry.relief sunken startup
    option add *Bindui*Listbox.relief raised startup
    # Default Listbox sizes
    option add *Bindui*key.width 18 startup
    option add *Bindui*cmd.width 25 startup
    option add *Bindui*Listbox.height 5 startup

    # A labeled entry at the top to hold the current
    # widget name or class.
    set t [frame $frame.top -bd 2]
    label $t.l -text "Bindings for" -width 11
    entry $t.e -textvariable bind(class)
    pack $t.l -side left
    pack $t.e -side left -fill x -expand true
    pack $t -side top -fill x

    bind $t.e <Return> [list Bind_Display $frame]

    # Command buttons
    button $t.quit -text Dismiss \
        -command [list destroy $frame]
    button $t.save -text Save \
        -command [list Bind_Save $frame]
    button $t.edit -text Edit \
        -command [list Bind_Edit $frame]
    button $t.new -text New \
        -command [list Bind_New $frame]
    pack $t.quit $t.save $t.edit $t.new -side right

    # A pair of listboxes and a scrollbar
    scrollbar $frame.s -orient vertical \
        -command [list BindYview \
            [list $frame.key $frame.cmd]]
    listbox $frame.key \
        -yscrollcommand [list $frame.s set] \
        -exportselection false
    listbox $frame.cmd \
        -yscrollcommand [list $frame.s set]
    pack $frame.s -side left -fill y
    pack $frame.key $frame.cmd -side left \
        -fill both -expand true

    foreach l [list $frame.key $frame.cmd] {
        bind $l <B2-Motion>\
            [list BindDragto %x %y $frame.key $frame.cmd]
```

```
        bind $l <Button-2> \
            [list BindMark %x %y $frame.key $frame.cmd]
        bind $l <Button-1> \
            [list BindSelect %y $frame.key $frame.cmd]
        bind $l <B1-Motion> \
            [list BindSelect %y $frame.key $frame.cmd]
        bind $l <Shift-B1-Motion> {}
        bind $l <Shift-Button-1> {}
    }
    # Initialize the display
    Bind_Display $frame
}
```

The `Bind_Interface` command takes a widget name or class as a parameter. It creates a toplevel window and gives it the `Bindui` class so that X resources can be set to control widget attributes. The `option add` command is used to set up the default listbox sizes. The lowest priority, `startup`, is given to these resources so that clients of the package can override the size with their own resource specifications.

At the top of the interface is a labeled entry widget. The entry holds the name of the class or widget for which the bindings are displayed. The `textvariable` option of the entry widget is used so that the entry's contents are available in a variable, `bind(class)`. Pressing `<Return>` in the entry invokes `Bind_Display` that fills in the display.

Example 27–2 `Bind_Display` presents the bindings for a widget or class.

```
proc Bind_Display { frame } {
    global bind
    $frame.key delete 0 end
    $frame.cmd delete 0 end
    foreach seq [bind $bind(class)] {
        $frame.key insert end $seq
        $frame.cmd insert end [bind $bind(class) $seq]
    }
}
```

The `Bind_Display` procedure fills in the display with the binding information. The `bind` command returns the events that have bindings, and what the command associated with each event is. `Bind_Display` loops through this information and fills in the listboxes.

A Pair of Listboxes Working Together

The two listboxes in the interface, `$frame.key` and `$frame.cmd`, are set up to work as a unit. A selection in one causes a parallel selection in the other. Only one listbox exports its selection as the X PRIMARY selection. Otherwise, the last listbox to assert the selection steals the selection rights from the other widget.

The following example shows the bind commands from Bind_Interface and the BindSelect routine that selects an item in both listboxes:

Example 27–3 Related listboxes are configured to select items together.

```
foreach l [list $frame.key $frame.cmd] {
    bind $l <Button-1> \
        [list BindSelect %y $frame.key $frame.cmd]
    bind $l <B1-Motion> \
        [list BindSelect %y $frame.key $frame.cmd]
}
proc BindSelect { y args } {
    foreach w $args {
        $w select clear 0 end
        $w select anchor [$w nearest $y]
        $w select set anchor [$w nearest $y]
    }
}
```

A single scrollbar scrolls both listboxes. This is achieved with some simple bindings that accept a variable number of arguments. The first arguments are coordinates, and then the rest are some number of listboxes that need to be operated on as a group.A single scrollbar is created and set up to control both listboxes. The next example shows the scrollbar command from Bind_Interface and the BindYview procedure that scrolls the listboxes:

Example 27–4 Controlling a pair of listboxes with one scrollbar.

```
scrollbar $frame.s -orient vertical \
    -command [list BindYview [list $frame.key $frame.cmd]]

proc BindYview { lists args } {
    foreach l $lists {
        eval {$l yview} $args
    }
}
```

The BindYview command is used to change the display of the listboxes associated with the scrollbar. Before the scroll command is evaluated some additional parameters are added that specify how to position the display. The details are essentially private between the scrollbar and the listbox. See page 180 for the details. The args keyword is used to represent these extra arguments, and eval is used to pass them through BindYview. The reasoning for using eval like this is explained in Chapter 6 on page 59.

The Listbox class bindings for <Button-2> and <B2-Motion> cause the listbox to scroll as the user drags the widget with the middle mouse button. These bindings are adjusted so that both listboxes move together. The following example shows the bind commands from the Bind_Interface procedure and the BindMark and BindDrag proceudures that scroll the listboxes:

Example 27–5 Drag-scrolling a pair of listboxes together.

```
bind $l <B2-Motion>\
    [list BindDragto %x %y $frame.key $frame.cmd]
bind $l <Button-2> \
    [list BindMark %x %y $frame.key $frame.cmd]

proc BindDragto { x y args } {
    foreach w $args {
        $w scan dragto $x $y
    }
}
proc BindMark { x y args } {
    foreach w $args {
        $w scan mark $x $y
    }
}
```

The `BindMark` procedure does a `scan mark` that defines an origin, and `BindDragto` does a `scan dragto` that scrolls the widget based on the distance from that origin. All Tk widgets that scroll support `yview`, `scan mark`, and `scan dragto`. Thus the `BindYview`, `BindMark`, and `BindDragto` procedures are general enough to be used with any set of widgets that scroll together.

The Editing Interface

Editing and defining a new binding is done in a pair of entry widgets. These widgets are created and packed into the display dynamically when the user presses the `New` or `Edit` button:

Example 27–6 An interface to define bindings.

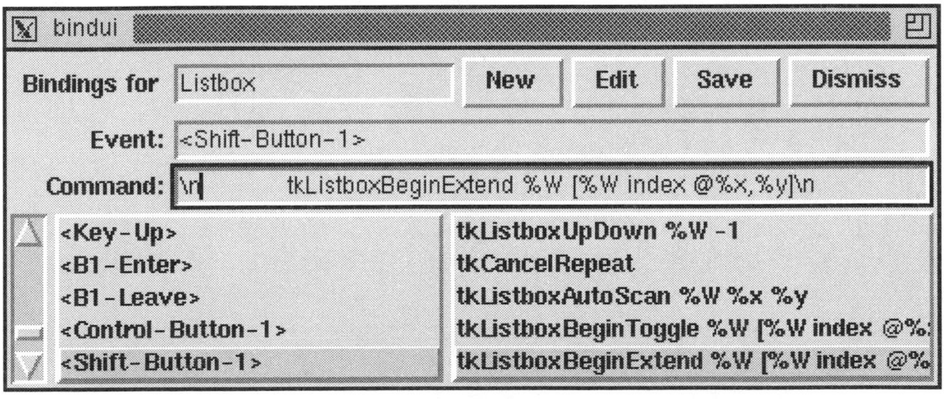


```
proc Bind_New { frame } {
    if [catch {frame $frame.edit} f] {
        # Frame already created
```

```
		set f $frame.edit
	} else {
		foreach x {key cmd} {
			set f2 [frame $f.$x]
			pack $f2 -fill x -padx 2
			label $f2.l -width 11 -anchor e
			pack $f2.l -side left
			entry $f2.e
			pack $f2.e -side left -fill x -expand true
			bind $f2.e <Return> [list BindDefine $f]
		}
		$f.key.l config -text Event:
		$f.cmd.l config -text Command
	}
	pack $frame.edit -after $frame.top -fill x
}
proc Bind_Edit { frame } {
	Bind_New $frame
	set line [$frame.key curselection]
	if {$line == {}} {
		return
	}
	$frame.key.e delete 0 end
	$frame.key.e insert 0 [$frame.key get $line]
	$frame.cmd.e delete 0 end
	$frame.cmd.e insert 0 [$frame.cmd get $line]
}
```

The `-width 11` and `-anchor e` attributes for the label widgets are specified so the `Event:` and `Command:` labels will line up with the `Bindings for` label at the top.

Saving and Loading Bindings

All that remains is the actual change or definition of a binding, and some way to remember the bindings the next time the application is run. The `BindDefine` procedure attempts a `bind` command that uses the contents of the entries. If it succeeds, then the edit window is removed by unpacking it.

The bindings are saved by `Bind_Save` as a series of Tcl commands that define the bindings. It is crucial that the `list` command be used to construct the commands properly.

`Bind_Read` uses the `source` command to read the saved commands. The application must call `Bind_Read` as part of its initialization to get the customized bindings for the widget or class. It also must provide a way to invoke `Bind_Interface`, such as a button, menu entry, or key binding.

Example 27–7 Defining and saving bindings.

```
proc BindDefine { f } {
    if [catch {
        bind [$f.top.e get] [$f.edit.key.e get] \
            [$f.edit.cmd.e get]
    } err] {
        Status $err
    } else {
        # Remove the edit window
        pack forget $f.edit
    }
}
proc Bind_Save { dotfile args } {
    set out [open $dotfile.new w]
    foreach w $args {
        foreach seq [bind $w] {
            # Output a Tcl command
            puts $out [list bind $w $seq [bind $w $seq]]
        }
    }
    close $out
    exec mv $dotfile.new $dotfile
}
proc Bind_Read { dotfile } {
    if [catch {
        if [file exists $dotfile] {
            # Read the saved Tcl commands
            source $dotfile
        }
    } err] {
        Status "Bind_Read $dotfile failed: $err"
    }
}
```

CHAPTER 28

Managing User Preferences

This chapter describes a user preferences package. The X resource database stores preference settings. Applications specify which Tcl variables are initialized from the database entries. A user interface lets the user browse and change their settings.

User customization is an important part of any complex application. There are always design decisions that could go either way. A typical approach is to choose a reasonable default, but then let users change the default setting through a preferences user interface. This chapter describes a preference package that works by tying together a Tcl variable, which the application uses, and an X resource specification, which the user sets. In addition, a user interface is provided so the user need not edit the resource database directly.

App-Defaults Files

We will assume that it is sufficient to have two sources of application defaults: a per-application database and a per-user database. In addition, we will allow for some resources to be specific to color and monochrome displays. The following example initializes the preference package by reading in the per-application and per-user resource specification files. There is also an initialization of the global array `pref` that will be used to hold state information about the preferences package. The `Pref_Init` procedure is called like this:

```
Pref_Init $library/foo-defaults ~/.foo-defaults
```

We assume `$library` is the directory holding support files for the `foo` application, and that per-user defaults will be kept in `~/.foo-defaults`.

Example 28–1 Preferences initialization.

```
proc Pref_Init { userDefaults appDefaults } {
	global pref

	set pref(uid) 0;# for a unique identifier for widgets
	set pref(userDefaults) $userDefaults
	set pref(appDefaults) $appDefaults

	PrefReadFile $appDefaults startup
	if [file exists $userDefaults] {
		PrefReadFile $userDefaults user
	}
}
proc PrefReadFile { basename level } {
	if [catch {option readfile $basename $level} err] {
		Status "Error in $basename: $err"
	}
	if {[tk colormodel .] == "color"} {
		if [file exists $basename-color] {
			if [catch {option readfile \
					$basename-color $level} err] {
				Status "Error in $basename-color: $err"
			}
		}
	} else {
		if [file exists $basename-mono] {
			if [catch {option readfile $basename-mono $level
				Status "Error in $basename-mono: $err"
			}
		}
	}
}
```

The `PrefReadFile` procedure reads a resource file and then looks for another file with the suffix `-color` or `-mono` depending on the color model of the display. The `tk colormodel` command returns what the toolkit thinks the display is capable of handling. The choices are either `color` or `monochrome`.

With this scheme a user would put generic settings in `~/.foo-defaults` . They would put color specifications in `~/.foo-defaults-color`. They would put specifications for black and white displays in `~/.foo-defaults-mono`. You could extend `PrefReadFile` to allow for per-host files as well.

Another approach is to use the `winfo visuals` command, which provides more detailed information about the display characteristics. You could detect a greyscale visual and support a third set of color possibilities. Visuals are discussed in Chapter 24.

Throughout this chapter we assume that the `Status` procedure displays messages to the user. It could be as simple as:

```
proc Status { s } { puts stderr $s }
```

Defining Preferences

This section describes the `Pref_Add` procedure that an application uses to define preference items. A preference item defines a relationship between a Tcl variable and an X resource name. The Tcl variable is undefined at the time `Pref_Add` is called, then it is set from the value for the resource, if it exists, otherwise it is set to the default value. A default value, a label, and a more extensive help string are associated with each item, which is represented by a Tcl list of five elements. A few short routines hide the layout of the item lists and make the rest of the code read better:

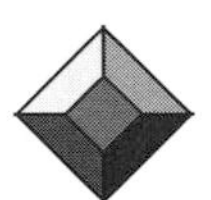

Example 28–2 Adding preference items.

```
proc PrefVar { item } { lindex $item 0 }
proc PrefXres { item } { lindex $item 1 }
proc PrefDefault { item } { lindex $item 2 }
proc PrefComment { item } { lindex $item 3 }
proc PrefHelp { item } { lindex $item 4 }

proc Pref_Add { prefs } {
    global pref
    append pref(items) $prefs
    foreach item $prefs {
        set varName [PrefVar $item]
        set xresName [PrefXres $item]
        set value [PrefValue $varName $xresName]
        if {$value == {}} {
            # Set variables that are still not set
            set default [PrefDefault $item]
            if {[llength $default] > 1} {
                if {[lindex $default 0] == "CHOICE"} {
                    PrefValueSet $varName [lindex $default 1]
                } else {
                    PrefValueSet $varName $default
                }
            } else {
                # Is it a boolean?
                if {$default == "OFF"} {
                    PrefValueSet $varName 0
                } elseif {$default == "ON"} {
                    PrefValueSet $varName 1
                } else {
                    # This is a string or numeric
                    PrefValueSet $varName $default
                }
            }
        } else {
            # Should map boolean resources to 0, 1 here.
        }
    }
}
```

The procedures `PrefValue` and `PrefValueSet` are used to query and set the value of the named variable, which can be an array element or a simple variable. The `upvar #0` command sets the variable in the global scope.

Example 28–3 Setting preference variables.

```
# PrefValue returns the value of the variable if it exists,
# otherwise it returns the X resource database value
proc PrefValue { varName xres } {
    upvar #0 $varName var
    if [info exists var] {
        return $var
    }
    set var [option get . $xres {}]
}
# PrefValueSet defines a variable in the global scope.
proc PrefValueSet { varName value } {
    upvar #0 $varName var
    set var $value
}
```

An important side effect of the `Pref_Add` call is that the variables in the preference item are defined at the global scope. It is also worth noting that `PrefValue` will honor any existing value for a variable, so if the variable is already set at the global scope then neither the resource value nor the default value will be used. It is easy to change `PrefValue` to always set the variable if this is not the behavior you want.

Example 28–4 Using the preferences package.

```
Pref_Add {
    {win(scrollside) scrollbarSide {CHOICE left right}
        "Scrollbar placement"
"Scrollbars can be positioned on either the left or
right side of the text and canvas widgets."}
    {win(typeinkills) typeinKills OFF
        "Type-in kills selection"
"This setting determines whether or not the selection
is deleted when new text is typed in."}
    {win(scrollspeed) scrollSpeed 15 "Scrolling speed"
"This parameter affects the scrolling rate when a selection
is dragged off the edge of the window. Smaller numbers
scroll faster, but can consume more CPU."}
}
```

Any number of preference items can be specified in a call to `Pref_Add`. The list-of-lists structure is created by proper placement of the curly braces, and it is preserved when the argument is appended to `pref(items)`, which is the master list of preferences. In this example `Pref_Add` gets passed a single argument that is a Tcl list with three elements. The Tcl variables are array elements, presumably related to the `Win` module of the application. The resource names are associated with the main application as opposed to any particular widget. They are specified in the database like this:

```
*scrollbarSide: left
*typeinKills: 0
*scrollSpeed: 15
```

The Preferences User Interface

The figure shows the interface for the items added with the `Pref_Add` command given in the previous section. The pop-up window with the extended help text appears after you click on "Scrollbar placement."

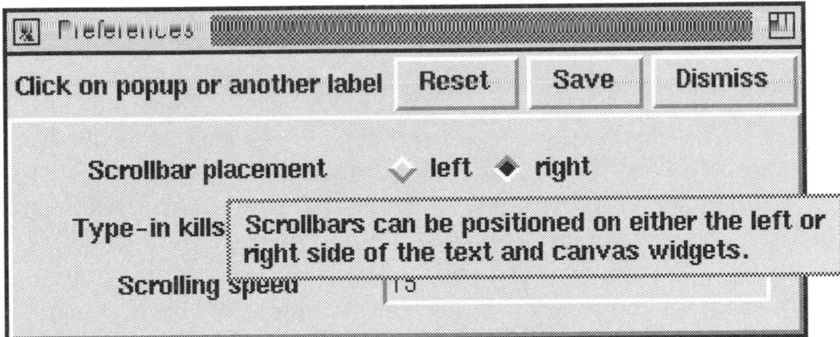

The user interface to the preference settings is table-driven. As a result of all the `Pref_Add` calls, a single list of all the preference items is built. The interface is constructed by looping through this list and creating a user interface item for each:

Example 28–5 A user interface to the preference items.

```
proc Pref_Dialog {} {
    global pref
    if [catch {toplevel .pref}] {
        raise .pref
    } else {
        wm title .pref "Preferences"
        set buttons [frame .pref.but]
        pack .pref.but -side top -fill x
        button $buttons.quit -text Dismiss \
            -command {PrefDismiss}
        button $buttons.save -text Save \
            -command {PrefSave}
        button $buttons.reset -text Reset \
            -command {PrefReset ; PrefDismiss}
        label $buttons.label \
             -text "Click labels for info on each item"
        pack $buttons.label -side left -fill x
        pack $buttons.quit $buttons.save $buttons.reset \
            -side right
```

```
        frame .pref.b -borderwidth 2 -relief raised
        pack .pref.b -fill both
        set body [frame .pref.b.b -bd 10]
        pack .pref.b.b -fill both

        set maxWidth 0
        foreach item $pref(items) {
            set len [string length [PrefComment $item]]
            if {$len > $maxWidth} {
                set maxWidth $len
            }
        }
        foreach item $pref(items) {
            PrefDialogItem $body $item $maxWidth
        }
    }
}
```

The interface supports three different types of preference items: boolean, choice, and general value. A boolean is implemented with a checkbutton that is tied to the Tcl variable, which will get a value of either 0 or 1. A boolean is identified by a default value that is either ON or OFF. A choice item is implemented as a set of radiobuttons, one for each choice. A choice item is identified by a default value that is a list with the first element equal to CHOICE. The remaining list items are the choices, with the first one being the default choice. If neither of these cases, boolean or choice, are detected, then an entry widget is created to hold the general value of the preference item:

Example 28–6 Interface objects for different preference types.

```
proc PrefDialogItem { frame item width } {
    global pref
    incr pref(uid)
    set f [frame $frame.p$pref(uid) -borderwidth 2]
    pack $f -fill x
    label $f.label -text [PrefComment $item] -width $width
    bind $f.label <1> \
        [list PrefItemHelp %X %Y [PrefHelp $item]]
    pack $f.label -side left
    set default [PrefDefault $item]
    if {([llength $default] > 1) &&
         ([lindex $default 0] == "CHOICE")} {
        foreach choice [lreplace $default 0 0] {
            incr pref(uid)
            radiobutton $f.c$pref(uid) -text $choice \
                -variable [PrefVar $item] -value $choice
            pack $f.c$pref(uid) -side left
        }
    } else {
        if {$default == "OFF" || $default == "ON"} {
            # This is a boolean
```

```
            set varName [PrefVar $item]
            checkbutton $f.check -text "On" -variable $varName
            pack $f.check -side left
        } else {
            # This is a string or numeric
            entry $f.entry -width 10 -relief sunken
            pack $f.entry -side left -fill x -expand true
            set pref(entry,[PrefVar $item]) $f.entry
            set varName [PrefVar $item]
            $f.entry insert 0 [uplevel #0 [list set $varName]]
            bind $f.entry <Return> "PrefEntrySet %W $varName"
        }
    }
}
proc PrefEntrySet { entry varName } {
    PrefValueSet $varName [$entry get]
}
```

In this interface, when the user clicks a radiobutton or a checkbutton, the Tcl variable is set immediately. To obtain a similar effect with the general preference item, the `<Return>` key is bound to a procedure that sets the associated Tcl variable to the value from the entry widget. `PrefEntrySet` is a one-line procedure that saves us from using the more awkward binding shown below. Grouping with double-quotes allows substitution of `$varName`, but then we must quote the square brackets to postpone command substitution:

```
bind $f.entry <Return> "PrefValueSet $varName \[%W get\]"
```

The binding on `<Return>` is done as opposed to using the `-textvariable` option because it interacts with traces on the variable a bit better. With `trace` you can arrange for a Tcl command to be executed when a variable is changed. An example appears on page 337. For a general preference item it is better to wait until the complete value is entered before responding to its new value.

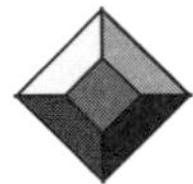

The other aspect of the user interface is the display of additional help information for each item. If there are lots of preference items then there isn't enough room to display this information directly. Instead, clicking on the short description for each item brings up a toplevel window with the help text for that item. The toplevel is marked `transient` so the window manager does not decorate it:

Example 28–7 Displaying the help text for an item.

```
proc PrefItemHelp { x y text } {
    catch {destroy .prefitemhelp}
    if {$text == {}} {
        return
    }
    set self [toplevel .prefitemhelp -class Itemhelp]
    wm title $self "Item help"
    wwm geometry $self +[expr $x+10]+[expr $y+10]
    wm transient $self .pref
    message $self.msg -text $text -aspect 1500
    pack $self.msg
```

```
    bind $self.msg <1> {PrefNukeItemHelp .prefitemhelp}
    .pref.but.label configure -text \
        "Click on pop-up or another label"
}
proc PrefNukeItemHelp { t } {
    .pref.but.label configure -text \
        "Click labels for info on each item"
    destroy $t
}
```

Managing the Preferences File

The preference settings are saved in the per-user file. The file is divided into two parts. The tail is automatically re-written by the preferences package. Users can manually add resource specifications to the beginning of the file and they will be preserved:

Example 28–8 Saving preferences settings to a file.

```
# PrefSave writes the resource specifications to the
# end of the per-user resource file, allowing users to
# add other resources to the beginning.
proc PrefSave {} {
    global pref
    if [catch {
        set old [open $pref(userDefaults) r]
        set oldValues [split [read $old] \n]
        close $old
    }] {
        set oldValues {}
    }
    if [catch {open $pref(userDefaults).new w} out] {
        .pref.but.label configure -text \
        "Cannot save in $pref(userDefaults).new: $out"
        return
    }
    foreach line $oldValues {
        if {$line == \
                "!!! Lines below here automatically added"} {
            break
        } else {
            puts $out $line
        }
    }
    puts $out "!!! Lines below here automatically added"
    puts $out "!!! [exec date]"
    puts $out "!!! Do not edit below here"
    foreach item $preferences {
        set varName [PrefVar $item]
        set xresName [PrefXres $item]
        if [info exists pref(entry,$varName)] {
```

```
            PrefEntrySet $pref(entry,$varName) $varName
        }
        set value [PrefValue $varName $xresName]
        puts $out [format "%s\t%s" *${xresName}: $value]
    }
    close $out
    set new [glob $pref(userDefaults).new]
    set old [file root $new]
    if [catch {exec mv $new $old} err] {
        Status "Cannot install $new: $err"
        return
    }
    PrefDismiss
}
```

There is one fine point in PrefSave. The value from the entry widget for general purpose items is obtained explicitly in case the user has not already pressed <Return> to update the Tcl variable.

The interface is rounded out with the PrefReset and PrefDismiss procedures. A reset is achieved by clearing the option database and reloading it, and then temporarily clearing the preference items and their associated variables and then redefining them with Pref_Add.

Example 28–9 Read settings from the preferences file.

```
proc PrefReset {} {
    global pref
    # Re-read user defaults
    option clear
    PrefReadFile $pref(appDefaults) startup
    PrefReadFile $pref(userDefaults) user
    # Clear variables
    set items $pref(items)
    set pref(items) {}
    foreach item $items {
        uplevel #0 [list unset [PrefVar $item]]
    }
    # Restore values
    Pref_Add $items
}
proc PrefDismiss {} {
    destroy .pref
    catch {destroy .prefitemhelp}
}
```

Tracing Changes to Preference Variables

Suppose, for example, we want to repack the scrollbars when the user changes their scrollside setting from left to right. This is done by setting a trace on the win(scrollside) variable. When the user changes that via the user interface, the trace routine is called. The `trace` command and its associated procedure are shown in the next example. The variable must be declared global before setting up the trace, which is not otherwise required if `Pref_Add` is the only command using the variable.

Example 28–10 Tracing a Tcl variable in a preference item.

```
Pref_Add {
    {win(scrollside) scrollbarSide {CHOICE left right}
        "Scrollbar placement"
"Scrollbars can be positioned on either the left or
right side of the text and canvas widgets."}
}
global win
set win(lastscrollside) $win(scrollside)
trace variable win(scrollside) w ScrollFixup
# Assume win(scrollbar) identifies the scrollbar widget
proc ScrollFixup { name1 name2 op } {
    global win
    if {$win(scrollside) != $win(lastscrollside)} {
        set parent [lindex [pack info $win(scrollbar)] 1]
        pack forget $win(scrollbar)
        set firstchild [lindex [pack slaves $parent] 0]
        pack $win(scrollbar) -in $parent -before $firstchild \
            -side $win(scrollside) -fill y
        set win(lastscrollside) $win(scrollside)
    }
}
```

Improving the Package

One small improvement can be made to `Pref_Add`. If a user specifies a boolean resource manually, they might use "true" instead of one and "false" instead of zero. `Pref_Add` should check for those cases and set the boolean variable to one or zero to avoid errors when the variables are used in expressions.

The interface lets you dismiss it without saving your preference settings. This is either a feature that lets users try out settings without committing to them, or it is a bug. Fixing this requires introducing a parallel set of variables to shadow the real variables until the user hits `Save`, which is tedious to implement. You can also use a *grab* as described in Chapter 18 to prevent the user from doing anything but setting preferences.

This preference package is a slightly simplified version of one I developed for *exmh*, which has so many preference items that a two-level scheme is necessary. The first level is a menu of preference sections, and each section is created with a single call to `Pref_Add`. This requires additional arguments to `Pref_Add` to provide a title for the section and some overall information about the preference section. The display code changes a small amount. The code for the *exmh* version is included with the sources on the floppy disk.

CHAPTER 29

C Programming and Tcl

This chapter explains how to extend the basic Tcl shells with new built-in commands. It describes how to include a Tcl interpreter in an existing application. The chapter reviews some of the support facilities provided by the Tcl C library, including a hash table package.

Tcl is designed to be easily extensible by writing new command implementations in C. A command implemented in C is more efficient than an equivalent Tcl procedure. A more pressing reason to write C code is that it may not be possible to provide the same functionality purely in Tcl. Suppose you have a new device, perhaps a color scanner or a unique input device. The programming interface to that device is through a set of C procedures that initialize and manipulate the state of the device. Without some work on your part, that interface is not accessible to your Tcl scripts. You are in the same situation if you have a C library that implements some specialized function such as a database. Fortunately, it is rather straight-forward to provide a Tcl interface that corresponds to the C interface. Unfortunately, it is not automatic. This chapter explains how to provide a Tcl interface as one or more new Tcl commands that you implement in C.

An alternative to writing new Tcl commands is to write stand-alone programs in C and use the Tcl `exec` command to run these programs. However, there is additional overhead in running an external program as compared to invoking a Tcl command that is part of the same application. There may be long-lived state associated with your application (e.g., the database), and it may make more sense for a collection of Tcl commands to provide an interface to this state than to run a program each time you want to access it. An external program is more suitable for one-shot operations like encrypting a file.

Another way to view Tcl is as a C library that is easy to integrate into your existing application. By adding the Tcl interpreter you can configure and control your application with Tcl scripts, and with Tk you can provide a nice graphical interface to it. This was the original model for Tcl. Applications would be largely application-specific C code and include a small amount of Tcl for configuration and the graphical interface. However, the basic Tcl shells proved so useful by themselves that relatively few Tcl programers need to worry about programming in C.

Using the Tcl C Library

This chapter does not provide a complete reference to the procedures exported by the Tcl C library. Instead, the general use of the procedures is explained at the end of this chapter, and a few of them appear in the code examples. Refer to the on-line manual pages for the routines for the specific details about each procedure. This approach differs from the rest of the chapters on the Tcl scripting commands, but space and time preclude a detailed treatment of the Tcl C library. Besides, their manual pages are an excellent source of information. The goal of this chapter is to give you an overall idea of what it is like to integrate C and Tcl, and to provide a few working examples.

Application Structure

This section describes the overall structure of an application that includes a Tcl interpreter. The relationship between the Tcl interpreter and the rest of your application can be set up in a variety of ways. Here is a general picture:

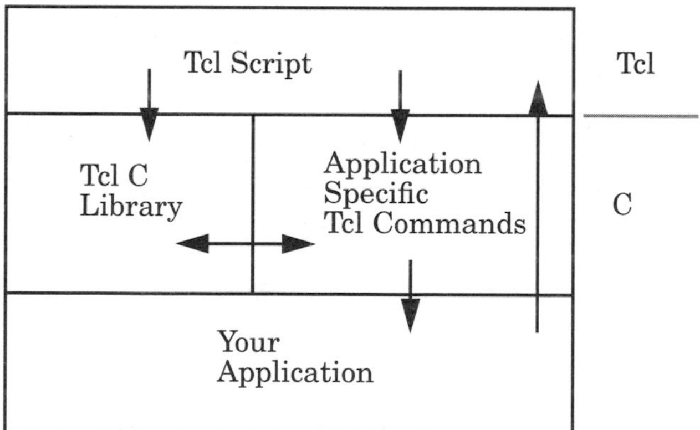

The Tcl C library implements the interpreter and the core Tcl commands such as `set`, `while`, and `proc`. Application-specific Tcl commands are implemented in C or C++ and registered as commands in the interpreter. The interpreter calls these *command procedures* when the script uses the application-specific Tcl command. The command procedures are typically thin layers over existing functionality in your application. By using `Tcl_Eval`, your application can invoke functionality programmed in the script layer. You can query and set

Tcl variables from C using the Tcl_SetVar and Tcl_GetVar procedures.

The application creates an interpreter with Tcl_CreateInterp and registers new commands with Tcl_CreateCommand. Then it evaluates a script to initialize the application by calling Tcl_EvalFile. The script can be as simple as defining a few variables that are parameters of a computation, or, it can be as ambitious as building a large user interface. The situation is slightly more complicated if you are using Tk and providing a graphical user interface, but not much more. Using Tk and C is described in the next chapter.

Tcl_Main and Tcl_AppInit

The Tcl library supports the basic application structure through the Tcl_Main procedure that is designed to be called from your main program. Tcl_Main does three things:

- It creates an interpreter that includes all the standard Tcl commands like set and proc. It also defines a few Tcl variables like argc and argv. These have the command line arguments that were passed to your application.
- It calls Tcl_AppInit, which is not part of the Tcl library. Instead, your application provides this procedure. In Tcl_AppInit you can register additional application-specific Tcl commands.
- It reads a script or goes into an interactive loop.

To use Tcl_Main you call it from your main program and provide an implementation of the Tcl_AppInit procedure. An example follows:

Example 29–1 A canonical Tcl main program and Tcl_AppInit.

```
/* main.c */
#include <tcl.h>

/*
 * Declarations for application-specific command procedures
 */
int RandomCmd(ClientData clientData,
             Tcl_Interp *interp,
             int argc, char *argv[]);

main(int argc, char *argv[]) {
   Tcl_Main(argc, argv);
   exit(0);
}
/*
 * Tcl_AppInit is called from Tcl_Main
 * after the Tcl interpreter has been created,
 * and before the script file
 * or interactive command loop is entered.
 */
int
```

```
Tcl_AppInit(Tcl_Interp *interp) {
    /*
     * Initialize packages
     * Tcl_Init sets up the Tcl library facility.
     */
    if (Tcl_Init(interp) == TCL_ERROR) {
        return TCL_ERROR;
    }
    /*
     * Register application-specific commands.
     */
    Tcl_CreateCommand(interp, "random", RandomCmd,
            (ClientData)NULL, (Tcl_CmdDeleteProc *)NULL);
    /*
     * Define startup filename. This file is read in
     * case the program is run interactively.
     */
    tcl_RcFileName = "~/.myapp.tcl";
    return TCL_OK;
}
```

The `main` program calls `Tcl_Main` with the `argc` and `argv` parameters passed into the program. These are the strings passed to the program on the command line, and `Tcl_Main` will store these values into Tcl variables by the same name. `Tcl_AppInit` is called by `Tcl_Main` with one argument, a handle on a newly created interpreter. There are three parts to the `Tcl_AppInit` procedure:

- The first part initializes the various packages the application uses. The example calls `Tcl_Init` to set up the script library facility. The core Tcl commands are defined by `Tcl_CreateInterp`, which is called by `Tcl_Main`.
- The second part of `Tcl_AppInit` does application-specific initialization. The example registers a command procedure, `RandomCmd` that implements a new Tcl command, `random`. When the Tcl script uses the `random` command, the `RandomCmd` procedure will be invoked by the Tcl library. The command procedure is described in the next section.
- The third part defines an application startup script, `tcl_RcFileName`, that executes if the program is used interactively.

The Standard Main in Tcl 7.3

The `Tcl_Main` procedure was added in Tcl 7.4. Before that, the Tcl library actually included a `main` procedure, so all you needed was a `Tcl_AppInit` procedure. There were some problems with using `main` from the library, especially with C++ programs, so `Tcl_Main` was introduced.

A C Command Procedure

The interface to a C command procedure is much like the interface to the `main` program. The arguments from the Tcl command are available as an array of strings defined by an `argv` parameter and counted by an `argc` parameter. In addition, the handle on the interpreter is passed, along with the client data that is registered when the command was defined. The client data is useful if the same command procedure is implementing many different commands. For example, a Tk command procedure can implement the commands corresponding to the various instances of a particular type of Tk widget. It that case, client data holds a pointer to the data structure defining the particular instance of the widget.

The return value of a Tcl command is either a string or an error message. A field in the `Tcl_Interp` data structure stores this value, and the command procedure returns either `TCL_OK` or `TCL_ERROR` to indicate success or failure. The procedure can also return `TCL_BREAK`, `TCL_CONTINUE`, or an application-specific code, which might be useful if you are implementing new kinds of built-in control structures. The examples in this book only use `TCL_OK` and `TCL_ERROR`. The use of the `result` field to return string values is described in the next section.

Example 29–2 The `RandomCmd` C command procedure.

```
/*
 * RandomCmd --
 * This implements the random Tcl command. With no arguments
 * the command returns a random integer.
 * With an integer valued argument "range",
 * it returns a random integer between 0 and range.
 */
int
RandomCmd(ClientData clientData, Tcl_Interp *interp,
		int argc, char *argv[])
{
	int rand, error;
	int limit = 0;
	if (argc > 2) {
		interp->result = "Usage: random ?range?";
		return TCL_ERROR;
	}
	if (argc == 2) {
		error = Tcl_GetInt(interp, argv[1], &limit);
		if (error != TCL_OK) {
			return error;
		}
	}
	rand = random();
	if (limit != 0) {
		rand = rand % limit;
	}
	sprintf(interp->result, "%d", rand);
	return TCL_OK;
}
```

The random implementation accepts an optional argument that is a range over which the random numbers should be returned. The argc parameter is tested to see if this argument has been given in the Tcl command. argc counts the command name as well as the arguments, so in our case argc == 2 indicates that the command has been invoked something like:

```
random 25
```

The procedure Tcl_GetInt converts the string-valued argument to an integer. It does error checking and sets the interpreter's result field in the case of error, so we can just return if it fails to return TCL_OK.

Finally, the real work of calling random is done, and the result is formatted directly into the result buffer. TCL_OK is returned to signal success.

Managing the Result's Storage

There is a simple protocol that manages the storage for a command procedure's result string. It involves two fields in the interpreter structure, interp->result, which holds the value, and interp->freeProc, which determines how the storage is cleaned up. When a command is called the interpreter provides default storage of TCL_RESULT_SIZE, which is 200 bytes. The default cleanup action is to do nothing. These defaults support two simple ways to define the result of a command. One way is to use sprintf to format the result in place:

```
sprintf(interp->result, "%d", rand);
```

Using sprintf is suitable if you know your result string is short, which is often the case. The other way is to set interp->result to the address of a constant string. In this case the original result buffer is not used, and there is no cleanup required because the string is compiled into the program:

```
interp->result = "Usage: random ?random?";
```

In more general cases the following procedures should be used to manage the result and freeProc fields:

```
Tcl_SetResult(interp, string, freeProc)
Tcl_AppendResult(interp, str1, str2, str3, (char *)NULL)
Tcl_AppendElement(interp, string)
```

Tcl_SetResult sets the return value to be *string*. The *freeProc* argument describes how the result should be disposed of. TCL_STATIC is used in the case where the result is a constant string allocated by the compiler. TCL_DYNAMIC is used if the result is allocated with malloc. TCL_VOLATILE is used if the result is in a stack variable. In this case the Tcl interpreter makes a copy of the result before calling any other command procedures. Finally, if you have your own memory allocator, pass in the address of the procedure that should free the result.

Tcl_AppendResult copies its arguments into the result buffer, reallocating the buffer if necessary. The arguments are concatenated onto the end of the existing result, if any. Tcl_AppendResult can be called several times to build a result.

Tcl_AppendElement adds the string to the result as a proper Tcl list element. It might add braces or backslashes to get the proper structure.

Invoking Scripts From C

The main program is not the only place you can evaluate a Tcl script. You can use the Tcl_Eval procedure essentially at any time to evaluate a Tcl command:

```
Tcl_Eval(Tcl_Interp *interp, char *command);
```

This is how the command associated with a button is invoked, for example. The only caveat is that the script may destroy the widget or Tcl command that invoked it. To guard against this, the Tk_Preserve, Tk_Release, and Tk_EventuallyFree procedures can be used to manage any data structures associated with the widget or Tcl command. These are described on page 001.

You should also be aware that Tcl_Eval may modify the string that is passed into it as a side effect of the way substitutions are performed. If you pass a constant string to Tcl_Eval, make sure your compiler has not put the string constant into read-only memory. If you use the *gcc* compiler you may need to use the -fwritable-strings option.

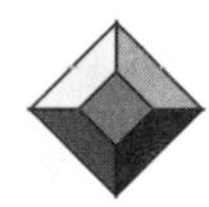

Bypassing Tcl_Eval

In a performance critical situation you may want to avoid some of the overhead associated with Tcl_Eval. David Nichols showed me a clever trick by which you can call the implementation of a C command procedure directly. The trick is facilitated by the Tcl_GetCommandInfo procedure that returns the address of the C command procedure for a Tcl command, plus its client data pointer. The Tcl_Invoke procedure shown in the next example implements this trick. It is used much like Tcl_VarEval, except that each of its arguments becomes an argument to the Tcl command without any substitutions being performed.

For example, you might want to insert a large chunk of text into a text widget without worrying about the parsing done by Tcl_Eval. You could use Tcl_Invoke like this:

```
Tcl_Invoke(interp, ".t", "insert", "insert", buf, NULL);
```

Or:

```
Tcl_Invoke(interp, "set", "foo", "$xyz [blah] {", NULL);
```

No substitutions are performed on any of the arguments because Tcl_Eval is out of the picture. The variable foo gets the following literal value:

```
$xyz [blah] {
```

Example 29–3 Calling C command procedure directly.

```
#include <varargs.h>
#include <tcl.h>
/*
 * Tcl_Invoke --
```

```
 * Call this somewhat like Tcl_VarEval:
 * Tcl_Invoke(interp, cmdName, arg1, arg2, ..., NULL);
 * Each arg becomes one argument to the command,
 * with no substitutions or parsing.
 */
int
Tcl_Invoke(va_alist)
    va_dcl          /* Variable number of arguments */
{
    Tcl_Interp *interp;
    char *cmd;
    char **argv;
    int argc, max;
    Tcl_CmdInfo info;
    va_list pvar;
    int result;

    va_start(pvar);
    interp = va_arg(pvar, Tcl_Interp *);
    cmd = va_arg(pvar, char *);
    /*
     * Build an argv vector out of the rest of the arguments.
     */
    max = 10;
    argv = (char **)malloc(max * sizeof(char *));
    argv[0] = cmd;
    argc = 1;
    while (1) {
        argv[argc] = va_arg(pvar, char *);
        if (argv[argc] == (char *)NULL) {
            break;
        }
        argc++;
        if (argc >= max) {
            /*
             * Allocate a bigger vector and copy old values in.
             */
            int i;
            char **oldargv = argv;
            argv = (char **)malloc(2*max * sizeof(char *));
            for (i=0 ; i<max ; i++) {
                argv[i] = oldargv[i];
            }
            free(oldargv);
            max = 2*max;
        }
    }
    Tcl_ResetResult(interp);
    /*
     * Map from the command name to a C procedure.
     */
    if (Tcl_GetCommandInfo(interp, cmd, &info)) {
        result = (*info.proc)(info.clientData, interp,
                argc, argv);
    } else {
```

```
        Tcl_AppendResult(interp, "Unknown command \"",
            cmd, "\"", NULL);
        result = TCL_ERROR;
    }
    va_end(pvar);
    free(argv);
    return result;
}
```

Putting A Tcl Program Together

Assuming you have put the examples into files named `tclMain.c`, `random.c`, and `tclInvoke.c` you are ready to try them. You need to know the locations of two things, the `tcl.h` include file and the Tcl C library. In this book we assume they are in `/usr/local/include` and `/usr/local/lib`, respectively, but you should check with your local system administrator.

Example 29–4 A Makefile for a simple Tcl C program.

```
INC = -I/usr/local/include
LIBS = -L/usr/local/lib -ltcl -lm
DEBUG = -g
CFLAGS =$(DEBUG) $(INC)

OBJS = tclMain.o random.o tclInvoke.o

mytcl : $(OBJS)
	$(CC) -o mytcl $(OBJS) $(LIBS)
```

The details in this `Makefile` may not be correct for your system. In some cases the math library (`-lm`) is included in the standard C library. You should consult a local expert and define a `Makefile` so you can record the details specific to your site.

Assuming you use `Tcl_Main`, which handles all the details about reading the script or prompting for interactive input, you can use *mytcl* like the other Tcl shells. You can specify your program in a script with the #! notation. If your program is stored in `/usr/joe/bin/mytcl`, start your script with:

```
#!/usr/joe/bin/mytcl
```

An Overview of the Tcl C library

This section provides a brief survey of other facilities provided by the Tcl C library. For the complete details about each procedure mentioned here, consult the on-line manual (man) pages. The manual pages describe groups of related C procedures. For example, `Tcl_CreateCommand` and `Tcl_DeleteCommand` are described in the `CrtCommand` man page. Your site may not have additional links set to let you utter "man Tcl_CreateCommand". Instead, you may have to use "man CrtCommand". For this reason, the name of the man page is noted in each section that introduces the procedures.

Application Initialization

The Tcl_Main and Tcl_AppInit procedures are described in the Tcl_Main and AppInit man pages, respectively.

Creating and Deleting Interpreters

A Tcl interpreter is created and deleted with the Tcl_CreateInterp and Tcl_DeleteInterp procedures, which are described in the CrtInterp man page. You can register a callback to occur when the interpreter is deleted with Tcl_CallWhenDeleted. Unregister the callback with Tcl_DontCallWhenDeleted. These two procedures are described in the CallDel man page.

Creating and Deleting Commands

Register a new Tcl command with Tcl_CreateCommand, and delete a command with Tcl_DeleteCommand. The Tcl_GetCommandInfo and Tcl_SetCommandInfo procedures query and modify the procedure that implement a Tcl command and the ClientData that is associated with the command. All of these are described in the CrtCommand man page.

Managing the Result String

The result string is managed through the Tcl_SetResult, Tcl_AppendResult, Tcl_AppendElement, and Tcl_ResetResult procedures. These are described in the SetResult man page. Error information is managed with the Tcl_AddErrorInfo, Tcl_SetErrorCode, and Tcl_PosixError procedures, which are described in the AddErrInfo man page.

Lists and Command Parsing

If you are reading commands, you can test for a complete command with Tcl_CommandComplete, which is described in the CmdCmplt man page. You can do backslash substitutions with Tcl_Backslash, which is described in the Backslash man page. The Tcl_Concat procedure, which is described in the Concat man page, concatenates its arguments with a space separator, just like the Tcl concat command.

You can chop a list up into its elements with Tcl_SplitList, which returns an array of strings. You can create a list out of an array of strings with Tcl_Merge. This behaves like the list command in that it will add syntax to the strings so that the list structure has one element for each of the strings. The Tcl_ScanElement and Tcl_ConvertElement procedures are used by Tcl_Merge. All of these are described in the SplitList man page.

Command Pipelines

The Tcl_CreatePipeline procedure does all the work of setting up a pipeline between processes. It handles file redirection and implements all the syntax supported by the exec and open commands. It is described by the CrtPipelin man page.

If the command pipeline is run in the background, then a list of process identifiers is returned. You can detach these processes with Tcl_DetachPids, and you can clean up after them with Tcl_ReapDetachedProcs. These are described in the DetachPid man page.

Tracing the Actions of the Tcl Interpreter

There are several procedures that let you trace the execution of the Tcl interpreter and provide control over its behavior. The Tcl_CreateTrace registers a procedure that is called before the execution of each Tcl command. Remove the registration with Tcl_DeleteTrace. These are described in the CrtTrace man page.

You can trace modifications and accesses to Tcl variables with Tcl_TraceVar and Tcl_TraceVar2. The second form is used with array elements. Remove the traces with Tcl_UntraceVar and Tcl_UntraceVar2. You can query the traces on variables with Tcl_VarTraceInfo and Tcl_VarTraceInfo2. These are all described in the TraceVar man page.

Evaluating Tcl Commands

The Tcl_Eval command evaluates a string as a Tcl command. Tcl_VarEval takes a variable number of string arguments and concatenates them before evaluation. The Tcl_EvalFile command reads commands from a file. Tcl_GlobalEval evaluates a string at the global scope. These are all described in the Eval man page.

If you are implementing an interactive command interpreter and want to use the history facility, then call Tcl_RecordAndEval. This records the command on the history list and then behaves like Tcl_GlobalEval. This is described in the RecordEval man page.

You can set the recursion limit of the interpreter with Tcl_SetRecursionLimit, which is described in the SetRecLmt man page.

If you are implementing a new control structure you may need to use the Tcl_AllowExceptions procedure. This makes it acceptable for Tcl_Eval and friends to return something other than TCL_OK and TCL_ERROR. This is described in the AllowExc man page.

Manipulating Tcl Variables

You can set a Tcl variable with Tcl_SetVar and Tcl_SetVar2. The second form is used for array elements. You can retrieve the value of a Tcl variable with

Tcl_GetVar and Tcl_GetVar2. You can delete variables with Tcl_UnsetVar and Tcl_UnsetVar2. These are all described in the SetVar man page.

You can link a Tcl variable and a C variable together with Tcl_LinkVar, and break the relationship with Tcl_UnlinkVar. Setting the Tcl variable modifies the C variable, and reading the Tcl variable returns the value of the C variable. These are described in the LinkVar man page.

Use the Tcl_UpVar and Tcl_UpVar2 procedures to link Tcl variables from different scopes together. You may need to do this if your command takes the name of a variable as an argument as opposed to a value. These procedures are used in the implementation of the upvar Tcl command, and they are described in the UpVar man page.

Evaluating Expressions

The Tcl expression evaluator is available through the Tcl_ExprLong, Tcl_ExprDouble, Tcl_ExprBool and Tcl_ExprString procedures. These all use the same evaluator, but they differ in how they return their result. They are described in the ExprLong man page.

You can register the implementation of new math functions by using the Tcl_CreateMathFunc procedure, which is described in the CrtMathFnc man page.

Converting Numbers

You can convert strings into numbers with the Tcl_GetInt, Tcl_GetDouble, and Tcl_GetBoolean procedures, which are described in the GetInt man page. The Tcl_PrintDouble procedure converts a floating point number to a string. Tcl uses it anytime it must do this conversion, and it honors the precision specified by the tcl_precision variable. It is described in the PrintDbl man page.

Hash Tables

Tcl has a nice hash table package that automatically grows the hash table data structures as more elements are added to the table. Because everything is a string, you may need to set up a hash table that maps from a string-valued key to an internal data structure. The procedures in the package are Tcl_InitHashTable, Tcl_DeleteHashTable, Tcl_CreateHashEntry, Tcl_DeleteHashEntry, Tcl_FindHashEntry, Tcl_GetHashValue, Tcl_SetHashValue, Tcl_GetHashKey, Tcl_FirstHashEntry, Tcl_NextHashEntry, and Tcl_HashStats. These are described in the Hash man page.

The next example uses a hash table to map from the first argument of a command procedure to the C procedure that handles the operation. The code is taken from *mxedit*, an editor built around a complex widget that supports many operations. The widget procedure looks up its first argument in a hash table instead of using many if statements to examine the argument:

Example 29–5 Using the `Hash` package.

```
static Tcl_HashTable mxInstanceCmdTable;

typedef struct {
    char *name;       /* Operation name. */
    int (*proc)();    /* Procedure to process operation. */
} CmdInfo;

static CmdInfo commands[] = {
    {"caret",     Mx_CaretCmd},
    {"clean",     Mx_CleanCmd},
    {"column",    Mx_ColumnCmd},
    {"configure", Mx_ConfigureCmd},
    /* Lines ommitted */
    {"write",     Mx_WriteCmd},
    {"written",   Mx_WrittenCmd},
    {(char *) NULL, (int (*)()) NULL}
};
/*
 * MxCmdInit creates a hash table of widget commands.
 * The hash table maps from argv[1] to C-procedures.
 */
void
MxCmdInit(mxwPtr)
 MxWidget *mxwPtr;
{
    CmdInfo *cmd;

    Tcl_InitHashTable(&mxInstanceCmdTable,
        TCL_STRING_KEYS);
    for (cmd = commands; cmd->name != NULL ; cmd++) {
        int newEntry;
        Tcl_HashEntry *entryPtr;
        entryPtr =
            Tcl_CreateHashEntry(&mxInstanceCmdTable,
            cmd->name, &newEntry);
        Tcl_SetHashValue(entryPtr, cmd->proc);
    }
    return;
}
/*
 * MxCmdFind uses the hash table to find the procedure
 * associated with an operation name.
 */
int (*
MxCmdFind(string))()
    char *string;
{
    Tcl_HashEntry *entryPtr;
    int (*handler)();
    entryPtr = Tcl_FindHashEntry(&mxInstanceCmdTable,
        string);
    if (entryPtr == NULL) {
        return NULL;
```

```
    }
    handler = (int(*)())Tcl_GetHashValue(entryPtr);
    return handler;
}
```

Dynamic Strings

The Tcl dynamic string package is designed for strings that get built up incrementally. You will need to use dynamic strings if you use the `Tcl_TildeSubst` procedure. The procedures in the package are `Tcl_DStringInit`, `Tcl_DStringAppend`, `Tcl_DStringAppendElement`, `Tcl_DStringStartSublist`, `Tcl_DStringEndSublist`, `Tcl_DStringLength`, `Tcl_DStringValue`, `Tcl_DStringSetLength`, `Tcl_DStringFree`, `Tcl_DStringResult`, and `Tcl_DStringGetResult`. These are described in the `DString` man page.

Regular Expressions and String Matching

The regular expression library used by Tcl is exported through the `Tcl_RegExpMatch`, `Tcl_RegExpCompile`, `Tcl_RegExpExec`, and `Tcl_RegExpRange` procedures. These are described in the `RegExp` man page. The string match function is available through the `Tcl_StringMatch` procedure, which is described in the `StrMatch` man page.

Tilde Substitution

The `Tcl_TildeSubst` procedure converts filenames that begin with tilde (`~`) into absolute pathnames. The `~` syntax is used to refer to the home directory of a user.

Working with Signals

Tcl provides a simple package for safely dealing with signals and other asynchronous events. You register a handler for an event with `Tcl_AsyncCreate`. When the event occurs, you mark the handler as ready with `Tcl_AsyncMark`. When the Tcl interpreter is at a safe point, it uses `Tcl_AsyncInvoke` to call all the ready handlers. Your application can call `Tcl_AsyncInvoke`, too. Use `Tcl_AsyncDelete` to unregister a handler. These are described in the `Async` man page.

CHAPTER 30

C Programming and Tk

This chapter explains how to include Tk in your application. It includes an overview of the Tk C library. The next chapter shows a sample widget implementation.

Tk can be extended by writing new features in C. You can implement new widgets, new canvas items, new image types, and new geometry managers. This chapter provides a brief introduction to these topics and some examples. Geometry managers are not described, although you can read about the table geometry manager provided by the BLT extension in the next chapter.

The structure of an application that uses Tk is a little different than the basic structure outlined in the previous chapter. After an initialization phase your program enters an event loop so it can process window system events. If you use certain extensions like Tcl-DP, you will also need an event loop. `Tk_MainLoop` is an event loop that processes window events, and `Tk_DoOneEvent` can be used if you build your own event loop. If you use `Tk_MainLoop`, you can have it call handlers for your own I/O streams by using `Tk_CreateFileHandler`. Thus there is some initial setup, the evaluation of a script, and then a processing loop.

Tk_Main and Tcl_AppInit

The Tk library supports the basic application structure through the `Tk_Main` procedure that is designed to be called from your `main` program. `Tk_Main` does the following things:

- It creates a Tcl interpreter and defines the argc and argv Tcl variables.
- It parses some window-related command line arguments.
- It creates the main window for your application by calling Tk_CreateMainWindow. It also defines the env(DISPLAY) variable.
- It calls Tcl_AppInit, which is provided by your application. Your Tcl_AppInit should call Tcl_Init and Tk_Init as shown in the example.
- It reads a script or sets up to read interactive commands.
- It enters an event loop in order to process window events and interactive commands.

Example 30–1 A canonical Tk main program and Tcl_AppInit.

```
/* main.c */
#include <tk.h>

main(int argc, char *argv[]) {
   Tk_Main(argc, argv);
   exit(0);
}
/*
 * New features added by this wish.
 */
int ClockCmd(ClientData clientData,
             Tcl_Interp *interp,
             int argc, char *argv[]);

/*
 * Tcl_AppInit is called from Tcl_Main
 * after the Tcl interpreter has been created,
 * and before the script file
 * or interactive command loop is entered.
 */
int
Tcl_AppInit(Tcl_Interp *interp) {
   /*
    * Initialize packages
    * Tcl_Init sets up the Tcl library facility.
    */
   if (Tcl_Init(interp) == TCL_ERROR) {
      return TCL_ERROR;
   }
   if (Tk_Init(interp) == TCL_ERROR) {
      return TCL_ERROR;
   }
   /*
    * Define application-specific commands here.
    */
   Tcl_CreateCommand(interp, "clock", ClockCmd,
      (ClientData)Tk_MainWindow(interp),
      (Tcl_CmdDeleteProc *)NULL);

   /*
```

```
     * Define startup filename. This file is read in
     * case the program is run interactively.
     */
    tcl_RcFileName = "~/.myapp.tcl";
    return TCL_OK;
}
```

The use of Tk_Main is very similar to Tcl_Main. Both procedures call Tcl_AppInit for initialization. If you are using Tk you need to call both Tcl_Init and Tk_Init from your Tcl_AppInit procedure. The first sets up the Tcl library, and the second sets up the script library used with the Tk widgets. This is important because much of the default behavior and event bindings for the Tk widgets are defined by its script library. Finally, this example sets up for the clock widget example that is the topic of Chapter 31.

A Custom Main Program

In more complex applications you may need to have complete control over the main program. This section gives an example that has a custom event loop. It shows much of the boiler-plate code needed to initialize a Tk application. In addition, it sets up an error handler for X protocol errors. This is mainly useful so you can set a breakpoint and find out what is causing the problem.

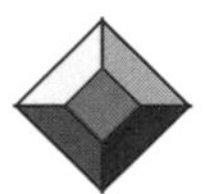

You should carefully consider whether a custom main program is really necessary. The primary point of this example is to give you an understanding of what goes on inside Tk_Main. In most cases Tk_Main should be sufficient for your needs.

Example 30–2 A custom Tk main program.

```
#include <tk.h>
/*
 * XErrorProc --
 *     Toe-hold for debugging X Protocol botches.
 */
static int
XErrorProc(data, errEventPtr)
    ClientData data;
    XErrorEvent *errEventPtr;
{
    Tk_Window w = (Tk_Window)data;
    fprintf(stderr, "X protocol error: ");
    fprintf(stderr, "error=%d request=%d minor=%d\n",
        errEventPtr->error_code, errEventPtr->request_code,
        errEventPtr->minor_code);
    /*
     * Claim to have handled the error.
     */
    return 0;
}
```

```
Tk_Window mainWindow;

/*
 * A table for command line arguments.
 */
static char *display = NULL;
static int debug = 0;
static char *geometry = NULL;

Tk_ArgvInfo argTable[] = {
   {"-display", TK_ARGV_STRING, (char *) NULL,
   (char *) &display, "Display to use"},
   {"-debug", TK_ARGV_CONSTANT, (char *) 1, (char *) &debug,
      "Set things up for gdb-type debugging"},
   {"", TK_ARGV_END, },
};
/*
 * This program takes one argument, which is the
 * name of a script to interpret.
 */
main(int argc, char *argv[])
{
   Tcl_Interp *interp;
   int error; char *trace;

   interp = Tcl_CreateInterp();
   if (Tk_ParseArgv(interp, (Tk_Window) NULL, &argc, argv,
      argTable, 0) != TCL_OK) {
      fprintf(stderr, "%s\n", interp->result);
      exit(1);
   }
   if (argc < 2) {
      fprintf(stderr, "Usage: %s filename\n", argv[0]);
      exit(1);
   }

   /*
    * Create the main window. The name of the application
    * for use with the send command is "myapp". The
    * class of the application for X resources is "Myapp".
    */
   mainWindow = Tk_CreateMainWindow(interp, display,
      "myapp", "Myapp");
   if (mainWindow == NULL) {
      fprintf(stderr, "%s\n", interp->result);
      exit(1);
   }
   /*
    * Register the X protocol error handler, and ask for
    * a synchronous protocol to help debugging.
    */
   Tk_CreateErrorHandler(Tk_Display(mainWindow), -1, -1, -1,
      XErrorProc, (ClientData)mainWindow);
   if (debug) {
      XSynchronize(Tk_Display(mainWindow), True);
```

```
    }
    /*
     * Grab an initial size and background.
     */
    Tk_GeometryRequest(mainWindow, 200, 200);
    Tk_SetWindowBackground(mainWindow,
        WhitePixelOfScreen(Tk_Screen(mainWindow)));

    /*
     * This is where Tcl_AppInit would be called.
     * In this case, we do the work right here.
     */
    if (Tcl_Init(interp) != TCL_OK) {
        fprintf(stderr, "Tcl_Init failed: %s\n",
             interp->result);
    }
    if (Tk_Init(interp) != TCL_OK) {
        fprintf(stderr, "Tk_Init failed: %s\n",
             interp->result);
    }
    error = Tcl_EvalFile(interp, argv[1]);
    if (error != TCL_OK) {
        fprintf(stderr, "%s: %s\n", argv[1],
               interp->result);
        trace = Tcl_GetVar(interp, "errorInfo",
               TCL_GLOBAL_ONLY);
        if (trace != NULL) {
            fprintf(stderr, "*** TCL TRACE ***\n");
            fprintf(stderr, "%s\n", trace);
        }
    }

    /*
     * Enter the custom event loop.
     */
    while (MyappExists()) {
        Tk_DoOneEvent(TK_ALL_EVENTS);
        MyappStuff();
    }
    /*
     * Call the Tcl exit to ensure that everything is
     * cleaned up properly.
     */
    Tcl_Eval(interp, "exit");
    return 0;
}
```

The command line arguments are parsed with `Tk_ParseArgv`. Then `Tcl_CreateInterp` creates an interpreter context, and `Tk_CreateMainWindow` creates the first window. As a side effect it defines all the Tk-related Tcl commands. The default window size is set, and the rest of the appearance is left up to the script. `Tcl_Init` and `Tk_Init` are called to complete the setup of these packages. `Tk_Init` has to be called after `Tk_CreateMainWindow`.

The handler for X protocol errors is installed with Tk_CreateErrorHandler. If the debug flag is set, then the X protocol is put into synchronous mode. This means that any protocol errors will occur as a direct result of your graphic operations, so you can put a breakpoint in XErrorProc and see what call causes the problems.

The application is really defined by the script, which is processed by the Tcl_EvalFile command. Its file name argument is argv[1], which is the first argument to the program when it is run from the command line. If the user types a bad file name, then Tcl_EvalFile will return an error so we can avoid checking for that ourselves.

This argument convention means that you can specify your program directly in the script with the #! notation. That is, if your program is named myapp, and it is stored as /usr/joe/bin/myapp, then you can begin a script with:

```
#!/usr/joe/bin/myapp
```

The script will be processed by your version of the Tcl interpreter. Remember there is a 32-character limit on this line in most UNIX systems, including the #!.

Much of the main program is devoted to handling any errors from the script. First, the return code from Tcl_EvalFile is checked. If it is not TCL_OK, then an error has occurred in the script. An error message is available in interp->result. We can provide even more detailed information to the user than the error message generated by the offending command. The interpreter maintains a variable errorInfo that is a stack trace of the commands that led up to the error. The Tcl_GetVar call returns us its value, or NULL if it is undefined. In practice, you would probably prompt the user before dumping the Tcl trace.

A Custom Event Loop

An event loop is used to process window system events and other events like timers and network sockets. The different event types are described later. All Tk applications must have an event loop so they function properly in the window system environment. Tk provides a standard event loop with the Tk_MainLoop procedure, which should be sufficient for most cases.

You can provide your own event loop as shown in the previous example. In this case you call Tk_DoOneEvent to process any outstanding Tk events. By default, Tk_DoOneEvent handles all event types and blocks if there are no events ready. It takes a bitmap of flag arguments that control what kind of events it will handle and whether or not it will block. Specify the TK_DONT_WAIT flag if you do not want it to block. In this case you typically want to process all outstanding requests and then go do some application-specific processing. Tk_DoOneEvent returns 1 if there are more events ready to process.

Example 30–3 Using `Tk_DoOneEvent` with `TK_DONT_WAIT`.

```
void
DoAllTkEvents() {
    while (Tk_DoOneEvent(TK_ALL_EVENTS|TK_DONT_WAIT)) {
        /* keep processing Tk events */
    }
}
```

The other way to customize the event loop is to register handlers for different events and use the `Tk_MainLoop` procedure. `Tk_MainLoop` takes no parameters and it returns when the last window is destroyed. It uses `Tk_DoOneEvent` to process events. Unless you have some really special requirements, using `Tk_MainLoop` and the registration procedures described below is preferable to using `Tk_DoOneEvent` directly.

There are four event classes, and they are handled in the following order by `Tk_DoOneEvent`:

- Window events. Use the `Tk_CreateEventHandler` procedure to register a handler for these events. Use the `TK_X_EVENTS` flag to process these in `Tk_DoOneEvent`.
- File events. Use these events to wait on slow devices and network connections. Register a handler with `Tk_CreateFileHandler`. Use the `TK_FILE_EVENTS` flag to process these in `Tk_DoOneEvent`.
- Timer events. You can set up events to occur after a specified time period. Use the `Tk_CreateTimerHandler` procedure to register a handler for the event. Use the `TK_TIMER_EVENTS` flag to process these in `Tk_DoOneEvent`.
- Idle events. These events are processed when there is nothing else to do. Virtually all the Tk widgets use idle events to display themselves. Use the `Tk_DoWhenIdle` procedure to register a procedure to call once at the next idle time. Use the `TK_IDLE_EVENTS` flag to process these in `Tk_DoOneEvent`.

An Overview of the Tk C library

The next few sections briefly introduce the facilities provided by the Tk C library. For the complete details you will need to consult the on line manual (man) pages. The man page for each set of routines is identified in the description so you can easily find the right on-line documentation. Your site may not be set up so that the man page is available by the name of the routine. You many need to know the name of the man page first.

Parsing Command Line Arguments

The `Tk_ParseArgv` procedure parses command line arguments. This procedure is designed for use by main programs. While you could use it for Tcl commands, the Tk_ConfigureWidget procedure might be better suited. The Tk_ParseArgv procedure is described by the ParseArgv man page.

The Standard Application Setup

The Tk_Main procedure does the standard setup for your application's main window and event loop. It is described by the Tk_Main man page.

Creating Windows

The Tk_CreateMainWindow procedure is what Tk_Main uses to create the main window for your application. The Tk_CreateWindow and Tk_CreateWindowFromPath are used to create windows for widgets. The actual creation of the window in the X server is delayed until an idle point. You can force the window to be created with Tk_MakeWindowExist, or destroy a window with Tk_DestroyWindow. These are described in the CrtMainWin man page.

The Tk_MainWindow procedure returns the handle on the applications main window. It is described in the MainWin man page. The Tk_MapWindow and Tk_UnmapWindow are used to display and withdraw a window, respectively. They are described in the MapWindow man page. The Tk_MoveToplevelWindow call is used to position a toplevel window. It is described in the MoveToplev man page.

Translate between window names and the Tk_Window type with Tk_Name, Tk_PathName, and Tk_NameToWindow. These are described in the Name man page.

Application Name for Send

The name of the application is defined or changed with Tk_SetAppName. This name is used when other applications send it Tcl commands using the send command. This procedure is described in the SetAppName man page.

Configuring Windows

The configuration of a window includes its width, height, cursor, and so on. Tk provides a set of routines that use Xlib routines to configure a window and also cache the results. This makes it efficient to query these settings because the X server does not need to be contacted. The window configuration routines are Tk_ConfigureWindow, Tk_MoveWindow, Tk_ResizeWindow, Tk_MoveResizeWindow, Tk_SetWindowBorderWidth, Tk_ChangeWindowAttributes, Tk_SetWindowBackground, Tk_SetWindowBackgroundPixmap, Tk_SetWindowBorder, Tk_SetWindowBorderPixmap, Tk_SetWindowColormap, Tk_DefineCursor, and Tk_UndefineCursor. These are described in the ConfigWind man page.

Window Coordinates

The coordinates of a widget relative to the root window (the main screen) are returned by Tk_GetRootCoords. This is described in the GetRootCrd man page. The Tk_GetVRootGeometry procedure returns the size and position of a window relative to the virtual root window. This is described by the GetVRoot man page. The Tk_CoordsToWindow procedure locates the window under a given coordinate. It is described in the CoordToWin man page.

Window Stacking Order

Control the stacking order of windows in the X window hierarchy with Tk_RestackWindow. This is described in the Restack man page.

Window Information

Tk keeps lots of information associated with each window, or widget. The following calls are fast macros that return the information without calling the X server: Tk_WindowId, Tk_Parent, Tk_Display, Tk_DisplayName, Tk_ScreenNumber, Tk_Screen, Tk_X, Tk_Y, Tk_Width, Tk_Height, Tk_Changes, Tk_Attributes, Tk_IsMapped, Tk_IsTopLevel, Tk_ReqWidth, Tk_ReqHeight, Tk_InternalBorderWidth, Tk_Visual, Tk_Depth, and Tk_Colormap. These are described in the WindowId man page.

Configuring Widget Attributes

The Tk_WidgetConfigure procedure parses command line specification of attributes and allocates resources like colors and fonts. Related procedures include Tk_Offset, Tk_ConfigureInfo, Tk_ConfigureValue, Tk_FreeOptions, and these are described in the ConfigWidg man page.

Safe Handling of the Widget Data Structure

If your widget makes callbacks to the script level it might invoke a Tcl command that deletes the widget. To avoid havoc in such situations, a simple reference counting scheme can be implemented for data structures. Call Tk_Preserve to increment the use count, and call Tk_Release to decrement the count. Then, when your widget is destroyed, use the Tk_EventuallyFree procedure to indirectly call the procedure that cleans up your widget data structure. If the data structure is in use, then the clean up call is delayed until after the last reference to the data structure is released with Tk_Release. These procedures are described in the Preserve man page.

The Selection and Clipboard

Retrieve the current selection with Tk_GetSelection. This is described in the GetSelect man page. Register a handler for X selection requests with Tk_CreateSelHandler. Unregister the handler with Tk_DeleteSelHandler. These are described in the CrtSelHdlr man page. Claim ownership of the selection with Tk_OwnSelection. This is described in the OwnSelect man page.

Manipulate the clipboard with Tk_ClipboardClear and Tk_ClipboardAppend, which are described in the Clipboard man page.

Event Bindings

The routines that manage bindings are exported by the Tk library so you can manage bindings your self. For example, the canvas widget does this to implement bindings on canvas items. The procedures are Tk_CreateBindingTable, Tk_DeleteBindingTable, Tk_CreateBinding, Tk_DeleteBinding, Tk_GetBinding, Tk_GetAllBindings, Tk_DeleteAllBindings, and Tk_BindEvent. These are described in the BindTable man page.

Event Loop Interface

The standard event loop is implemented by Tk_MainLoop. If you write your own event loop you need to call Tk_DoOneEvent so Tk can handle its events. If you read X events directly, (e.g., through Tk_CreateGenericHandler) you can dispatch to the correct handler for the event with Tk_HandleEvent. These are described in the DoOneEvent man page.

If you want to use the Tk event loop mechanism without using the rest of the Tk toolkit, which requires a connection to an X server, then call Tk_EventInit to set up the event registration mechanism. You can create handlers for file, timer, and idle events after this call.

Restrict or delay events with the Tk_RestrictEvent procedure, which is described in the RestrictEv man page.

Handling X Events

Use Tk_CreateEventHandler to set up a handler for specific X events. Widget implementations need a handler for expose and resize events, for example. Remove the registration with Tk_DeleteEventHandler. These are described in the EventHndlr man page.

You can set up a handler for all X events with Tk_CreateGenericHandler. This is useful in some modal interactions where you have to poll for a certain event. Delete the handler with Tk_DeleteGenericHandler. These are described in the CrtGenHdlr man page.

File Handlers

Use Tk_CreateFileHandler to register handlers for I/O streams. You set up the handlers to be called when the I/O stream is ready for reading or writing, or both. Or, you can use the lower-level Tk_CreateFileHandler2, which is called every time through the event loop so it can decide for itself if the I/O stream is ready. File handlers are called after X event handlers.

Timer Events

Register a callback to occur at some time in the future with `Tk_CreateTimerHandler`. The handler is only called once. If you need to delete the handler before it gets called, use `Tk_DeleteTimerHandler`. These are described in the `Tk_TimerToken` man page.

Idle Callbacks

If there are no outstanding events, the Tk makes idle callbacks before waiting for new events to arrive. In general, Tk widgets queue their display routines to be called at idle time. Use `Tk_DoWhenIdle` to queue an idle callback, and use `Tk_CancelIdleCall` to remove the callback from the queue. These are described in the `DoWhenIdle` man page.

Sleeping

The `Tk_Sleep` procedure delays execution for a specified number of milliseconds. It is described in the `Sleep` man page.

Reporting Script Errors

If your widget makes a callback into the script level, what do you do when the callback returns an error? Use the `Tk_BackgroundError` procedure that invokes the standard `tkerror` procedure to report the error to the user. This is described in the `BackgdErr` man page.

Handling X Protocol Errors

You can handle X protocol errors by registering a handler with `Tk_CreateErrorHandler`. Unregister it with `Tk_DeleteErrorHandler`. These are described in the `CrtErrHdlr` man page. Because X has an asynchronous interface, the error will be reported sometime after the offending call was made. You can call the Xlib `XSynchronize` routine to turn off the asynchronous behavior in order to help you debug.

Using the X Resource Database

The `Tk_GetOption` procedure looks up items in the X resource database. This is described in the `GetOption` man page.

The resource class of a window is set with `Tk_SetClass`, and the current class setting is retrieved with `Tk_Class`. These are described in the `SetClass` man page.

Managing Bitmaps

Tk maintains a registry of bitmaps by name, (e.g. gray50 and questhead). You can define new bitmaps with Tk_DefineBitmap, and you can get a handle on the bitmap from its name with Tk_GetBitmap. Related procedures include Tk_NameOfBitmap, Tk_SizeOfBitmap, Tk_FreeBitmap, and Tk_GetBitmapFromData. These are described in the GetBitmap man page.

Creating New Image Types

The Tk_CreateImageType procedure is used to register the implementation of a new image type. The registration includes several procedures that callback into the implementation to support creation, display, and deletion of images. The interface to an image implementation is described in the CrtImgType man page.

When an image changes, the widgets that display it are notified by calling Tk_ImgChanged. This is described in the ImgChanged man page.

Using an Image in a Widget

The following routines support widgets that display images. Tk_GetImage maps from the name to a Tk_Image data structure. Tk_RedrawImage causes the image to update its display. Tk_SizeOfImage tells you how big it is. When the image is no longer in use, call Tk_FreeImage. These are described in the GetImage man page.

Photo Image Types

One of the image types is photo, which has its own C interface for defining new formats. The job of a format handler is to read and write different image formats such as GIF or JPEG so that the photo image can display them. The Tk_CreatePhotoImageFormat procedure sets up the interface, and it is described in the CrtPhImgFmt man page.

There are several support routines for photo format handlers. The Tk_FindPhoto procedure maps from a photo name to its associated Tk_PhotoHandle data structure. The image is updated with Tk_PhotoBlank, Tk_PhotoPutBlock, and Tk_PhotoPutZoomedBlock. The image values can be obtained with Tk_PhotoGetImage. The size of the image can be manipulated with Tk_PhotoExpand, Tk_PhotoGetSize, and Tk_PhotoSetSize. These support routines are described in the FindPhoto man page.

Canvas Object Support

The C interface for defining new canvas items is exported via the Tk_CreateItemType procedure. The description for a canvas item includes a set of procedures that the canvas widget uses to call the implementation of the canvas item type. This interface is described in detail in the CrtItemType man page.

There are support routines for the managers of new item types. The CanvTkwin man page describes Tk_CanvasTkwin, Tk_CanvasGetCoord, Tk_CanvasDrawableCoords, Tk_CanvasSetStippleOrigin, Tk_CanvasWindowCoords, and Tk_CanvasEventuallyRedraw. The following procedures help with the generation of postscript: Tk_CanvasPsY, Tk_CanvasPsBitmap, Tk_CanvasPsColor, Tk_CanvasPsFont, Tk_CanvasPsPath, and Tk_CanvasPsStipple. These are described by the CanvPsY man page. If you are manipulating text items directly, then you can use the Tk_CanvasTextInfo procedure to get a description of the selection state and other details about the text item. This procedure is described in the CanvTxtInfo man page.

Geometry Management

A widget requests a certain size with the Tk_GeometryRequest procedure. If it draws a border inside that area, it calls Tk_SetInternalBorder. The geometry manager responds to these requests, although the widget may get a different size. These are described in the GeomReq man page.

The Tk_ManageGeometry procedure sets up the relationship between the geometry manager and a widget. This is described in the ManageGeom man page.

The Tk_MaintainGeometry arranges for one window to stay at a fixed position relative to another widget. This is used by the place geometry manager. The relationship is broken with the Tk_UnmaintainGeometry call. These are described in the MaintGeom man page.

The Tk_SetGrid enabled gridded geometry management. The grid is turned off with Tk_UnsetGrid. These are described in the SetGrid man page.

String Identifiers (UIDS)

Tk maintains a database of string values such that a string only appears in it once. The Tk_Uid type refers to such a string. You can test for equality by using the value of Tk_Uid, which is the strings address, as an identifier. A Tk_Uid is used as a name in the various GetByName calls introduced below. The Tk_GetUid procedure installs a string into the registry. It is described in the GetUid man page.

Colors and Colormaps

Use Tk_GetColor and Tk_GetColorByValue to allocate a color. You can retrieve the string name of a color with Tk_NameOfColor. When you are done using a color you need to call Tk_FreeColor. Colors are shared among widgets, so it is important to free them when you are done using them. These are described in the GetColor man page.

Use Tk_GetColormap and Tk_FreeColormap to allocate and free a colormap. Colormaps are shared, if possible, so you should use these routines instead of the lower-level X routines to allocate colormaps. These are described in the GetClrmap man page.

The color model used by the screen can be set and queried with Tk_SetColorModel and Tk_GetColorModel. For example, you can force a window into monochrome mode when it runs on a color screen. These are described in the SetCModel man page.

The window's visual type is set with Tk_SetWindowVisual. This is described in the SetVisual man page.

3D Borders

The three dimensional relief used for widget borders is supported by a collection of routines described by the 3DBorder man page. The routines are Tk_Get3DBorder, Tk_Draw3DRectangle, Tk_Fill3DRectangle, Tk_Draw3DPolygon, Tk_Fill3DPolygon, Tk_3DVerticalBevel, Tk_3DHorizontalBevel, Tk_SetBackgroundFromBorder, Tk_NameOf3DBorder, Tk_3DBorderColor, Tk_3DBorderGC, and Tk_Free3DBorder.

Mouse Cursors

Allocate a cursor with Tk_GetCursor and Tk_GetCursorFromData. Map back to the name of the cursor with Tk_NameOfCursor. Release the cursor resource with Tk_FreeCursor. These are described in the GetCursor man page.

Font Structures

Allocate a font with Tk_GetFontStruct. Get the name of a font with Tk_NameOfFontStruct. Release the font with Tk_FreeFontStruct. These are described in the GetFontStr man page.

Graphics Contexts

Allocate a graphics context with Tk_GetGC, and free it with Tk_FreeGC. These are described in the GetGC man page.

Allocate a Pixmap

Allocate and free pixmaps with Tk_GetPixmap and Tk_FreePixmap. These are described in the GetPixmap man page.

Screen Measurements

Translate between strings like 4c or 72p and screen distances with Tk_GetPixels and Tk_GetScreenMM. The first call returns pixels (integers), the second returns millimeters as a floating point number. These are described in the GetPixels man page.

Relief Style

Translate between relief styles and names with `Tk_GetRelief` and `Tk_NameOfRelief`. These are described in the `GetRelief` man page.

Text Anchor Positions

Translate between strings and anchor positions with `Tk_GetAnchor` and `Tk_NameOfAnchor`. These are described in the `GetAnchor` man page.

Line Cap Styles

Translate between line cap styles and names with `Tk_GetCapStyle` and `Tk_NameOfCapStyle`. These are described in the `GetCapStyl` man page.

Line Join Styles

Translate between line join styles and names with `Tk_GetJoinStyle` and `Tk_NameOfJoinStyle`. These are described in the `GetJoinStl` man page.

Text Justification Styles

Translate between line justification styles and names with `Tk_GetJustify` and `Tk_NameOfJustify`. These are described in the `GetJustify` man page.

Atoms

An atom is an integer that references a string that has been registered with the X server. Tk maintains a cache of the atom registry to avoid contacting the X server when atoms are used. Use `Tk_InternAtom` to install an atom in the registry, and `Tk_GetAtomName` to return the name given an atom. These are described by the `InternAtom` man page.

X Resource ID Management

Each X resource like a color or pixmap has a resource ID associated with it. The `Tk_FreeXId` call releases an ID so it can be reused. This is used, for example, by routines like `Tk_FreeColor` and `Tk_FreePixmap`. It is described in the `FreeXId` man page.

CHAPTER 31

Writing a Tk Widget in C

This chapter describes in the implementation of a simple clock widget.

A custom widget implemented in C has the advantage of being efficient and flexible. However, it is more work, too. This chapter illustrates the effort by explaining the implementation of a clock widget. It is a digital clock that displays the current time according to a format string. The formatting is done by the `strftime` library procedure, so you can use any format supported by that routine. The implementation of a widget includes:

- A data structure to describe one instance of the widget.
- A set of configuration options for the widget.
- A command procedure to create a new instance of the widget.
- A command procedure to operate on an instance of the widget.
- A configuration procedure used when creating and reconfiguring the widget.
- An event handling procedure.
- A display procedure.
- Other widget-specific procedures.

The Widget Data Structure

Each widget is associated with a data structure that describes it. Any widget structure will need a pointer to the Tcl interpreter, the Tk window, and the X display. The interpreter is used in many of the Tcl and Tk library calls, and it provides a way to call out to the script or query and set Tcl variables. The Tk window is needed for various Tk operations, and the X display is used when doing low-level graphic operations. The rest of the information in the data structure depends on the widget. The structure for the clock widget follows. The different types will be explained as they are used in the rest of the code.

Example 31–1 The `Clock` widget data structure.

```
#include "tkPort.h"
#include "tk.h"

typedef struct {
    Tk_Window tkwin; /* The window for the widget */
    Display *display;/* X's handle on the display */
    Tcl_Interp *interp;/* Interpreter of the widget */
    /*
     * Clock specific attributes.
     */
    int borderWidth; /* Size of 3-D border */
    int relief;      /* Style of 3-D border */
    Tk_3DBorder background;/* Color for border, background */
    XColor *foreground;/* Color for the text */
    XColor *highlight;/* Color for the highlight */
    int highlightWidth;/* Thickness of highlight rim */
    XFontStruct *fontPtr;/* Font info for the text */
    char *format;    /* Format for the clock text */
    /*
     * Graphic contexts and other support.
     */
    GC highlightGC;  /* Highlight graphics context */
    GC textGC;       /* Text graphics context */
    Tk_TimerToken token;/* For periodic callbacks */
    char *clock;     /* Pointer to the clock string */
    int numChars;    /* in the text */
    int textWidth;   /* in pixels */
    int textHeight;  /* in pixels */
    int flags;       /* Flags defined below */
} Clock;
/*
 * Flag bit definitions.
 */
#define REDRAW_PENDING0x1
#define GOT_FOCUS   0x2
#define TICKING  0x4
```

Specifying Widget Attributes

Several of the fields in the `Clock` structure are attributes that can be set when the widget is created or reconfigured with the `configure` operation. The default values, their resource names, and their class names are specified with an array of `Tk_ConfigSpec` records, and this array is processed by the

Tk_ConfigureWidget operation. The specifications for the Clock structure are given in the next example.

Example 31–2 Configuration specs for the clock widget.

```
static Tk_ConfigSpec configSpecs[] = {
    {TK_CONFIG_BORDER, "-background", "background",
        "Background", "light blue",
        Tk_Offset(Clock, background), TK_CONFIG_COLOR_ONLY},
    {TK_CONFIG_BORDER, "-background", "background",
        "Background", "white", Tk_Offset(Clock, background),
        TK_CONFIG_MONO_ONLY},
    {TK_CONFIG_SYNONYM, "-bg", "background", (char *) NULL,
        (char *) NULL, 0, 0},

    {TK_CONFIG_SYNONYM, "-bd", "borderWidth", (char *) NULL,
        (char *) NULL, 0, 0},
    {TK_CONFIG_PIXELS, "-borderwidth", "borderWidth",
        "BorderWidth","2", Tk_Offset(Clock, borderWidth), 0},
    {TK_CONFIG_RELIEF, "-relief", "relief", "Relief",
        "ridge", Tk_Offset(Clock, relief), 0},

    {TK_CONFIG_COLOR, "-foreground", "foreground",
        "Foreground", "black", Tk_Offset(Clock, foreground),
        0},
    {TK_CONFIG_SYNONYM, "-fg", "foreground", (char *) NULL,
        (char *) NULL, 0, 0},

    {TK_CONFIG_COLOR, "-highlightcolor", "highlightColor",
        "HighlightColor", "red", Tk_Offset(Clock, highlight),
        TK_CONFIG_COLOR_ONLY},
    {TK_CONFIG_COLOR, "-highlightcolor", "highlightColor",
         "HighlightColor", "black",
        Tk_Offset(Clock, highlight),TK_CONFIG_MONO_ONLY},
    {TK_CONFIG_PIXELS, "-highlightthickness",
        "highlightThickness","HighlightThickness",
        "2", Tk_Offset(Clock, highlightWidth), 0},

    {TK_CONFIG_STRING, "-format", "format", "Format",
        "%H:%M:%S", Tk_Offset(Clock, format), 0},
    {TK_CONFIG_FONT, "-font", "font", "Font",
        "*courier-medium-r-normal-*-18-*",
         Tk_Offset(Clock, fontPtr), 0},

    {TK_CONFIG_END, (char *) NULL, (char *) NULL,
         (char *) NULL, (char *) NULL, 0, 0}
};
```

The initial field is a type, such as TK_CONFIG_BORDER. Colors and borders will be explained shortly. The next field is the command line flag for the attribute, (e.g., -background). Then comes the resource name and the class name. The default value is next, (e.g., light blue). The offset of a structure member is next, and the Tk_Offset macro is used to compute this offset. The last field is a bitmask of flags. The two used in this example are TK_CONFIG_COLOR_ONLY and TK_CONFIG_MONO_ONLY, which restrict the application of the configuration setting to color and monochrome displays, respectively. You can define additional flags and pass them into Tk_ConfigureWidget if you have a family of widgets that share most, but not all, of their attributes. The tkButton.c file in the Tk sources has an example of this.

Table 31–1 Configuration flags and corresponding C types.

TK_CONFIG_ACTIVE_CURSOR	Cursor
TK_CONFIG_ANCHOR	Tk_Anchor
TK_CONFIG_BITMAP	Pixmap
TK_CONFIG_BOOLEAN	int (0 or 1)
TK_CONFIG_BORDER	Tk_3DBorder *
TK_CONFIG_CAP_STYLE	int (see Tk_GetCapStyle)
TK_CONFIG_COLOR	XColor *
TK_CONFIG_CURSOR	Cursor
TK_CONFIG_CUSTOM	
TK_CONFIG_DOUBLE	double
TK_CONFIG_END	(signals end of options)
TK_CONFIG_FONT	XFontStruct *
TK_CONFIG_INT	int
TK_CONFIG_JOIN_STYLE	int (see Tk_GetJoinStyle)
TK_CONFIG_JUSTIFY	Tk_Justify
TK_CONFIG_MM	double
TK_CONFIG_PIXELS	int
TK_CONFIG_RELIEF	int (see Tk_GetRelief)
TK_CONFIG_STRING	char *
TK_CONFIG_SYNONYM	(alias for other option)
TK_CONFIG_UID	Tk_Uid
TK_CONFIG_WINDOW	Tk_Window

Table 31–1 lists the correspondence between the configuration type passed Tk_ConfigureWidget and the type of the associated field in the widget data structure. The complete details are given in the ConfigWidg man page. Some of the table entries reference a Tk procedure like Tk_GetCapStyle. In those cases

an integer-valued field takes on a few limited values that are described in the man page for that procedure.

The Widget Class Command

The Tcl command that creates an instance of a widget is known as the *class command*. In our example, the `clock` command creates a clock widget. The command procedure for `clock` follows. The procedure allocates the `Clock` data structure. It registers an event handler that gets called when the widget is exposed, resized, or gets focus. It creates a new Tcl command that operates on the widget. Finally, it calls `ClockConfigure` to set up the widget according to the attributes specified on the command line and the default configuration specifications.

Example 31–3 The `ClockCmd` command procedure.

```
int
ClockCmd(clientData, interp, argc, argv)
    ClientData clientData;/* Main window of the app */
    Tcl_Interp *interp;/* Current interpreter. */
    int argc;        /* Number of arguments. */
    char **argv;     /* Argument strings. */
{
    Tk_Window main = (Tk_Window) clientData;
    Clock *clockPtr;
    Tk_Window tkwin;

    if (argc < 2) {
        Tcl_AppendResult(interp, "wrong # args: should be '",
             argv[0], " pathName ?options?'", (char *) NULL);
        return TCL_ERROR;
    }
    tkwin = Tk_CreateWindowFromPath(interp, main,
             argv[1], (char *) NULL);
    if (tkwin == NULL) {
        return TCL_ERROR;
    }
    Tk_SetClass(tkwin, "Clock");
    /*
     * Allocate and initialize the widget record.
     */
    clockPtr = (Clock *) ckalloc(sizeof(Clock));
    clockPtr->tkwin = tkwin;
    clockPtr->display = Tk_Display(tkwin);
    clockPtr->interp = interp;
    clockPtr->borderWidth = 0;
    clockPtr->highlightWidth = 0;
    clockPtr->relief = TK_RELIEF_FLAT;
    clockPtr->background = NULL;
    clockPtr->foreground = NULL;
    clockPtr->highlight = NULL;
    clockPtr->fontPtr = NULL;
```

```
    clockPtr->textGC = None;
    clockPtr->highlightGC = None;
    clockPtr->token = NULL;
    clockPtr->clock = NULL;
    clockPtr->numChars = 0;
    clockPtr->textWidth = 0;
    clockPtr->textHeight = 0;
    clockPtr->flags = 0;
    /*
     * Register a handler for when the window is
     * exposed or resized.
     */
    Tk_CreateEventHandler(clockPtr->tkwin,
       ExposureMask|StructureNotifyMask|FocusChangeMask,
       ClockEventProc, (ClientData) clockPtr);
    /*
     * Create a Tcl command that operates on the widget.
     */
    Tcl_CreateCommand(interp, Tk_PathName(clockPtr->tkwin),
       ClockInstanceCmd,
       (ClientData) clockPtr, (void (*)()) NULL);
    /*
     * Parse the command line arguments.
     */
    if (ClockConfigure(interp, clockPtr,
           argc-2, argv+2, 0) != TCL_OK) {
       Tk_DestroyWindow(clockPtr->tkwin);
       return TCL_ERROR;
    }
    interp->result = Tk_PathName(clockPtr->tkwin);
    return TCL_OK;
}
```

The Widget Instance Command

For each instance of a widget a new command is created that operates on that widget. This is called the *widget instance command*. Its name is the same as the Tk pathname of the widget. In the clock example, all that is done on instances is to query and change their attributes. Most of the work is done by `Tk_ConfigureWidget` and `ClockConfigure`, which is shown in the next section. The `ClockInstanceCmd` command procedure is shown in the next example:

Example 31–4 The `ClockInstanceCmd` command procedure.

```
static int
ClockInstanceCmd(clientData, interp, argc, argv)
    ClientData clientData;/* A pointer to a Clock struct */
    Tcl_Interp *interp;/* The interpreter */
    int argc;          /* The number of arguments */
    char *argv[];      /* The command line arguments */
{
```

```
    Clock *clockPtr = (Clock *)clientData;
    int result = TCL_OK;
    char c;
    int length;

    if (argc < 2) {
        Tcl_AppendResult(interp, "wrong # args: should be '",
            argv[0], " option ?arg arg ...?'", (char *) NULL);
        return TCL_ERROR;
    }
    c = argv[1][0];
    length = strlen(argv[1]);
    if ((c == 'c') && (strncmp(argv[1], "cget", length) == 0)
            && (length >= 2)) {
        if (argc != 3) {
            Tcl_AppendResult(interp,
                 "wrong # args: should be '",
                argv[0], " cget option'",
                (char *) NULL);
            return TCL_ERROR;
        }
        result = Tk_ConfigureValue(interp, clockPtr->tkwin,
             configSpecs, (char *) clockPtr, argv[2], 0);
    } else if ((c == 'c') &&
            (strncmp(argv[1], "configure", length) == 0)
            && (length >= 2)) {
        if (argc == 2) {
            /*
             * Return all configuration information.
             */
            result = Tk_ConfigureInfo(interp, clockPtr->tkwin,
                configSpecs, (char *) clockPtr,
                (char *) NULL,0);
        } else if (argc == 3) {
            /*
             * Return info about one attribute, like cget.
             */
            result = Tk_ConfigureInfo(interp, clockPtr->tkwin,
                configSpecs, (char *) clockPtr, argv[2], 0);
        } else {
            /*
             * Change one or more attributes.
             */
            result = ClockConfigure(interp, clockPtr, argc-2,
                argv+2,TK_CONFIG_ARGV_ONLY);
        }
    } else {
        Tcl_AppendResult(interp, "bad option '", argv[1],
            "': must be cget, configure, position, or size",
            (char *) NULL);
        return TCL_ERROR;
    }
    return result;
}
```

Configuring and Reconfiguring Attributes

When the widget is created or reconfigured, then the implementation needs to allocate the resources implied by the attribute settings. Each clock widget uses some colors and a font. These are described by graphics contexts. X uses a graphics context to parameterize operations. Instead of specifying every possible attribute in the X calls, a graphics context is initialized with a subset of the parameters and this is passed into the X drawing commands. The context can specify the foreground and background colors, clip masks, line styles, and so on. In the example, two different graphics contexts are used, one for the highlight rectangle and one for the text and background. They use different colors, so different contexts are needed. The graphics contexts are allocated once and reused each time the widget is displayed.

There are two kinds of color resources used by the widget. The focus highlight and the text foreground are simple colors. The background is a Tk_3DBorder, which is a set of colors used to render 3D borders. The background color is specified in the attribute, and the other colors are computed based on that color. The code uses `Tk_3DBorderColor` to map back to the original color for use in the background of the widget.

After the resources are set up, a call to redisplay the widget is scheduled for the next idle period. This is a standard idiom for Tk widgets. It means that you can create and reconfigure a widget in the middle of a script, and all the changes only result in one redisplay. The `REDRAW_PENDING` flag is used to ensure that only one redisplay is queued up at any time. The `ClockConfigure` procedure is shown in the next example:

Example 31–5 `ClockConfigure` allocates resources for the widget.

```
static int
ClockConfigure(interp, clockPtr, argc, argv, flags)
    Tcl_Interp *interp;/* Needed for return values and errors
*/
    Clock *clockPtr; /* The per-instance data structure */
    int argc;        /* Number of valid entries in argv */
    char *argv[];    /* The command line arguments */
    int flags;       /* Tk_ConfigureClock flags */
{
    XGCValues gcValues;
    GC newGC;

    /*
     * Tk_ConfigureWidget parses the command line arguments
     * and looks for defaults in the resource database.
     */
    if (Tk_ConfigureWidget(interp, clockPtr->tkwin,
            configSpecs, argc, argv, (char *) clockPtr, flags)
                != TCL_OK) {
        return TCL_ERROR;
    }
```

```
    /*
     * Give the widget a default background so it doesn't get
     * a random background between the time it is initially
     * displayed by the X server and we paint it
     */
    Tk_SetWindowBackground(clockPtr->tkwin,
        Tk_3DBorderColor(clockPtr->background)->pixel);
    /*
     * Set up the graphics contexts to display the widget.
     * These contexts are all used to draw off-screen
     * pixmaps, so turn off exposure notifications.
     */
    gcValues.graphics_exposures = False;
    gcValues.background = clockPtr->highlight->pixel;
    newGC = Tk_GetGC(clockPtr->tkwin,
        GCBackground|GCGraphicsExposures, &gcValues);
    if (clockPtr->highlightGC != None) {
        Tk_FreeGC(clockPtr->display, clockPtr->highlightGC);
    }
    clockPtr->highlightGC = newGC;

    gcValues.background =
        Tk_3DBorderColor(clockPtr->background)->pixel;
    gcValues.foreground = clockPtr->foreground->pixel;
    gcValues.font = clockPtr->fontPtr->fid;
    newGC = Tk_GetGC(clockPtr->tkwin,
        GCBackground|GCForeground|GCFont|GCGraphicsExposures,
        &gcValues);
    if (clockPtr->textGC != None) {
        Tk_FreeGC(clockPtr->display, clockPtr->textGC);
    }
    clockPtr->textGC = newGC;

    /*
     * Determine how big the widget wants to be.
     */
    ComputeGeometry(clockPtr);

    /*
     * Set up a call to display ourself.
     */
    if ((clockPtr->tkwin != NULL) &&
            Tk_IsMapped(clockPtr->tkwin)
            && !(clockPtr->flags & REDRAW_PENDING)) {
        Tk_DoWhenIdle(ClockDisplay, (ClientData) clockPtr);
        clockPtr->flags |= REDRAW_PENDING;
    }
    return TCL_OK;
}
```

Displaying the Clock

There are two parts to a widget's display. First the size must be determined. This is done at configuration time, and then that space is requested from the geometry manager. When the widget is later displayed, it should use the `Tk_Width` and `Tk_Height` calls to find out how much space it was actually allocated by the geometry manager. The next example shows `ComputeGeometry`.

Example 31–6 `ComputeGeometry` computes the widget's size.

```
static void
ComputeGeometry(Clock *clockPtr)
{
    int width, height;
    struct tm *tmPtr;/* Time info split into fields */
    struct timeval tv;/* BSD-style time value */
    int offset = clockPtr->highlightWidth +
                 clockPtr->borderWidth
                 + 2;/* Should be padX attribute */
    char clock[1000];

    /*
     * Get the time and format it to see how big it will be.
     * gettimeofday returns the current time.
     * localtime parses this into day, hour, etc.
     * strftime formats this into a string.
     */
    gettimeofday(&tv, NULL);
    tmPtr = localtime(&tv.tv_sec);
    strftime(clock, 1000, clockPtr->format, tmPtr);
    if (clockPtr->clock != NULL) {
        ckfree(clockPtr->clock);
    }
    clockPtr->clock = ckalloc(1+strlen(clock));
    clockPtr->numChars = strlen(clock);
    /*
     * Let Tk tell us how big the string will be.
     */
    TkComputeTextGeometry(clockPtr->fontPtr, clock,
        clockPtr->numChars, 0, &clockPtr->textWidth,
        &clockPtr->textHeight);
    width = clockPtr->textWidth + 2*offset;
    height = clockPtr->textHeight + 2*offset;
    /*
     * Request size and border from the geometry manager.
     */
    Tk_GeometryRequest(clockPtr->tkwin, width, height);
    Tk_SetInternalBorder(clockPtr->tkwin, offset);
}
```

Finally we get to the actual display of the widget! The routine is careful to check that the widget still exists and is mapped. This is important because the redisplay is scheduled asynchronously. The current time is converted to a string. This uses library procedures that exist on SunOS. There might be different routines on your system. The string is painted into a pixmap, which is a drawable region of memory that is off-screen. After the whole display has been painted, the pixmap is copied into on-screen memory to avoid flickering as the image is cleared and repainted. The text is painted first, then the borders. This ensures that the borders overwrite the text if the widget has not been allocated enough room by the geometry manager.

This example allocates and frees the off-screen pixmap for each redisplay. This is the standard idiom for Tk widgets. They temporarily allocate the off-screen pixmap each time they redisplay. In the case of a clock that updates every second, it might be reasonable to permanently allocate the pixmap and store its pointer in the `Clock` data structure. Make sure to reallocate the pixmap if the size changes.

After the display is finished, another call to the display routine is scheduled to happen in one second. If you were to embellish this widget, you might want to make the uptime period a parameter. The `TICKING` flag is used to note that the timer callback is scheduled. It is checked when the widget is destroyed so that the callback can be canceled. The next example shows `ClockDisplay`.

Example 31–7 The `ClockDisplay` procedure.

```
static void
ClockDisplay(ClientData clientData)
{
   Clock *clockPtr = (Clock *)clientData;
   Tk_Window tkwin = clockPtr->tkwin;
   Pixmap pixmap;
   int offset, x, y;
   struct tm *tmPtr;/* Time info split into fields */
   struct timeval tv;/* BSD-style time value */
   /*
    * Make sure the button still exists
    * and is mapped onto the display before painting.
    */
   clockPtr->flags &= ~(REDRAW_PENDING|TICKING);
   if ((clockPtr->tkwin == NULL) || !Tk_IsMapped(tkwin)) {
      return;
   }
   /*
    * Format the time into a string.
    * localtime chops up the time into fields.
    * strftime formats the fields into a string.
    */
   gettimeofday(&tv, NULL);
   tmPtr = localtime(&tv.tv_sec);
   strftime(clockPtr->clock, clockPtr->numChars+1,
      clockPtr->format, tmPtr);
   /*
    * To avoid flicker when the display is updated, the new
    * image is painted in an offscreen pixmap and then
```

```
 * copied onto the display in one operation.
 */
pixmap = Tk_GetPixmap(clockPtr->display,
    Tk_WindowId(tkwin),Tk_Width(tkwin),
    Tk_Height(tkwin), Tk_Depth(tkwin));
Tk_Fill3DRectangle(clockPtr->display, pixmap,
    clockPtr->background, 0, 0, Tk_Width(tkwin),
    Tk_Height(tkwin), 0, TK_RELIEF_FLAT);
/*
 * Paint the text first.
 */
offset = clockPtr->highlightWidth +
         clockPtr->borderWidth;
x = (Tk_Width(tkwin) - clockPtr->textWidth)/2;
if (x < 0) x = 0;
y = (Tk_Height(tkwin) - clockPtr->textHeight)/2;
if (y < 0) y = 0;

TkDisplayText(clockPtr->display, pixmap,
    clockPtr->fontPtr, clockPtr->clock,
    clockPtr->numChars, x, y, clockPtr->textWidth,
    TK_JUSTIFY_CENTER, -1, clockPtr->textGC);
/*
 * Display the borders, so they overwrite any of the
 * text that extends to the edge of the display.
 */
if (clockPtr->relief != TK_RELIEF_FLAT) {
    Tk_Draw3DRectangle(clockPtr->display, pixmap,
        clockPtr->background, clockPtr->highlightWidth,
        clockPtr->highlightWidth,
        Tk_Width(tkwin) - 2*clockPtr->highlightWidth,
        Tk_Height(tkwin) - 2*clockPtr->highlightWidth,
        clockPtr->borderWidth, clockPtr->relief);
}
if (clockPtr->highlightWidth != 0) {
    GC gc;
    if (clockPtr->flags & GOT_FOCUS) {
        gc = clockPtr->highlightGC;
    } else {
        gc = Tk_3DBorderGC(clockPtr->background,
            TK_3D_FLAT_GC);
    }
    TkDrawFocusHighlight(tkwin, gc,
        clockPtr->highlightWidth, pixmap);
}
/*
 * Copy the information from the off-screen pixmap onto
 * the screen, then delete the pixmap.
 */
XCopyArea(clockPtr->display, pixmap, Tk_WindowId(tkwin),
    clockPtr->textGC, 0, 0, Tk_Width(tkwin),
    Tk_Height(tkwin), 0, 0);
Tk_FreePixmap(clockPtr->display, pixmap);
/*
 * Queue another call to ourselves.
```

```
      */
    clockPtr->token = Tk_CreateTimerHandler(1000,
        ClockDisplay, (ClientData)clockPtr);
    clockPtr->flags |= TICKING;
}
```

The Window Event Procedure

Each widget registers an event handler for expose and resize events. If it implements and focus highlight, it also needs to be notified of focus events. If you have used other toolkits, you may expect to register callbacks for mouse and keystroke events too. You should not need to do that. Instead, use the regular Tk bind facility and define your bindings in Tcl. That way they can be customized by applications.

Example 31–8 The `ClockEventProc` handles window events.

```
static void
ClockEventProc(ClientData clientData, XEvent *eventPtr)
{
    Clock *clockPtr = (Clock *) clientData;
    if ((eventPtr->type == Expose) &&
        (eventPtr->xexpose.count == 0)) {
            goto redraw;
    } else if (eventPtr->type == DestroyNotify) {
        Tcl_DeleteCommand(clockPtr->interp,
            Tk_PathName(clockPtr->tkwin));
        /*
         * Zapping the tkwin lets the other procedures
         * know we are being destroyed.
         */
        clockPtr->tkwin = NULL;
        if (clockPtr->flags & REDRAW_PENDING) {
            Tk_CancelIdleCall(ClockDisplay,
                (ClientData) clockPtr);
            clockPtr->flags &= ~REDRAW_PENDING;
        }
        if (clockPtr->flags & TICKING) {
            Tk_DeleteTimerHandler(clockPtr->token);
            clockPtr->flags &= ~TICKING;
        }
        /*
         * This results in a call to ClockDestroy.
         */
        Tk_EventuallyFree((ClientData) clockPtr,
            ClockDestroy);
    } else if (eventPtr->type == FocusIn) {
        if (eventPtr->xfocus.detail != NotifyPointer) {
            clockPtr->flags |= GOT_FOCUS;
            if (clockPtr->highlightWidth > 0) {
                goto redraw;
```

```
            }
        }
    } else if (eventPtr->type == FocusOut) {
        if (eventPtr->xfocus.detail != NotifyPointer) {
            clockPtr->flags &= ~GOT_FOCUS;
            if (clockPtr->highlightWidth > 0) {
                goto redraw;
            }
        }
    }
    return;
redraw:
    if ((clockPtr->tkwin != NULL) &&
            !(clockPtr->flags & REDRAW_PENDING)) {
        Tk_DoWhenIdle(ClockDisplay, (ClientData) clockPtr);
        clockPtr->flags |= REDRAW_PENDING;
    }
}
```

Final Cleanup

When a widget is destroyed you need to free up any resources it has allocated. The resources associated with attributes are cleaned up by `Tk_FreeOptions`. The others you must take care of yourself. The `ClockDestroy` procedure is called as a result of the `Tk_EventuallyFree` call in the `ClockEventProc`. The `Tk_EventuallyFree` procedure is part of a protocol that is needed for widgets that might get deleted when in the middle of processing. Typically the `Tk_Preserve` and `Tk_Release` procedures are called at the beginning and end of the widget instance command to mark the widget as being in use. `Tk_EventuallyFree` will wait until `Tk_Release` is called before calling the cleanup procedure. The next example shows `ClockDestroy`.

Example 31–9 The `ClockDestroy` cleanup procedure.

```
static void
ClockDestroy(clientData)
 ClientData clientData;/* Info about entry widget. */
{
    register Clock *clockPtr = (Clock *) clientData;

    /*
     * Free up all the stuff that requires special handling,
     * then let Tk_FreeOptions handle resources associated
     * with the widget attributes.
     */
    if (clockPtr->highlightGC != None) {
        Tk_FreeGC(clockPtr->display, clockPtr->highlightGC);
    }
    if (clockPtr->textGC != None) {
        Tk_FreeGC(clockPtr->display, clockPtr->textGC);
```

```
    }
    if (clockPtr->clock != NULL) {
        ckfree(clockPtr->clock);
    }
    if (clockPtr->flags & TICKING) {
        Tk_DeleteTimerHandler(clockPtr->token);
    }
    if (clockPtr->flags & REDRAW_PENDING) {
        Tk_CancelIdleCall(ClockDisplay,
            (ClientData) clockPtr);
    }
    /*
     * This frees up colors and fonts and any allocated
     * storage associated with the widget attributes.
     */
    Tk_FreeOptions(configSpecs, (char *) clockPtr,
        clockPtr->display, 0);
    ckfree((char *) clockPtr);
}
```

CHAPTER 32

Tcl Extension Packages

This chapter surveys a few of the more popular Tcl extension packages.

Extension packages add suites of Tcl commands, usually as a combination of new built-in commands written in C and associated Tcl procedures. Some extensions provide new Tk widgets and geometry managers. This chapter surveys a few of the more popular extensions. Some are complex enough to deserve their own book, so this chapter is just meant to give you a feel for what these packages have to offer. For the details, consult the documentation that comes with the packages. This chapter briefly describes the following packages:

- *Extended Tcl* adds commands that provide access to more UNIX libraries and system calls. It adds new list operations and new loop constructs. It adds profiling commands so you can analyze the performance of your Tcl scripts.
- *Expect* adds commands that let you control interactive programs. Programs that insist on having a conversation with a user can be fooled by *expect* into doing work for you automatically.
- *Tcl debugger*. Part of the *Expect* package includes a small Tcl debugger that lets you set breakpoints and step through scripts.
- *Tcl-dp* adds commands that set up network connections among Tcl interpreters. You can set up distributed systems using *Tcl-dp*.
- *BLT* provides a table geometry manager for Tk, a graph widget, and more.
- [incr Tcl] provides an object system for Tcl. The scope for variables and pro-

cedures can be limited by using classes, and multiple inheritance can be used to set up a class hierarchy. The Tk-like interface with attributes and values is well supported by the package so you can create mega-widgets that look and feel like native Tk widgets to the programmer.

There are many more extensions available on the internet, and there is not enough time or space to describe even these extensions in much detail. This chapter provides a few tips on how to integrate these extensions into your application and what they can provide for you.

Extended Tcl

Extended Tcl, or TclX, provides many new built-in commands and support procedures. It provides access to more UNIX system calls and library procedures, and it provides tools that are useful for developing large Tcl applications. Over time, features from TclX have been adopted by John Ousterhout for use in the core language. For example, arrays originated from TclX.

The TclX extension is a little different from other applications because it assumes a more fundamental role. It provides its own script library mechanism, which is described later in more detail, and its own interactive shell. The extended Tcl shell is normally installed as *tcl*, and the Extended Tcl/Tk shell is normally installed as *wishx*.

There is one main manual page for TclX that describes all the commands and Tcl procedures provided by the package. The system also comes with a built-in help system so you can easily browse the man pages for standard Tcl and Extended tcl. The *tclhelp* program provides a graphical interface to the help system, or use the `help` command when running under the Extended Tcl shell, *tcl*.

Extended Tcl was designed and implemented by Karl Lehenbauer and Mark Diekhans, with help in the early stages from Peter da Silva. Extended Tcl is freely distributable, including for commercial use and resale. You can fetch the TclX distribution from the following FTP site:

```
ftp.neosoft.com:/pub/tcl/distrib/tclX7.4a.tar.gz
```

Adding TclX to Your Application

TclX has a different script library mechanism that makes integrating it into your application a little different than other extension packages. The main thing is that you need to call `TclX_Init` in your `Tcl_AppInit` procedure, not the standard `Tcl_Init` procedure. A version of the `tclAppInit.c` that is oriented toward Extended Tcl is provided with its distribution. The TclX library facility can read the `tclIndex` files of the standard library mechanism, so you can still use other packages.

It is possible, but rather awkward, to use the TclX commands and procedures with the standard library mechanism, which is described in Chapter 9. Instead of calling `TclX_Init`, you call `TclXCmd_Init` that only registers the built-in commands provided by TclX. However, gaining access to the Tcl procedures added by TclX is awkward because TclX insists on completely overriding the standard tcl library. It goes so far as to change the result of the `info library` call if you use its script library mechanism. This means that you can use one library directory or the other, but not both at the same time. You must copy the `tcl.tlib` file out of the TclX library directory into another location, or teach your application where to find it. It is probably easiest to use the TclX library system if you are using Extended Tcl.

More UNIX System Calls

Extended Tcl provides several UNIX-related commands. Most of the following should be familiar to a UNIX programmer: `alarm`, `chgrp`, `chmod`, `chown`, `chroot`, `convertclock`, `dup`, `execl`, `fmtclock`, `fork`, `getclock`, `kill`, `link`, `mkdir`, `nice`, `pipe`, `readdir`, `rmdir`, `select`, `signal`, `sleep`, `system`, `sync`, `times`, `umask`, `unlink`, and `wait`. The `id` command provides several operations on user, group, and process IDs.

File Operations

The `bsearch` command does a binary search of a sorted file. The `copyfile` command copies a file, and `frename` changes the name of a file. Low-level file controls are provided with `fcntl`, `flock`, `funlock`, and `fstat`. Use `lgets` to read the next complete Tcl list into a list variable. The `read_file` and `write_file` commands provide basic I/O operations. The `recursive_glob` command matches file names in a directory hierarchy.

New Loop Constructs

The `loop` command is an optimized version of the `for` loop that works with constant start, end, and increment values. The `for_array_keys` command loops over the contents of an array. The `for_recursive_glob` command loops over file names that match a pattern, possibly descending into directories. The `for_file` command loops over lines in a file.

Command Line Additions

A script can explicitly enter an interactive command loop with the `commandloop` command. The `echo` command makes it easy to print values. The `dirs`, `pushd`, and `popd` commands provide a stack of working directories. The `infox` command provides information like the application name, the version number, and so on.

Debugging and Development Support

The `cmdtrace` procedure shows what commands are being executed. The `profile` command sets up a profile of the CPU time used by each procedure or command. The profile results are formatted with the `profrep` command. Use `showprocs` to display a procedure definition, `edprocs` to bring up an editor on a procedure, and `saveprocs` to save procedure definitions to a file.

TCP/IP Access

The `server_info` command returns name, address, and alias information about servers. The `server_open` command opens a TCP socket to specified host and port. The `fstat remotehost` command returns the IP address of the remote peer if the file is an open socket. Once a socket is opened, it can be read and written with the regular file I/O commands, and `select` can be used to wait for the socket to be ready for I/O.

File Scanning

You can search for patterns in files and then execute commands when lines match those patterns. This provides a similar sort of functionality as *awk*. The process starts by defining a context with the `scancontext` command. The `scanmatch` command registers patterns and commands. The `scanfile` command reads a file and does matching according to a context. When a line is matched, information is placed into the `matchInfo` array for use by the associated command.

Math Functions as Commands

Procedures are defined that let you use the math functions as command names. The commands are implemented like this:

```
proc sin {x} { uplevel [list expr sin($x)] }
```

List Operations

New built-in list operations are provided. The `lvarpop` command removes an element from a list and returns its value, which is useful for processing command line arguments. The `lvarpush` command is similar to `linsert`. The `lassign` command assigns a set of variables values from a list. The `lmatch` command returns all the elements of a list that match a pattern. The `lempty` command is a shorthand for testing the list length against zero. The `lvarcat` command is similar to the `lappend` command.

There are four procedures that provide higher level list operations. The `intersect` procedure returns the common elements of two lists. The `intersect3` procedure returns three lists: the elements only in the first list, the elements in both lists, and the elements only in the second list. The `union` procedure merges two lists. The `lrmdups` procedure removes duplicates from a list.

Keyed List Data Structure

A keyed list is a list where each element is a key-value pair. The value can also be a keyed list, leading to a recursive data structure. Extended Tcl provides built-in support to make accessing keyed lists efficient. The `keylset` command sets the value associated with a key. The `keylkeys` returns a list of the keys in a keyed list. The `keylget` command returns the value associated with a key. The `keyldel` command deletes a key-value pair.

String Utilities

Several built-in commands provide the same function as uses of the `string` command. The `cequal` command is short for checking `string compare` with zero. The `clength` command is short for `string length`. The `crange` command is short for `string range`. The `cindex` command is short for `string index`. The `collate` command is short for string compare, plus it has locale support for different character sets. Because these are built-in commands, they are faster that writing Tcl procedures to obtain the shorthand, and a tiny bit faster than the `string` command because there is less argument checking.

The `ctype` command provides several operations on strings, such as checking for spaces, alphanumerics, and digits. It can also convert between characters and their ordinal values.

The `cexpand` command expands backslash sequences in a string. The `replicate` command creates copies of a string. The `translit` command maps characters in a string to new values in a similar fashion as the UNIX *tr* program.

XPG/3 Message Catalog

The XPG/3 message catalog supports internationalization of your program. You build a catalog that has messages in different languages. The `catopen` command returns a handle on a catalog. The `catgets` command takes a default string, looks for it in the catalog, and returns the right string for the current locale setting. The `catclose` command closes the handle on the catalog.

Memory Debugging

Extended Tcl provides both C library hooks to help you debug memory problems, and a Tcl interface that dumps out a map of how your dynamic memory arena is being used. Consult the Memory man page that comes with TclX for details.

Expect: Controlling Interactive Programs

Expect gives you control over interactive programs. For example, you can have two instances of the *chess* program play each other. More practical applications include automated access to FTP sites or navigation through network firewalls. If you are stuck with a program that does something useful but insists on an interactive interface, then you can automate its use with expect. It provides sophisticated control over processes and UNIX pseudo-terminals, so you can do things with expect that you just cannot do with ordinary shell scripts.

The *expect* shell program includes the core Tcl commands and the additional expect commands. The *expectk* shell also includes Tk, so you can have a graphical interface. If you have a custom C program you can include the expect commands by linking in its C library, `libexpect.a`. You can use the C interface directly, but in nearly all cases you will find it easier to drive expect (and the rest of your application) from Tcl.

The expect package was designed and implemented by Don Libes. Historically it is the first extension package. Libes wrote the initial version in about two weeks after he first heard about Tcl. He had long wanted to write something like expect, and Tcl provided just the infrastructure that he needed to get started. By now the expect package is quite sophisticated. Libes has an excellent book about expect, *Exploring Expect*, published by O'Reilly & Associates, Inc.

As of this writing, the current version of expect is 5.13, and it is compatible with Tcl 7.4. A version 5.14 is expected, which will take advantage of some of the new features in Tcl and improve the debugger that comes with expect. You can always fetch the latest version of expect by FTP from the following site and file name.

```
ftp.cme.nist.gov:/pub/expect/expect.tar.Z
```

The rest of this section provides a short overview of expect and gives a few tips that may help you understand how expect works. Expect is a rich facility, however, and this section only scratches the surface.

The Core Expect Commands

There are four fundamental commands added by expect: `spawn`, `exp_send`, `expect`, and `interact`. The `spawn` command executes a program and returns a handle that is used to control I/O to the program. The `exp_send` command sends input to the program. (If you are not also using Tk, then you can shorten this command to `send`.) The `expect` command pattern matches on output from the program. The `expect` command is used somewhat like the Tcl `switch` command. There are several branches that have different patterns, and a block of Tcl commands is associated with each pattern. When the program generates output that matches a pattern, the associated Tcl commands are executed.

The `send_user` and `expect_user` commands are analogous to `exp_send` and `expect`, but they use the I/O connection to the user instead of the process. A common idiom is to `expect` a prompt from the process, `expect_user` the response, and then `exp_send` the response to the program. Generally, the user sees everything so you do not need to `send_user` all the program output.

The `interact` command reconnects the program and the user so you can interact with the program directly. The `interact` command also does pattern matching, so you can set up Tcl commands to execute when you type certain character sequences or when the program emits certain strings. Thus you can switch back and forth between human interaction and program controlled interaction. Expect is quite powerful!

Pattern Matching

The default pattern matching used by expect is *glob*-style. You can use regular expression matching by specifying the `-re` option to the `expect` command. Most of the work in writing an expect script is getting the patterns right. When writing your patterns, it is important to remember that expect relies on the Tcl parser to expand backslash sequences like `\r\n` (carriage return, newline), which is often an important part of an expect pattern. There is often a `\n` and or `\r` at the end of a pattern to make sure that a whole line is matched, for example. You need to group your patterns with double-quotes, not braces, to allow backslash substitutions.

If you use regular expressions the quoting can get complicated. You have to worry about square brackets and dollar signs, which have different meanings to Tcl and the regular expression parser. Matching a literal backslash is the most tedious because it is special to both Tcl and the regular expression parser. You will need four backslashes, which Tcl maps into two, which the regular expression interprets as a single literal backslash.

There are a few pattern keywords. If an expect does not match within the timeout period, the `timeout` pattern is matched. If the process closes its output stream, then the `eof` pattern is matched.

Important Variables

Expect uses a number of global variables. A few of the more commonly used variables are described here.

The `spawn` command returns a value that is also placed into the `spawn_id` variable. If you spawn several programs, you can implement a sort of job control by changing the value of the global `spawn_id` variable. This affects which process is involved with `exp_send`, `expect`, and `interact` commands. You can also specify the ID explicitly with a `-i` argument to those commands.

If you use `spawn` in a procedure, you probably need to declare `spawn_id` as a `global` variable. Otherwise, an `exp_send` or `expect` in anther context will not see the right value for `spawn_id`. It is not strictly necessary to make `spawn_id` global, but it is certainly necessary if you use it in different contexts.

The `timeout` variable controls how long expect waits for a match. Its value is in seconds.

When a pattern is matched by expect, the results are put into the `expect_out` array. The `expect_out(0,string)` element has the part of the input that matched the pattern. If you use subpatterns in your regular expressions, the parts that match those are available in `expect_out(1,string)`, `expect_out(2,string)`, and so on. The `expect_out(buffer)` element has the input that matched the pattern, plus everything read before the match since the last `expect` match.The `interact` command initializes an array called `interact_out`, which has a similar structure.

The `log_user` variable controls whether or not the user sees the output from the process. For some programs you may want to suppress all the output. In other cases it may be important for the user to see what is happening so they know when to type responses, such as passwords.

An Example expect Script

The following example demonstrates the usefulness of *expect*. The situation is an FTP server that uses a challenge response security system. Without *expect*, the user needs two windows. In one window they run FTP. In the other window they run a program that computes the response to the challenge from FTP. They use cut and paste to feed the challenge from FTP to the *key* program, and use it again to feed the response back to FTP. It is a tedious task that can be fully automated with *expect*.

Example 32–1 A sample expect script.

```
#!/usr/local/bin/expect -f
# This logs into the FTP machine and
# handles the S/Key authentication dance.

# Setup global timeout action. Any expect that does not match
# in timeout seconds will trigger this action.
expect_after timeout {
    send_user "Timeout waiting for response\n"
    exit 1
}
set timeout 30    ;# seconds

# Run ftp and wait for Name prompt
spawn ftp parcftp.xerox.com
expect {*Name *:}

# Get the name from the user pass it to FTP
expect_user "*\n"
exp_send $expect_out(buffer)

# Wait for Skey Challenge, which looks like:
# 331 Skey Challenge "s/key 664 be42066"
expect -re {331.*s/key ([^"]+)"} {
    set skey $expect_out(1,string)
}
```

```
# Save the spawn ID of ftp and then
# run the key program with the challenge as the argument
set ftpid $spawn_id
eval {spawn key} $skey

# Read password with no echoing, pass it to key
system stty -echo
expect {password:}
expect_user "*\n" { send_user \n }
exp_send $expect_out(buffer)

# Wait for the key response
expect -re "\n(.+)\[\r\n\]" {
   set response $expect_out(1,string)
}
# Close down the connection to the key program
close
system stty echo

# Pull ftp back into the foreground
set spawn_id $ftpid
exp_send $response\n

# Interact with FTP normally
expect {*ftp>*} { interact }
```

The example uses the `expect_after` command to set up a global timeout action. The alternative is to include a timeout pattern on each expect command. In that case the commands would look like this:

```
expect {*Name *:} { # Do nothing } \
     timeout { send_user "You have to login!\n" ; exit 1 }
```

The `system` command is used to run UNIX programs. It is like exec, except that the output is not returned and a /bin/sh is used to interpret the command. The `stty echo` command turns off echoing on the terminal so the user doesn't see their password being typed.

Debugging expect Scripts

The *expect* shell takes a `-d` flag that turns on debugging output. This shows you all the characters generated by a program and all the attempts at pattern matching. This is very useful. You become very aware of little details. Remember that programs actually generate `\r\n` at the end of a line, even though their `printf` only includes `\n`. The terminal driver converts a simple newline into a carriage return, line feed sequence. Conversely, when you send data to a program, you need to explicitly include a `\n`, but you don't send `\r`.

Expect includes a debugger, which is described in the next section and in Chapter 8. If you specify the `-D 1` command line argument to the *expect* shell, then this debugger is entered before your script starts execution. If you specify the `-D 0` command line argument, then the debugger is entered if you generate a keyboard interrupt (`SIGINT`).

Expect's Tcl Debugger

The expect package includes a Tcl debugger. It lets you set breakpoints and look at the Tcl execution stack. This section explains what you need to add to your C program to make the debugger available to scripts. The interactive use of the debugger is described in Chapter 8 on page 84.

The Dbg C Interface

The debugger is implemented in one file, `Dbg.c`, that is part of the expect library. You can make the debugger separately from expect, but it is easiest to link against the expect library. The core procedures are `Dbg_On` and `Dbg_Off`.*

```
void *Dbg_On(Tcl_Interp *interp, int immediate);
void *Dbg_Off(Tcl_Interp *interp);
```

If `immediate` is 1, then `Dbg_On` enters an interactive command loop right away. Otherwise the debugger waits until just before the next command is evaluated. It is reasonable to call `Dbg_On` with `immediate` set to zero from inside a `SIGINT` interrupt handler.

The `Dbg_ArgcArgv` call lets the debugger make a copy of the command line arguments. It wants to print this information as part of its call stack display. If the *`copy`* argument is 1, a copy of the argument strings is made and a pointer to the allocated memory is returned. Otherwise it just retains a pointer and returns 0. The copy may be necessary because the `Tk_ParseArgv` procedure will modify the argument list. Call `Dbg_ArgcArgv` first.

```
char **Dbg_ArgcArgv(int argc, char *argv[], int copy);
```

The `Dbg_Active` procedure returns 1 if the debugger is currently on. It does no harm, by the way, to call `Dbg_On` if the debugger is already active.

```
int Dbg_Active(Tcl_Interp *interp);
```

The remaining procedures are only needed if you want to refine the behavior of the debugger. You can change the command interpreter, and you can filter out commands so the debugger ignores them.

The `Dbg_Interactor` procedure registers a command loop implementation and a client data pointer. It returns the previously registered procedure.

```
Dbg_InterProc
Dbg_Interactor(Tcl_Interp *interp,
    Dbg_InterpProc *inter_proc, ClientData data);
```

The command loop procedure needs to have the following signature.

```
int myinteractor(Tcl_Interp *interp);
```

Look in the `Dbg.c` file at the simpler_interactor procedure to see how the command loop works. In practice the default interactor is just fine.

---

* I will give the C signatures for the procedures involved because I no longer see them in the standard Expect documentation. You must read `Dbg.h`. Don Libes described the debugger in a nice little paper, "A Debugger for Tcl Applications," which appeared in the 1993 Tcl/Tk workshop.

The Dbg_IgnoreFuncs procedure registers a filtering function that decides what Tcl commands should be ignored. It returns the previously registered filter procedure. The filter should be relatively efficient because it is called before every command when the debugger is enabled.

```
Dbg_IgnoreFuncsProc
Dbg_IgnoreFuncs(Tcl_Interp *interp,
    Dbg_IgnoreFuncsProc *ignoreproc);
```

The ignoreproc procedure just takes a string as an argument, which is the name of the command about to be executed. It returns 1 if the command should be ignored.

```
int ignoreproc(char *s);
```

Handling SIGINT

A common way to enter the debugger is in response to a keyboard interrupt. The details of signal handling vary a little from system to system, so you may have to adjust Example 32–2 somewhat. The Sig_Setup procedure is meant to be called early in your main program. It does two things. It registers a signal handler, and it registers a Tcl asynchronous event. It isn't safe to do much more than set a variable value inside a signal handler, and it certainly is not safe to call Tcl_Eval in a signal handler. However, the Tcl interpreter lets you register procedures to be called at a safe point. The registration is done with Tcl_AsyncCreate, and the handler is enabled with Tcl_AsyncMark. Finally, within the async handler the debugger is entered by calling Dbg_On.

Example 32–2 A SIGINT handler.

```
#include <signal.h>
/*
 * Token and handler procedure for async event.
 */
Tcl_AsyncHandler sig_Token;
int Sig_HandleSafe(ClientData data,
   Tcl_Interp *interp, int code);
/*
 * Set up a signal handler for interrupts.
 * This also registers a handler for a Tcl asynchronous
 * event, which is enabled in the interrupt handler.
 */
void
Sig_Setup(interp)
   Tcl_Interp *interp;
{
   RETSIGTYPE (*oldhandler)();
   oldhandler = signal(SIGINT, Sig_HandleINT);
   if ((int)oldhandler == -1) {
      perror("signal failed");
      exit(1);
   }
```

```
    sig_Token = Tcl_AsyncCreate(Sig_HandleSafe, NULL);
#if !defined(__hpux) & !defined(SVR4)
    /*
     * Ensure that wait() kicks out on interrupt.
     */
    siginterrupt(SIGINT, 1);on interrupt */
#endif
}
/*
 * Invoked upon interrupt (control-C)
 */
RETSIGTYPE
Sig_HandleINT(sig, code, scp, addr)
    int sig, code;
    struct sigcontext *scp;
    char *addr;
{
    Tcl_AsyncMark(sig_Token);
}
/*
 * Invoked at a safe point sometime after Tcl_AsyncMark
 */
int
Sig_HandleSafe(data, interp, code)
    ClientData data;
    Tcl_Interp *interp;
    int code;
{
    Dbg_On(interp, 1);/* Enter the Tcl debugger */
}
```

BLT

The BLT package has a number of Tk extensions: a bar graph widget, an X-Y graph widget, a drag-and-drop facility, a table geometry manager, a busy window, and more. This section provides an overview of this excellent collection of extensions. The gadgets in BLT where designed and built by George Howlett, and Michael McLennan built the drag and drop facility. As of this writing BLT version 1.7 is compatible with Tk 3.6 and Tcl 7.3. A 1.8 (or 2.0) release is expected shortly that will be compatible with Tk 4.0 and Tcl 7.4. You can find the BLT package in the Tcl archives in the extensions directory:

`ftp.aud.alcatel.com:tcl/extensions/BLT-1.7.tar.gz`

The BLT package is very clean to add to your application. All the commands and variables that it defines begin with the `blt_` prefix. Initialization simply requires calling `Blt_Init` in your `Tcl_AppInit` procedure.

Drag and Drop

The drag and drop paradigm lets you "pick up" an object in one window and drag it into another window, even if that window is in another application. The `blt_drag&drop` command provides a drag and drop capability for Tk applications. A right click in a window creates a token window that you drag into another window. When the object is released, the TK send command is used to communicate between the sender and the receiver.

Hypertext

The `blt_htext` widget combines text and other widgets in the same scrollable window. The widget lets you embed Tcl commands in the text, and these commands are invoked as the text is parsed and displayed. Tk 4.0 added similar functions to the standard Tk `text` widget, except for the embedded Tcl commands in the text.

Graphs

The `blt_graph` widget provides an X-Y plotting widget. You can configure the graph in a variety of ways. The elements of the graph can have tags that are similar to the canvas widget object tags. The `blt_barchart` widget provides a bar graph display. It also has a tag facility.

Table Geometry Manager

The `table` geometry manager lets you position windows on a grid, which makes it easy to line things up. The interface is designed by defining a grid that can have uneven spacing for the rows and columns. Widgets are positioned by specifying a grid location and the number of rows and columns the widget can span. You can constrain the size of the widget in various ways. A table geometry manager will probably be added to the standard Tk library in a future release.

Bitmap Support

In standard Tk, the only way to define new bitmaps in Tcl is to specify a file that contains its definition. The `blt_bitmap` command lets you define a new bitmap and give it a symbolic name. It also lets you query the names and sizes of existing bitmaps.

Background Exec

The `blt_bgexec` command runs a pipeline of processes in the background. The output is collected into a Tcl variable. You use `tkwait variable` to detect when the pipeline has completed operation.

Busy Window

The `blt_busy` command creates an invisible window that covers your application, provides a different cursor, and prevents the user from interacting with your application.

Tracing Tcl Commands

The `blt_watch` provides a Tcl interface to the Tcl trace facility. It lets you register Tcl commands to be called before and after the execution of all commands. You can implement logging and profiling with this facility. The `blt_debug` command displays each Tcl command before and after substitutions are performed.

The Cutbuffer

Old versions of X programs may still use the out-dated cutbuffer facility. The `blt_cutbuffer` command provides an interface to the cutbuffer. This can help improve your interoperation with other tools, although you should use the regular selection mechanism by default.

Tcl-DP

The Tcl-DP extension creates network connections between Tcl interpreters using the TCP protocol. It provides a client-server model so you can execute Tcl commands in other interpreters. This is similar to the Tk `send` command, except that Tcl-DP is not limited to applications on the same display. You can have Tcl-DP without Tk, too, for clients or servers that have no graphical interface.

There are three shell programs: *dpwish* includes Tk and Tcl-DP. *dptcl* just has the Tk event loop and Tcl-DP. The *dpsh* shell includes Tk, but can be started with a `-notk` argument to prevent it from opening a display. Of course, all of these include the standard Tcl commands, too.

The low-level networking functions are exported to both Tcl and C. For example, the `dp_packetSend` Tcl command sends a network packet. The same function is available from C with the `Tdp_PacketSend` procedure. Other C procedures include `Tdp_FindAddress`, `Tdp_CreateAddress`, `Tdp_PacketReceive`, and `Tdp_RPC`. These are bundled into the `libdpnetwork.a` library archive.

Tcl-DP was designed and built by Brian Smith and Professor Lawrence Rowe of the University of California, Berkeley. Version 3.2 is compatible with Tcl 7.3 and Tk 3.6. When it is released, version 3.3 will be compatible with Tcl 7.4 and Tk 4.0. You can find the Tcl-DP distribution at the following FTP site:

```
mm-ftp.cs.berkeley.edu
/pub/multimedia/Tcl-DP/tcl-dp3.2.tar.Z
```

Remote Procedure Call

The dp_MakeRPCServer command sets up the server's network socket. The dp_MakeRPCClient command sets up the client and connects to the server. The dp_RPC command invokes a Tcl command in the server. The do_RDO command is similar, except that it does not wait for completion of the command. It takes an optional callback command so you can get notified when the asynchronous operation completes. The dp_CancelRPC is used to cancel asynchronous RPCs. The dp_CloseRPC shuts down one end of a connection.

Servers are identified by a network address and port number. No higher-level name service is provided, although you can often do quite well by using a file in your shared network file system. The developers of Tcl-DP are currently working on a simple name server that will help client applications locate server processes. The server can be configured to "auto-start" a server requested by a client that is not running. In addition, the name server is replicated so that if it fails, a backup name server will take over. This name server will be included in the v3.3 release.

A simple form of security is provided. A server can define a set of trusted hosts with the dp_Host command. Connections will only be accepted from clients on those trusted hosts. Each command can be verified before execution. The dp_SetCheckCmd registers a procedure that is called to verify a client request. You could use the verification hook to enforce an authentication dialog, although the TCP connect is not encrypted.

Connection Setup

The dp_connect -server command is used by servers to create a listening socket. Servers then use the dp_accept command to wait for new connections from clients. Clients use the dp_connect command (without -server) to connect to a server. The connect uses TCP by default. The -udp option creates a UDP connection. The dp_socketOption provides an interface to the setsockopt and getsockopt system calls. The dp_shutdown command is used to close down a connection. The dp_atclose command registers a command to be called just before a connection is closed. The dp_atexit command registers a command to be called when the process is exiting. These commands are used by the RPC-related procedures described above.

Sending Network Data

The regular puts and gets commands can be used to transfer line-oriented data over a connection. If you use these commands, it is necessary to use the eof command to detect a closed connection.

The dp_send and dp_receive commands transfer data across a connection. The dp_packetSend and dp_packetReceive transfer blocks of data while preserving message boundaries. These use the TCP protocol, and they automatically handle closed connections.

Using UDP

The dp_sendTo and dp_receiveFrom commands transfer packets using the UDP protocol. These commands take an argument that specifies the remote network address with which to communicate. These arguments are returned by dp_address command, which maintains an address table.

Event Processing

Tcl-DP uses the Tk event loop mechanism to wait for network data. It provides several commands that relate to the event loop processing. The dp_filehandler command registers a command to be called when data is ready on a connection. The dp_isready command indicates if data is available on a connection. The dp_whenidle command schedules a command to occur at the next idle point.

The following commands are provided by Tcl-DP in case Tk is not available. The dp_update command forces a trip through the event loop. The dp_after command executes a command after a specified time interval. dp_waitvariable waits for a variable to be modified. These are equivalent to the following Tk commands: update, after, and tkwait variable.

Replicated Objects

A simple replicated object package is built on top of Tcl-DP. In the model, an object is a procedure with methods and slot values. Every object must implement the configure, slotvalue, and destroy methods. The configure method is used to query and set slot values, much like the Tk widget configure operation. The slotvalue method returns the value of a slot, much like the cget operation of a Tk widget.

An object is replicated on one or more sites, and updates to an object are reflected in all copies. You can register callbacks that are invoked when the object is modified. The dp_setf command sets a replicated slot value. The dp_getf command returns a slot value. The dp_DistributeObject command arranges for an object to be replicated on one or more sites. The dp_UndistributeObject breaks the shared relationship among distributed objects. The dp_SetTrigger, dp_AppendTrigger, and dp_AppendTriggerUnique commands register a Tcl command to be called when a slot is modified. The dp_GetTriggers command returns the registered triggers. The dp_ReleaseTrigger removes one trigger, and the dp_ClearTrigger removes all triggers from a slot.

An object can be implemented by a command procedure written in C. All it has to do is adhere to the conventions outlined above about what methods it supports. The method is just the first argument to the procedure. The object will be invoked as follows:

```
objName method ?args?
```

Obviously, there must also be a command that creates instances of the object. This should have the following form:

```
makeCmd objName ?-slot value? ?-slot value? ...
```

You can also implement objects with Tcl procedures. Several commands are provided to support this: `dp_objectCreateProc`, `dp_objectExists`, `dp_objectFree`, `dp_objectConfigure` `dp_objectSlot`, `dp_objectSlotSet`, `dp_objectSlotAppend`, and `dp_objectSlots`.

The [incr Tcl] Object System

The [incr Tcl] extension provides an object system for Tcl. It was designed and built by Michael McLennan. Its funny name is an obvious spoof on C++. This extension adds classes with multiple inheritance to Tcl. A class has methods, class procedures, private variables, public variables, and class variables. All of these items are contained within their own scope. The class procedures and class variables are shared by all objects in a class. The methods, private variables, and public variables are per-object. A public variable is a lot like the attributes for Tk widgets. Its value is defined when the object is created, or changed later with a `config` method. The `config` syntax looks like the syntax used with Tk widgets and their attributes.

The following summary of the [incr Tcl] commands is taken straight from the man page for the package:

Example 32–3 Summary of [incr Tcl] commands.

```
itcl_class className {
   inherit baseClass ?baseClass...?

   constructor args body
   destructor body
   # A method is per-object
   method name args body
   # proc creates class procedures
   proc name args body

   # public vars have a config syntax to set their value
   public varName ?init? ?config?
   # protected variables are per-object
   protected varName ?init?
   # common variables are shared by the whole class
   common varName ?init?
}

# Create an object. The second form chooses the name.
className objName ?args...?
className #auto ?args...?

# Invoke a class procedure proc from the global scope
className :: proc ?args...?

# Invoke an object method
```

```
objName method ?args...?

# Built-in methods
objName isa className
objName delete
objName info option ?args?

# Get info about classes and objects
itcl_info classes ?pattern?
itcl_info objects ?pattern? ?-class className? ?-isa
className?

# Commands available within class methods/procs:
global varName ?varName...?
# Run command in the scope of the parent class (up)
previous command ?args...?
# Run command in the scope of the most-specific class (down)
virtual command ?args...?
```

The most important contribution of [incr Tcl] is the added scope control. The elements of a class are hidden inside its scope, so they do not clutter the global Tcl name space. When you are inside a method or class procedure, you can directly name other methods, class procedures, and the various class variables. When you are outside a class, you can only invoke its methods through an object. It is also possible to access class procedures with the `::` syntax shown in the previous example. The scope control is implemented by creating a new Tcl interpreter for each class, although this is hidden from you when you use the extension.

There is one restriction on the multiple inheritance provided by [incr Tcl]. The inheritance graph must be a tree, not a more general directed-acyclic-graph. For example, if you have a very general class called `Obj` that two classes `A` and `B` inherit, then class `C` cannot inherit from both `A` and `B`. That causes the elements of `Obj` to be inherited by two paths, and the implementation of [incr Tcl] does not allow this. You would have to replicate the elements of `Obj` in `A` and `B` in this example.

Tcl_AppInit with Extensions

Example 32–4 shows a `Tcl_AppInit` that initializes several packages in addition to the new commands and widgets from the previous chapters. Most of the packages available from the Tcl archive have been structured so you can initialize them with a single call to their *`Package_Init`* procedure. Your `main` program and the `Tcl_AppInit` routine are linked with the libraries for Tcl and the various extensions being used. Example 32–5 shows the `Makefile` for the program.

Example 32–4 `Tcl_AppInit` and extension packages.

```
/* supertcl.c */
#include <stdio.h>
#include <tk.h>
#include <tclExtend.h>

extern char *exp_argv0;/* For expect */

/*
 * Our clock widget.
 */
int ClockCmd(ClientData clientData,
             Tcl_Interp *interp,
             int argc, char *argv[]);
/*
 * Our pixmap image type.
 */
extern Tk_ImageType tkPixmapImageType;

main(int argc, char *argv[]) {
   /*
    * Save arguments for expect and its debugger.
    */
   exp_argv0 = argv[0];/* Needed by expect */
   Dbg_ArgcArgv(argc, argv, 1);
   /*
    * Create the main window. This calls
    * back into Tcl_AppInit.
    */
   Tk_Main(argc, argv);
   exit(0);
}

int
Tcl_AppInit(Tcl_Interp *interp) {
   char *value;
   Tk_Window main = Tk_MainWindow(interp);
   /*
    * Initialize extensions
   */
   if (TclX_Init(interp) == TCL_ERROR) {
      /* TclX_Init is called instead of Tcl_Init */
      return TCL_ERROR;
   }
   if (Tk_Init(interp) == TCL_ERROR) {
      return TCL_ERROR;
   }
   if (Tdp_Init(interp) == TCL_ERROR) {/* Tcl-DP */
      return TCL_ERROR;
   }
   if (Blt_Init(interp) == TCL_ERROR) {/* BLT */
      return TCL_ERROR;
   }
   if (Exp_Init(interp) == TCL_ERROR) {/* Expect */
```

```
        return TCL_ERROR;
    }
    /*
     * This affects X resource names.
     */
    Tk_SetClass(main, "SuperTcl");
    /*
     * Our own extra commands.
     */
    Tcl_CreateCommand(interp, "clock", ClockCmd,
        (ClientData)Tk_MainWindow(interp),
        (Tcl_CmdDeleteProc *)NULL);

    Tk_CreateImageType(&tkPixmapImageType);
    /*
     * The remaining lines are similar to code in TkX_Init.
     * The tclApp variables define info returned by infox
     * The Tcl_SetupSigInt is a TclX utility that lets
     * keyboard interrupts stop the current Tcl command.
     */
    tclAppName = "SuperTcl";
    tclAppLongname = "Tcl-Tk-TclX-DP-BLT-Expect-incr_Tcl";
    tclAppVersion = "1.0";
    /*
    * If we are going to be interactive,
    * Setup SIGINT handling.
    */
    value = Tcl_GetVar (interp, "tcl_interactive",
         TCL_GLOBAL_ONLY);
    if ((value != NULL) && (value [0] != '0'))
        Tcl_SetupSigInt ();

    return TCL_OK;
}
```

Because Extended Tcl is being used, `TclX_Init` is called instead of `Tcl_Init`. This is an unfortunate inconsistency, but Extended Tcl insists on duplicating some things in Tcl and Tk, so this is necessary to avoid linker problems. In protest, the example calls `Tk_Init` instead of `TkX_Init`, which is recommended by the TclX documentation. However, this means it does much of the same work by calling `Tcl_SetupSigInt` and defining the various `tclApp` variables. The `Tcl_SetupSigInt` procedure is part of Extended Tcl, and it sets up an interrupt handler so users can stop Tcl commands with a keyboard interrupt.

The Makefile for the *supertcl* program is given in the next example. The program uses a mixture of shared and static libraries. Ideally, all the packages can be set up as shared libraries in order to reduce the size of the shell programs. Shared libraries are described in Chapter 9.

Example 32–5 Makefile for *supertcl*.

```
# At our site all the Tcl packages have their
# libraries in /import/tcl/lib, and the files
# have the version number in them explicitly
# The .so files are shared libraries

TCL_LIB = /import/tcl/lib/libtcl7_4_g.a
TK_LIB = /import/tcl/lib/libtk4_0_g.a

BLT_LIB = /import/tcl/lib/libBLT1_7.a
DP_LIB = /import/tcl/lib/libdpnetwork.so.3.2
EXP_LIB = /import/tcl/lib/libexpect5_13.a
TCLX_LIB = /import/tcl/lib/libtclx7_4.a
TKX_LIB = /import/tcl/lib/libtkx4_0.a
INCR_LIB = /import/tcl/lib/libitcl.so.1.3

# The include files are also organized under
# /import/tcl/include in directories that
# reflect the packages' version numbers.
INCS = -I/import/tcl/include/tk4.0 \
   -I/import/tcl/include/tclX7.4a \
   -I/import/tcl/include/tcl7.4 \
   -I/import/X11R4/usr/include
CFLAGS = -g $(INCS)
CC = gcc

# The order of these libraries is important, especially
# having TKX TK TCLX TCL come last.
# Your site may not need -lm for the math library
ALL_LIBS = $(DP_LIB) $(EXP_LIB) $(BLT_LIB) $(INCR_LIB) \
   $(TKX_LIB) $(TK_LIB) $(TCLX_LIB) $(TCL_LIB) -lX11 -lm

OBJS = supertcl.o tkWidget.o tkImgPixmap.o
supertcl: $(OBJS)
   $(CC) -o supertcl $(TRACE) $(OBJS) $(ALL_LIBS)
```

Other Extensions

There are lots of contributed Tcl packages. You should check out the Tcl FTP archive sites that are listed in the introduction. The docs directory contains an excellent set of Frequently Asked Questions files that are maintained by Larry Virden. Volumes 4 and 5 of the FAQ list the contributed applications and the contributed extensions, respectively. There is a separate list of commercial uses of Tcl and Tk. The following list of Tcl applications and extensions is just a hint of the tools available in the Tcl archive:

- The *jstools* package is based around an extensible text editor. There are a collection of text management procedures and other tools in the package. Contributed by Jay Sekora.

- The *TIX* package provides many compound widgets and an object system that is designed to support them. Contributed by Ioi Kim Lam. `http://www.cis.upenn.edu/%7Eioi/tix/3.9a/tix3.9a.html`
- The *shells* package supports dynamic linking and facilitates management of multiple extensions. Look for `shells-1.1.tar.gz` in the archive.
- The *DejaGnu* package provides a framework based on *expect* for testing other software. `ftp://ftp.cygnus.com/pub/dejagnu/dejagnu-1.2.tar.z`
- The *minterp* package adds Tcl commands to manage multiple interpreter contexts. Contributed by David Herron.
- The *TkSteal* extension lets you embed another application's window into a Tk interface. Contributed by Sven Delmas.
- The *GroupKit* toolkit provides a set of tools for building groupware applications. Contributed by Mark Roseman and Dr. Saul Greenberg. `http://www.cpsc.ucalgary.ca/projects/grouplab/groupkit/groupkit.html`
- The *Elsbeth* text editor and *Teacher* hypertools include facilities for dynamically modifying other Tk applications. Contributed by David Svoboda.
- The *emil* mail conversion program handles MIME, Eudora, Mailtool, PC client, and Mac client mail formats. Contributed by Martin Wendel. `ftp://scr.doc.ic.ac.uk/computing/mail/emil`
- The *exmh* program is a graphical front end for MH mail. It supports the MIME standard for multimedia mail, and the PGP tool for encryption and digital signatures. It is designed for extensibility. Contributed by Brent Welch. `ftp://parcftp.xerox.com/pub/exmh/html/index.html`
- The *tkman* program provides a great user interface to the UNIX man pages. Contributed by Tom Phelps.
- The *tkinspect* program lets you browse the state of other Tk applications. This is an excellent debugging aid. Contributed by Sam Shen.
- The *ical* program is a very useful calendar manager. Contributed by Sanjay Ghemawat. `http://clef.lcs.mit.edu/%7Esanjay/ical/ftp.html`
- The *mxedit* editor is a port of John Ousterhout's *mx* editor into the Tk framework. Contributed by Brent Welch.
- The *XF* interface builder lets you interactively create Tk interfaces. Contributed by Sven Delmas.

This list is by no means complete. Be sure to check the FAQ and the on-line Tcl archives for the up-to-date set of applications and extension packages.

CHAPTER 33

Porting to Tk 4.0

This chapter has notes about upgrading your application from earlier versions of Tk such as Tk 3.6. This includes notable new features that you may want to take advantage of as well as things that need to be fixed because of incompatible changes.

Porting your scripts from any of the Tk version 3 releases is easy. Not that many things have changed. The sections in this chapter summarize what has changed in Tk 4.0 and what some of the new commands are.

wish

The *wish* shell no longer requires a `-file` (or `-f`) argument, so you can drop this from your script header lines. This flag is still valid, but no longer necessary.

The class name of the application is set from the name of the script file instead of always being `Tk`. If the script is `/usr/local/bin/foobar`, then the class is set to `Foobar`, for example.

Obsolete Features

Several features that were replaced in previous versions are now completely unsupported.

The variable that contains the version number is `tk_version`. The ancient (version 1) `tkVersion` is no longer supported.

Button widgets no longer have `activate` and `deactivate` operations. Instead, configure their `state` attribute.

Menus no longer have `enable` and `disable` operations. Instead, configure their `state` attribute.

The cget Operation

All widgets support a `cget` operation that returns the current value of the specified configuration option. The following two commands are equivalent:

```
lindex [$w config option] 4
$w cget option
```

Nothing breaks with this change, but you should enjoy this feature.

Input Focus Highlight

Each widget can have an input focus highlight, which is a border that is drawn in color when the widget has the input focus. This border is outside the border used to draw the 3D relief for widgets. It has the pleasant visual effect of providing a little bit of space around widgets, even when they do not have the input focus. The addition of the input focus highlight does not break anything, but it changes the appearance of your interfaces a little. In particular, the highlight on a canvas obscures objects that are at its edge. See Chapter 23 for a description of the generic widget attributes related to the input focus highlight.

Bindings

The hierarchy of bindings has been fixed so that it is actually useful to define bindings at each of the global (i.e., `all`), class, and instance levels. The new `bindtags` command defines the order among these sources of binding information. You can also introduce new binding classes, (e.g. `InsertMode`), and bind things to that class. Use the `bindtags` command to insert this class into the binding hierarchy. The order of binding classes in the bindtags command determines the order in which bindings are triggered. Use `break` in a binding command to stop the progression, or use `continue` to go on to the next level.

```
bindtags $w [list all Text InsertMode $w]
```

The various `Request` events have gone away: `CirculateRequest`, `ConfigureRequest`, `MapRequest`, and `ResizeRequest`.

Extra modifier keys are ignored when matching events. While you can still use the `Any` wild card modifier, it is no longer necessary. The `Alt` and `Meta` modifiers are set up in a general way so they are associated with the `Alt_L`, `Alt_R`, `Meta_L`, and `Meta_R` keysyms.

Scrollbar Interface

The interface between scrollbars and the scrollable widgets has changed. Happily, the change is transparent to most scripts. If you hook your scrollbars to widgets in the straight-forward way, the new interface is compatible. If you use the `xview` and `yview` widget commands directly, however, you might need to modify your code. The old interface still works, but there are new features of these operations that give you even better control. You can also query the view state so you do not need to watch the scroll set commands to keep track of what is going on. Finally, scrollable widgets are constrained so that the end of their data remains stuck at the bottom (right) of their display. In most cases, nothing is broken by this change.

Pack info

Version 3 of Tk introduced a new syntax for the `pack` command, but the old syntax was still supported. This continues to be true in nearly all cases except the `pack info` command. If you are still using the old packer format, you should probably take this opportunity to convert to the new packer syntax.

The problem with `pack info` is that its semantics changed. The new operation used to be known as `pack newinfo`. In the old packer, `pack info` returned a list of all the slaves of a window and their packing configuration. Now `pack info` returns the packing configuration for a particular slave. You must first use the `pack slaves` command to get the list of all the slaves, and then use the (new) `pack info` to get their configuration information.

Focus

The focus mechanism has been cleaned up to support different focus windows on different screens. The focus command now takes a `-displayof` argument because of this. Tk now remembers which widget inside each toplevel has the focus. When the focus is given to a toplevel by the window manager, Tk automatically assigns focus to the right widget. The `-lastfor` argument queries which widget in a toplevel will get the focus by this means.

The `focus default` and `focus none` commands are no longer supported. There is no real need for `focus default` anymore, and `focus none` can be achieved by passing an empty string to the regular `focus` command.

The `tk_focusFollowsMouse` procedure changes from the default explicit focus model where a widget must claim the focus to one in which moving the mouse into a widget automatically gives it the focus.

The `tk_focusNext` and `tk_focusPrev` procedures implement keyboard traversal of the focus among widgets. Most widgets have bindings for `<Tab>` and `<Shift-Tab>` that cycle the focus among widgets.

Send

The `send` command has been changed so that it does not time out after 5 seconds, but instead waits indefinitely for a response. Specify the `-async` option if you do not want to wait for a result. You can also specify an alternate display with the `-displayof` option.

The name of an application can be set and queried with the new `tk appname` command. Use this instead of `winfo name "."`.

Because of the changes in the `send` implementation, it is not possible to use `send` between Tk 4.0 applications and earlier versions.

Internal Button Padding

Buttons and labels have new defaults for the amount of padding around their text. There is more padding now, so your buttons get bigger if you use the default `padX` and `padY` attributes. The old defaults were one pixel for both attributes. The new defaults are `3m` for `padX` and `1m` for `padY`, which map into three pixels and ten pixels on my display.

There is a difference between buttons and the other button-like widgets. An extra 2 pixels of padding is added, in spite of all padX and padY settings in the case of simple buttons. If you want your checkbuttons, radiobuttons, menubuttons, and buttons all the same dimensions, you'll need two extra pixels of padding for everything but simple buttons.

Radio Button Value

The default value for a radio button is no longer the name of the widget. Instead, it is an empty string. Make sure you specify a `-value` option when setting up your radio buttons.

Entry Widget

The `scrollCommand` attribute changed to `xScrollCommand` to be consistent with other widgets that scroll horizontally. The `view` operation changed to the `xview` operation for the same reason.

The `delete` operation has changed the meaning of the second index so that the second index refers to the character just after the affected text. The selection operations have changed in a similar fashion. The `sel.last` index refers to the character just after the end of the selection, so deleting from `sel.first` to `sel.last` still works. The default bindings have been updated, of course, but if you have custom bindings you must fix them.

Menus

The `menu` associated with a `menubutton` must be a child widget of the `menubutton`. Similarly, the `menu` for a cascade menu entry must be a child of the `menu`.

The `@y` index for a menu always returns a valid index, even if the mouse cursor is outside any entry. In this case, it simply returns the index of the closest entry, instead of `none`.

The `selector` attribute is now `selectColor`.

Listboxes

Listboxes have changed quite a bit in Tk 4.0. See Chapter 17 for all the details. There are now four Motif-like selection styles, and two of these support disjoint selections. The `tk_listboxSingleSelect` procedure no longer exists. Instead, configure the `selectMode` attribute of the listbox. A listbox has an active element, which is drawn with an underline. It is referenced with the `active` index keyword.

The selection commands for listboxes have changed. Change:

```
$listbox select from index1
$listbox select to index2
```

To:

```
$listbox select anchor index1
$listbox select set anchor index2
```

The `set` operation takes two indices, and `anchor` is a valid index, which typically corresponds to the start of a selection.

You can selectively clear the selection, and query if there is a selection in the listbox. The command to clear the selection has changed. It requires one or two indices. Change:

```
$listbox select clear
```

To:

```
$listbox select clear 0 end
```

No geometry Attribute

The `frame`, `toplevel`, and `listbox` widgets no longer have a `geometry` attribute. Use the `width` and `height` attributes instead. The `geometry` attribute got confused with geometry specifications for toplevel windows. The use of `width` and `height` is more consistent. Note that for listboxes the width and height is in terms of lines and characters, while for frames and toplevels it is in screen units.

Text Widget

The tags and marks of the text widgets have been cleaned up a bit, justification and spacing is supported, and you can embed widgets in the text display.

A mark now has a gravity, either left or right, that determines what happens when characters are inserted at the mark. With right gravity you get the old behavior: the mark gets pushed along by the inserted text by sticking to the right-hand character. With left gravity it remains stuck. The default is right gravity. The `mark gravity` operation changes it.

When text is inserted, it only picks up tags that are present on both sides of the insert point. Previously it would inherit the tags from the character to the left of the insert mark. You can also override this default behavior by supplying tags to the insert operation.

The widget scan operation supports horizontal scrolling. Instead of using marks like `@y`, you need a mark like `@x,y`.

For a description of the new features, see Chapter 19.

Color Attributes

Table 33–1 lists the names of the color attributes that changed.

Table 33–1 Changes in color attribute names.

Tk 3.6	Tk4.0
selector	selectColor
Scrollbar.activeForeground	Scrollbar.activeBackground
Scrollbar.background	troughColor
Scrollbar.foreground	Scrollbar.background
Scale.activeForeground	Scale.activeBackground
Scale.background	troughColor
Scale.sliderForeground	Scale.background
(did not exist)	highlightColor

Canvas scrollincrement

The canvas widget changed the `scrollIncrement` attribute to a pair of attributes: `xScrollIncrement` and `yScrollIncrement`. The default for these is now one tenth the width (height) of the canvas instead of one pixel. Scrolling by one page scrolls by nine tenths of the canvas display.

The Selection

The selection support has been generalized in Tk 4.0 to allow use of other selections such as the CLIPBOARD and SECONDARY selections. The changes do not break anything, but you should check out the new `clipboard` command. Some other toolkits, notably OpenLook, can only paste data from the clipboard.

The bell Command

The `bell` command rings the bell associated with the X display. You need to use the *xset* program to modify the parameters of the bell such as volume and duration.

Index

A

- abbreviation of commands 92
- access time, file 65
- activeBackground, widget attribute 286
- activeBorderWidth, widget attribute 280
- activeForeground, widget attribute 286
- activeRelief, widget attribute 280
- addinput. See fileevent.
- after, Tk command 267
- anchor position, in C 367
- anchor position, pack 124
- anchor, widget attribute 282
- animation with update 125, 208
- animation, with images 290
- Any modifer, bindings 142
- app-defaults file 165, 329
- append mode, open 69
- append, Tcl command 21
- appplication name 319
- arc canvas item 241
- args, example 186, 279
- args, keyword 50, 59
- argv 12, 43, 312
- arithmetic on text indices 220
- arithmetic operators 15
- array parameters 54
- arrays 36
- array, Tcl command 37
- arrow keys 138
- arrow on canvas 244
- aspect ratio, message widget 175, 278
- aspect ratio, of window 311
- asynchronous RPCs 399
- atom 317
- atom, in C 367
- attribute 98
  - activeBackground 286
  - activeBorderWidth 280
  - activeForeground 286
  - activeRelief 280
  - anchor 282
  - aspect 278
  - background 286
  - bitmap 290
  - borderWidth 280
  - colormap 288
  - colors, all 286
  - configuring in C 361, 371
  - cursor 295
  - disabledForeground 286
  - exportSelection 302
  - font 297
  - foreground 286
  - geometry, old 411
  - height 278
  - highlightColor 281, 286
  - highlightThickness 281
  - image 289
  - insertBackground 286, 295
  - insertBorderWidth 295
  - insertOffTime 295
  - insertOnTime 295
  - insertWidth 295
  - justify 301
  - length 278
  - orient 278
  - padX 282
  - padY 282
  - relief 280
  - resources for 212
  - selectBackground 286, 302
  - selectBorderWidth 302
  - selectColor 286
  - selectForeground 286, 302
  - setgrid 301
  - size 279
  - text tag 223
  - troughColor 286
  - types, in C 372
  - visual 288
  - width 278
  - wrapLength 301
- attributes, file 66
- automatic program execution 65, 92
- auto_index for library 91
- auto_noexec 65, 92
- auto_noload, disable library 91
- auto_path search path 91
- awk-like functionality 388

B

- background errors 86, 363
- background execution, in BLT 397
- background proceses, in C 349
- background, execute in 64
- background, widget attribute 286
- backslash character 14
- backslash sequences 6, 13, 14
- backslash-newline, in quoted string 175
- backspace character 14

BackSpace key 138
barchart widget 397
bd. Synonym for borderwidth.
beep 184
bell character 14
bell, Tk command 184
bg. Synonym for background.
binary search of a sorted file 387
binding 133
    adding to 134
    arrow keys 138
    break 136
    button modifiers 140
    canvas text objects 250
    class 134
    continue 136
    destroy window 139
    dialog box 212
    double click 140
    entry widget 187
    event syntax 137
    event types 137
    global 135
    in C code 362
    keyboard events 138
    Meta and Escape 142
    mouse events 139
    on canvas object 237, 239
    order of execution 135
    scale widget 178
    scrollbar widget 182
    sequence of events 142
    tab key 204
    text tags 227
    text widget 230
    Tk 3.6 differences 136, 138, 142
    Tk 4.0 changes 408
    user interface for 321
    window changes size 139
    x, y coordinates 144
bindtags, Tk command 134
bind, Tk command 133
bitmap
    canvas item 242
    definition in C code 364
    definition in Tcl 397
    image type 290
    in label 173
    widget attribute 290
black and white 319
BLT extension package 396
bold text 224, 298
boolean expressions 39
boolean preference item 334
borders vs. padding, example 283
borderWidth, widget attribute 280
bounding box of canvas items 239
box on canvas 248
breakpoints 84
break, in bindings 136
break, Tcl command 45
browser, example 109
busy window 398
button 145
    as event modifiers 140
    attributes 151
    attributes by resource 212
    operations 153
    padding 410
    problems with command 146
    row of 105, 117
    scope of command 145
    Tk widget 145
    user defined 167

C

C library for Tcl 347
C library for Tk 359
call by name 53
call stack, viewing 77
canvas 235
    arc object 241
    arrow 244
    attributes 258
    bindings on objects 239
    bindings, text object 250
    bitmap object 242
    bounding box 239
    C interface 364
    circle 246
    coordinate space 235
    coordinates, large 259
    drag object 236
    embedded window 252
    events coordinates 259
    hints 259
    hit detection 250, 260
    image object 243
    line object 244
    moving objects 237
    object bindings 237
    objects with many points 260
    operations 254
    oval object 246
    polygon object 247
    postscript rendering 256
    rectangle object 248
    resources for objects 260
    rotation 260

scaling objects 239, 259
scroll increment 254
scroll region 236, 259
spline 244
tag on object 237, 241
text object 249
text object attributes 252
text object bindings 250
carriage return character 14
cascaded menu 112
case. See switch.
catch, Tcl command 45
cd, Tcl command 72
cells in colormap 318
centimeters 235
cget, widget operation 278
change directory 72
changing widgets 98, 277
character code 14
checkbox. See checkbutton.
checkbutton, Tk widget 149
child windows 315
choice preference item 334
circle, canvas object 246
class, event binding 134
class, of application 407
class, resource 164, 212, 315
class, widget 97
click-to-type focus model 205
client machine 313
client-server model. See Tcl-DP.
CLIPBOARD selection 263
clipboard, Tk command 263
clock widget 369
close a window 139, 311
close, Tcl command 72
coding conventions 94
color 285
allocating in C 376
attributes 286
convert to number 318
model, in C 366
monochrome, test for 319
name 287
of text 224
resources 166
reverse video 285
RGB specification 287
Tk 4.0 new attributes 412
values, in C 365
colormap cells 318
colormap, for frame 172
colormap, in C 365
colormap, widget attribute 288
command 3
abbreviation 92
body 9
command line arguments 12, 43, 312
command line arguments, in C 356, 359
complete Tcl command 78
history 80, 92
implement in C 343, 348
profile, TclX 387
reading commands 78
substitution 4
trace, TclX 387
comments 12
comment, in resource file 165
comment, in switch 42
concatenate strings 32
concat, Tcl command 32
configure, widget operation 98, 277
configuring a window, in C 360
connection setup, TCP 399
containing window 317
continue in bindings 136
continue, Tcl command 45
controlling terminal 69
convert strings into numbers, in C 350
coordinate space, canvas 235
coordinates of mouse event 134
coordinates of window, in C 360
corner grips 130
create an interpreter 348
create file, open 69
create windows, in C 360
creating commands in C 348
curly braces 3
curly braces vs. double quotes 7
current directory 72
cursor, in C 366
cursor, mouse 294
cursor, text insert 295
cursor, widget attribute 295
cut and paste 262
cutbuffer extension 398
C++ programs 342

D

date 63
Dbg_ArgcArgv 403
debug memory problems 389
debugger for Tcl 84, 394
debugging 83
declaring variables 4
default parameter values 50
delete list elements 34
deleting text 220
Delmas, Sven 406

depth, screen 318
destroy widget 208
destroy window 206
destroy window event 139
destroy, Tk command 208
detached window 172
dialog box, message for 175
dialog box, window for 172
dictionary. See array.
Diekhans, Mark 386
directory, current 72
directory, file test 65
directory, listing 214
disable library 91
disabledForeground, widget attribute 286
display space, with pack 119, 120
dollar sign 13
double click 140
double quotes vs. curly braces 7
dpwish, Tcl-DP/Tk shell 398
dp_send 62
drag and drop 397
drag object on canvas 236
dynamic linking 92
dynamic string package, in C 352

E

editable text 219
elseif. See if.
else. See if.
embedded widget in text 228
embedded window on canvas 252
end-of-file condition 71
entry 185
- attributes 188
- bindings 187
- indices 189
- long strings in 191
- operations 190
- read-only 189
- Tk 4.0 changes 410
- Tk widget 185
- variable for value 189
- with label 185

environment variable 74
eof, Tcl command 71
error
- background, in Tk 363
- catching 45
- errorCode, variable 47
- errorInfo, variable 45, 47
- handler for Tk 86
- information in C 348
- Tcl command 46

Escape key 138
eval server 276
evaluate Tcl command from C 349
eval, example 170, 186, 222
eval, Tcl command 57
event
- bindings 133
- handler, in C 362
- handler, resize in C 381
- I/O 268
- loop 96, 360, 362
- loop, in C 358
- loop, in Tcl-DP 400
- modifier 140
- sequences 142
- syntax, bindings 137
- types, binding 137

exception. See catch.
exclusive open 69
executable, is file 65
executing programs 107
exec, Tcl command 63
exit, Tcl command 73
expect, example script 392
expect, extension and shell 390
exportSelection, widget attribute 302
expressions, from C code 350
expr, Tcl command 5
Extended Tcl 386
extension, file name 65

F

fg. Synonym for foreground.
fifo, special file 66
file 65
- access time 65
- attributes 66
- base name 66
- current script 78
- end-of-file 71
- equality test 67
- exists 65
- extension 65
- fifo 66
- find by name 73
- is executable 65
- is plain 65
- modify time 65
- name completion 217
- name patterns 72
- open 68
- ownership 65
- partial re-write 336
- read loop 71

read symlink value 66
selection dialog 209
size 66
symbolic link 66
Tcl command 65
tilde in names 73
type 66
fileevent, Tk command 108, 268
find file by name 73
fixed font 297
flush, Tcl command 70
focus 203
click-to type 205
follows-mouse 204
grab 205
highlight 408
introduction 96
model of window 313
tab binding 204
Tk 4.0 changes 409
Tk command 204
tk_focusNext 204
font
all possible 304
family 298
fixed width 297
in C code 366
missing 168
resource 164
selection example 302
widget attribute 297
foreach, Tcl command 43
foreground, widget attribute 286
form feed character 14
format, Tcl command 21
for, Tcl command 44
frame
as container 96
attributes 172
colormap 172
nested for packing 119
positioned on canvas 252
reparented 313
size 116
Tk widget 171
function definition. See procedure

G

geometry
gridding 301, 310
management, in C 365
manager 95
canvas 252
pack 115, 128
place 129
table 397
text 228
of widget 316
of window 311
old attribute 411
gets, Tcl command 71
Ghemawat, Sanjay 406
GIF. See photo.
global binding 135
global, Tcl command 52
glob, string matching 24
glob, Tcl command 72
goto 45
grab, Tk command 205
graph widget 397
graphics context 366, 376
gravity, of text mark 222
Greenberg, Saul 406
gridded geometry 301, 310
gridded geometry, in C 365
grips on corners 130
group leader, window 311, 313
grouping rules 13

H

hash table 36
hash table package, in C 350
hbox 117
height, of widget 316
height, virtual root window 317
height, widget attribute 278
Herron, David 406
highlightColor, widget attribute 281, 286
highlightThickness, widget attribute 281
history, Tcl command 80
horizontal layout 117
Hot Tip
abbreviate history commands 80
args and eval 59
array elements on demand 79
array for module data 94
attribute resource names 99
bind callback is in global scope 134
borders, padding, and highlight 282
braces get stripped off 3, 32
button command procedures 147
canvas hints 259
canvas stroke example 245
careful file open 69
color, convert to RGB 287
comments at the end of line 12
comments in switch 42
curly brace placement 40

cut and paste, OpenLook 263
debug Tk with tkinspect 86
do not declare Tcl variables 4
double-click warning 140
entry, displaying end of string 191
entry, variable for contents 189
errors on close 72
eval and double-quotes 60
eval and list 58
expect, newlines in output 393
expect, spawn_id as a global 391
find file by name 70
font, fall back to fixed 300
geometry gridding side-effect 301
global arrays 53
global inside procedures 52
group expressions with braces 10
grouping before substitution 11
grouping regular expressions 27
I/O operations and fileevent 268
labels that change size 173
limit on interpreter pathname 2
list handling in C code 348
list with foreach 43
lists are slow 87
lists vs. arrays 31
list, after, and send 61
menu accelerator, consistent 161
menu index pattern 156
message text layout 175
mouse cursors, all shown 294
open a process pipeline 70
pack the scrollbar first 126
packing widgets to a side 118
parentheses do not group 37
pipelines and error output 107
procedures to hide list structure 331
profiling scripts, TclX 387
recursive makedir 67
resources, general patterns first 165
result string, managing in C 344
scrollbar for two listboxes 324
scrollbars, layout of two 192
scrolling widgets on a canvas 252
send requires X authority 270
send, constructing commands 272
single round of interpretation 6
size not set until mapped 315
string conversions by expr 20
Tcl C library, survey 347
TclX script libraries 386
Tcl_AppInit with extensions 402
Tcl_Eval may modify its string 345
text mark gravity 222
Tk C library, survey 359
tkwait on global variable 206
traces on entry values 335
update, using safely 209
variable for widget name 98
virtual root window coordinates 317
widget data, safety in C 382
window session protocol 312
window size, getting correct 254
X protocol error handler 355
Howlett, George 396
hypertext 397

I

icon for window 311
icon, position 312
icon, window for 312
idle events, in C 359, 363
if, Tcl command 40
image on canvas 243
image, Tk command 289
image, using in C code 364
image, widget attribute 289
inch 235
[incr Tcl] 401
increment a variable 9
incr, Tcl command 9, 54
indices, canvas text object 249
indices, entry widget 189
indices, text widget 219
infinite loop 10
info, Tcl command 75
init.tcl 93
input focus 96, 106, 204
input focus highlight 408
insertBackground, widget attribute 286, 295
insertBorderWidth, widget attribute 295
inserting text 220
insertOffTime, widget attribute 295
insertOnTime, widget attribute 295
insertWidth, widget attribute 295
inspector, tkinspect 86
interactive resize 107, 311
interpreter internals 75
interpreter registry 314
interpreter, creating in C 348
interprocess communication. See send.
interrupt, from keyboard 404
italic text 224, 298
I/O events, in C 359, 362
I/O redirection 63

J

join, Tcl command 36
justification of text 223, 225

justify, widget attribute 301

K

- keyboard
  - events 138
  - grab 205
  - interrupt 404
  - map 141
  - selection, menu 155
- keycode 143
- keyed list 389
- keysym 138, 144

L

- label attributes 174
- label, lining up 326, 334
- label, multi-line 175
- label, Tk widget 173
- Lam, Ioi Kim 406
- lappend, Tcl command 32
- ldelete, Tcl procedure 34
- Lehenbauer, Karl 386
- length, widget attribute 278
- Libes, Don 84, 390
- library 89
  - index 90
  - of procedures 89
  - search path 91
  - TclX mechanism 386
- library directory, Tcl 78
- limit on interpreter pathname 2, 12
- lindex, Tcl command 33
- line cap styles, in C 367
- line join styles, in C 367
- line justification styles, in C 367
- line on canvas 244
- linsert, Tcl command 34
- list 31
  - append elements 32
  - constructing commands 58, 147, 170, 272, 326
  - extensions by TclX 388
  - extract element 33
  - insert elements 34
  - join into string 36
  - keyed 389
  - length of 33
  - manipulation in C code 348
  - replace elements 34
  - searching a 34
  - splice together 32
  - split string into 35
  - sublist 33
  - summary of operations 31
  - Tcl command 32
- listbox 191
  - pair working together 323
  - scrollbar alignment 192
  - scrollbar for 193
  - selection example 217
  - Tk 4.0 changes 411
  - Tk widget 191
- llength, Tcl command 33
- load, Tcl command 92
- location of icon 312
- loop
  - break & continue 45
  - for 44
  - foreach 43
  - optimizing 87
  - reading input 71, 111
  - TclX extensions 387
  - while 44
- LoVerso, John 167
- lower, Tk command 131
- lrange, Tcl command 33
- lreplace, example 300
- lreplace, Tcl command 34
- lsearch, Tcl command 34

M

- Macintosh 95
- Makefile for a Tcl C program 347
- Makefile for Tcl with extensions 404
- manual pages, Tk 99
- map window event 139
- mapping windows 97
- mark position in text 108, 221
- math expressions 5
- math functions, built-in 16
- maximum size, window 311
- McLennan, Michael 396, 401
- memory debugging 389
- menu 153
  - accelerator 158, 161
  - attributes 157
  - button for 153
  - cascade 112
  - entry index 156
  - example 154
  - keyboard selection 155
  - operations on entries 156
  - packing a menubar 123
  - pop-up 155
  - tear off 157
  - Tk widget 153
  - user-defined 168
- menubutton, Tk widget 153

message attributes 176
message catalog, XPG/3 389
message, Tk widget 175
Meta key 142
millimeters 235
min max scale, example 238
minimum size, window 311
missing font 168
modify time, file 65
module support 94
monochrome, test for 319
mouse cursor 294
mouse events 139
mouse event, coordinates 134
multi-line labels 175
multiple inheritance 401
multi-way branch 41

N

name
  of all interpreters 314
  of atom 318
  of color 287
  of interpreter, in C 360
  of interpreter, send 270, 314, 319
  on icon 312
naming widgets 98
nested frames 119
network, send packet 398
newline character 14
Nichols, David 345
non-blocking I/O 69
numeric value, widget for 177

O

object code, dynamic linking 92
object package, in Tcl-DP 400
object system, [incr Tcl] 401
open a window 311
open a window, binding 139
OpenLook, cut and paste 263
open, Tcl command 68
operators, arithmetic 15
option, Tk command 165
orient, widget attribute 278
oval, canvas object 246
override redirect 143, 313
ownership, file 65

P

pack 115
  display space 119, 120
  nested frames 119
  packing order 125
  padding 122
  resizing windows 122
  scrollbar example 193
  scrollbars first 126
  space for 119
  Tk 4.0 changes 409
  Tk command 128
padding around widgets 122
padding in buttons 410
padX, widget attribute 282
padY, widget attribute 282
parent directory 65
parent window 315
parsing command line arguments 43
paste, example 261
patch level, Tcl release 78
pathname from window ID 318
pattern match
  glob, file name match 72
  glob, string match 24
  in expect 391
  menu entries 156
  regular expressions 25
  resource database 164
  switch command 41
performance tuning 87
Phelps, Tom 406
photo image type 291
photo, C interface 364
pid, Tcl command 73
pie slice, canvas 241
pipeline 72
pipeline and fileevent 269
pipeline setup in C 349
pipeline, closing 108
pixmap, in C 366
pixmap, off screen 379
pixmap. See photo.
place, Tk command 130
plain file 65
plus, in bindings 134
points per pixel 298
polygon, canvas item 247
position in text 221
position in virtual root window 317
position, relative to widget 129
POSIX file access 68
POSIX, errorCode 47
postscript from canvas 256
PPM format 292
preference package 329
preserve widget data 361
PRIMARY selection 261
PrintByName, Tcl procedure 151
printenv 74

printer points 235
printf. See format
print. See puts.
private procedure 94
procedure definition 8, 49, 77
procedure library 89
process ID 73
proc, Tcl command 8, 49
profiling Tcl code 87
protocol handler, window manager 313
pseudo-tty. See expect.
puts, Tcl command 70
pwd, Tcl command 72

Q

query widget attributes 99
quit application protocol 312
quit button 104

R

radiobutton, Tk widget 149
raise an error 46
raise, Tk command 131
random number generator 52
random, in C 344
read only, open 69
readable, file 66
reading commands from a file 2
reading Tcl commands 78
readline. See gets.
readlink 66
read-only entry widget 189
read-only text widget 112
read, Tcl command 71
rectangle on canvas 248
redefining procedures 50
redisplay. See update.
redo. See history.
reference count widget data 361
regexp, Tcl command 27
register image format, in C 364
regsub, example 308
regsub, Tcl command 28
regular expression C library 352
regular expressions 25
relative position of windows 129
relief, in C 366, 367
relief, widget attribute 280
rename, Tcl command 50
reparented frame 313
replicated object package, Tcl-DP 400
requested hight of widget 316
resizing windows, interactive 110
resizing windows, layout 122
resource 163
    associated with Tcl variable 331
    attribute names 99
    class 164
    color 166
    database 163
    example 212, 322
    font 164
    for canvas objects 260
    loading 165, 330
    lookup in C code 363
    non-standard 169
    order of patterns 165
    specifications 99
RESOURCE_MANAGER property 164
Return key 138
return, Tcl command 8, 47
reverse video 285
RGB, color specification 287
ring the bell 184
root window ID 144
root, file name 66
Roseman, Mark 406
rotation not supported 260
row of buttons 117
Rowe, Lawrence 398
running programs 63

S

saving state as Tcl commands 326
scale 177
    attributes 178
    bindings 178
    operations 179
    Tk widget 177
    variable 177
    with two values 238
scaling canvas objects 239
scanf. See scan
scan, Tcl command 23
scope control, in [incr Tcl] 402
scope, global 52
scope, local 51
screen
    depth 318
    for toplevel 172
    height 316
    identifier 317
    measurement units 235, 279
        converting 316
        in C 366
    multiple 172
    position of window 317
    relative coordinates 317

width 316
script library 89
script, current 78
scrollbar 180
alignment 192
attributes 182
bindings 182
example 181
for canvas 236
for two widgets 324
operations 183
Tk widget 180
with text 107
scrolling multiple widgets 324
scrolling widgets on a canvas 252
searching arrays 38
seek, Tcl command 72
Sekora, Jay 405
selectBackground, widget attribute 286, 302
selectBorderWidth, widget attribute 302
selectColor, widget attribute 286
selectForeground, widget attribute 286, 302
selection 262
CLIPBOARD 263
example 264
exporting to X 301
in C 361
ownership 263
PRIMARY 261
text widget 227
Tk command 262
select. See fileevent.
send 269
command to another application 271
constructing remote command 272
name of interpreter 270, 314
network packet 398
timeout changed in Tk 4.0 410
Tk command 269
X authority required 270
server connection 399
session, window system 312
setgrid, widget attribute 301
set, Tcl command 4, 29
shell, supertcl 404
shell, tclsh 1
shell, wish 1
Shen, Sam 86, 406
shrinking frames 116
signal handling, in C 352, 395
significant digits 6
Silva, Peter da 386
size of label 173
size, file 66
size, relative to widget 129
size, widget attribute 279
sleep, Tk_Sleep 363
sleep. See after.
Smith, Brian 398
socket, special file 66
source, example 326
source, Tcl command 2
space around widgets 122
spaces in array indices 37
spline curve on canvas 244
split, Tcl command 35
square brackets 13
stack 55
stack trace 358
stack trace. See errorInfo.
stacking order, in C 361
stacking order, window 127, 131
standard options 100
state of window 312
Status, Tcl procedure 330
stat, file 66
stat, symlink 65
stderr, standard error output 3
stdin, standard input 3
stdout, standard output 3
string 19
comparison 21
continuation of 175
display. See label.
facilities in TclX 389
identifiers, in C 365
match. See pattern match.
Tcl command 20
stroke, canvas example 245
substitution rules 13
substitutions, no eval 62
subst, Tcl command 62
supertcl, extended Tcl shell 404
Svoboda, David 406
switch, example 170
switch, Tcl command 41
symbolic link 66
symbolic link, stat 65
syntax 13
character code 14
command 3
curly braces 3
dollar sign 13
square brackets 13

T

tab character 14
Tab key 138
table geometry manager 397

tab, default binding 204
tag characters in text 222
tag on canvas object 237, 241
tail, file name 66
Tcl applications and extensions 405
Tcl C library, survey 347
Tcl command 17
- append 21
- array 37
- break 45
- catch 45
- cd 72
- close 72
- concat 32
- continue 45
- eof 71
- error 46
- eval 57
- exec 63
- exit 73
- expr 5
- file 65
- flush 70
- for 44
- foreach 43
- format 21
- gets 71
- glob 72
- global 52
- history 80
- if 40
- incr 9
- incr, improved 54
- info 75
- join 36
- lappend 32
- lindex 33
- linsert 34
- list 32
- list-related commands 31
- llength 33
- load 92
- lrange 33
- lreplace 34
- lsearch 34
- number executed 78
- open 68
- pid 73
- proc 8, 49
- puts 70
- pwd 72
- read 71
- regexp 27
- regsub 28
- rename 50
- return 8, 47
- scan 23
- seek 72
- set 4, 29
- source 2
- split 35
- string 20
- subst 62
- switch 41
- tell 72
- time 87
- trace 79
- unknown 89
- unset 30
- uplevel 60
- upvar 53
- while 44
- writing commands to files 326

Tcl debugger 394
Tcl library 78
Tcl patch level 78
Tcl shell, supertcl 404
Tcl version 78
Tcl-DP and fileevent 268
Tcl-DP extension 398
tclIndex file 90
tclsh, Tcl shell 1
TclX extension package 386
Tcl_AppendElement 344
Tcl_AppendResult 344, 375
Tcl_AppInit, example 342, 354, 403
Tcl_CmdInfo 346
Tcl_CreateCommand 342, 354, 374
Tcl_CreateHashEntry 351
Tcl_CreateInterp 356
Tcl_DeleteCommand 381
Tcl_Eval runs Tcl commands from C 345
Tcl_EvalFile 357
Tcl_FindHashEntry 351
Tcl_GetCommandInfo 346
Tcl_GetInt 343
Tcl_GetVar 357
Tcl_Init 342, 354, 357
Tcl_InitHashTable 351
Tcl_Invoke bypasses Tcl_Eval 345
TCL_LIBRARY, environment 93
tcl_precision variable 6
tcl_RcFileName 342, 355
Tcl_SetHashValue 351
Tcl_SetResult 344
TCP protocol 399
TCP/IP access 388
tell, Tcl command 72
terminal emulator 113
terminal, controlling 69

- terminate process 73
- text 219
  - attributes 234
  - attributes for tags 223
  - bindings 230
  - bold 224
  - color 224
  - embedded widgets 228
  - entry widget 185
  - index arithmatic 220
  - indices 219
  - insert cursor 295
  - italic 224
  - justification 223, 225
  - mark 221
  - mark gravity 222
  - on canvas 249
  - operations 232
  - read-only 112
  - selection 227
  - tag 222
  - tag bindings 227
  - Tk 4.0 changes 412
  - Tk widget 219
  - underlined 224
  - with scrollbar 107
- then. See if.
- tilde in file names 73
- tilde key, asciicircum 138
- tilde substitution, in C 352
- timer events, in C 359, 363
- timer. See after.
- time, Tcl command 87
- title, of window 310
- title, supressing 313
- Tk 4.0, porting issues 407
- Tk C library survey 359
- Tk command 100
  - after 267
  - bell 184
  - bind 133
  - bindtags 134
  - clipboard 263
  - destroy 208
  - fileevent 268
  - focus 204
  - grab 205
  - image 289
  - lower 131
  - option 165
  - pack 128
  - place 130
  - raise 131
  - See also widgets.
  - selection 262
  - send 269
  - tk 319
  - tkerror 86, 363
  - tkwait 206
  - update 209
  - winfo 314
  - wm 309
- TkDisplayText 380
- TkDrawFocusHighlight 380
- tkerror, Tcl procedure 86, 363
- tkinspect, inspector program 86
- tkwait, Tk command 206
- tk, Tk command 319
- tk.tcl 93
- Tk_3DBorderGC 380
- Tk_CancelIdleCall 381
- Tk_ConfigSpec 371
- Tk_ConfigureInfo 375
- Tk_ConfigureValue 375
- Tk_CreateErrorHandler 356
- Tk_CreateEventHandler 374
- Tk_CreateImageType 404
- Tk_CreateMainWindow 356
- Tk_CreateTimerHandler 381
- Tk_CreateWindowFromPath 373
- Tk_DeleteTimerHandler 381
- Tk_DoOneEvent 357
- Tk_DoWhenIdle 382
- Tk_EventuallyFree 381
- Tk_Fill3DRectangle 380
- tk_focusFollowsMouse 204
- tk_focusNext, Tcl procedure 204
- Tk_FreeGC 382
- Tk_FreeOptions 383
- Tk_FreePixmap 380
- Tk_GeometryRequest 357
- Tk_GetPixmap 380
- Tk_Init 354, 357
- tk_library 93
- TK_LIBRARY, environment 93
- tk_listboxSingleSelect 411
- Tk_Main 353
- Tk_MainWindow 354
- Tk_ParseArgv 356
- Tk_SetClass 373
- Tk_SetWindowBackground 357
- toplevel of widget 317
- toplevel, attributes 172
- toplevel, Tk widget 172
- trace 79
  - example 304, 338
  - execution, in BLT 398
  - execution, in C 349
  - Tcl command 79
  - variables, in C 349

transient window 313
translit, TclX command 389
trig functions 16
triple click 140
troughColor, widget attribute 286
truncate file, open 69
two screens 172
typeface. See font.
type-in widget 185
type, file 66

U

UDP protocol 400
underlined text 224
UNIX system calls, TclX 387
unknown, Tcl command 89
unmap widget 127
unmap window 312
unmap window event 139
unset, Tcl command 30
update, Tk command 209
uplevel, Tcl command 60
upvar, example 151, 332
upvar, Tcl command 53
user customization 329
user-defined buttons 167
User-defined menus 168

V

variable
- args 50
- argv 12, 43, 312
- argv0 312
- array 36
- assignment 4
- auto_index 91
- auto_noexec 65, 92
- auto_noload 91
- auto_path 91
- call by name 53
- command line arguments 12
- convert array to list 38
- currently defined 76
- deleting 30
- entry widget text 189
- environment 74
- errorCode 47
- errorInfo 45, 47
- for scale widget 177
- increment 9
- manipulate from C code 349
- names 4
- predefined 15
- PrintByName 151
- read-only 79
- tcl_precision 6
- test if defined 30
- text of label 173
- tk_library 93
- trace access 79
- wait for modification 206

vbox 117
version number, Tcl 78
vertical layout 117
vertical tab character 14
Virden, Larry 405
virtual root window 317
visual class, widget attribute 288, 318
volume, of bell 184

W

wait for Tk event 206
Welch, Brent 406
Wendel, Martin 406
while, Tcl command 44
white space 3, 36
widget
- attributes 98
- class 97
- class command, in C 373
- container. See frame.
- containing 317
- data structure, in C 369
- definition 95
- destroy, in C 382
- display in C 378
- embed in text 228
- geometry 316
- height 316
- implemented in C 369
- instance command, in C 374
- naming 98
- preserving C data structure 361
- reconfigure 98
- screen of 317
- screen position 317
- toplevel of 317
- unmapping 127
- width 316
- x, y coordinate 317

widgets 95
- button 145
- canvas 235
- checkbutton 149
- entry 185
- frame 96, 171
- label 173
- listbox 191

menu 153
menubutton 153
message 175
radiobutton 149
scale 177
scrollbar 180
text 219
toplevel 172
width of widget 316
width, virtual root window 317
width, widget attribute 278
window 313
aspect ratio 311
binding on open 139
changes size 139
children 315
class, resource 315
close 311
color model 319, 330
configuration in C 360
coordinates, in C 360
creating in C 360
deiconify 312
deleting 208
detached 172
embedded in canvas 252
events, in C 359
exists 315
focus model 313
general information in C 361
geometry 311
geometry manager 315
gridding 310
group 311, 313
hierarchy 95
icon 312
iconbitmap 311
iconify 312
ID 318
manager 105, 309
mapped 315
maxsize 311
minsize 311
open 311
open, is 315
override redirect 313
parent 315
pathname 318
position from 311
protocol handler 313
resize, interactive 107, 110
rooms 317
session state 312
size from 311
stacking order, in C 361
startup command 313
state 312
title 105, 310
transient 313
unmap 312
virtual root 317
visual 318
wait for destroy 206
wait for visibility 206
withdraw 312
Windows 95
winfo, Tk command 314
wish, Tcl/Tk shell 1
withdraw window 312
wm, Tk command 309
WM_DELETE_WINDOW 312
wrapLength, widget attribute 301
writable, file 66
write only, open 69

X

X authority, send 270
X ID for resource, in C 367
X protocol errors 355, 363
X resource database 163
Xdefaults. See resource database.
xfontsel, UNIX program 299
xlsfonts, UNIX program 299
xmodmap, program 141
XPG/3 message catalog 389
xrdb. See option.
xset program 184
x, y coordinate of widget 317
x, y coordinates, in event 144